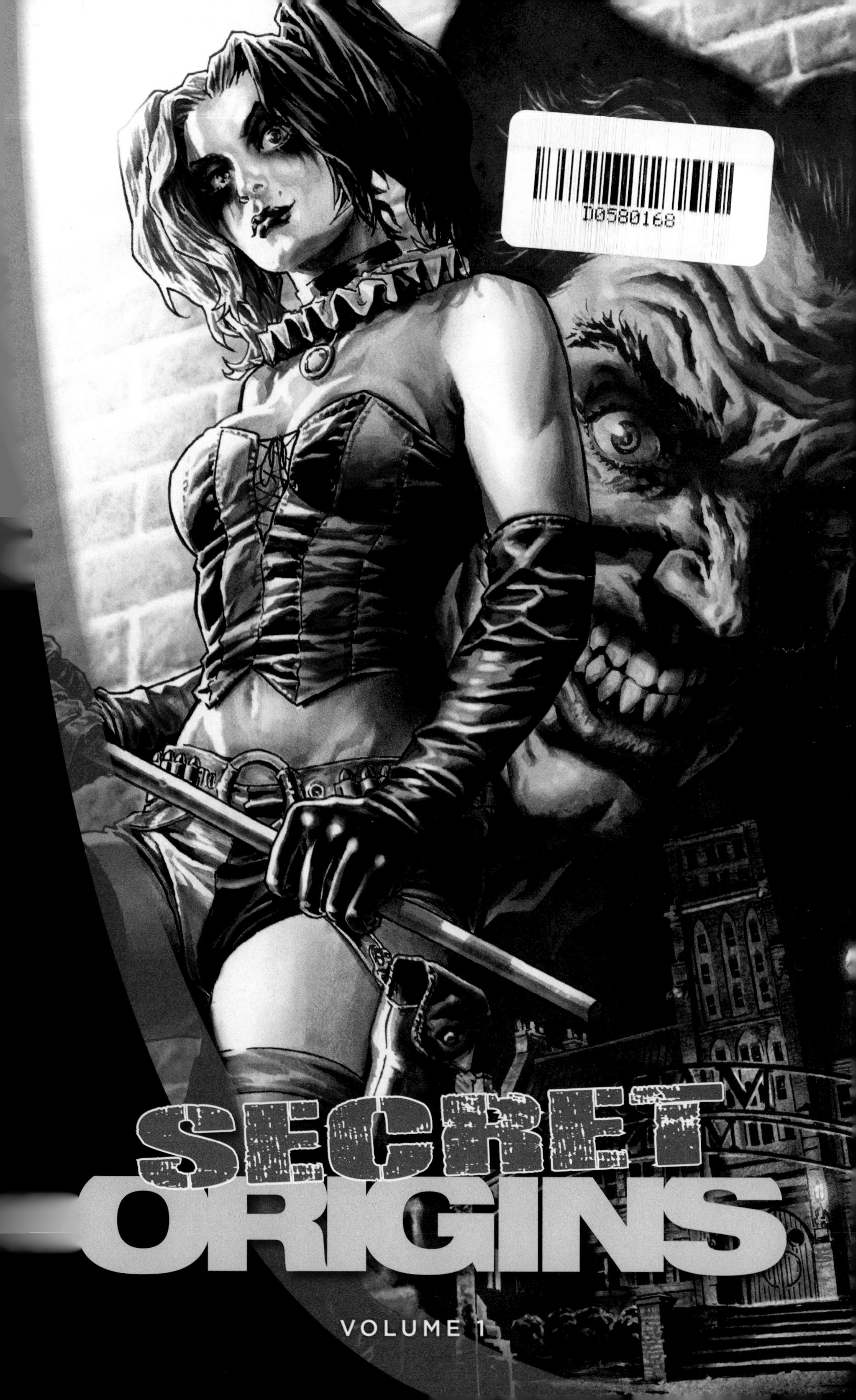
SECRET
ORIGINS
VOLUME 1

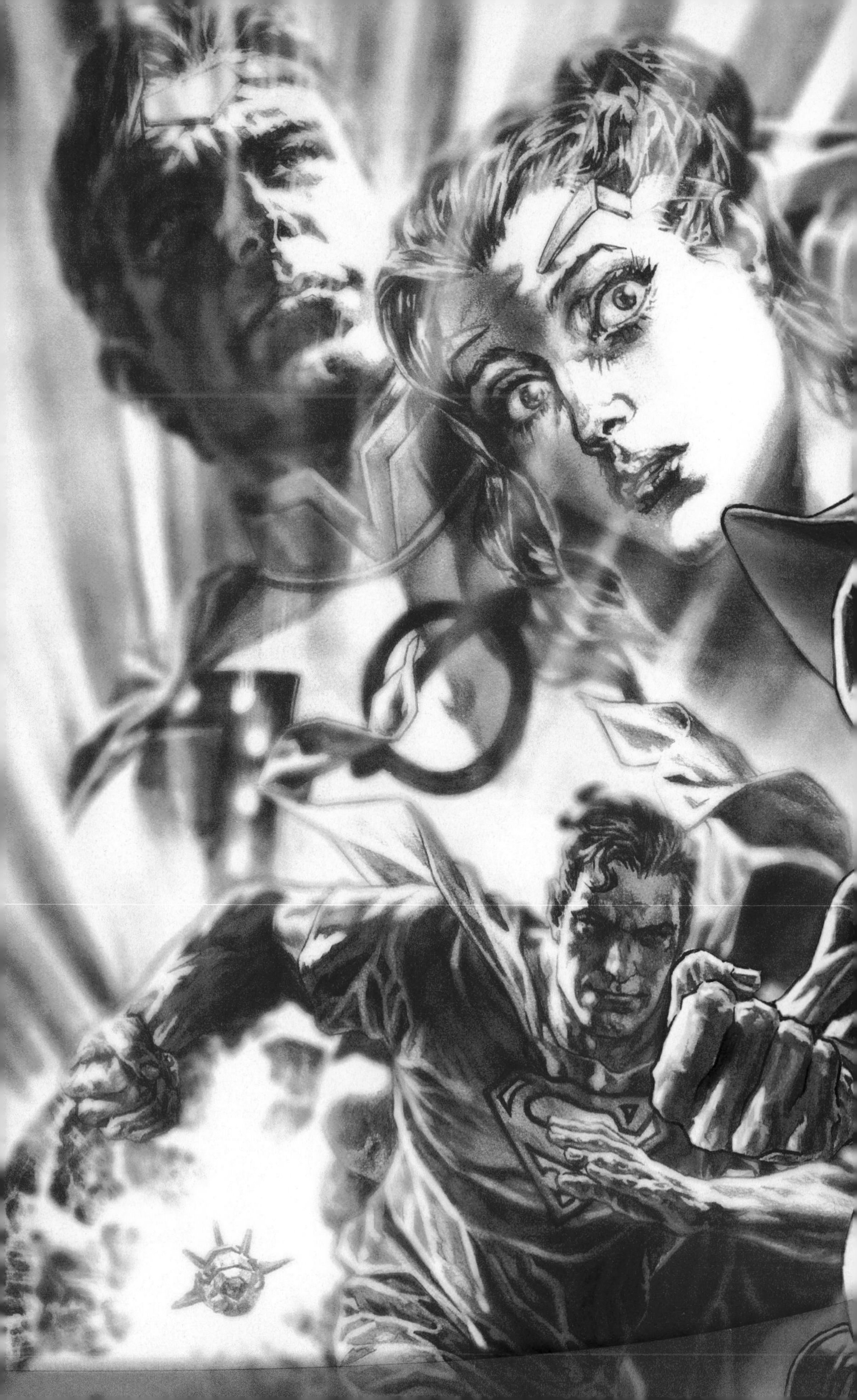

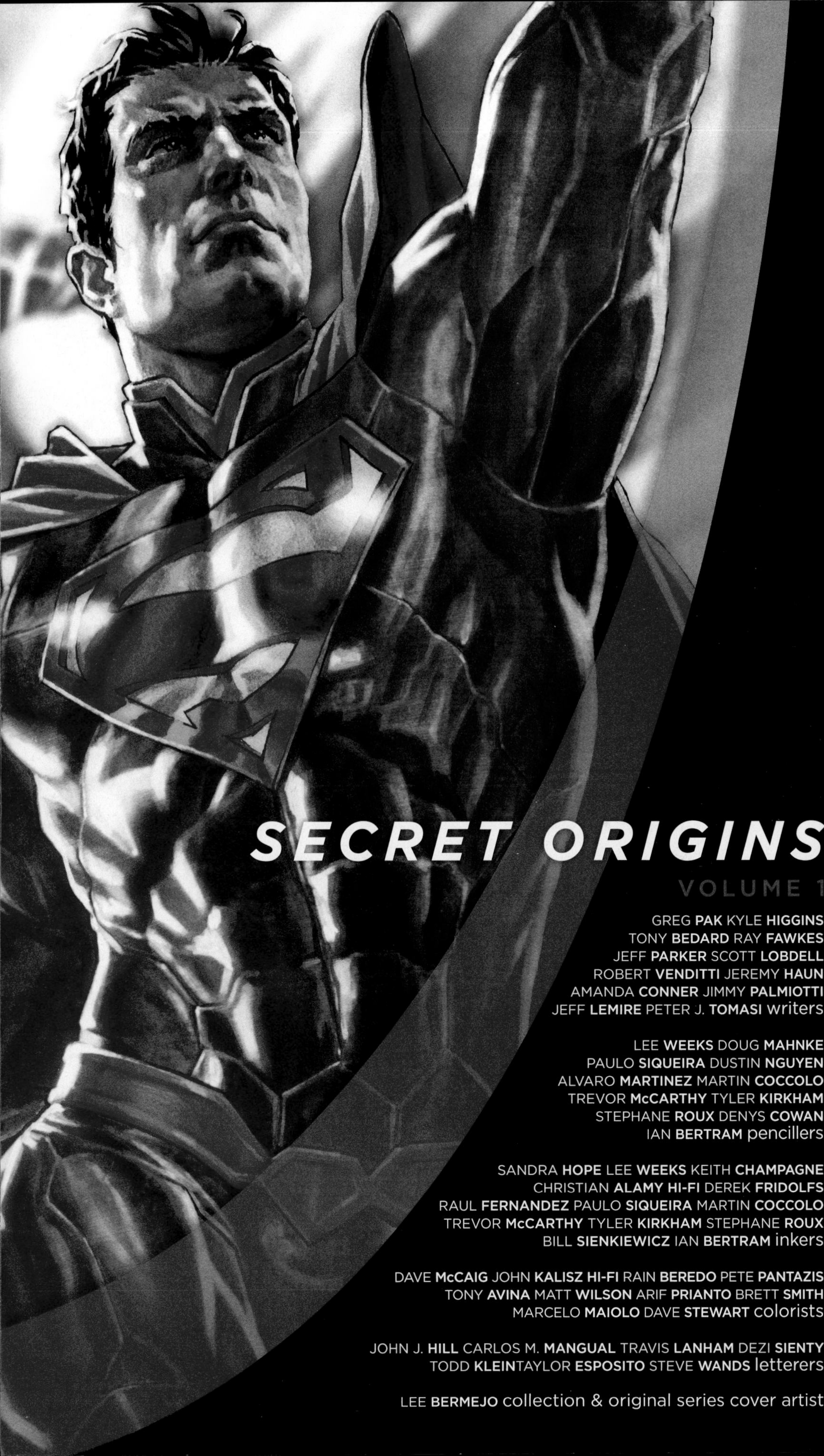

SECRET ORIGINS

VOLUME 1

GREG **PAK** KYLE **HIGGINS**
TONY **BEDARD** RAY **FAWKES**
JEFF **PARKER** SCOTT **LOBDELL**
ROBERT **VENDITTI** JEREMY **HAUN**
AMANDA **CONNER** JIMMY **PALMIOTTI**
JEFF **LEMIRE** PETER J. **TOMASI** writers

LEE **WEEKS** DOUG **MAHNKE**
PAULO **SIQUEIRA** DUSTIN **NGUYEN**
ALVARO **MARTINEZ** MARTIN **COCCOLO**
TREVOR **McCARTHY** TYLER **KIRKHAM**
STEPHANE **ROUX** DENYS **COWAN**
IAN **BERTRAM** pencillers

SANDRA **HOPE** LEE **WEEKS** KEITH **CHAMPAGNE**
CHRISTIAN **ALAMY** **HI-FI** DEREK **FRIDOLFS**
RAUL **FERNANDEZ** PAULO **SIQUEIRA** MARTIN **COCCOLO**
TREVOR **McCARTHY** TYLER **KIRKHAM** STEPHANE **ROUX**
BILL **SIENKIEWICZ** IAN **BERTRAM** inkers

DAVE **McCAIG** JOHN **KALISZ** **HI-FI** RAIN **BEREDO** PETE **PANTAZIS**
TONY **AVINA** MATT **WILSON** ARIF **PRIANTO** BRETT **SMITH**
MARCELO **MAIOLO** DAVE **STEWART** colorists

JOHN J. **HILL** CARLOS M. **MANGUAL** TRAVIS **LANHAM** DEZI **SIENTY**
TODD **KLEIN**TAYLOR **ESPOSITO** STEVE **WANDS** letterers

LEE **BERMEJO** collection & original series cover artist

EDDIE BERGANZA CHRIS CONROY MIKE COTTON BRIAN CUNNINGHAM MARK DOYLE RACHEL GLUCKSTERN
MATT IDELSON KATIE KUBERT RICKEY PURDIN HARVEY RICHARDS Editors – Original Series
MATT HUMPHREYS ANTHONY MARQUES DARREN SHAN Assistant Editors – Original Series RACHEL PINNELAS Editor
ROBBIN BROSTERMAN Design Director – Books ROBBIE BIEDERMAN Publication Design

BOB HARRAS Senior VP – Editor-in-Chief, DC Comics

DIANE NELSON President DAN DIDIO and JIM LEE Co-Publishers GEOFF JOHNS Chief Creative Officer
AMIT DESAI Senior VP – Marketing and Franchise Management
AMY GENKINS Senior VP – Business and Legal Affairs NAIRI GARDINER Senior VP – Finance
JEFF BOISON VP – Publishing Planning MARK CHIARELLO VP – Art Direction and Design
JOHN CUNNINGHAM VP – Marketing TERRI CUNNINGHAM VP – Editorial Administration
LARRY GANEM VP – Talent Relations and Services ALISON GILL Senior VP – Manufacturing and Operations
HANK KANALZ Senior VP – Vertigo and Integrated Publishing JAY KOGAN VP – Business and Legal Affairs, Publishing
JACK MAHAN VP – Business Affairs, Talent NICK NAPOLITANO VP – Manufacturing Administration SUE POHJA VP – Book Sales
FRED RUIZ VP – Manufacturing Operations COURTNEY SIMMONS Senior VP – Publicity BOB WAYNE Senior VP – Sales

SECRET ORIGINS VOLUME 1

DC Comics, 1700 Broadway, New York, NY 10019
A Warner Bros. Entertainment Company.
Printed by RR Donnelley, Owensville, MO, USA. 1/9/15. First Printing.
ISBN: 978-1-4012-5049-2

Library of Congress Cataloging-in-Publication Data

Lemire, Jeff, author.
Secret Origins / Jeff Lemire, Greg Pak ; [illustrated by] Doug Mahnke.
volumes cm. — (The New 52!)

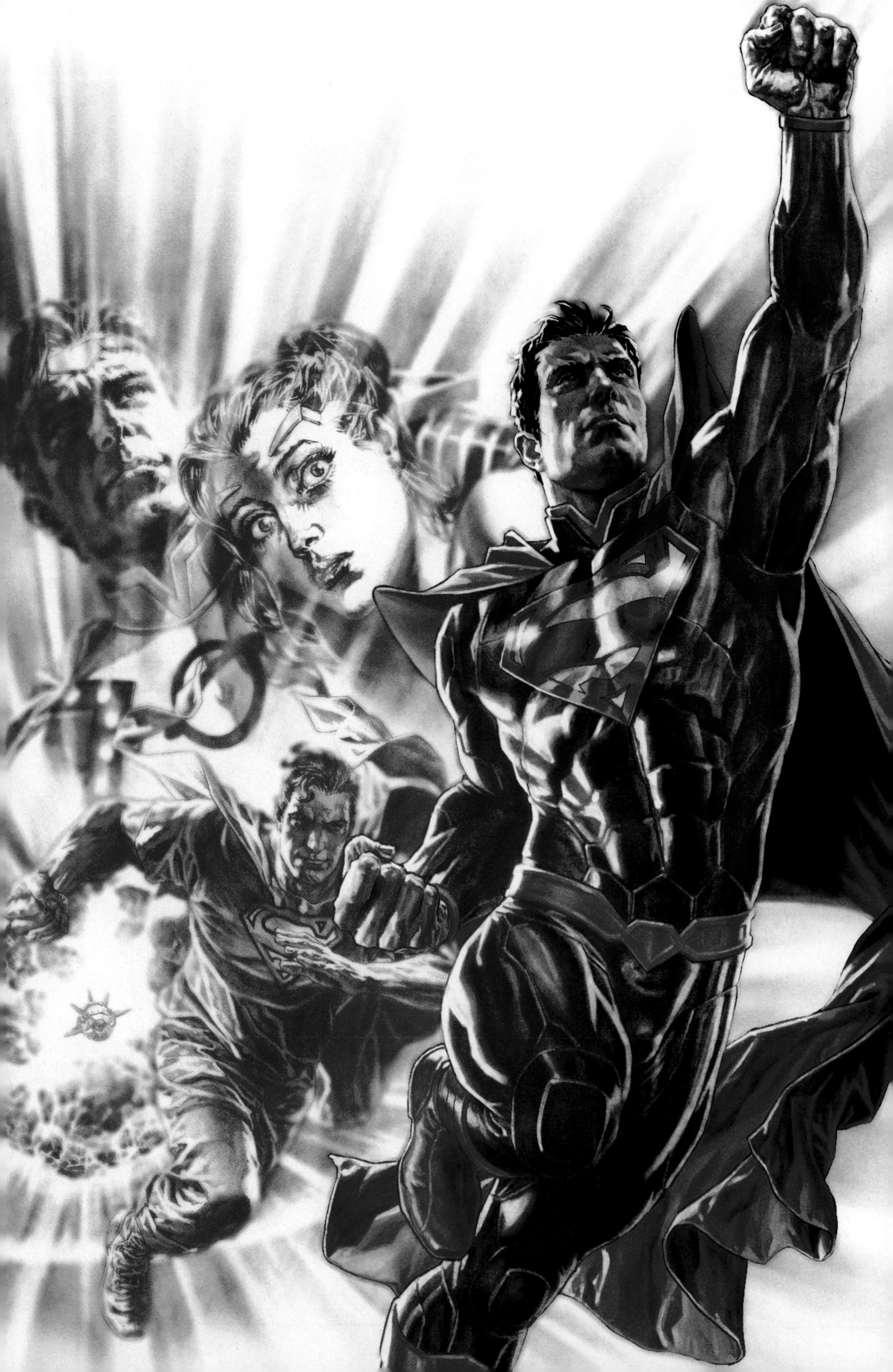

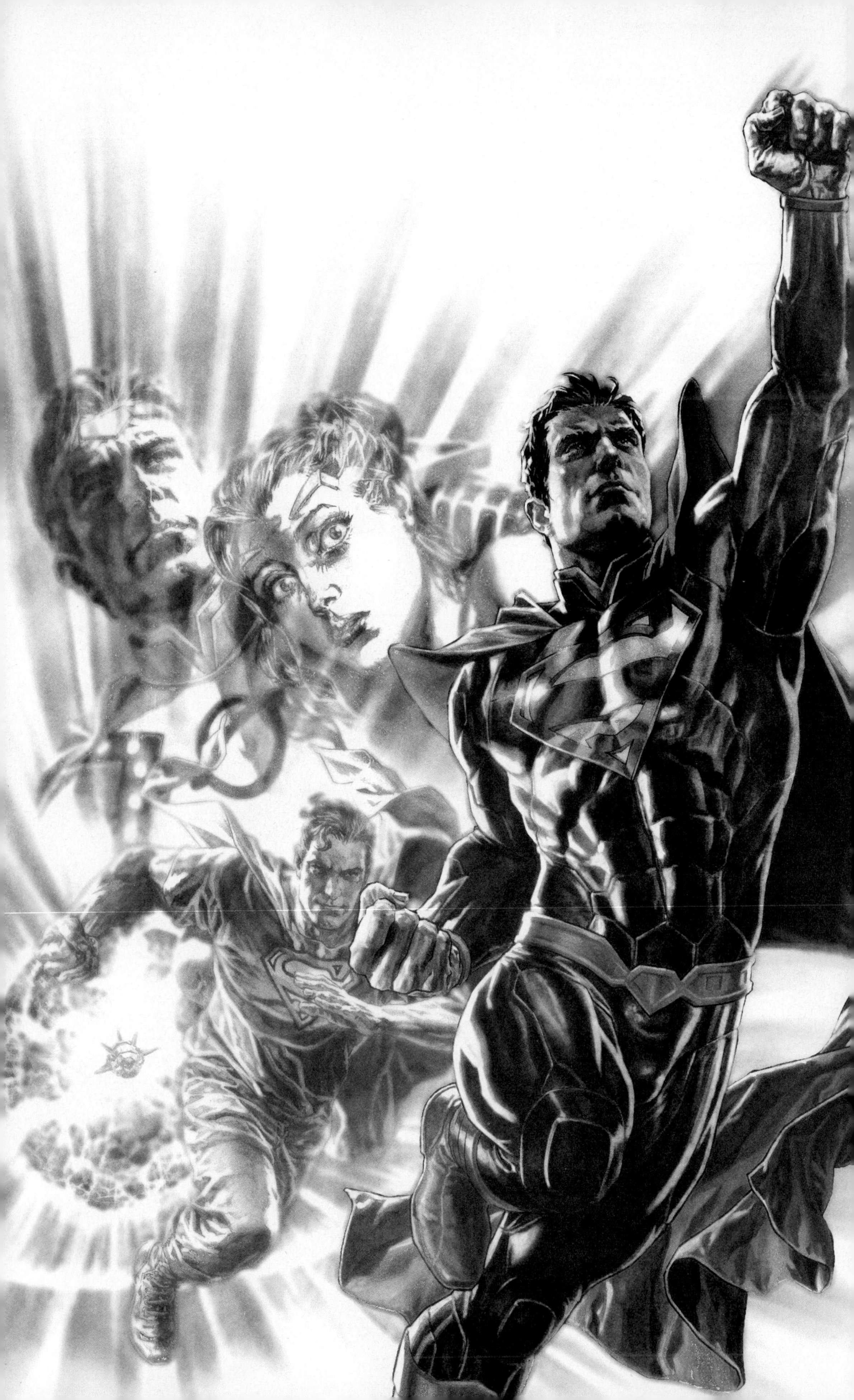

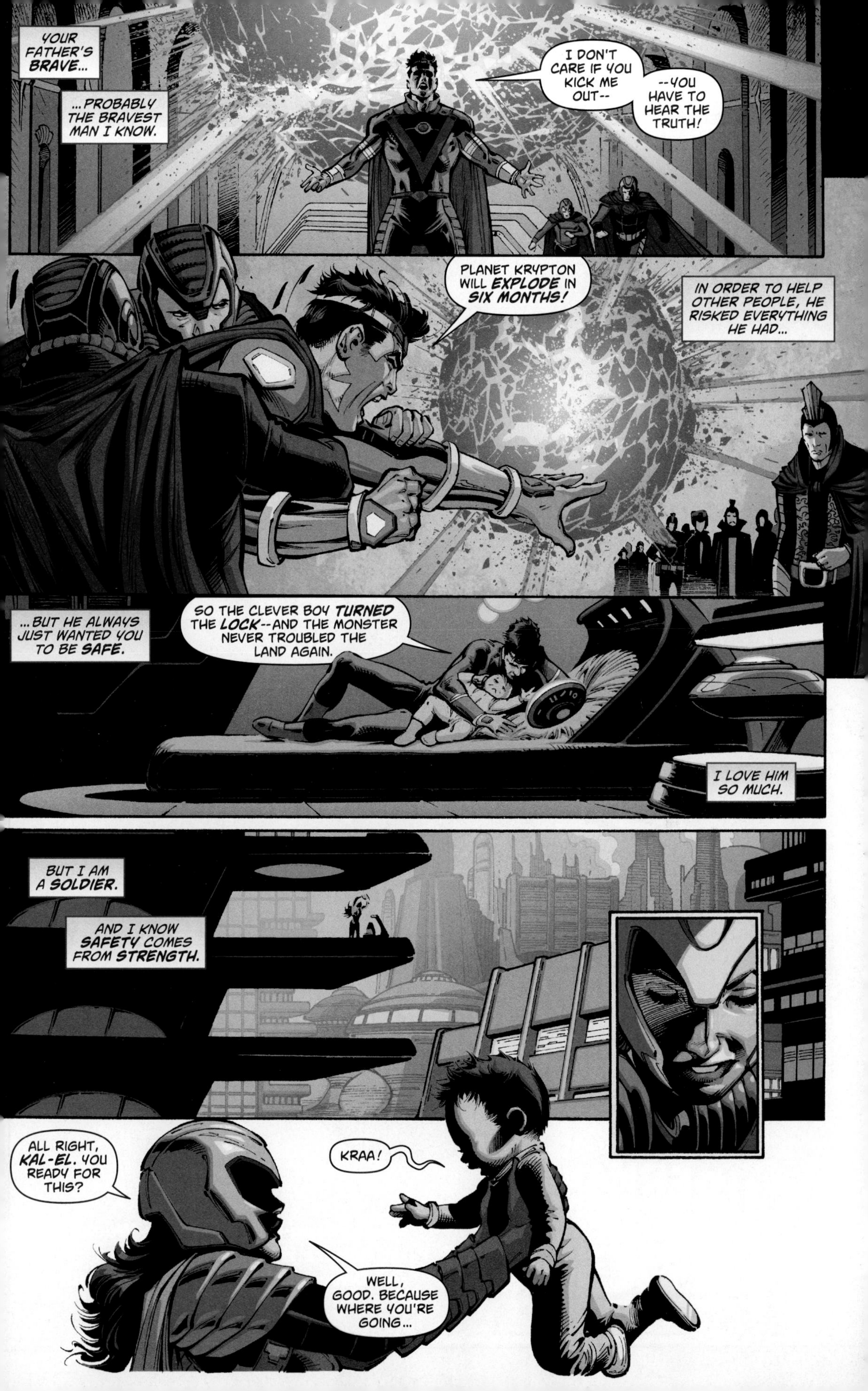
YOUR FATHER'S BRAVE...
...PROBABLY THE BRAVEST MAN I KNOW.
I DON'T CARE IF YOU KICK ME OUT--
--YOU HAVE TO HEAR THE TRUTH!
PLANET KRYPTON WILL EXPLODE IN SIX MONTHS!
IN ORDER TO HELP OTHER PEOPLE, HE RISKED EVERYTHING HE HAD...
...BUT HE ALWAYS JUST WANTED YOU TO BE SAFE.
SO THE CLEVER BOY TURNED THE LOCK--AND THE MONSTER NEVER TROUBLED THE LAND AGAIN.
I LOVE HIM SO MUCH.
BUT I AM A SOLDIER.
AND I KNOW SAFETY COMES FROM STRENGTH.
ALL RIGHT, KAL-EL. YOU READY FOR THIS?
KRAA!
WELL, GOOD. BECAUSE WHERE YOU'RE GOING...

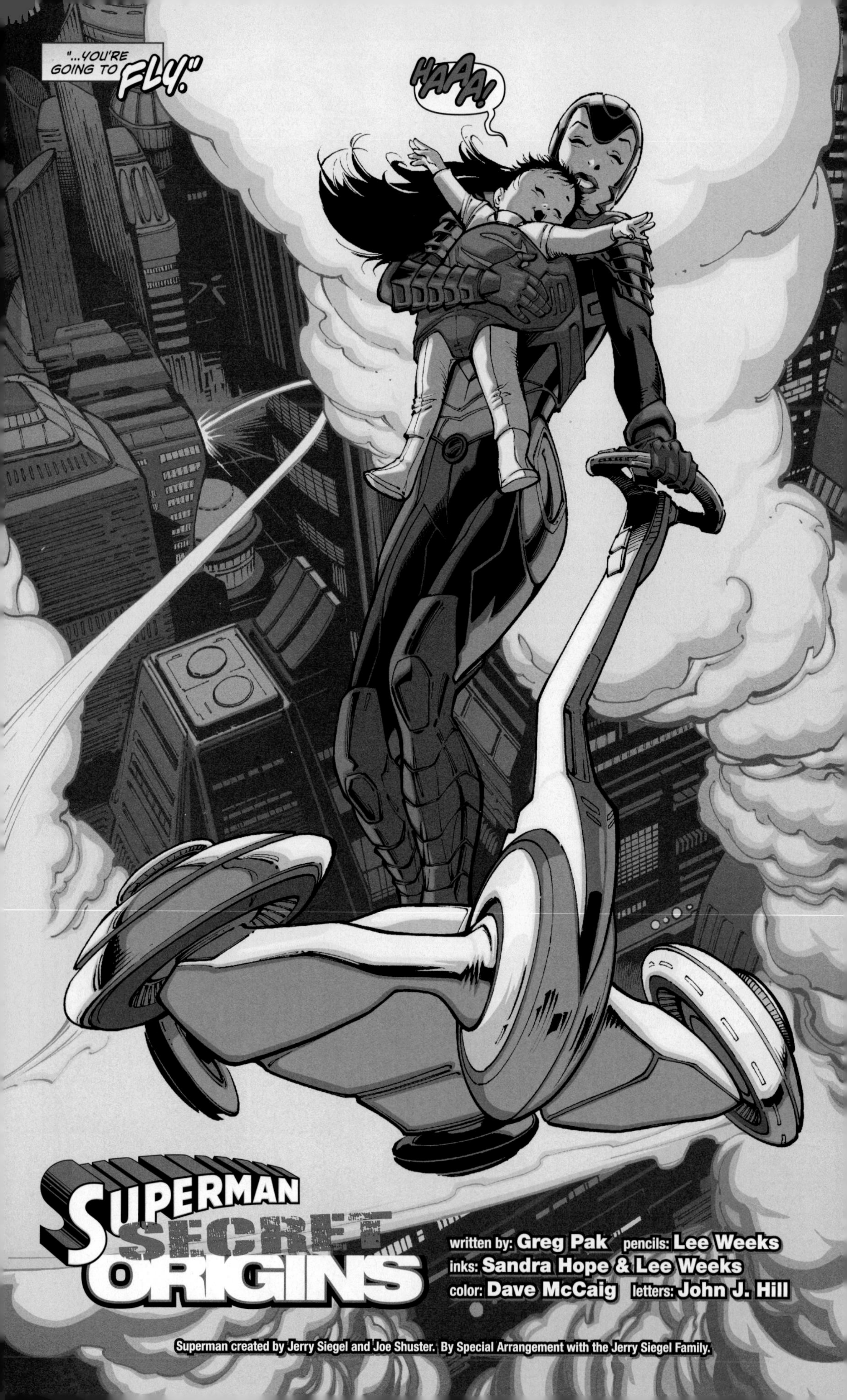
"...YOU'RE GOING TO FLY."
HAAAA!
SUPERMAN SECRET ORIGINS
written by: Greg Pak pencils: Lee Weeks
inks: Sandra Hope & Lee Weeks
color: Dave McCaig letters: John J. Hill
Superman created by Jerry Siegel and Joe Shuster. By Special Arrangement with the Jerry Siegel Family.

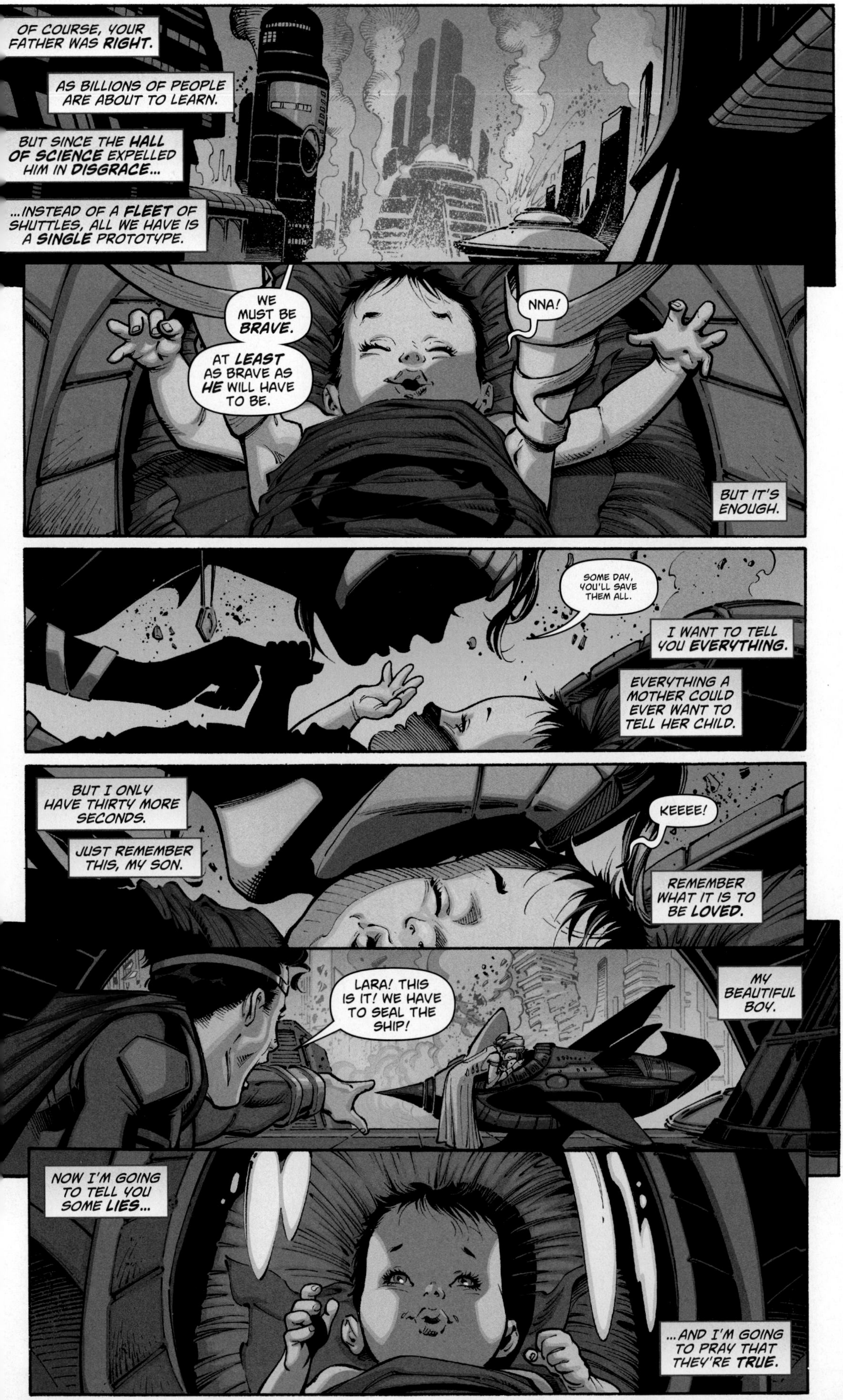
OF COURSE, YOUR FATHER WAS RIGHT.
AS BILLIONS OF PEOPLE ARE ABOUT TO LEARN.
BUT SINCE THE HALL OF SCIENCE EXPELLED HIM IN DISGRACE...
...INSTEAD OF A FLEET OF SHUTTLES, ALL WE HAVE IS A SINGLE PROTOTYPE.
WE MUST BE BRAVE.
AT LEAST AS BRAVE AS HE WILL HAVE TO BE.
NNA!
BUT IT'S ENOUGH.
SOME DAY, YOU'LL SAVE THEM ALL.
I WANT TO TELL YOU EVERYTHING.
EVERYTHING A MOTHER COULD EVER WANT TO TELL HER CHILD.
BUT I ONLY HAVE THIRTY MORE SECONDS.
JUST REMEMBER THIS, MY SON.
KEEEE!
REMEMBER WHAT IT IS TO BE LOVED.
LARA! THIS IS IT! WE HAVE TO SEAL THE SHIP!
MY BEAUTIFUL BOY.
NOW I'M GOING TO TELL YOU SOME LIES...
...AND I'M GOING TO PRAY THAT THEY'RE TRUE.

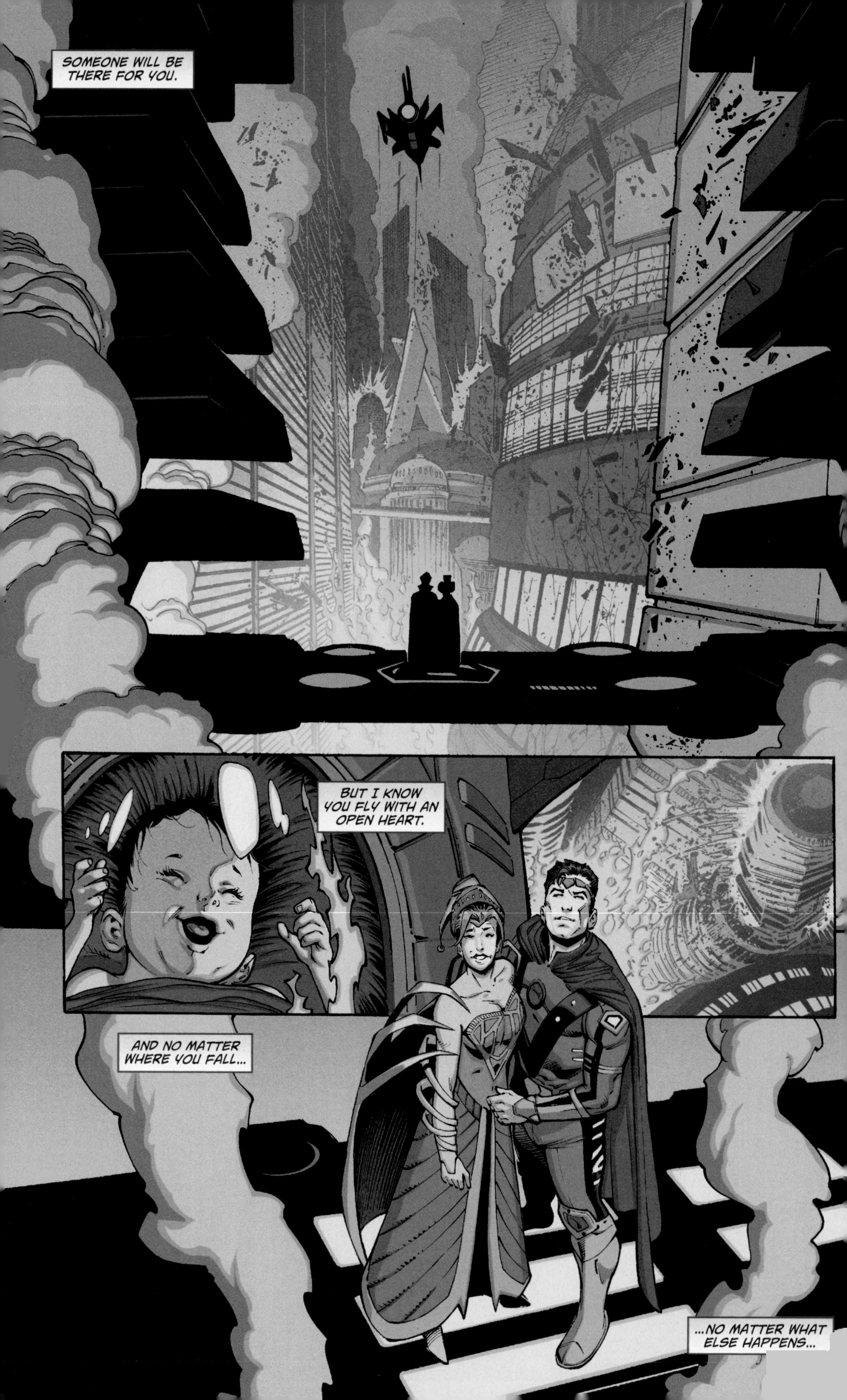
SOMEONE WILL BE THERE FOR YOU.
BUT I KNOW YOU FLY WITH AN OPEN HEART.
AND NO MATTER WHERE YOU FALL...
...NO MATTER WHAT ELSE HAPPENS...

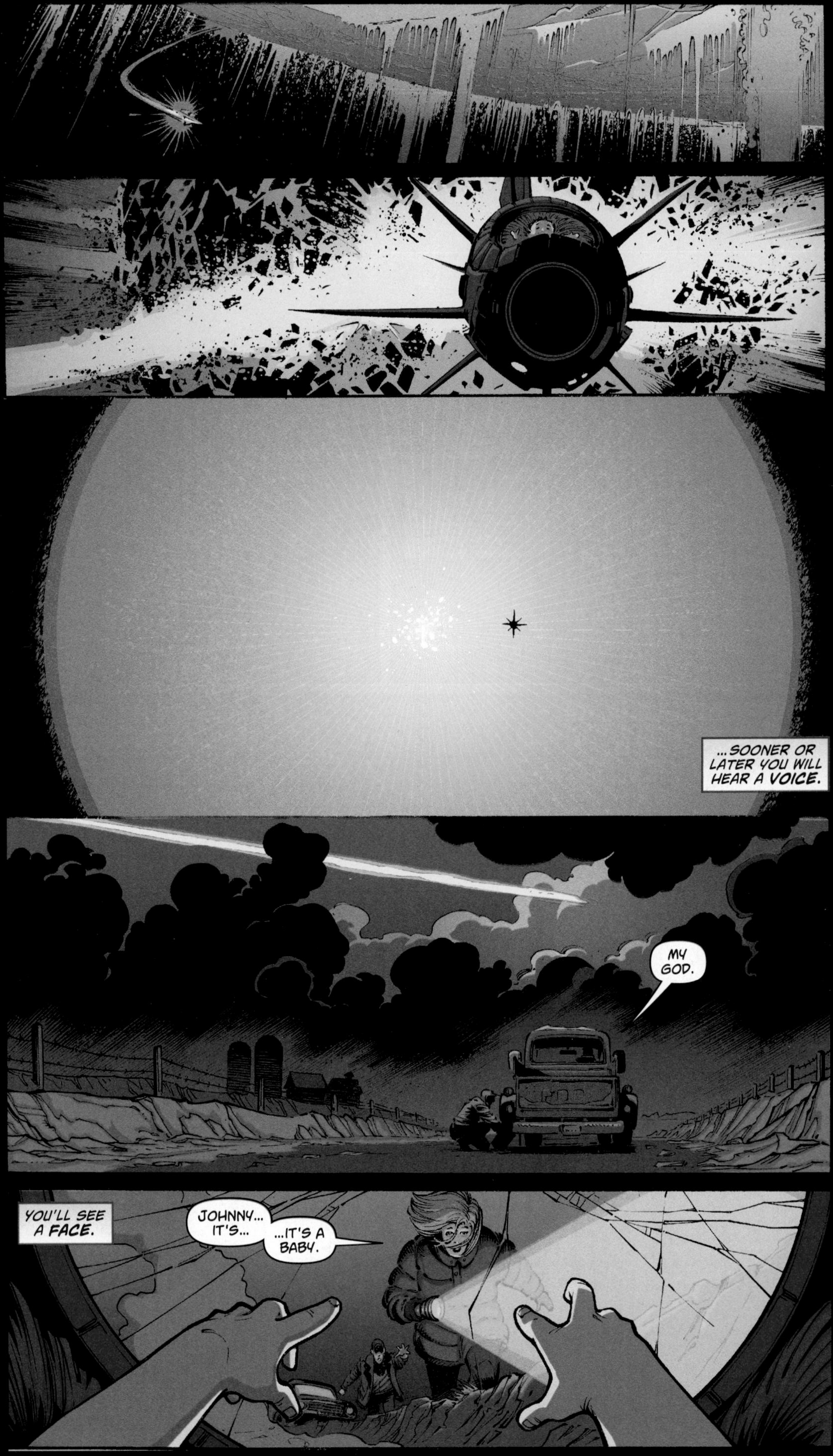
...SOONER OR LATER YOU WILL HEAR A VOICE.
MY GOD.
YOU'LL SEE A FACE.
JOHNNY... IT'S...
...IT'S A BABY.

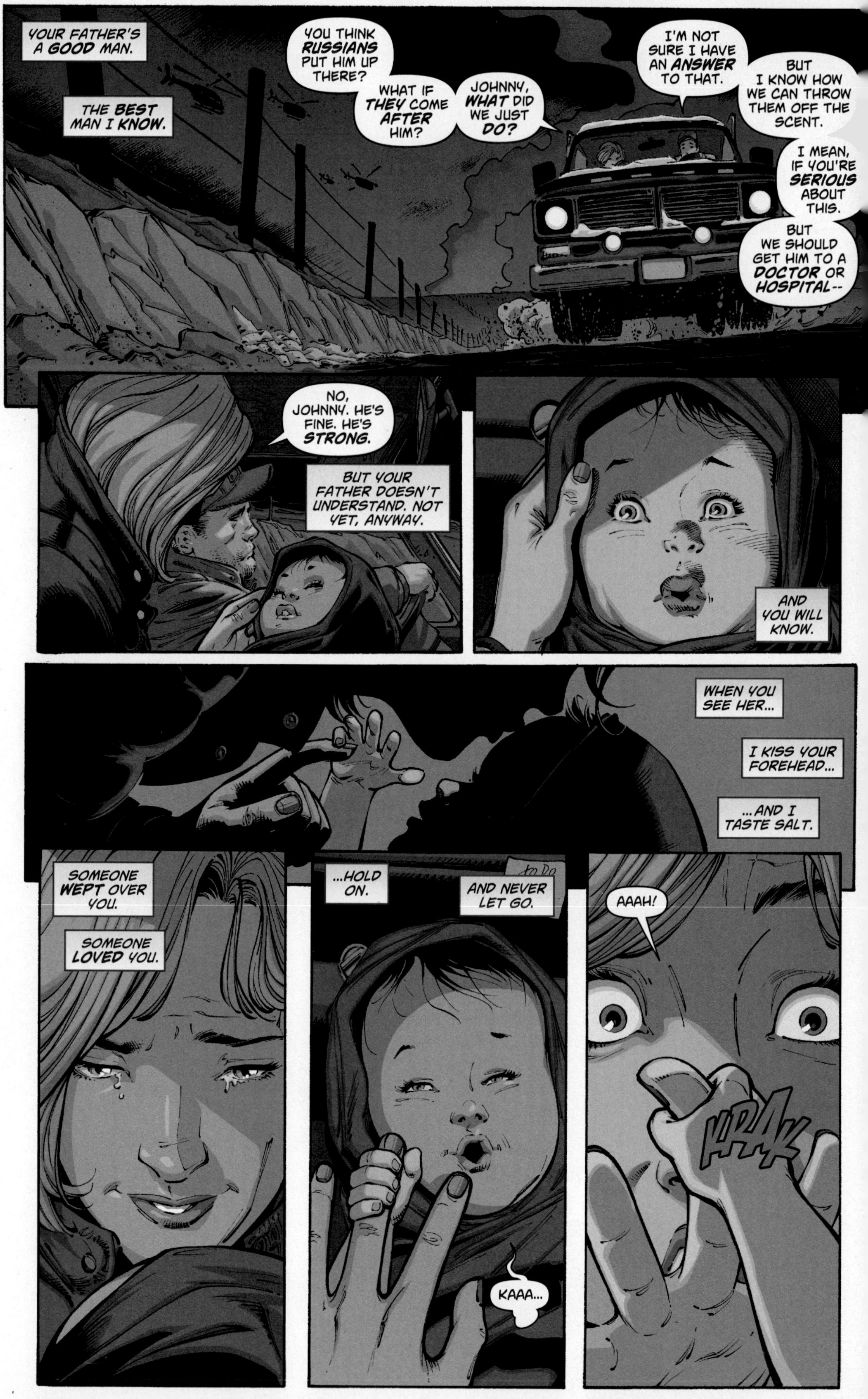
YOUR FATHER'S A GOOD MAN.
THE BEST MAN I KNOW.
YOU THINK RUSSIANS PUT HIM UP THERE?
WHAT IF THEY COME AFTER HIM?
JOHNNY, WHAT DID WE JUST DO?
I'M NOT SURE I HAVE AN ANSWER TO THAT.
BUT I KNOW HOW WE CAN THROW THEM OFF THE SCENT.
I MEAN, IF YOU'RE SERIOUS ABOUT THIS.
BUT WE SHOULD GET HIM TO A DOCTOR OR HOSPITAL--
NO, JOHNNY. HE'S FINE. HE'S STRONG.
BUT YOUR FATHER DOESN'T UNDERSTAND. NOT YET, ANYWAY.
AND YOU WILL KNOW.
WHEN YOU SEE HER...
I KISS YOUR FOREHEAD...
...AND I TASTE SALT.
SOMEONE WEPT OVER YOU.
SOMEONE LOVED YOU.
...HOLD ON.
AND NEVER LET GO.
KAAA...
AAAH!
KRAK

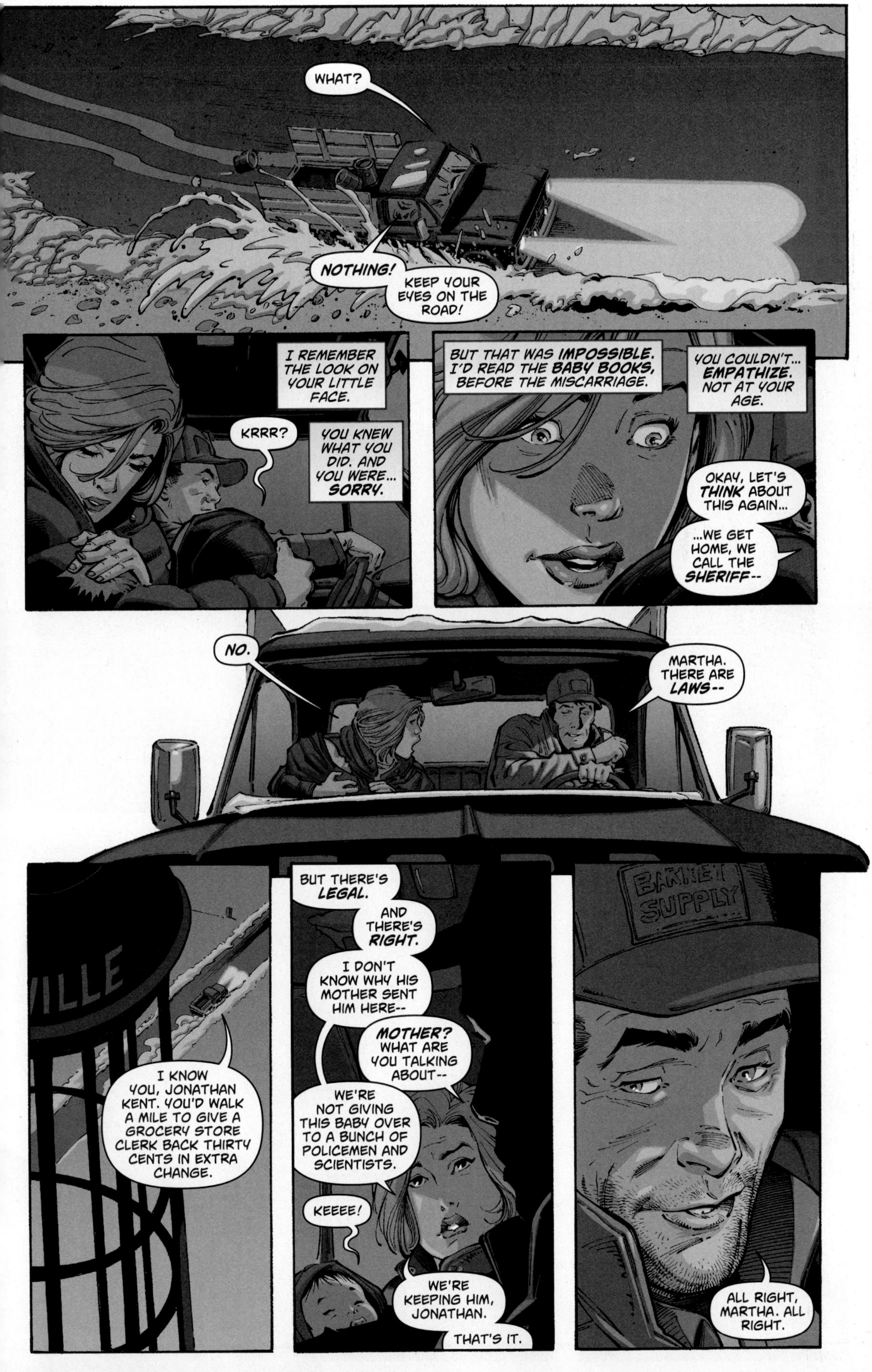
WHAT?
NOTHING!
KEEP YOUR EYES ON THE ROAD!
I REMEMBER THE LOOK ON YOUR LITTLE FACE.
KRRR?
YOU KNEW WHAT YOU DID. AND YOU WERE... SORRY.
BUT THAT WAS IMPOSSIBLE. I'D READ THE BABY BOOKS, BEFORE THE MISCARRIAGE.
YOU COULDN'T... EMPATHIZE. NOT AT YOUR AGE.
OKAY, LET'S THINK ABOUT THIS AGAIN...
...WE GET HOME, WE CALL THE SHERIFF--
NO.
MARTHA. THERE ARE LAWS--
VILLE
I KNOW YOU, JONATHAN KENT. YOU'D WALK A MILE TO GIVE A GROCERY STORE CLERK BACK THIRTY CENTS IN EXTRA CHANGE.
BUT THERE'S LEGAL.
AND THERE'S RIGHT.
I DON'T KNOW WHY HIS MOTHER SENT HIM HERE--
MOTHER? WHAT ARE YOU TALKING ABOUT--
WE'RE NOT GIVING THIS BABY OVER TO A BUNCH OF POLICEMEN AND SCIENTISTS.
KEEEE!
WE'RE KEEPING HIM, JONATHAN.
THAT'S IT.
SUPPLY
ALL RIGHT, MARTHA. ALL RIGHT.

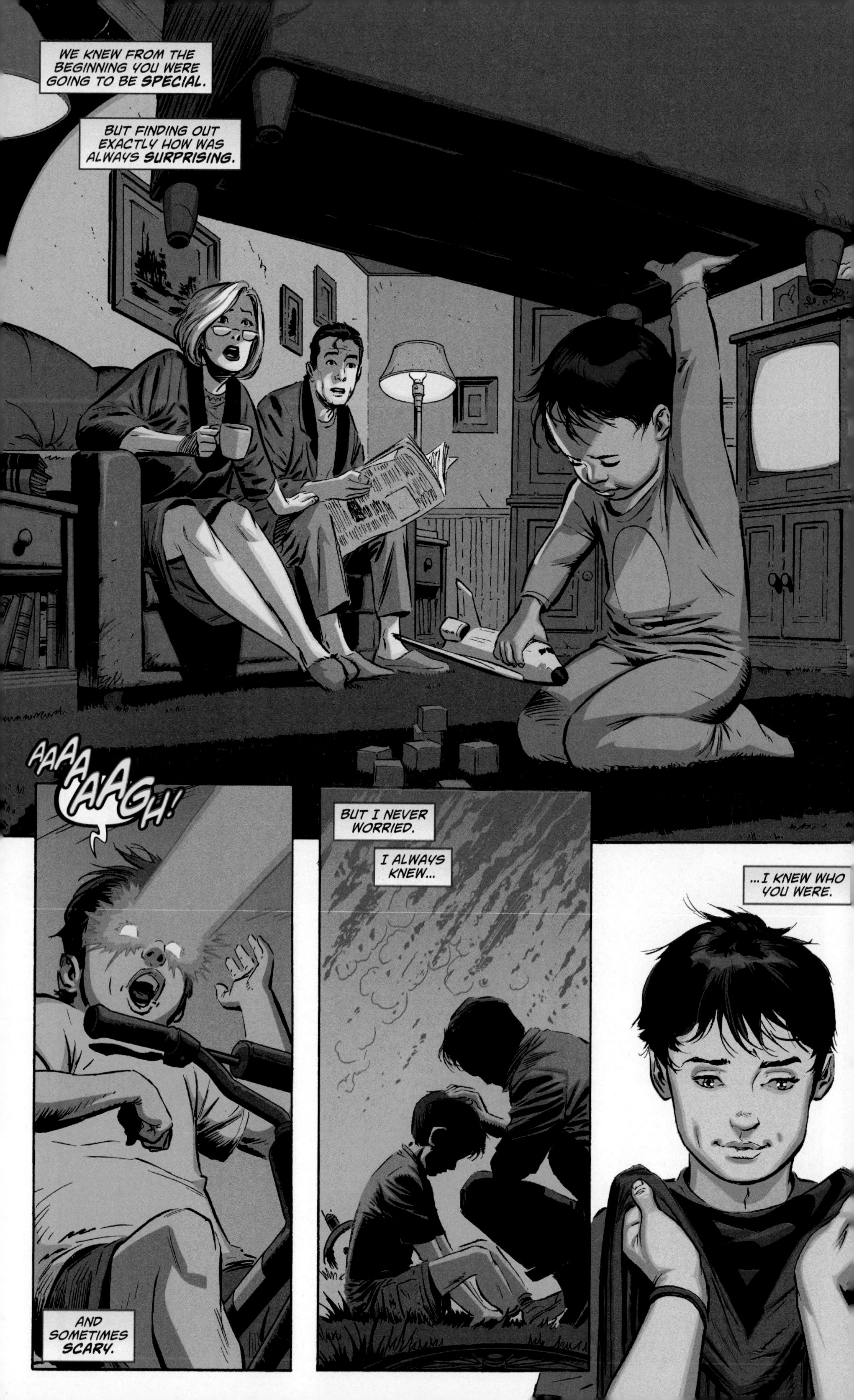

WE KNEW FROM THE BEGINNING YOU WERE GOING TO BE SPECIAL.
BUT FINDING OUT EXACTLY HOW WAS ALWAYS SURPRISING.
AAAAAAAGH!
AND SOMETIMES SCARY.
BUT I NEVER WORRIED.
I ALWAYS KNEW...
...I KNEW WHO YOU WERE.

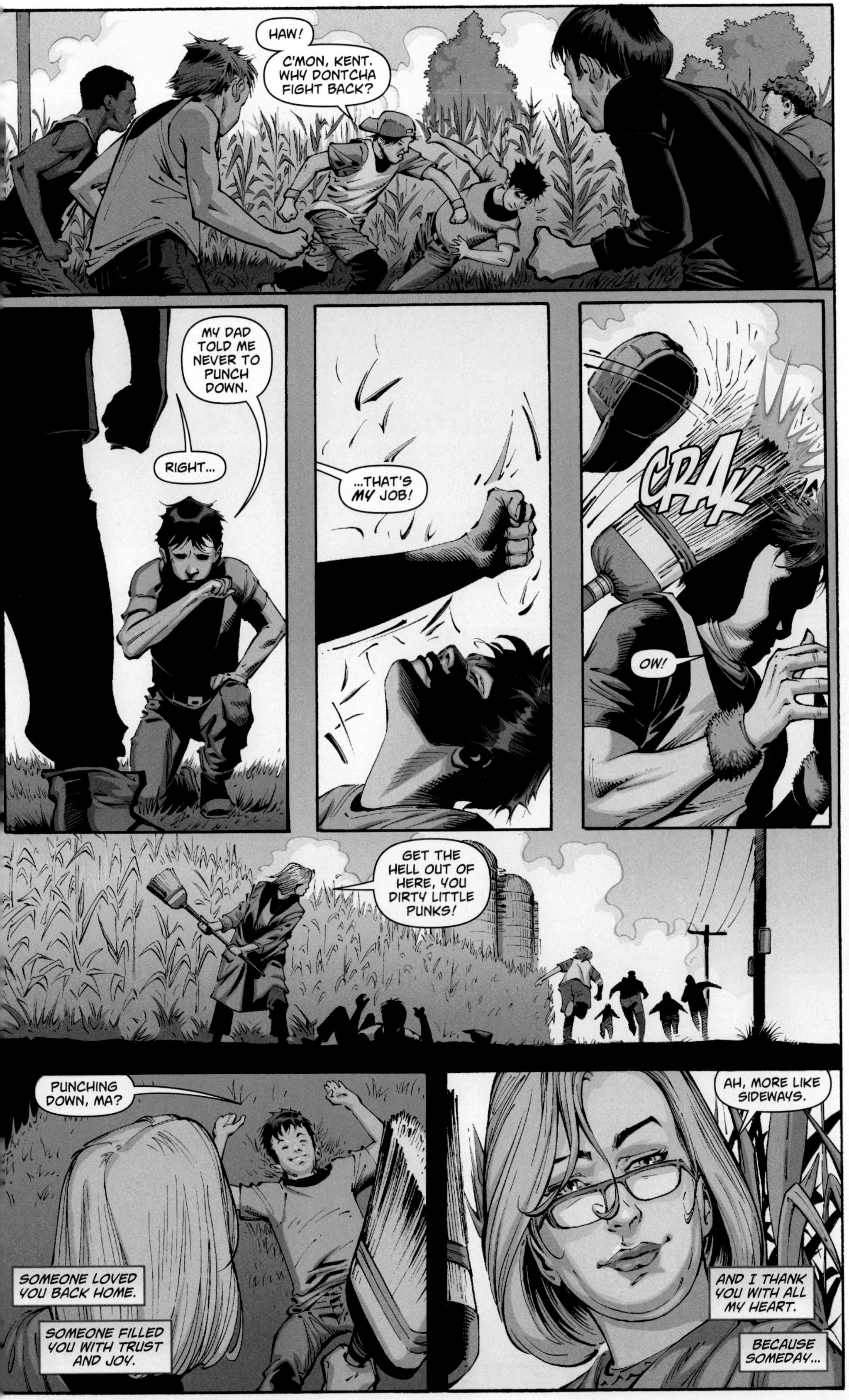
HAW!
C'MON, KENT. WHY DONTCHA FIGHT BACK?
MY DAD TOLD ME NEVER TO PUNCH DOWN.
RIGHT...
...THAT'S MY JOB!
CRAK
OW!
GET THE HELL OUT OF HERE, YOU DIRTY LITTLE PUNKS!
PUNCHING DOWN, MA?
SOMEONE LOVED YOU BACK HOME.
SOMEONE FILLED YOU WITH TRUST AND JOY.
AH, MORE LIKE SIDEWAYS.
AND I THANK YOU WITH ALL MY HEART.
BECAUSE SOMEDAY...

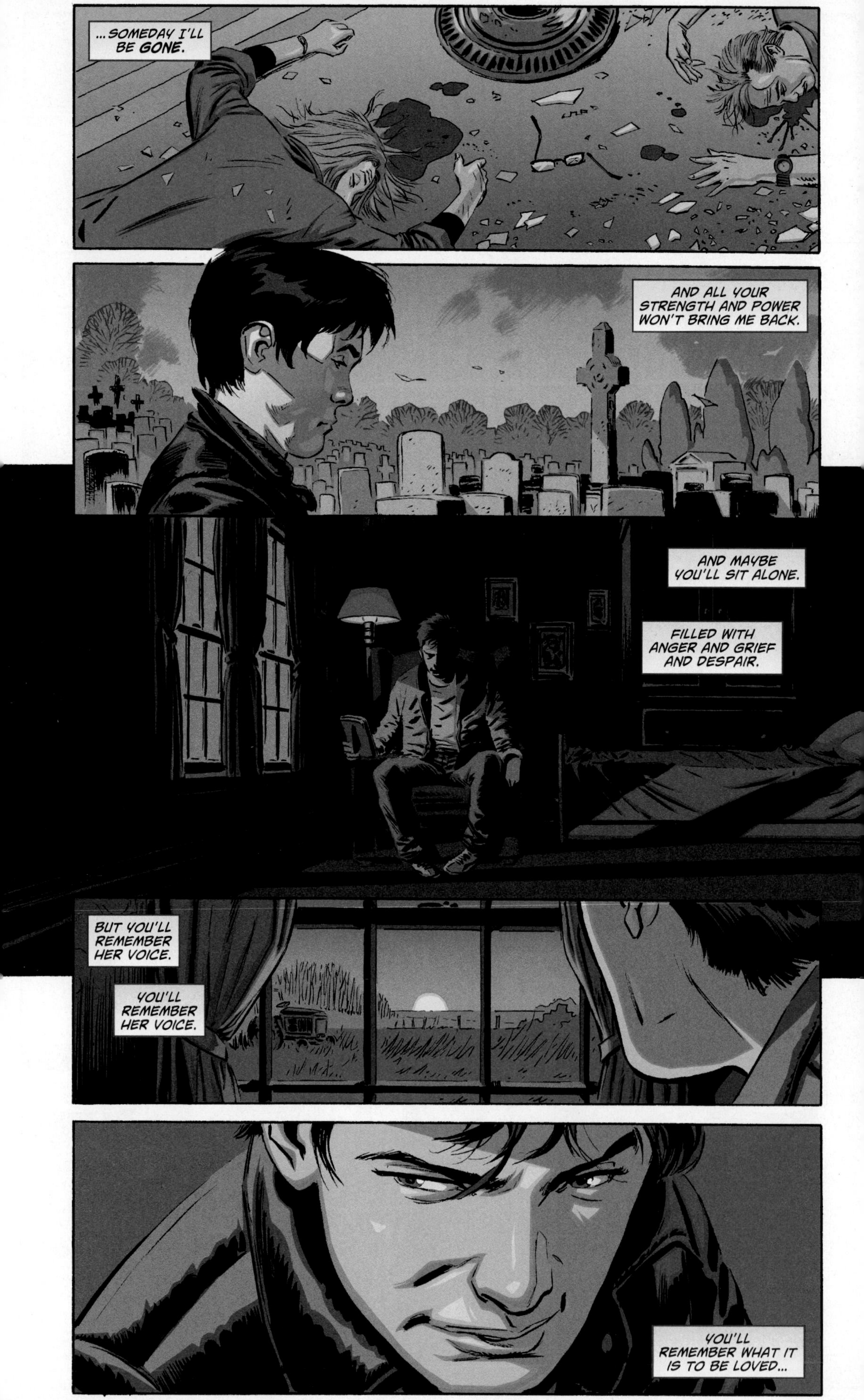
...SOMEDAY I'LL BE GONE.
AND ALL YOUR STRENGTH AND POWER WON'T BRING ME BACK.
AND MAYBE YOU'LL SIT ALONE.
FILLED WITH ANGER AND GRIEF AND DESPAIR.
BUT YOU'LL REMEMBER HER VOICE.
YOU'LL REMEMBER HER VOICE.
YOU'LL REMEMBER WHAT IT IS TO BE LOVED...

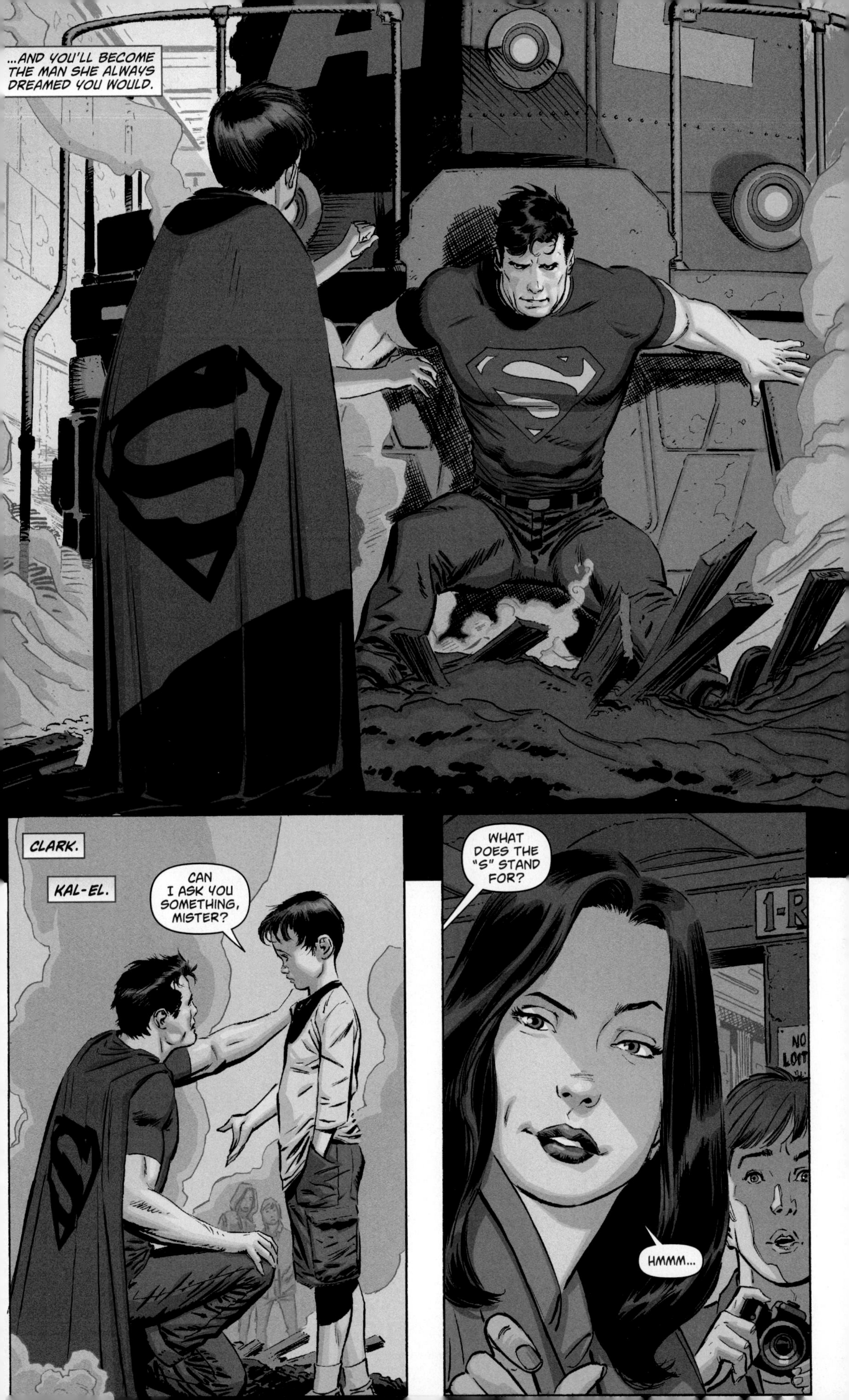
...AND YOU'LL BECOME THE MAN SHE ALWAYS DREAMED YOU WOULD.
CLARK.
KAL-EL.
CAN I ASK YOU SOMETHING, MISTER?
WHAT DOES THE "S" STAND FOR?
HMMM...
1-R
NO LOI

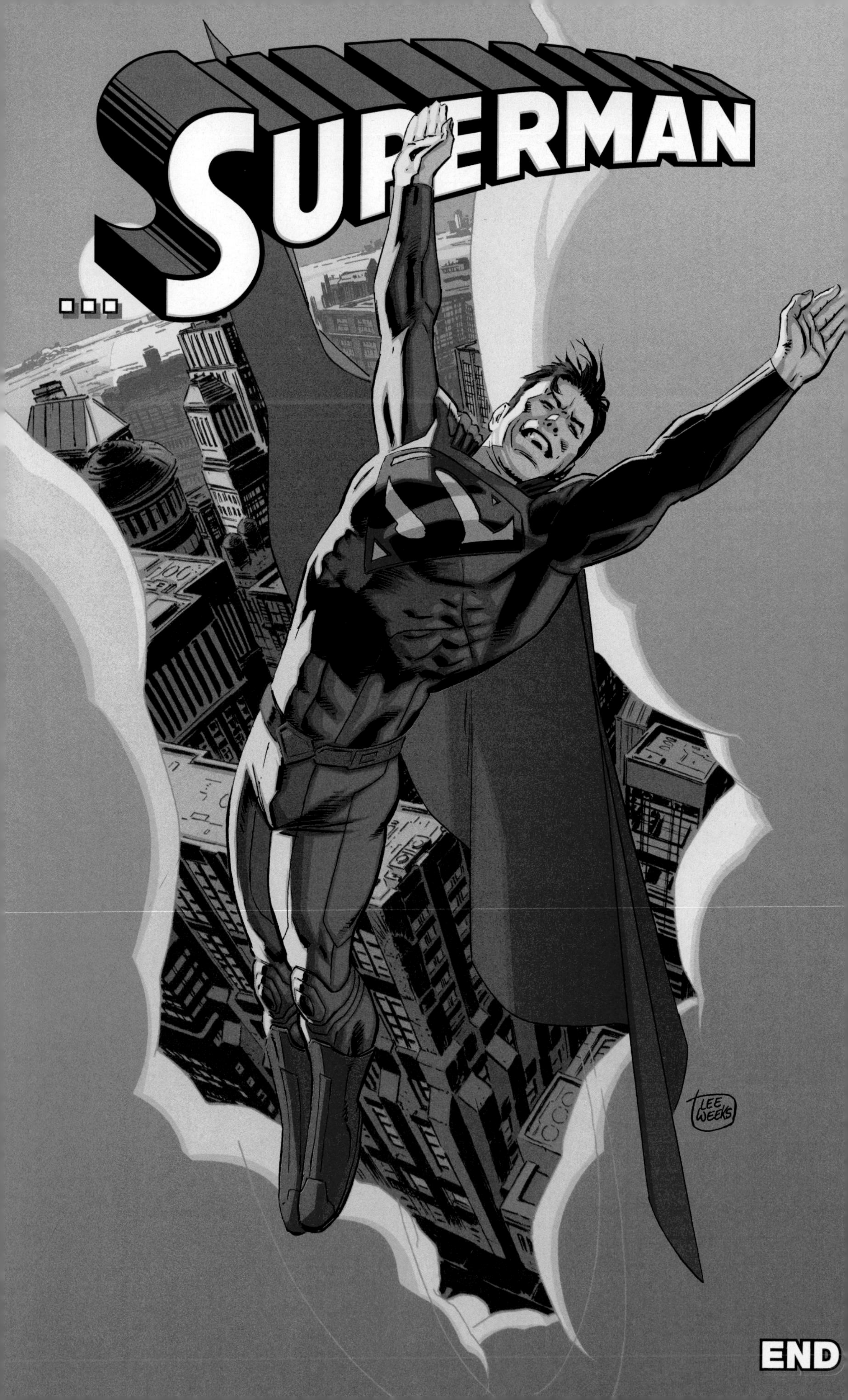
SUPERMAN
...
LEE WEEKS
END

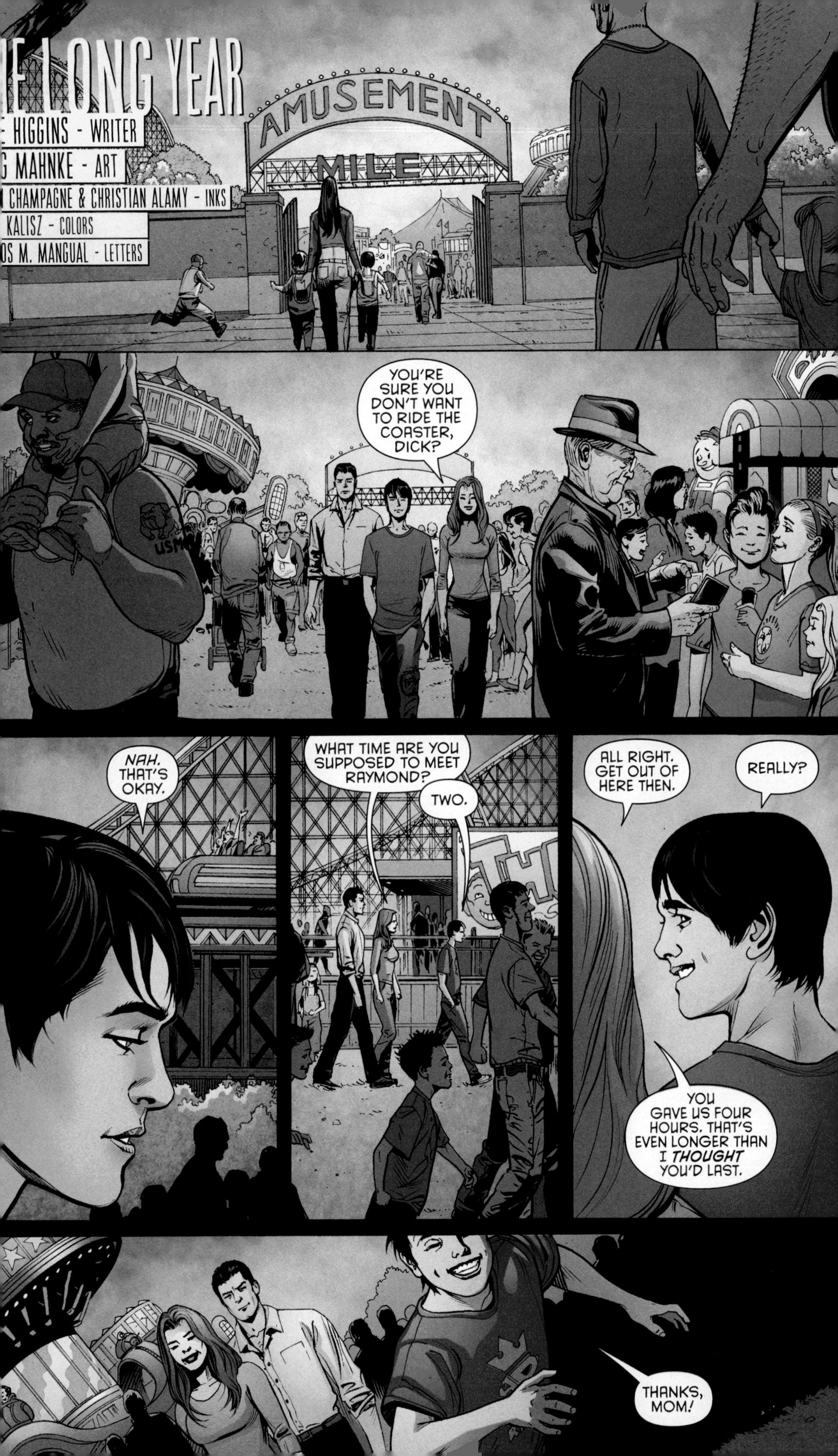
LONG YEAR
HIGGINS - WRITER
MAHNKE - ART
CHAMPAGNE & CHRISTIAN ALAMY - INKS
KALISZ - COLORS
M. MANGUAL - LETTERS
AMUSEMENT
MILE
YOU'RE SURE YOU DON'T WANT TO RIDE THE COASTER, DICK?
NAH. THAT'S OKAY.
WHAT TIME ARE YOU SUPPOSED TO MEET RAYMOND?
TWO.
ALL RIGHT. GET OUT OF HERE THEN.
REALLY?
YOU GAVE US FOUR HOURS. THAT'S EVEN LONGER THAN I *THOUGHT* YOU'D LAST.
THANKS, MOM!

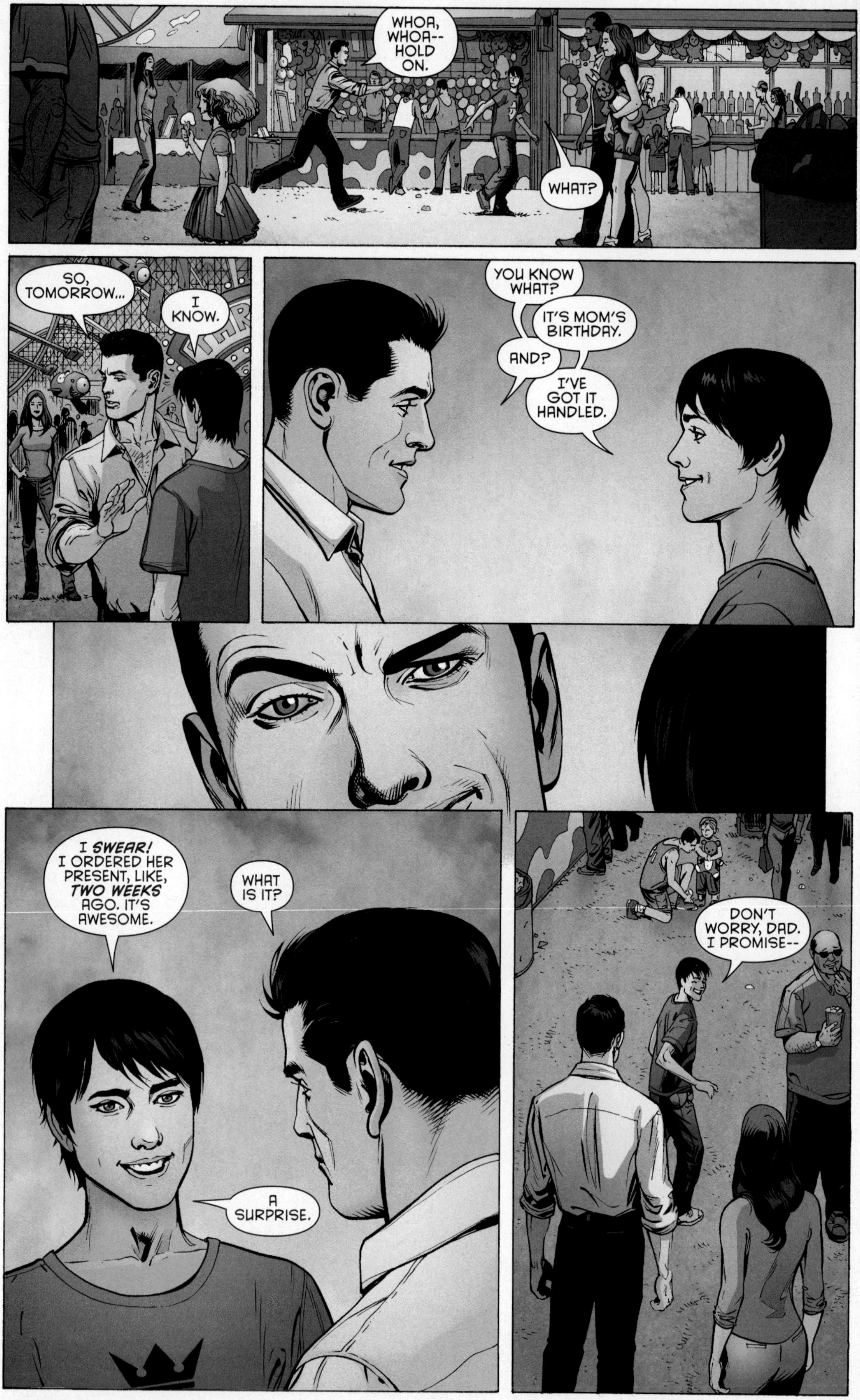
WHOA, WHOA-- HOLD ON.
WHAT?
SO, TOMORROW...
I KNOW.
YOU KNOW WHAT?
IT'S MOM'S BIRTHDAY.
AND?
I'VE GOT IT HANDLED.
I SWEAR! I ORDERED HER PRESENT, LIKE, TWO WEEKS AGO. IT'S AWESOME.
WHAT IS IT?
A SURPRISE.
DON'T WORRY, DAD. I PROMISE--

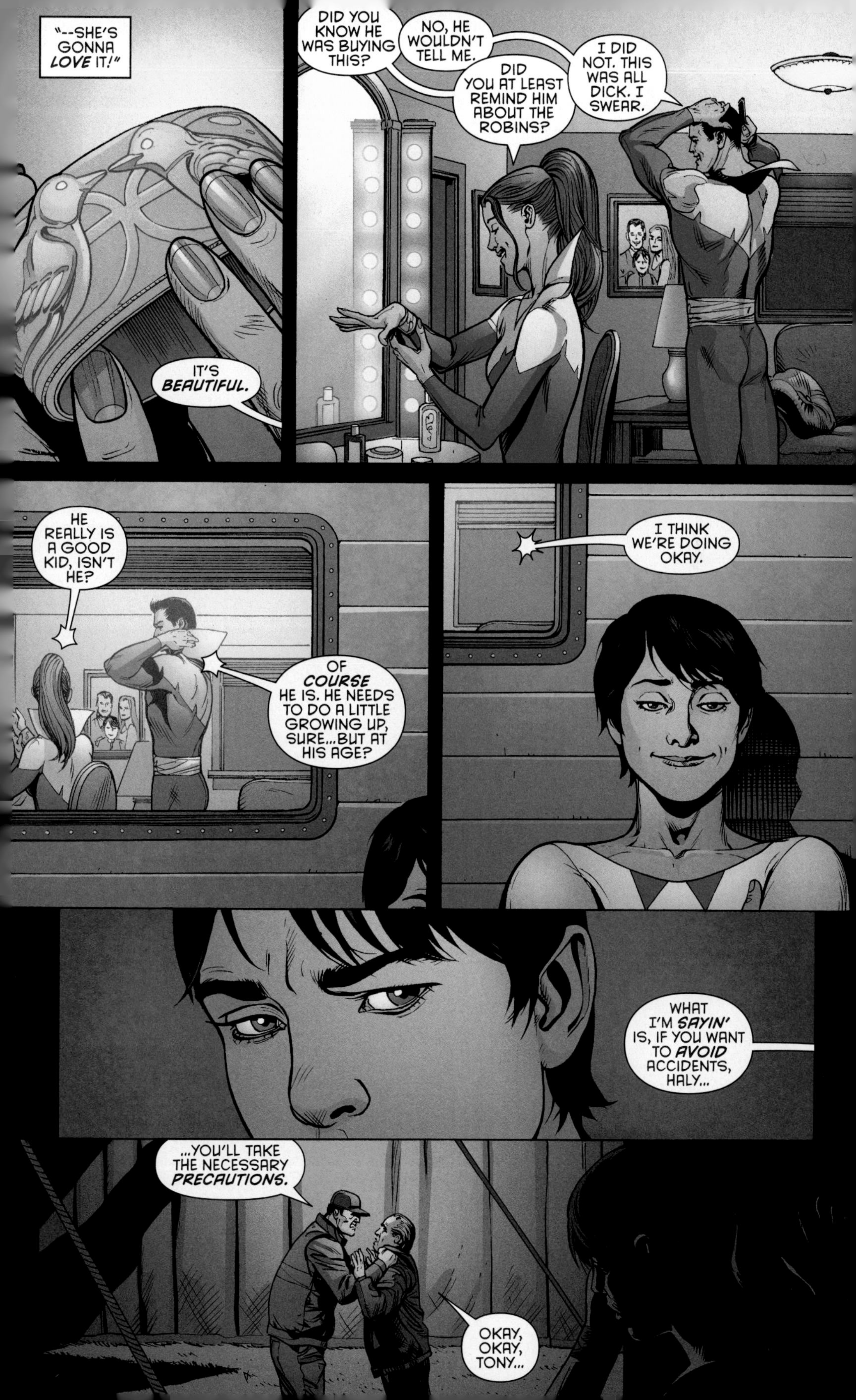
"--SHE'S GONNA *LOVE* IT!"
IT'S *BEAUTIFUL.*
DID YOU KNOW HE WAS BUYING THIS?
NO, HE WOULDN'T TELL ME.
DID YOU AT LEAST REMIND HIM ABOUT THE ROBINS?
I DID NOT. THIS WAS ALL DICK. I SWEAR.
HE REALLY IS A GOOD KID, ISN'T HE?
OF *COURSE* HE IS. HE NEEDS TO DO A LITTLE GROWING UP, SURE...BUT AT HIS AGE?
I THINK WE'RE DOING OKAY.
WHAT I'M *SAYIN'* IS, IF YOU WANT TO *AVOID* ACCIDENTS, HALY...
...YOU'LL TAKE THE NECESSARY *PRECAUTIONS.*
OKAY, OKAY, TONY...

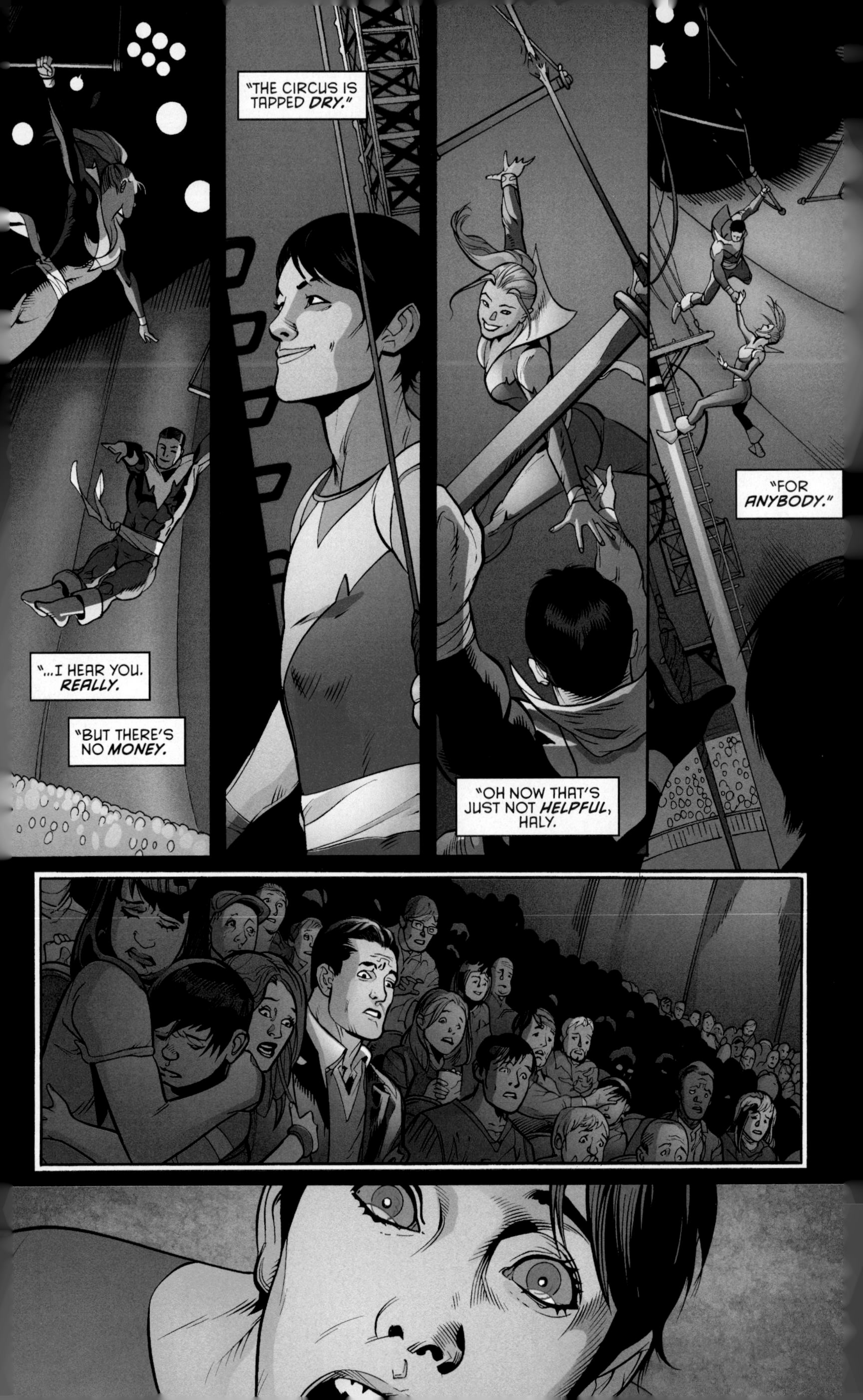
"...I HEAR YOU. REALLY.
"BUT THERE'S NO MONEY.
"THE CIRCUS IS TAPPED DRY."
"OH NOW THAT'S JUST NOT HELPFUL, HALY.
"FOR ANYBODY."

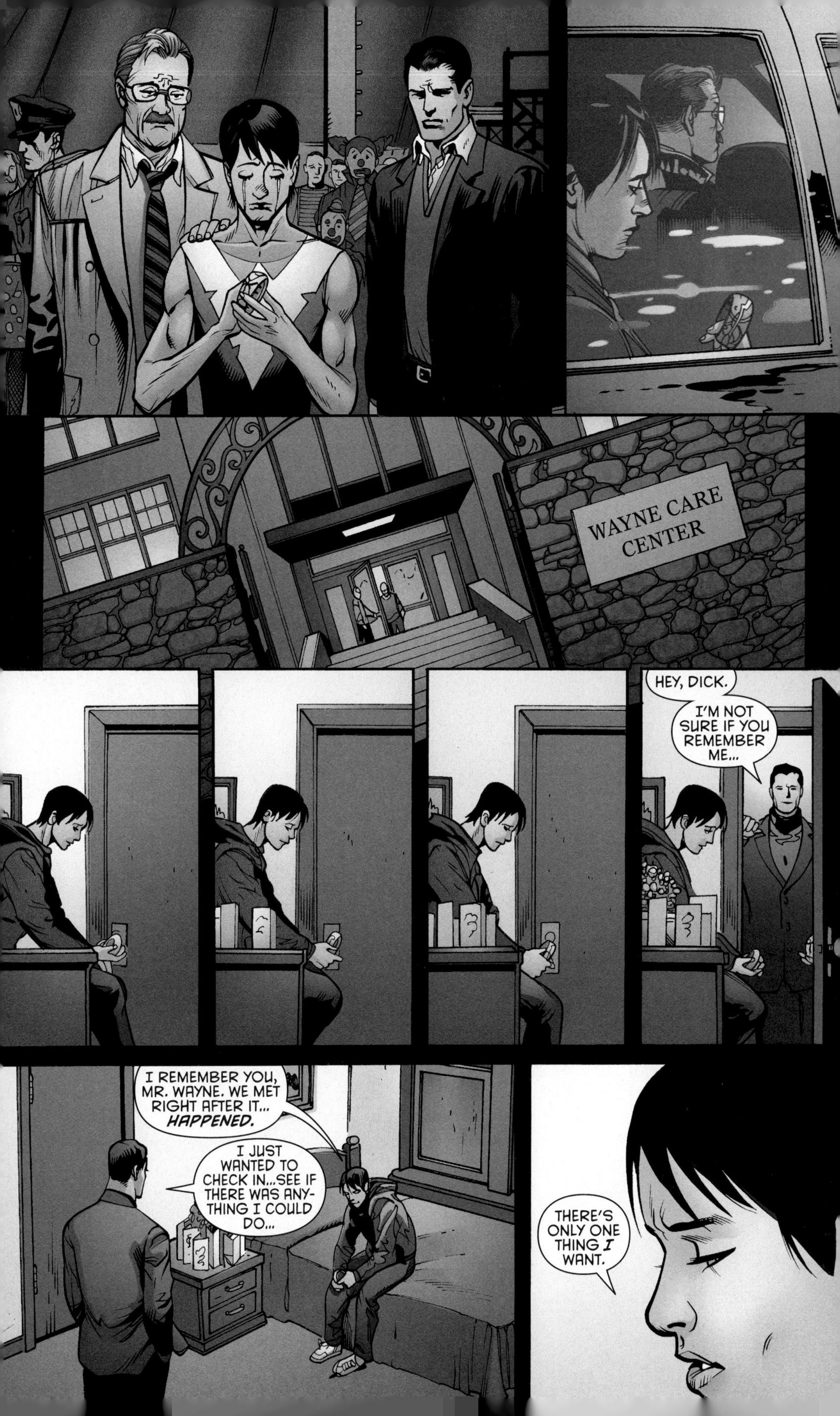
WAYNE CARE CENTER
HEY, DICK.
I'M NOT SURE IF YOU REMEMBER ME...
I REMEMBER YOU, MR. WAYNE. WE MET RIGHT AFTER IT... HAPPENED.
I JUST WANTED TO CHECK IN...SEE IF THERE WAS ANY-THING I COULD DO...
THERE'S ONLY ONE THING I WANT.

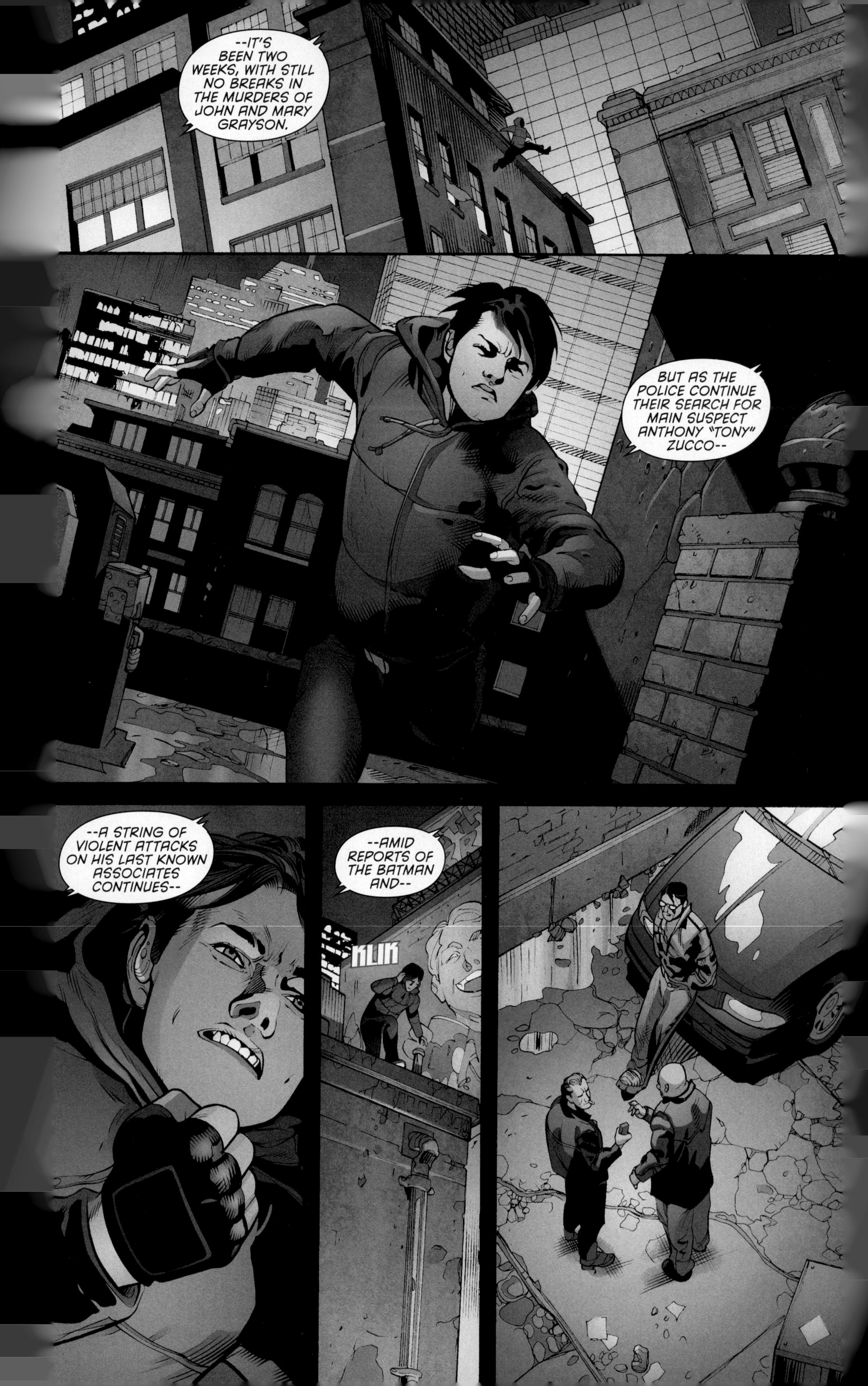
--IT'S BEEN TWO WEEKS, WITH STILL NO BREAKS IN THE MURDERS OF JOHN AND MARY GRAYSON.
BUT AS THE POLICE CONTINUE THEIR SEARCH FOR MAIN SUSPECT ANTHONY "TONY" ZUCCO--
--A STRING OF VIOLENT ATTACKS ON HIS LAST KNOWN ASSOCIATES CONTINUES--
--AMID REPORTS OF THE BATMAN AND--
KLIK

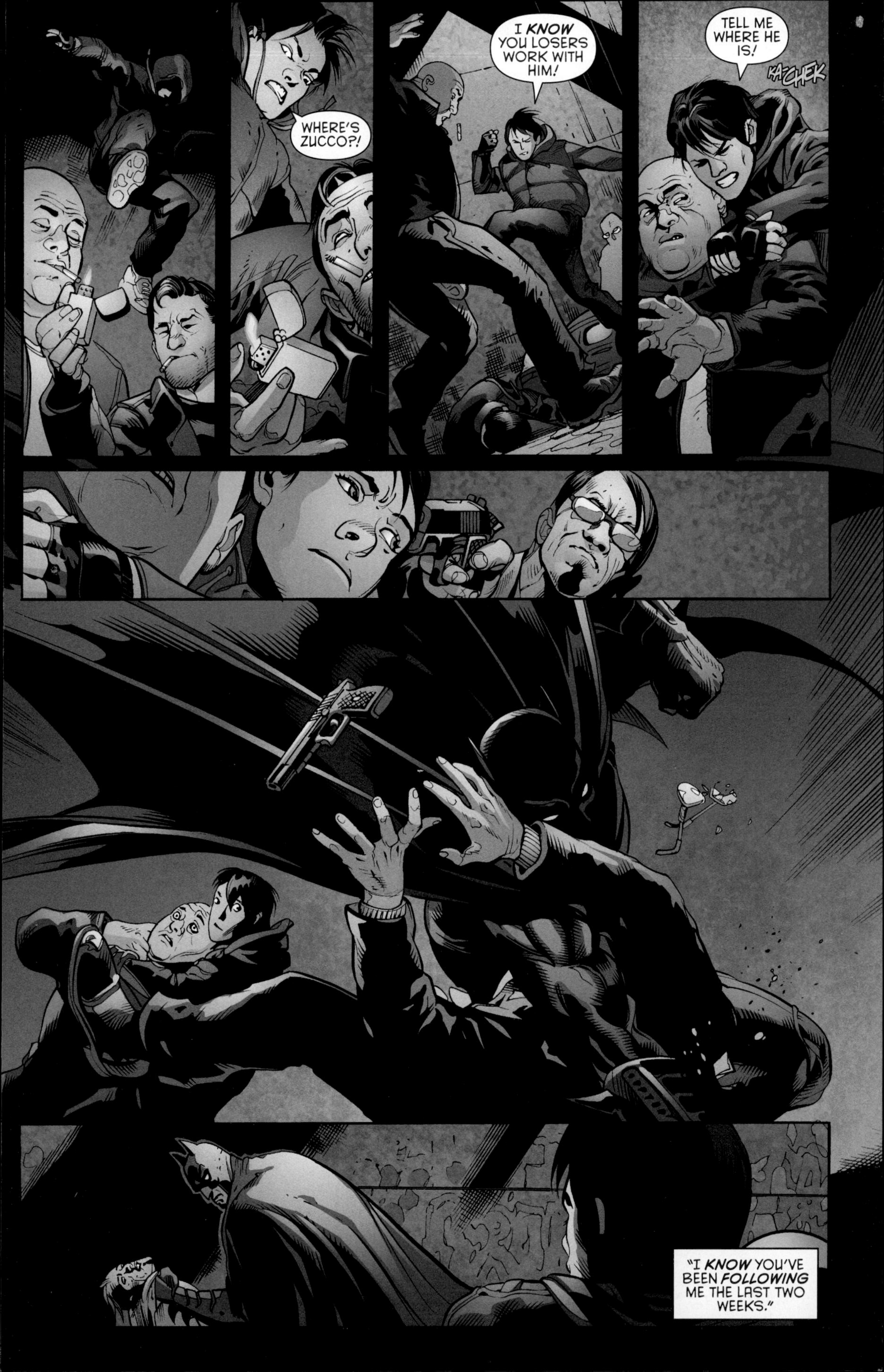
WHERE'S ZUCCO?!
I *KNOW* YOU LOSERS WORK WITH HIM!
TELL ME WHERE HE IS!
KA-CHEK
"I *KNOW* YOU'VE BEEN *FOLLOWING* ME THE LAST TWO WEEKS."

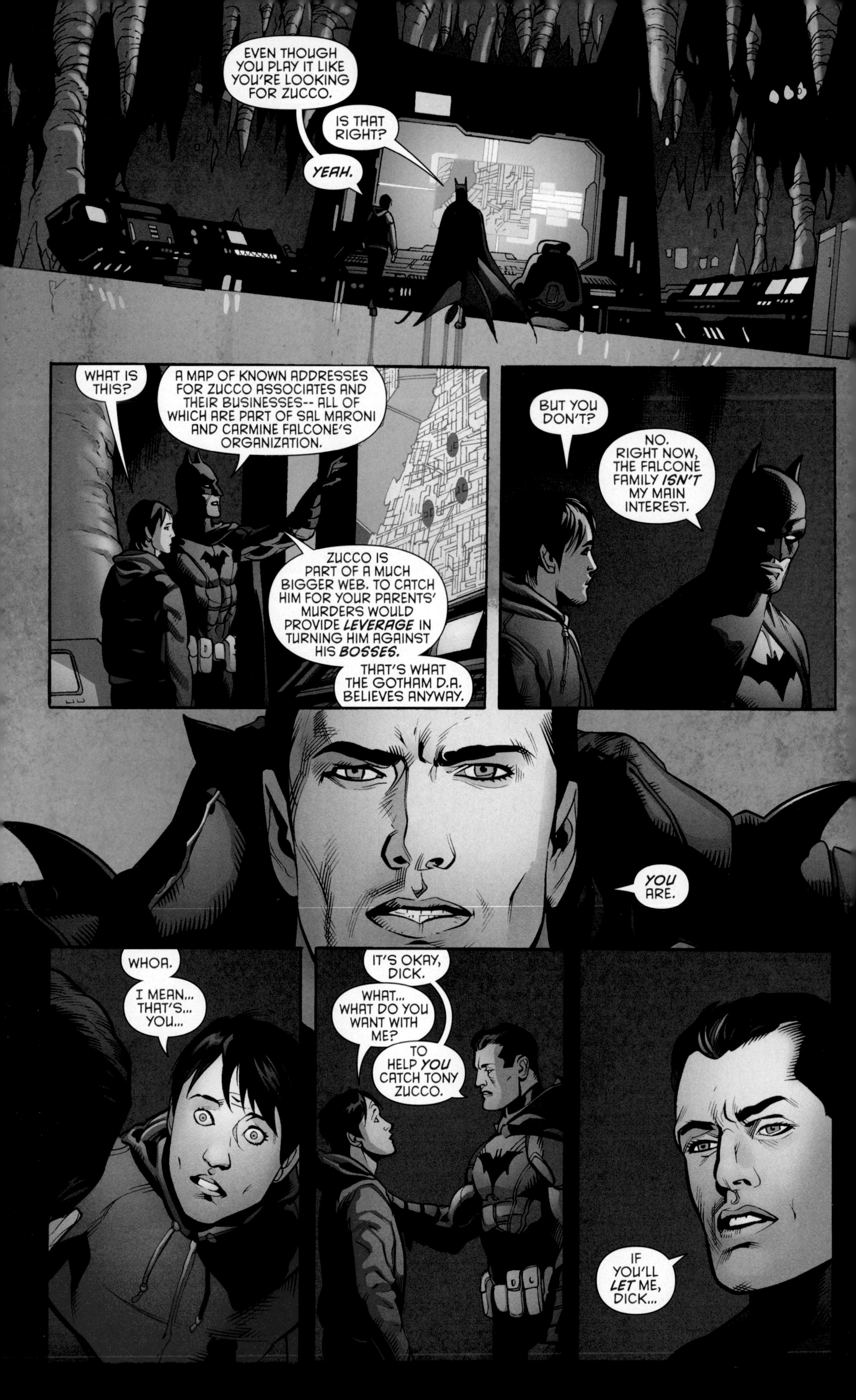
EVEN THOUGH YOU PLAY IT LIKE YOU'RE LOOKING FOR ZUCCO.
IS THAT RIGHT?
YEAH.
WHAT IS THIS?
A MAP OF KNOWN ADDRESSES FOR ZUCCO ASSOCIATES AND THEIR BUSINESSES-- ALL OF WHICH ARE PART OF SAL MARONI AND CARMINE FALCONE'S ORGANIZATION.
ZUCCO IS PART OF A MUCH BIGGER WEB. TO CATCH HIM FOR YOUR PARENTS' MURDERS WOULD PROVIDE LEVERAGE IN TURNING HIM AGAINST HIS BOSSES.
THAT'S WHAT THE GOTHAM D.A. BELIEVES ANYWAY.
BUT YOU DON'T?
NO. RIGHT NOW, THE FALCONE FAMILY ISN'T MY MAIN INTEREST.
YOU ARE.
WHOA.
I MEAN... THAT'S... YOU...
IT'S OKAY, DICK.
WHAT... WHAT DO YOU WANT WITH ME?
TO HELP YOU CATCH TONY ZUCCO.
IF YOU'LL LET ME, DICK...

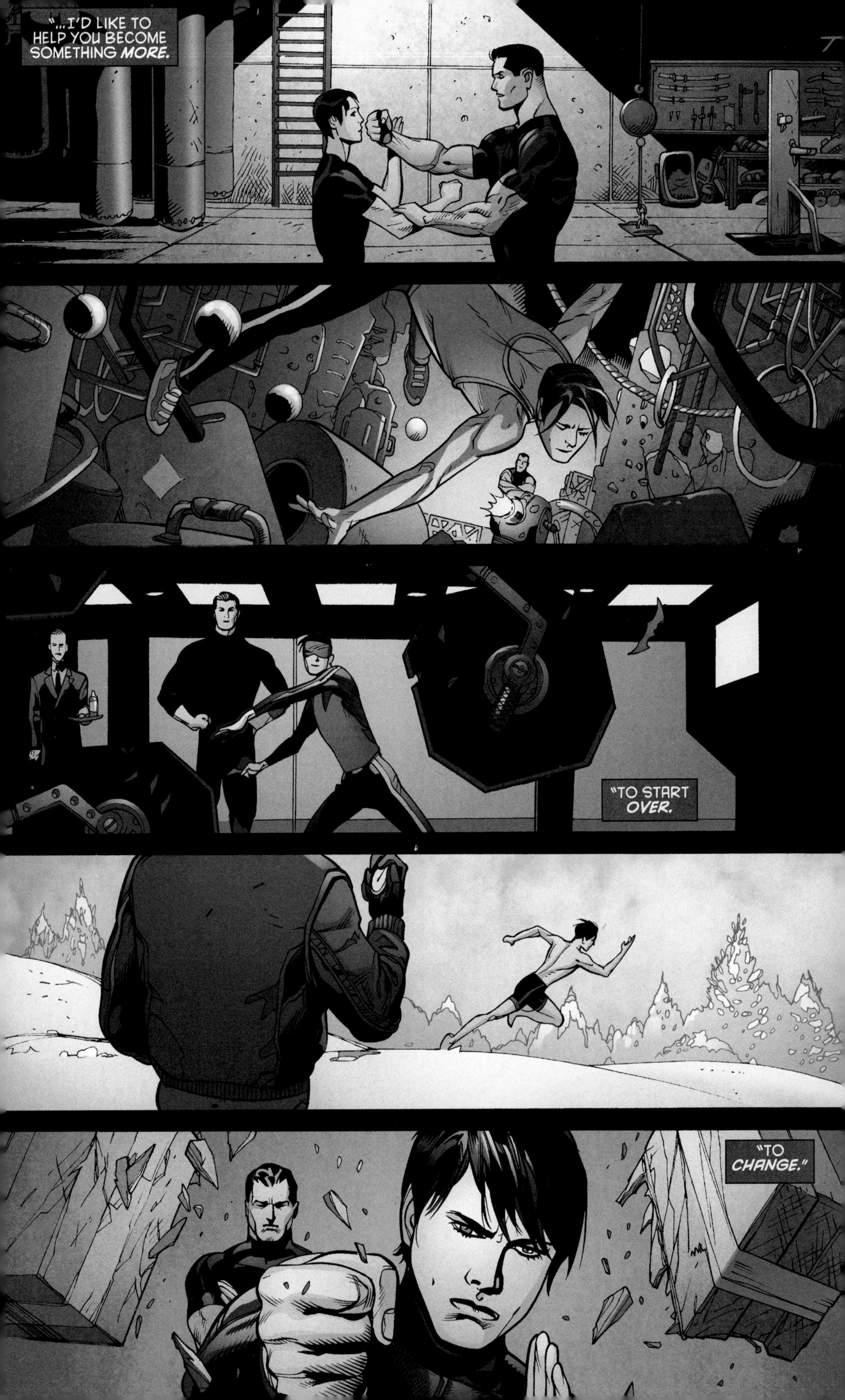
"...I'D LIKE TO HELP YOU BECOME SOMETHING *MORE*.
"TO START *OVER*.
"TO *CHANGE*."

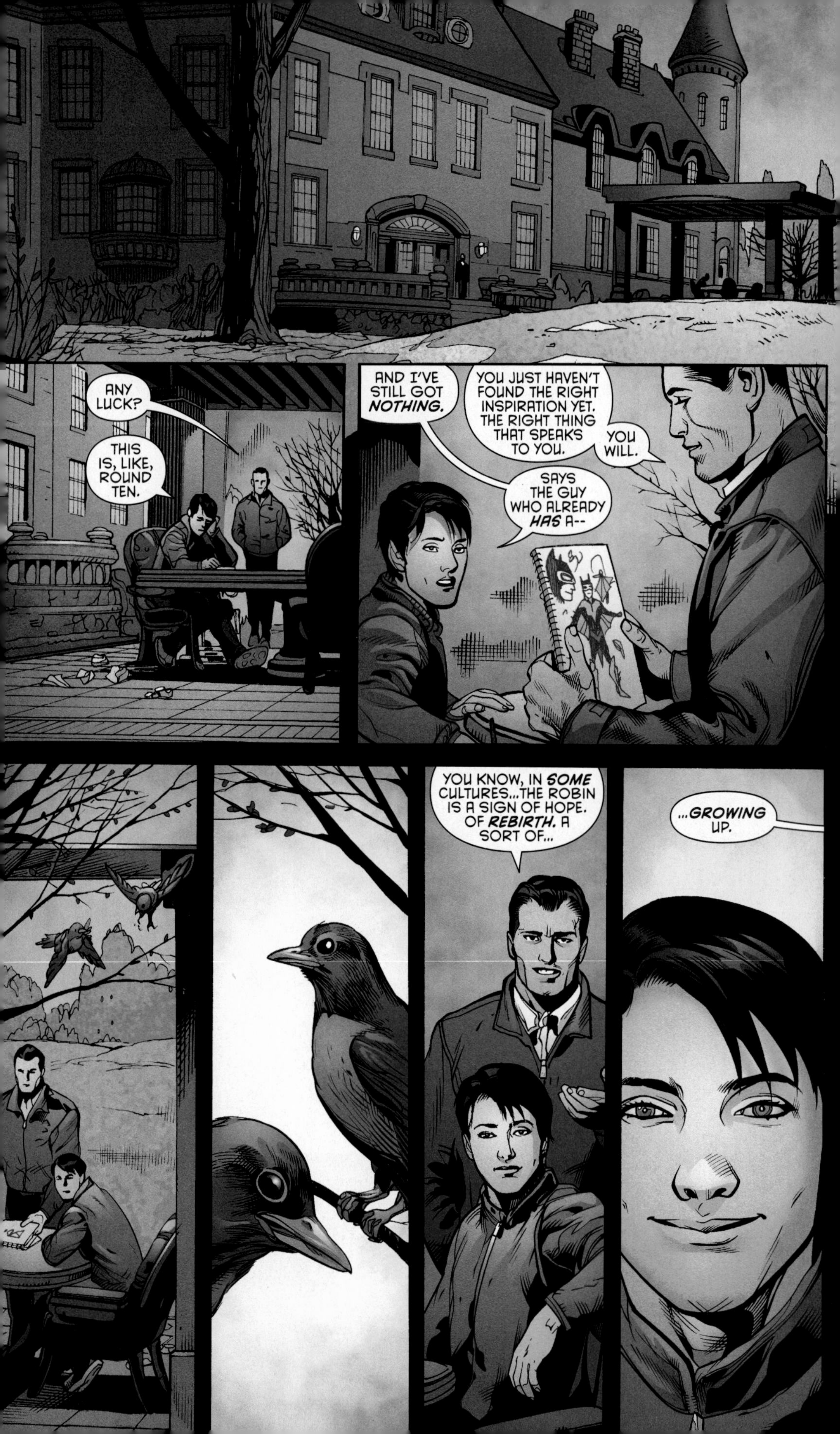
ANY LUCK?
THIS IS, LIKE, ROUND TEN.
AND I'VE STILL GOT NOTHING.
YOU JUST HAVEN'T FOUND THE RIGHT INSPIRATION YET. THE RIGHT THING THAT SPEAKS TO YOU.
YOU WILL.
SAYS THE GUY WHO ALREADY HAS A--
YOU KNOW, IN SOME CULTURES...THE ROBIN IS A SIGN OF HOPE. OF REBIRTH. A SORT OF...
...GROWING UP.

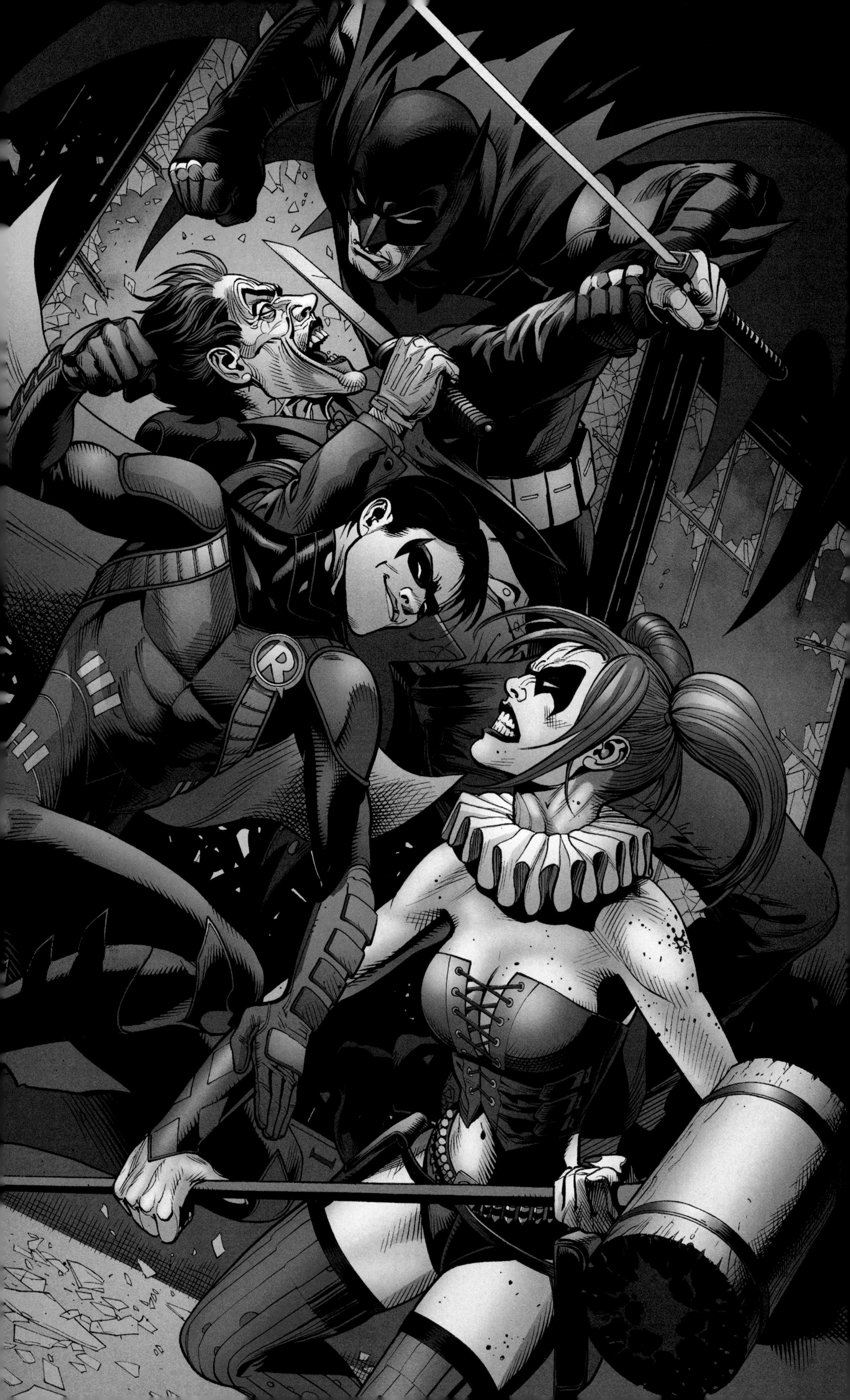

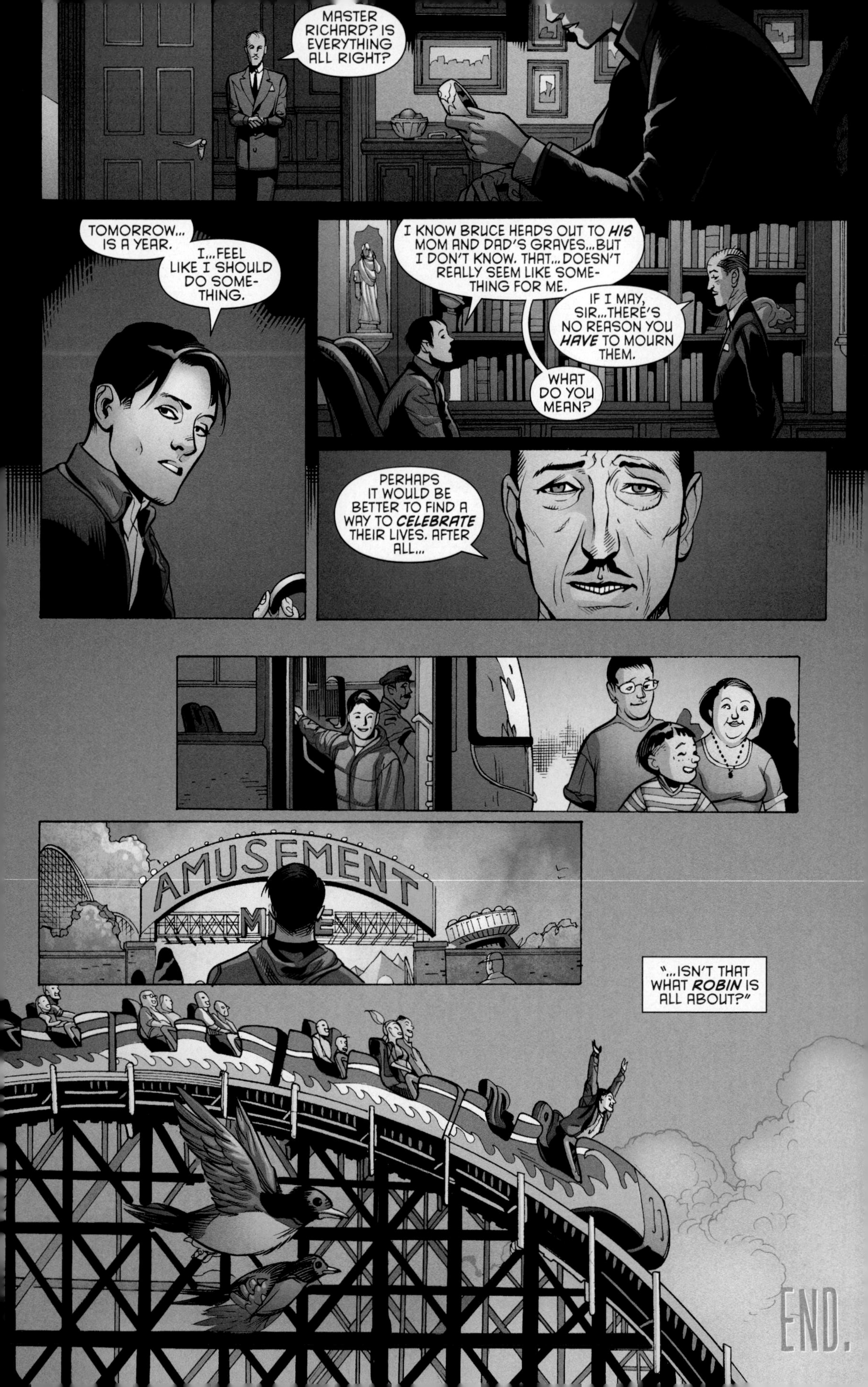
MASTER RICHARD? IS EVERYTHING ALL RIGHT?
TOMORROW... IS A YEAR.
I...FEEL LIKE I SHOULD DO SOME-THING.
I KNOW BRUCE HEADS OUT TO HIS MOM AND DAD'S GRAVES...BUT I DON'T KNOW. THAT...DOESN'T REALLY SEEM LIKE SOME-THING FOR ME.
IF I MAY, SIR...THERE'S NO REASON YOU HAVE TO MOURN THEM.
WHAT DO YOU MEAN?
PERHAPS IT WOULD BE BETTER TO FIND A WAY TO CELEBRATE THEIR LIVES. AFTER ALL...
AMUSEMENT
"...ISN'T THAT WHAT ROBIN IS ALL ABOUT?"
END.

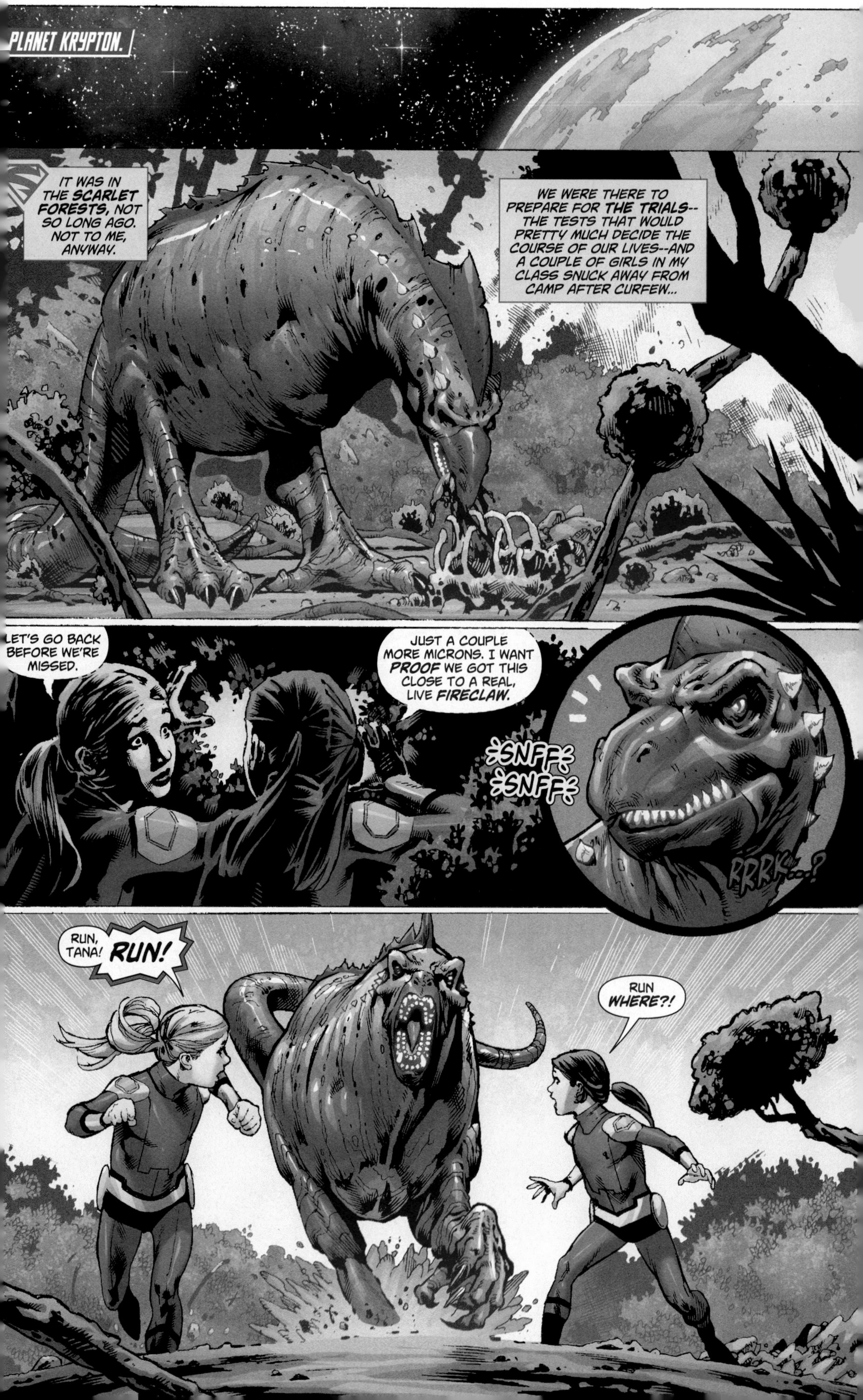
PLANET KRYPTON.
IT WAS IN THE SCARLET FORESTS, NOT SO LONG AGO. NOT TO ME, ANYWAY.
WE WERE THERE TO PREPARE FOR THE TRIALS-- THE TESTS THAT WOULD PRETTY MUCH DECIDE THE COURSE OF OUR LIVES--AND A COUPLE OF GIRLS IN MY CLASS SNUCK AWAY FROM CAMP AFTER CURFEW...
LET'S GO BACK BEFORE WE'RE MISSED.
JUST A COUPLE MORE MICRONS. I WANT PROOF WE GOT THIS CLOSE TO A REAL, LIVE FIRECLAW.
SNFF SNFF
RRRK...?
RUN, TANA! RUN!
RUN WHERE?!

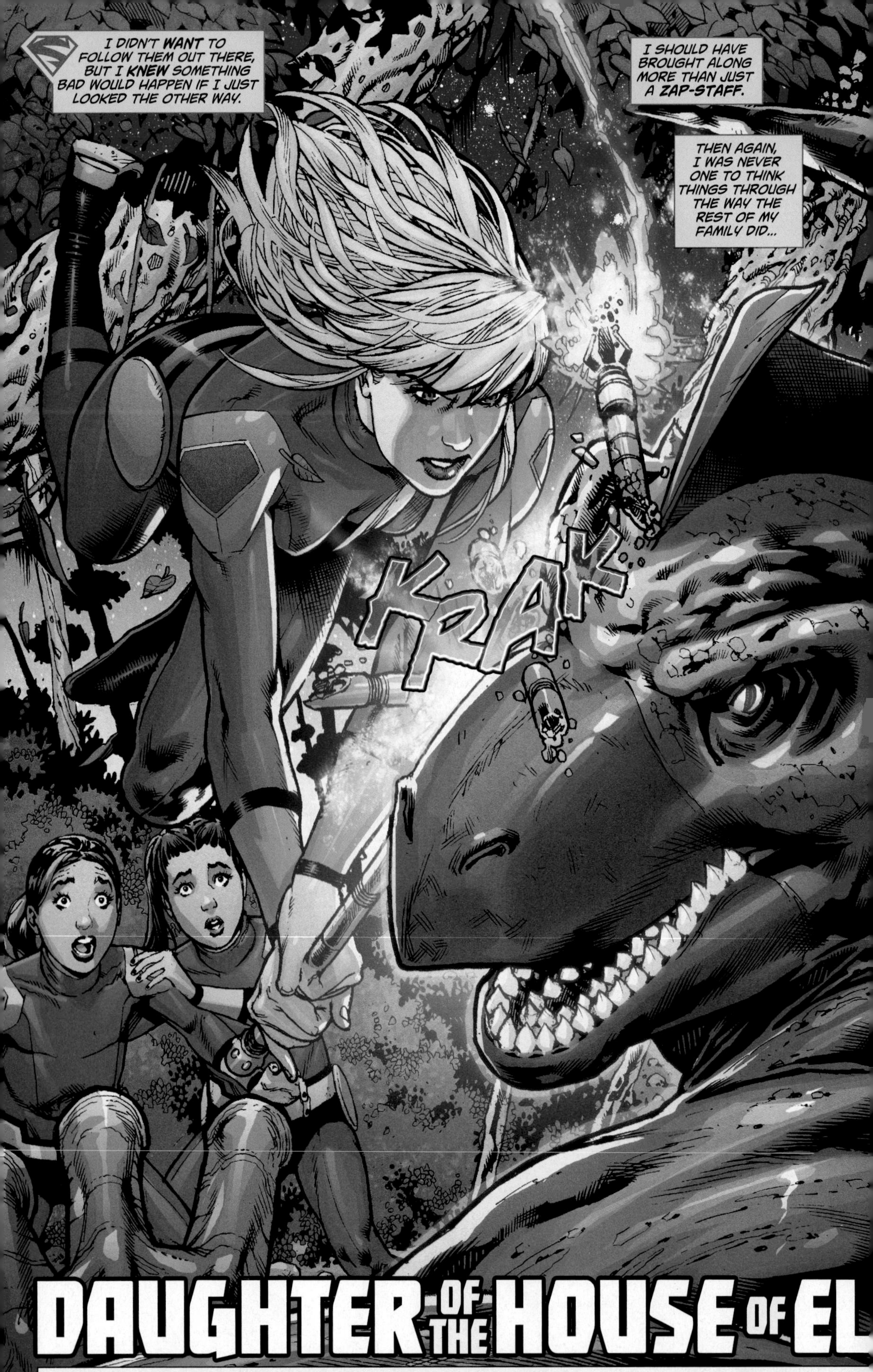
I DIDN'T WANT TO FOLLOW THEM OUT THERE, BUT I KNEW SOMETHING BAD WOULD HAPPEN IF I JUST LOOKED THE OTHER WAY.
I SHOULD HAVE BROUGHT ALONG MORE THAN JUST A ZAP-STAFF.
THEN AGAIN, I WAS NEVER ONE TO THINK THINGS THROUGH THE WAY THE REST OF MY FAMILY DID...
KRAK

DAUGHTER OF THE HOUSE OF EL

TONY BEDARD: writer PAULO SIQUEIRA: pencils HI-FI: inks/colors TRAVIS LANHAM: letters
Based on the characters created by JERRY SIEGEL and JOE SHUSTER. By special arrangement with the JERRY SIEGEL FAMILY.

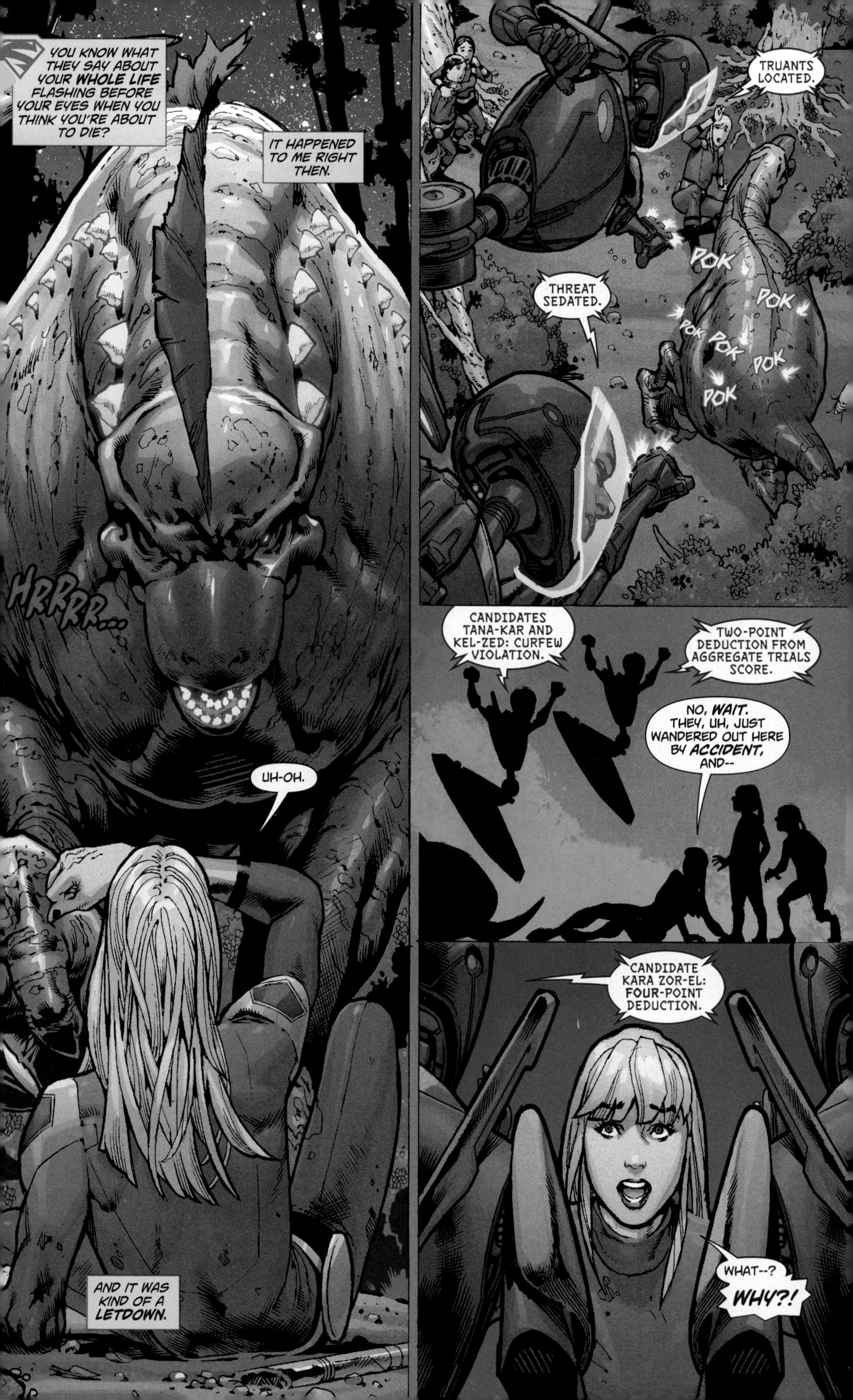

YOU KNOW WHAT THEY SAY ABOUT YOUR WHOLE LIFE FLASHING BEFORE YOUR EYES WHEN YOU THINK YOU'RE ABOUT TO DIE?
IT HAPPENED TO ME RIGHT THEN.
HRRRR...
UH-OH.
AND IT WAS KIND OF A LETDOWN.
TRUANTS LOCATED.
THREAT SEDATED.
POK
POK
POK
POK
POK
POK
CANDIDATES TANA-KAR AND KEL-ZED: CURFEW VIOLATION.
TWO-POINT DEDUCTION FROM AGGREGATE TRIALS SCORE.
NO, WAIT. THEY, UH, JUST WANDERED OUT HERE BY ACCIDENT, AND--
CANDIDATE KARA ZOR-EL: FOUR-POINT DEDUCTION.
WHAT--? WHY?!

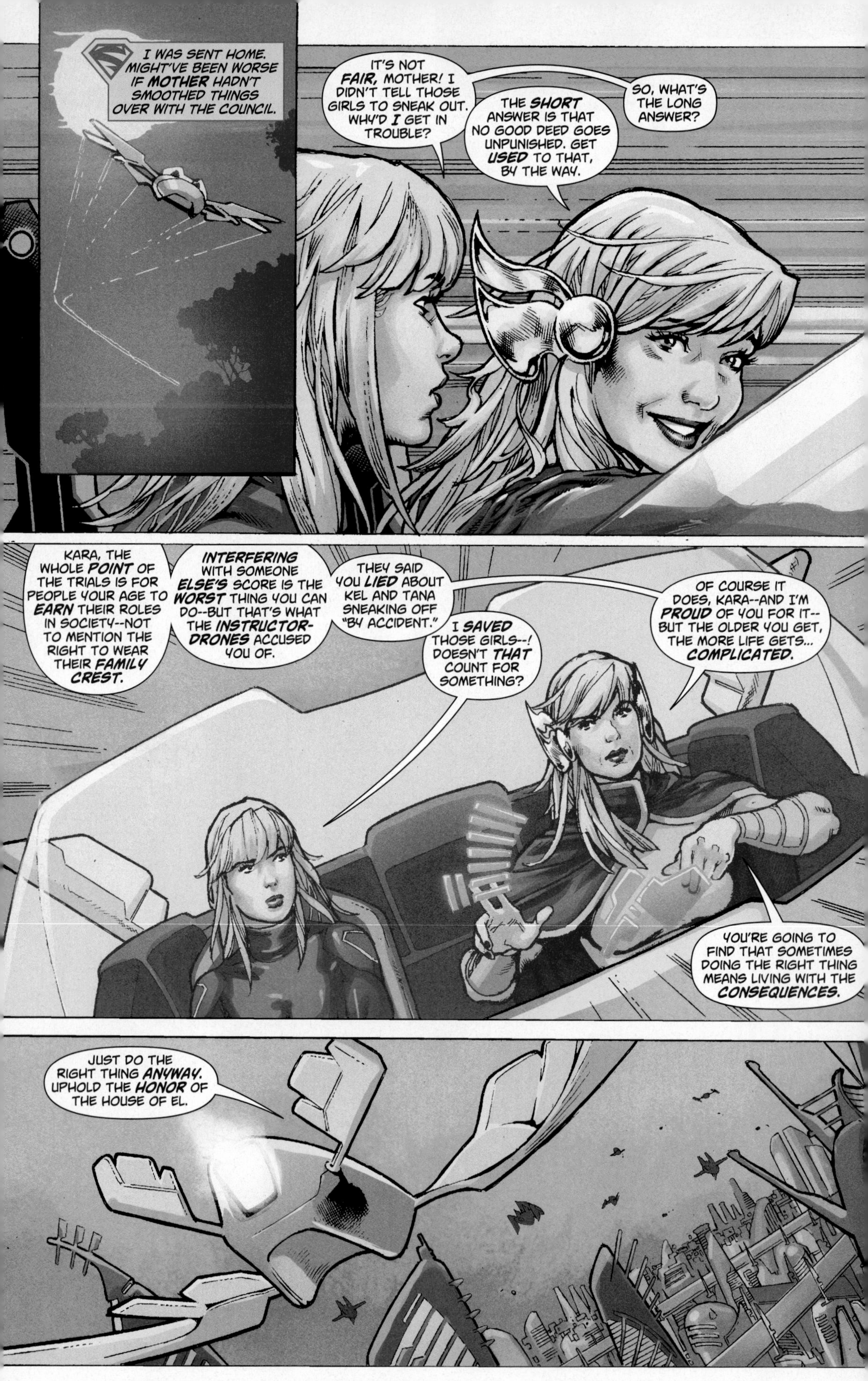
I WAS SENT HOME. MIGHT'VE BEEN WORSE IF MOTHER HADN'T SMOOTHED THINGS OVER WITH THE COUNCIL.
IT'S NOT FAIR, MOTHER! I DIDN'T TELL THOSE GIRLS TO SNEAK OUT. WHY'D I GET IN TROUBLE?
THE SHORT ANSWER IS THAT NO GOOD DEED GOES UNPUNISHED. GET USED TO THAT, BY THE WAY.
SO, WHAT'S THE LONG ANSWER?
KARA, THE WHOLE POINT OF THE TRIALS IS FOR PEOPLE YOUR AGE TO EARN THEIR ROLES IN SOCIETY--NOT TO MENTION THE RIGHT TO WEAR THEIR FAMILY CREST.
INTERFERING WITH SOMEONE ELSE'S SCORE IS THE WORST THING YOU CAN DO--BUT THAT'S WHAT THE INSTRUCTOR-DRONES ACCUSED YOU OF.
THEY SAID YOU LIED ABOUT KEL AND TANA SNEAKING OFF "BY ACCIDENT."
I SAVED THOSE GIRLS--! DOESN'T THAT COUNT FOR SOMETHING?
OF COURSE IT DOES, KARA--AND I'M PROUD OF YOU FOR IT--BUT THE OLDER YOU GET, THE MORE LIFE GETS... COMPLICATED.
YOU'RE GOING TO FIND THAT SOMETIMES DOING THE RIGHT THING MEANS LIVING WITH THE CONSEQUENCES.
JUST DO THE RIGHT THING ANYWAY. UPHOLD THE HONOR OF THE HOUSE OF EL.

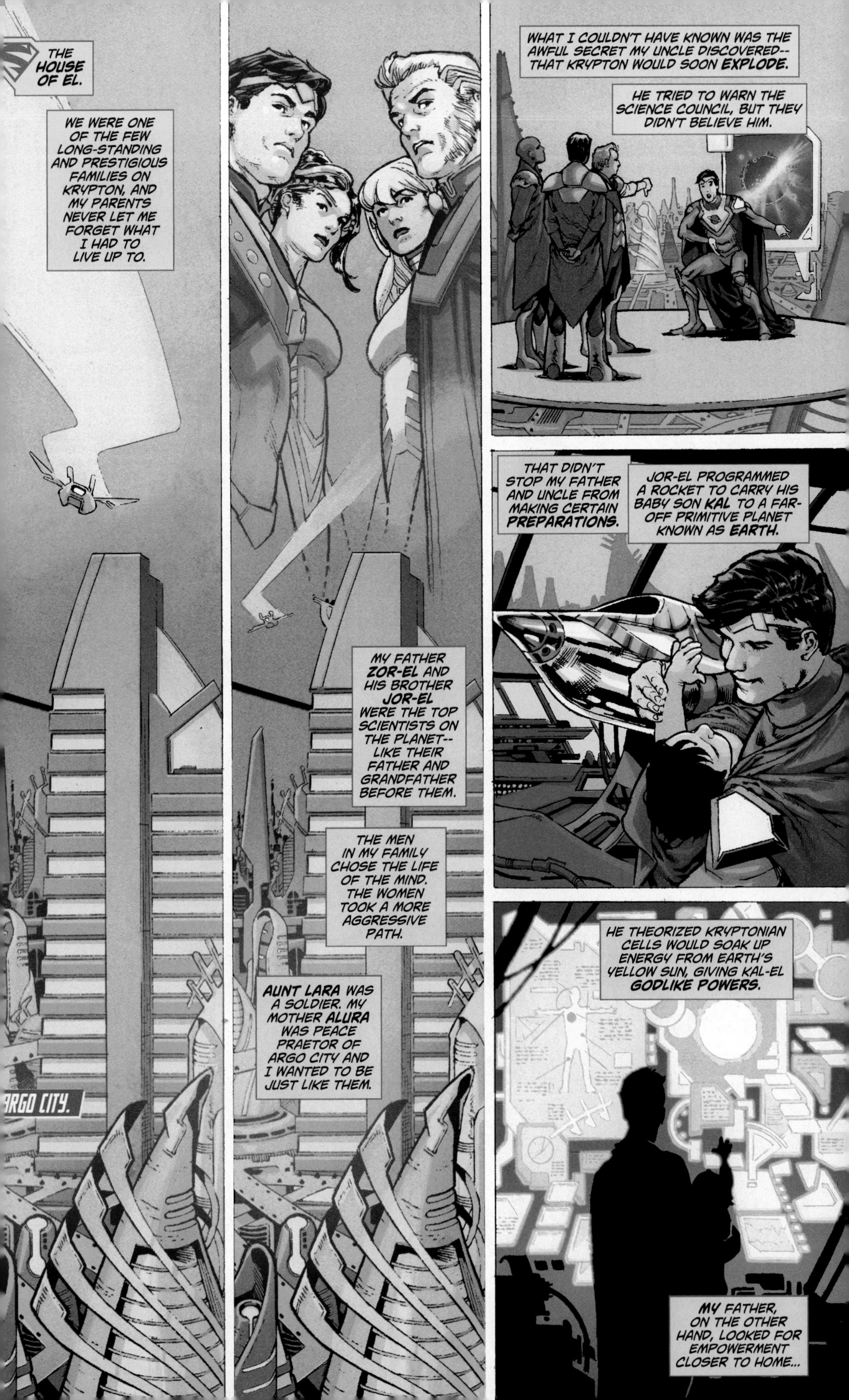
THE HOUSE OF EL.
WE WERE ONE OF THE FEW LONG-STANDING AND PRESTIGIOUS FAMILIES ON KRYPTON, AND MY PARENTS NEVER LET ME FORGET WHAT I HAD TO LIVE UP TO.
ARGO CITY.
MY FATHER ZOR-EL AND HIS BROTHER JOR-EL WERE THE TOP SCIENTISTS ON THE PLANET--LIKE THEIR FATHER AND GRANDFATHER BEFORE THEM.
THE MEN IN MY FAMILY CHOSE THE LIFE OF THE MIND. THE WOMEN TOOK A MORE AGGRESSIVE PATH.
AUNT LARA WAS A SOLDIER. MY MOTHER ALURA WAS PEACE PRAETOR OF ARGO CITY AND I WANTED TO BE JUST LIKE THEM.
WHAT I COULDN'T HAVE KNOWN WAS THE AWFUL SECRET MY UNCLE DISCOVERED--THAT KRYPTON WOULD SOON EXPLODE.
HE TRIED TO WARN THE SCIENCE COUNCIL, BUT THEY DIDN'T BELIEVE HIM.
THAT DIDN'T STOP MY FATHER AND UNCLE FROM MAKING CERTAIN PREPARATIONS.
JOR-EL PROGRAMMED A ROCKET TO CARRY HIS BABY SON KAL TO A FAR-OFF PRIMITIVE PLANET KNOWN AS EARTH.
HE THEORIZED KRYPTONIAN CELLS WOULD SOAK UP ENERGY FROM EARTH'S YELLOW SUN, GIVING KAL-EL GODLIKE POWERS.
MY FATHER, ON THE OTHER HAND, LOOKED FOR EMPOWERMENT CLOSER TO HOME...

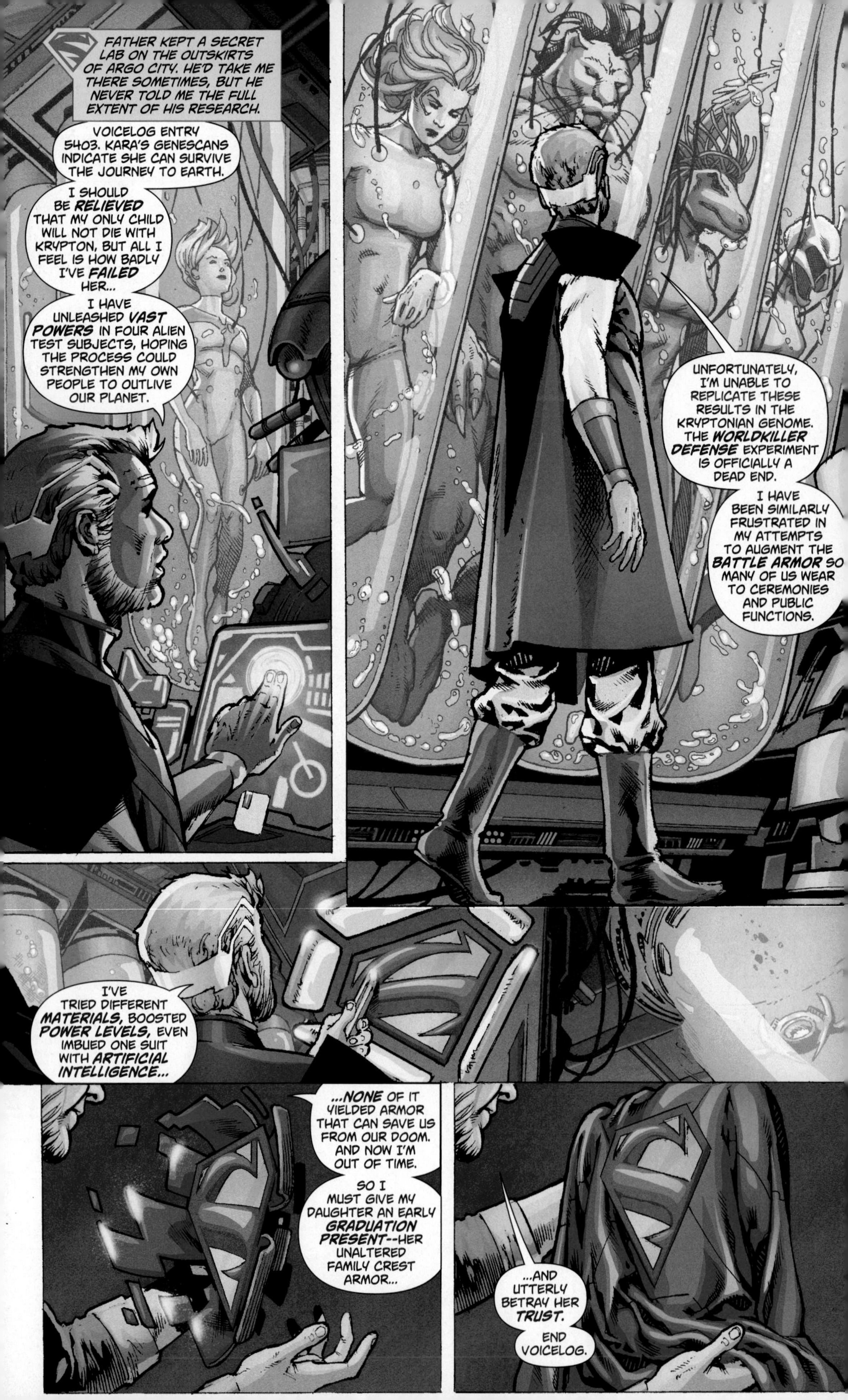

FATHER KEPT A SECRET LAB ON THE OUTSKIRTS OF ARGO CITY. HE'D TAKE ME THERE SOMETIMES, BUT HE NEVER TOLD ME THE FULL EXTENT OF HIS RESEARCH.
VOICELOG ENTRY 5403. KARA'S GENESCANS INDICATE SHE CAN SURVIVE THE JOURNEY TO EARTH.
I SHOULD BE RELIEVED THAT MY ONLY CHILD WILL NOT DIE WITH KRYPTON, BUT ALL I FEEL IS HOW BADLY I'VE FAILED HER...
I HAVE UNLEASHED VAST POWERS IN FOUR ALIEN TEST SUBJECTS, HOPING THE PROCESS COULD STRENGTHEN MY OWN PEOPLE TO OUTLIVE OUR PLANET.
UNFORTUNATELY, I'M UNABLE TO REPLICATE THESE RESULTS IN THE KRYPTONIAN GENOME. THE WORLDKILLER DEFENSE EXPERIMENT IS OFFICIALLY A DEAD END.
I HAVE BEEN SIMILARLY FRUSTRATED IN MY ATTEMPTS TO AUGMENT THE BATTLE ARMOR SO MANY OF US WEAR TO CEREMONIES AND PUBLIC FUNCTIONS.
I'VE TRIED DIFFERENT MATERIALS, BOOSTED POWER LEVELS, EVEN IMBUED ONE SUIT WITH ARTIFICIAL INTELLIGENCE...
...NONE OF IT YIELDED ARMOR THAT CAN SAVE US FROM OUR DOOM. AND NOW I'M OUT OF TIME.
SO I MUST GIVE MY DAUGHTER AN EARLY GRADUATION PRESENT--HER UNALTERED FAMILY CREST ARMOR...
...AND UTTERLY BETRAY HER TRUST.
END VOICELOG.

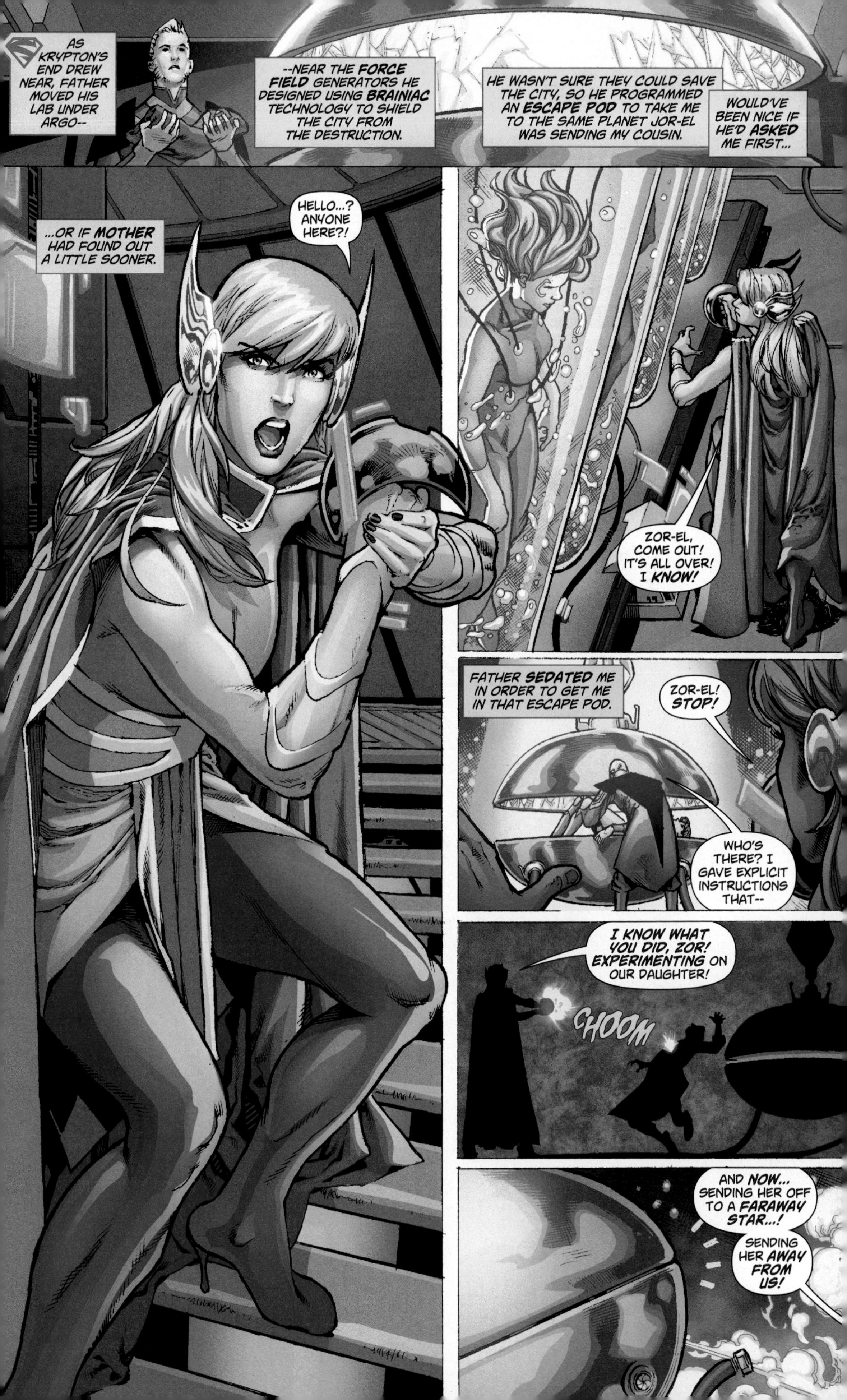
AS KRYPTON'S END DREW NEAR, FATHER MOVED HIS LAB UNDER ARGO--
--NEAR THE FORCE FIELD GENERATORS HE DESIGNED USING BRAINIAC TECHNOLOGY TO SHIELD THE CITY FROM THE DESTRUCTION.
HE WASN'T SURE THEY COULD SAVE THE CITY, SO HE PROGRAMMED AN ESCAPE POD TO TAKE ME TO THE SAME PLANET JOR-EL WAS SENDING MY COUSIN.
WOULD'VE BEEN NICE IF HE'D ASKED ME FIRST...
...OR IF MOTHER HAD FOUND OUT A LITTLE SOONER.
HELLO...? ANYONE HERE?!
ZOR-EL, COME OUT! IT'S ALL OVER! I KNOW!
FATHER SEDATED ME IN ORDER TO GET ME IN THAT ESCAPE POD.
ZOR-EL! STOP!
WHO'S THERE? I GAVE EXPLICIT INSTRUCTIONS THAT--
I KNOW WHAT YOU DID, ZOR! EXPERIMENTING ON OUR DAUGHTER!
CHOOM
AND NOW... SENDING HER OFF TO A FARAWAY STAR...!
SENDING HER AWAY FROM US!

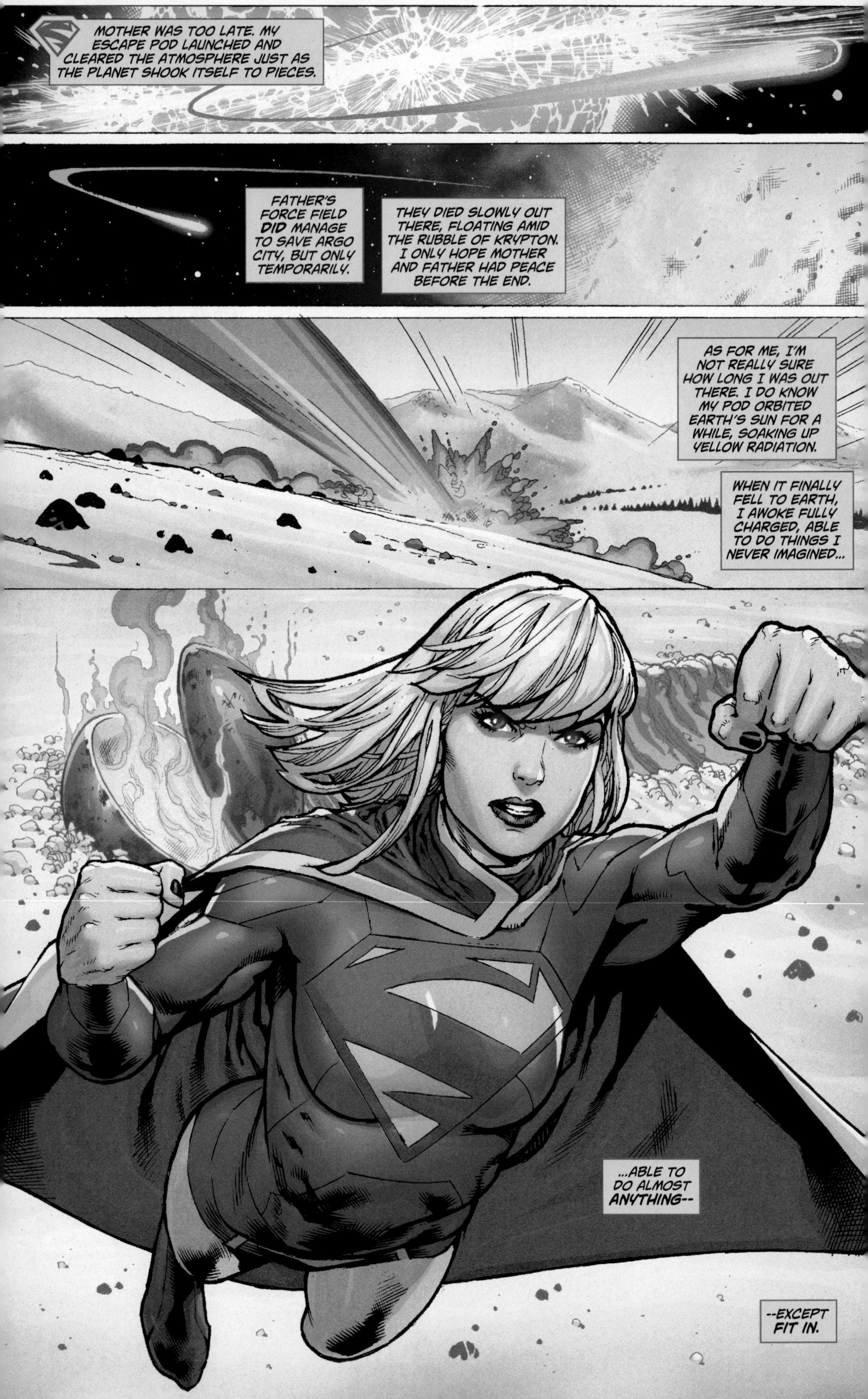
MOTHER WAS TOO LATE. MY ESCAPE POD LAUNCHED AND CLEARED THE ATMOSPHERE JUST AS THE PLANET SHOOK ITSELF TO PIECES.
FATHER'S FORCE FIELD DID MANAGE TO SAVE ARGO CITY, BUT ONLY TEMPORARILY.
THEY DIED SLOWLY OUT THERE, FLOATING AMID THE RUBBLE OF KRYPTON. I ONLY HOPE MOTHER AND FATHER HAD PEACE BEFORE THE END.
AS FOR ME, I'M NOT REALLY SURE HOW LONG I WAS OUT THERE. I DO KNOW MY POD ORBITED EARTH'S SUN FOR A WHILE, SOAKING UP YELLOW RADIATION.
WHEN IT FINALLY FELL TO EARTH, I AWOKE FULLY CHARGED, ABLE TO DO THINGS I NEVER IMAGINED...
...ABLE TO DO ALMOST ANYTHING--
--EXCEPT FIT IN.

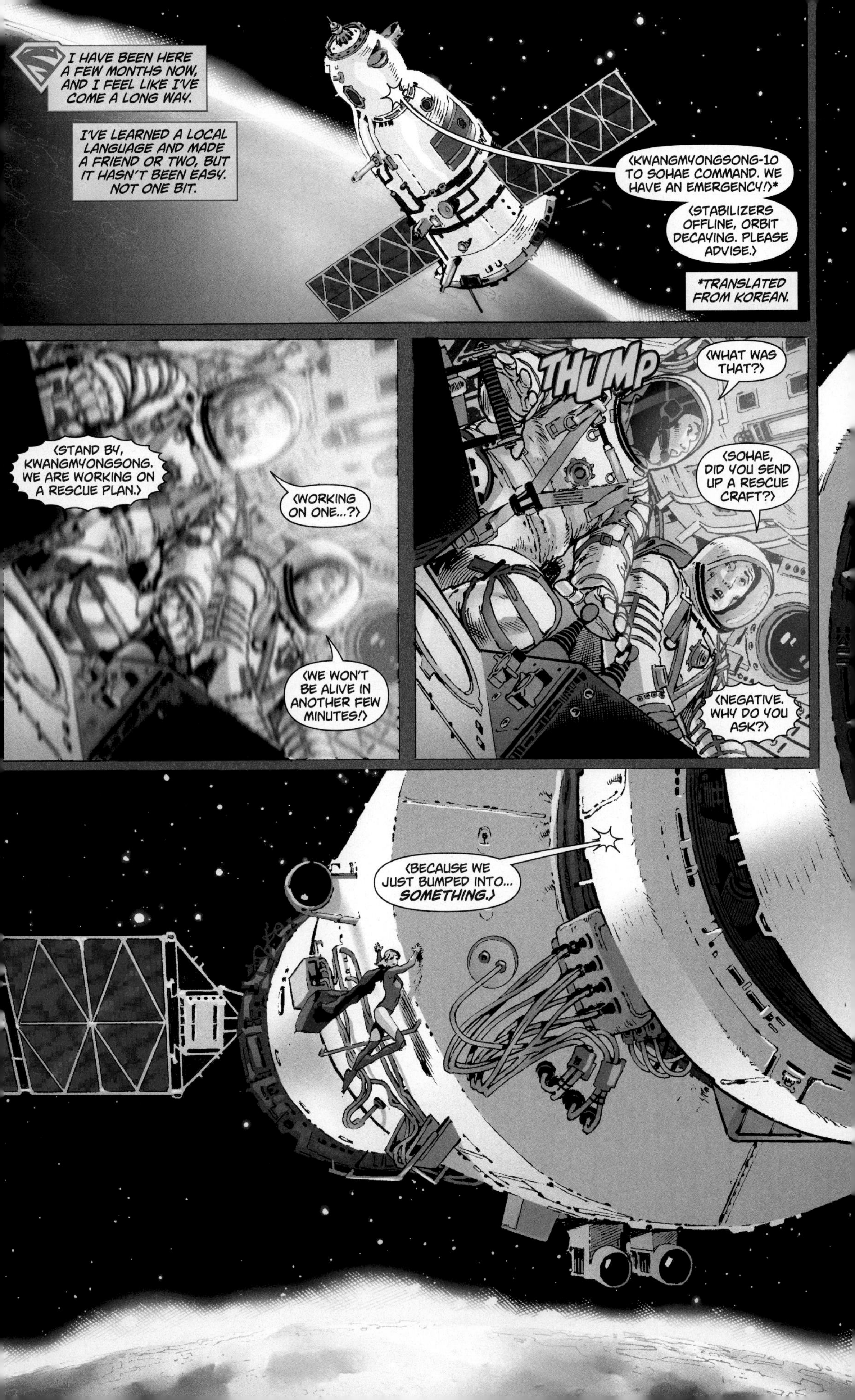
I HAVE BEEN HERE A FEW MONTHS NOW, AND I FEEL LIKE I'VE COME A LONG WAY.
I'VE LEARNED A LOCAL LANGUAGE AND MADE A FRIEND OR TWO, BUT IT HASN'T BEEN EASY. NOT ONE BIT.
‹KWANGMYONGSONG-10 TO SOHAE COMMAND. WE HAVE AN EMERGENCY!›*
‹STABILIZERS OFFLINE, ORBIT DECAYING. PLEASE ADVISE.›
*TRANSLATED FROM KOREAN.
‹STAND BY, KWANGMYONGSONG. WE ARE WORKING ON A RESCUE PLAN.›
‹WORKING ON ONE...?›
‹WE WON'T BE ALIVE IN ANOTHER FEW MINUTES!›
THUMP
‹WHAT WAS THAT?›
‹SOHAE, DID YOU SEND UP A RESCUE CRAFT?›
‹NEGATIVE. WHY DO YOU ASK?›
‹BECAUSE WE JUST BUMPED INTO... SOMETHING.›

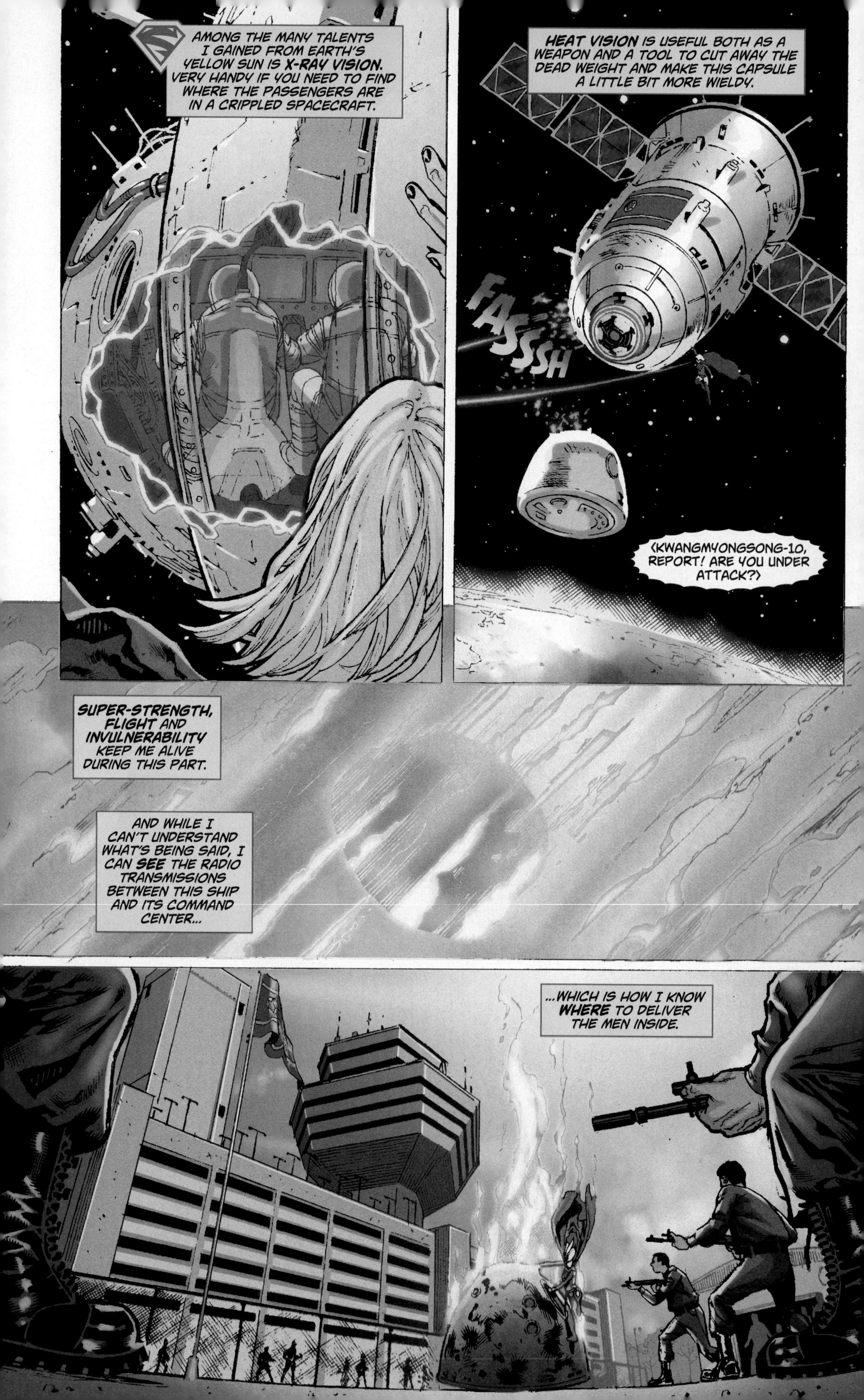
AMONG THE MANY TALENTS I GAINED FROM EARTH'S YELLOW SUN IS X-RAY VISION. VERY HANDY IF YOU NEED TO FIND WHERE THE PASSENGERS ARE IN A CRIPPLED SPACECRAFT.
HEAT VISION IS USEFUL BOTH AS A WEAPON AND A TOOL TO CUT AWAY THE DEAD WEIGHT AND MAKE THIS CAPSULE A LITTLE BIT MORE WIELDY.
FASSSH
<KWANGMYONGSONG-10, REPORT! ARE YOU UNDER ATTACK?>
SUPER-STRENGTH, FLIGHT AND INVULNERABILITY KEEP ME ALIVE DURING THIS PART.
AND WHILE I CAN'T UNDERSTAND WHAT'S BEING SAID, I CAN SEE THE RADIO TRANSMISSIONS BETWEEN THIS SHIP AND ITS COMMAND CENTER...
...WHICH IS HOW I KNOW WHERE TO DELIVER THE MEN INSIDE.

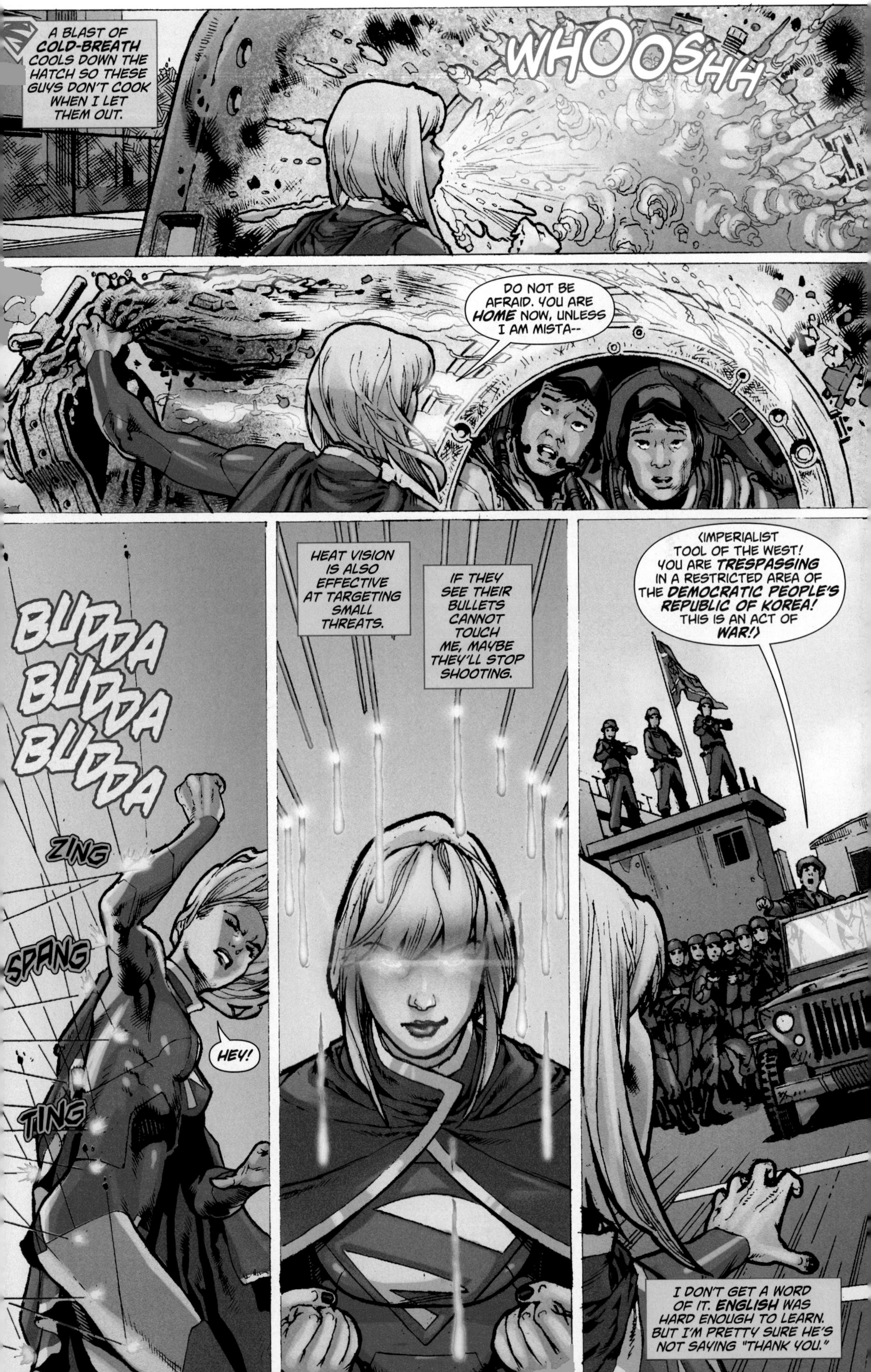
A BLAST OF COLD-BREATH COOLS DOWN THE HATCH SO THESE GUYS DON'T COOK WHEN I LET THEM OUT.
WHOOSHH
DO NOT BE AFRAID. YOU ARE HOME NOW, UNLESS I AM MISTA--
BUDDA BUDDA BUDDA
ZING
SPANG
HEY!
TING
HEAT VISION IS ALSO EFFECTIVE AT TARGETING SMALL THREATS.
IF THEY SEE THEIR BULLETS CANNOT TOUCH ME, MAYBE THEY'LL STOP SHOOTING.
‹IMPERIALIST TOOL OF THE WEST! YOU ARE TRESPASSING IN A RESTRICTED AREA OF THE DEMOCRATIC PEOPLE'S REPUBLIC OF KOREA! THIS IS AN ACT OF WAR!›
I DON'T GET A WORD OF IT. ENGLISH WAS HARD ENOUGH TO LEARN. BUT I'M PRETTY SURE HE'S NOT SAYING "THANK YOU."

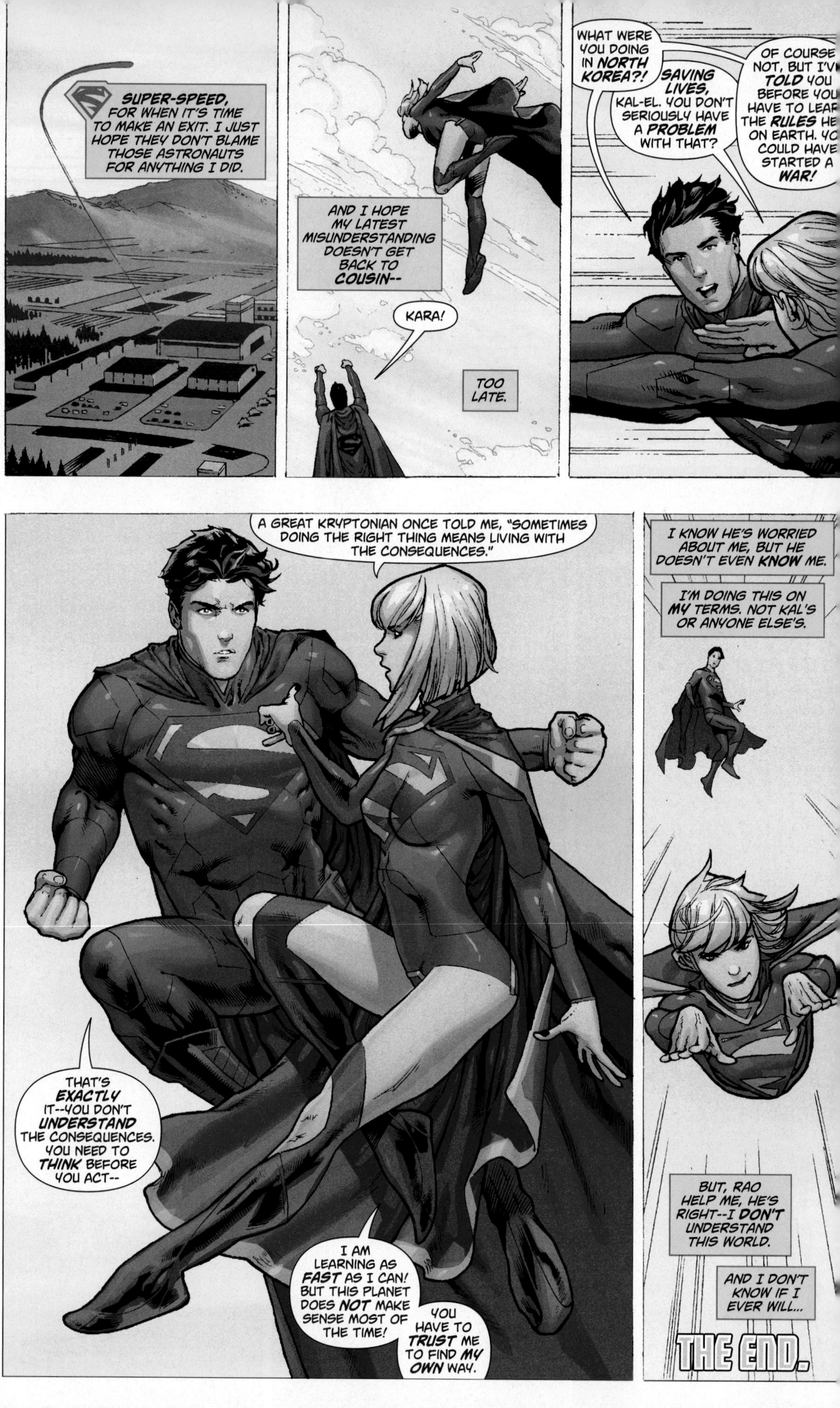
SUPER-SPEED, FOR WHEN IT'S TIME TO MAKE AN EXIT. I JUST HOPE THEY DON'T BLAME THOSE ASTRONAUTS FOR ANYTHING I DID.
AND I HOPE MY LATEST MISUNDERSTANDING DOESN'T GET BACK TO COUSIN--
KARA!
TOO LATE.
WHAT WERE YOU DOING IN NORTH KOREA?!
SAVING LIVES, KAL-EL. YOU DON'T SERIOUSLY HAVE A PROBLEM WITH THAT?
OF COURSE NOT, BUT I'V TOLD YOU BEFORE YOU HAVE TO LEAR THE RULES HE ON EARTH. YO COULD HAVE STARTED A WAR!
A GREAT KRYPTONIAN ONCE TOLD ME, "SOMETIMES DOING THE RIGHT THING MEANS LIVING WITH THE CONSEQUENCES."
THAT'S EXACTLY IT--YOU DON'T UNDERSTAND THE CONSEQUENCES. YOU NEED TO THINK BEFORE YOU ACT--
I AM LEARNING AS FAST AS I CAN! BUT THIS PLANET DOES NOT MAKE SENSE MOST OF THE TIME!
YOU HAVE TO TRUST ME TO FIND MY OWN WAY.
I KNOW HE'S WORRIED ABOUT ME, BUT HE DOESN'T EVEN KNOW ME.
I'M DOING THIS ON MY TERMS. NOT KAL'S OR ANYONE ELSE'S.
BUT, RAO HELP ME, HE'S RIGHT--I DON'T UNDERSTAND THIS WORLD.
AND I DON'T KNOW IF I EVER WILL...
THE END.

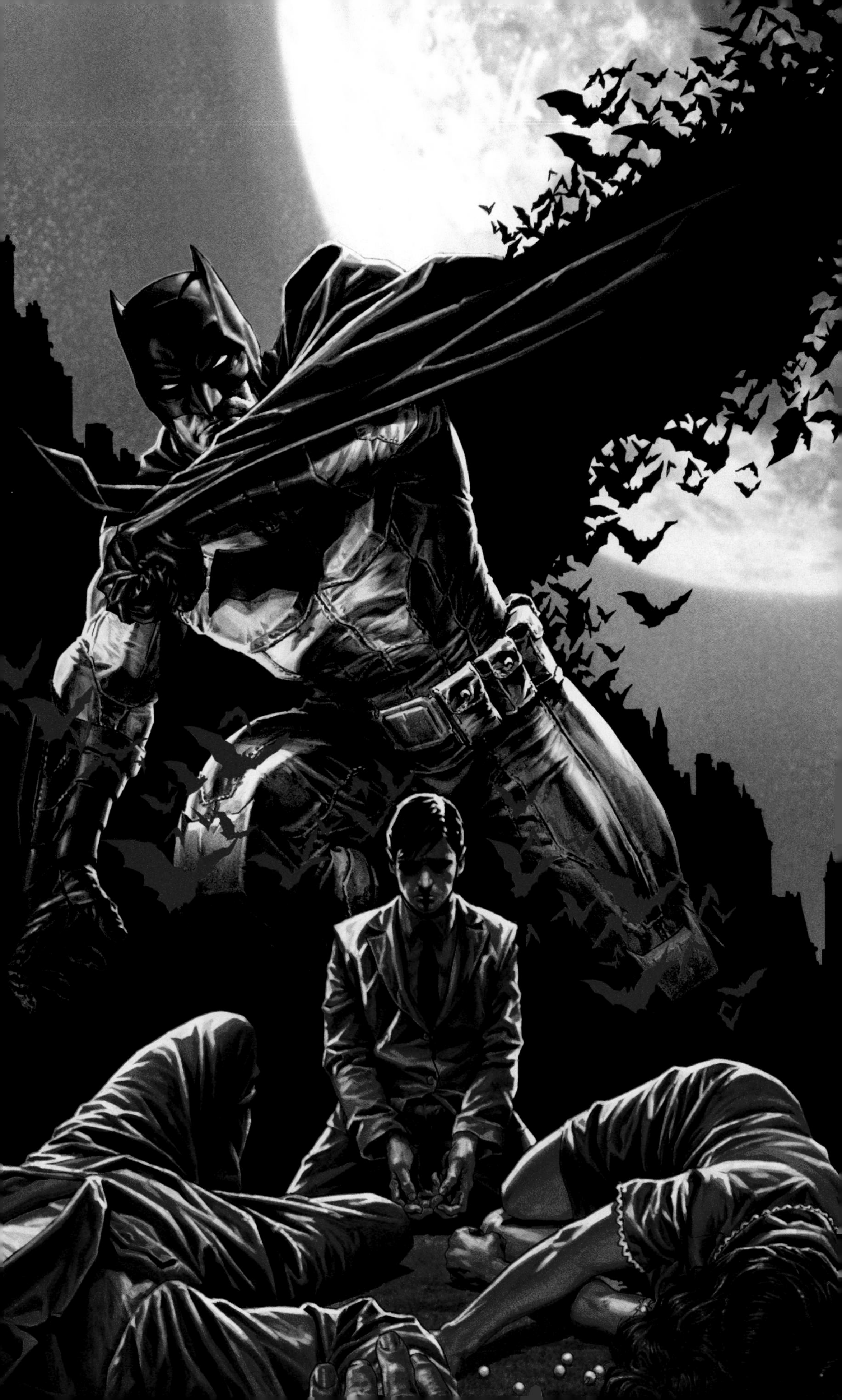

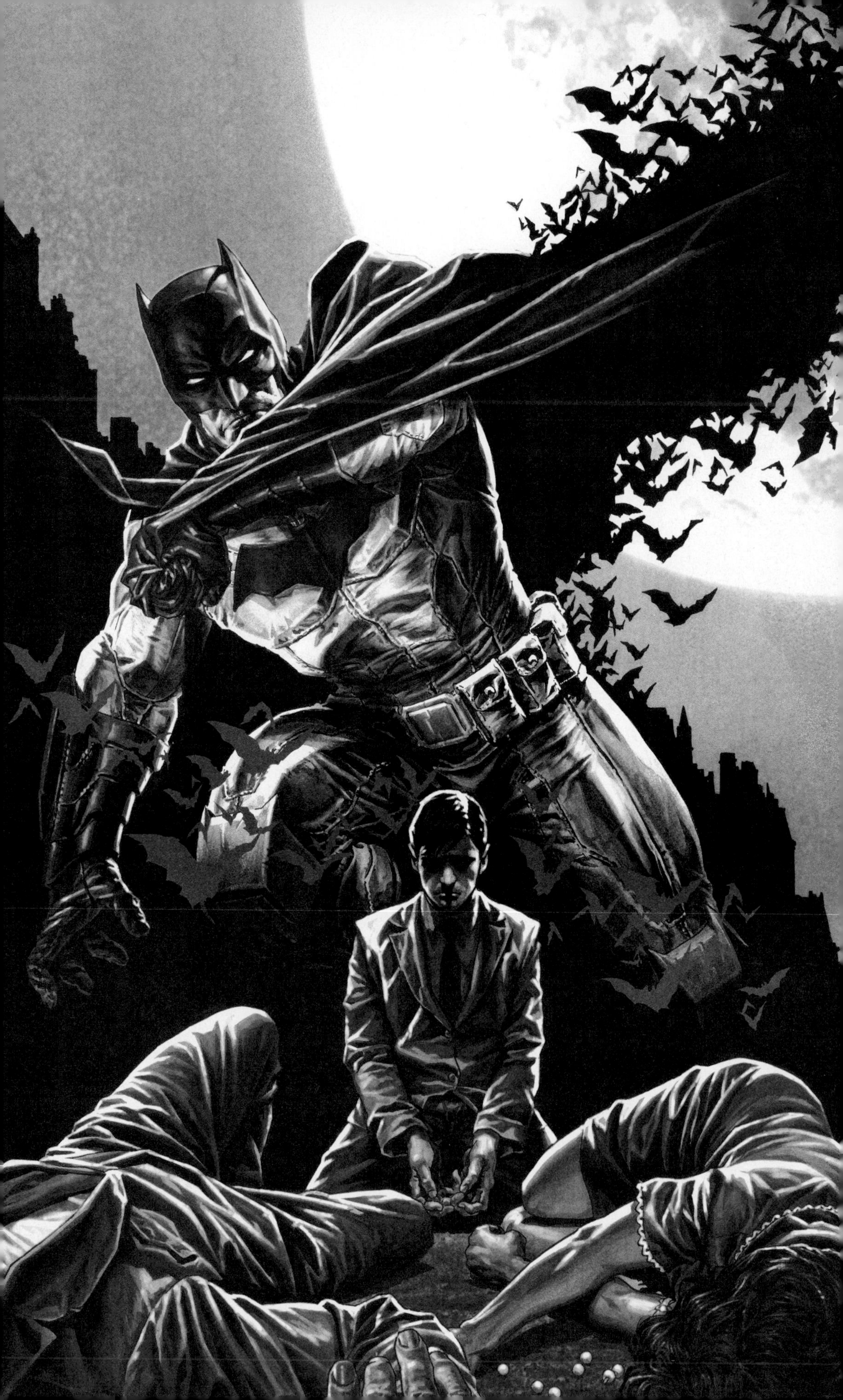

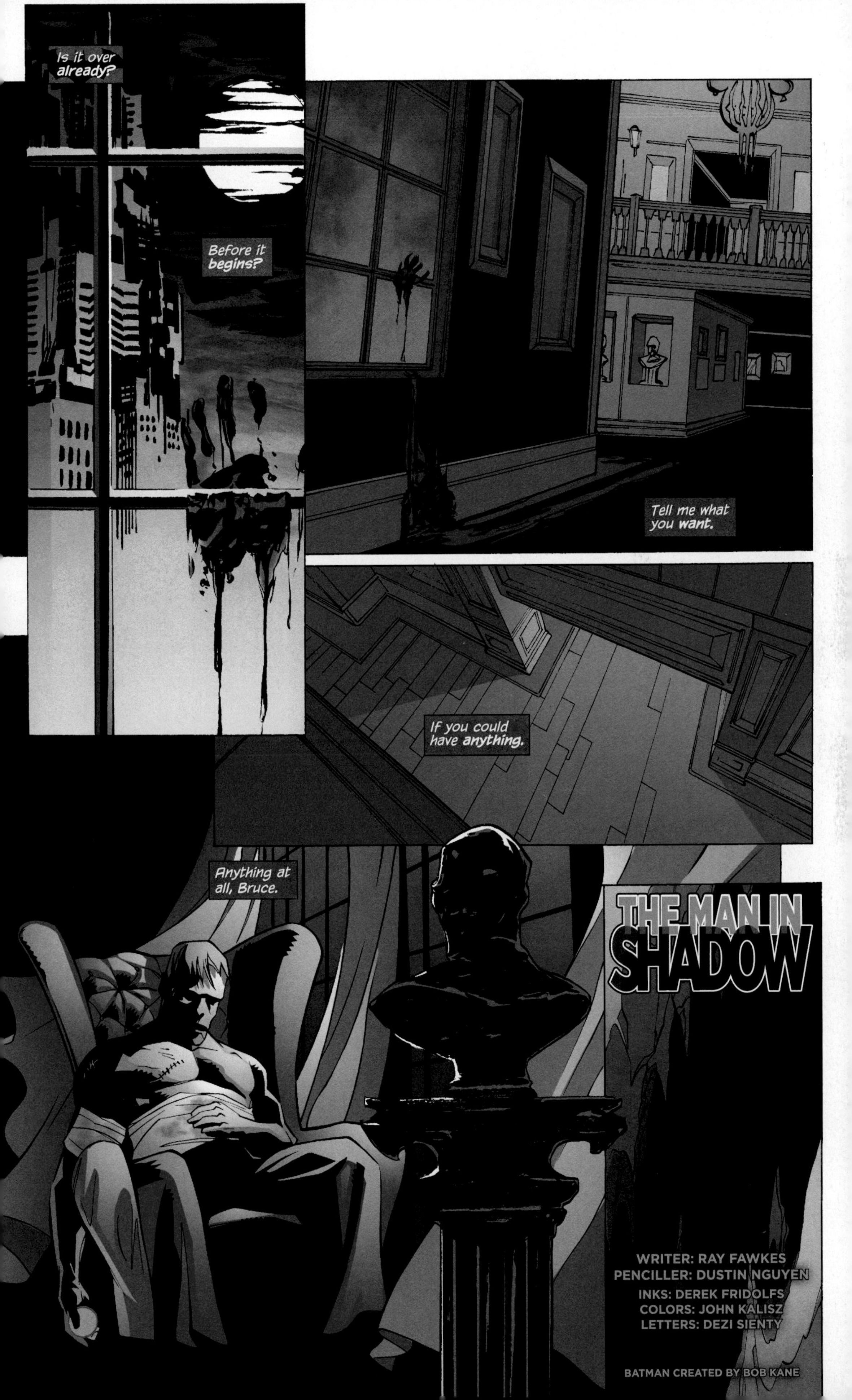
Is it over already?
Before it begins?
Tell me what you want.
If you could have anything.
Anything at all, Bruce.
THE MAN IN SHADOW
WRITER: RAY FAWKES
PENCILLER: DUSTIN NGUYEN
INKS: DEREK FRIDOLFS
COLORS: JOHN KALISZ
LETTERS: DEZI SIENTY
BATMAN CREATED BY BOB KANE

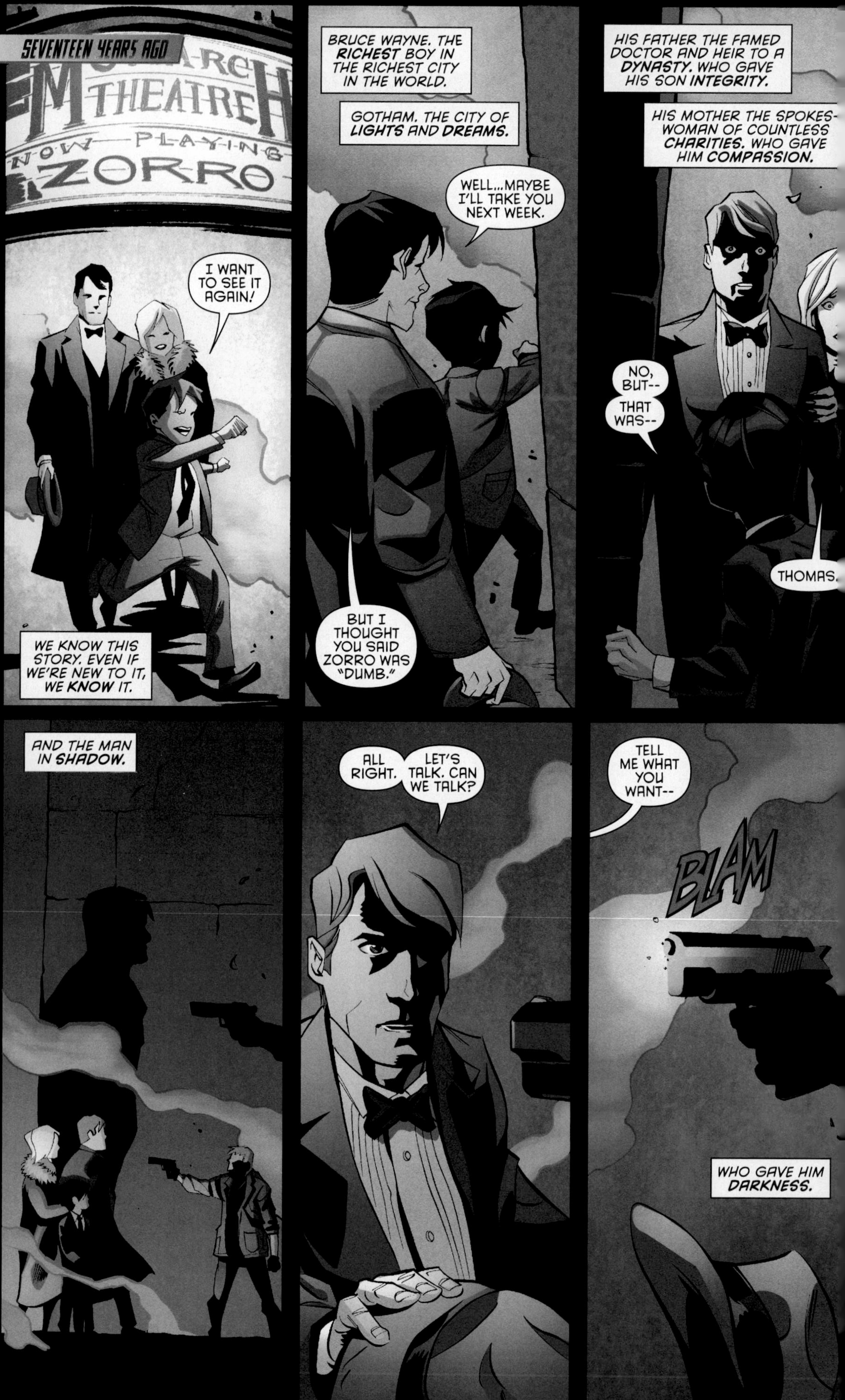
SEVENTEEN YEARS AGO
MONARCH THEATRE
NOW PLAYING
ZORRO
I WANT TO SEE IT AGAIN!
WE KNOW THIS STORY. EVEN IF WE'RE NEW TO IT, WE KNOW IT.
BRUCE WAYNE. THE RICHEST BOY IN THE RICHEST CITY IN THE WORLD.
GOTHAM. THE CITY OF LIGHTS AND DREAMS.
WELL...MAYBE I'LL TAKE YOU NEXT WEEK.
BUT I THOUGHT YOU SAID ZORRO WAS "DUMB."
HIS FATHER THE FAMED DOCTOR AND HEIR TO A DYNASTY. WHO GAVE HIS SON INTEGRITY.
HIS MOTHER THE SPOKES-WOMAN OF COUNTLESS CHARITIES. WHO GAVE HIM COMPASSION.
NO, BUT--
THAT WAS--
THOMAS.
AND THE MAN IN SHADOW.
ALL RIGHT.
LET'S TALK. CAN WE TALK?
TELL ME WHAT YOU WANT--
BLAM
WHO GAVE HIM DARKNESS.

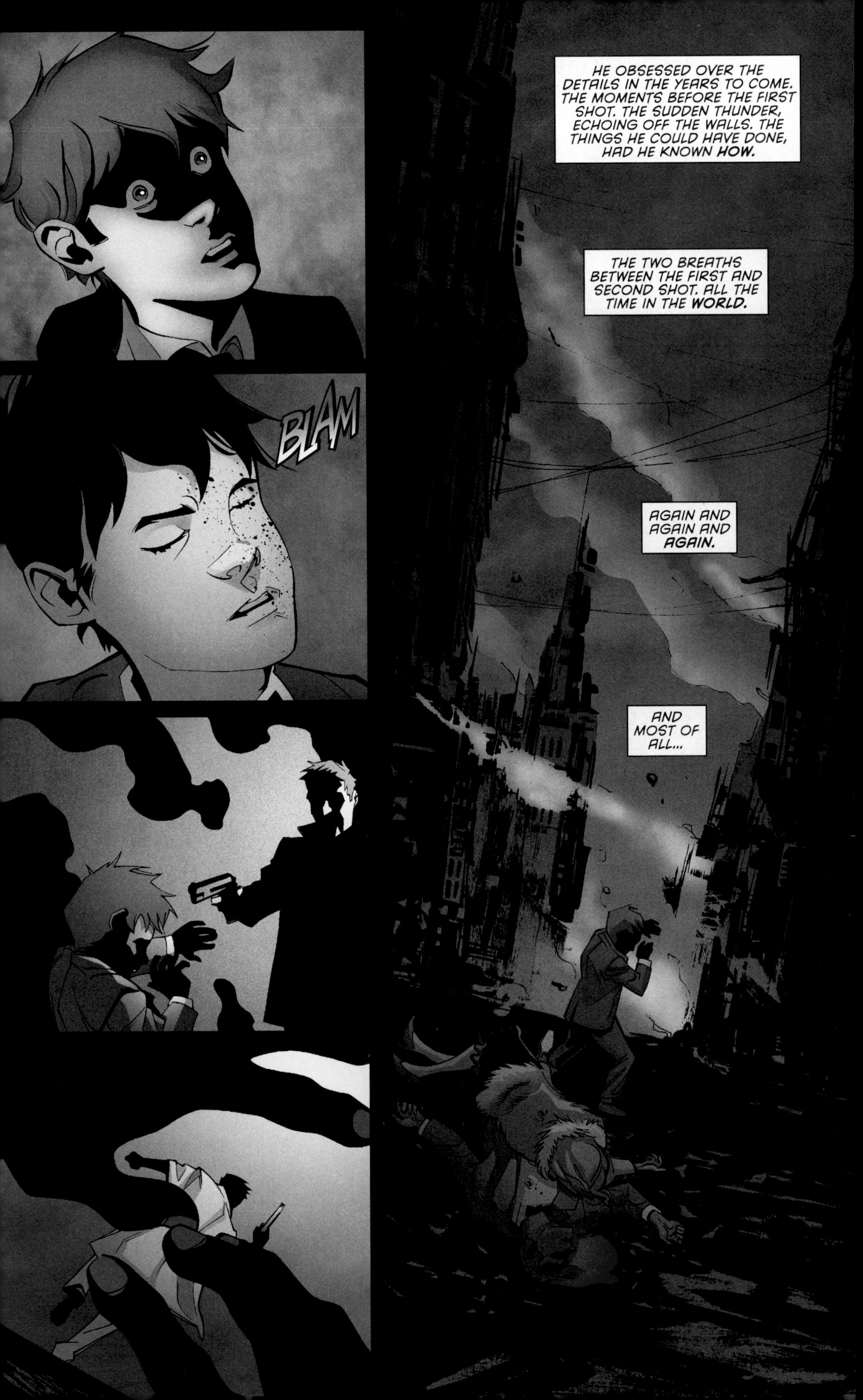
HE OBSESSED OVER THE DETAILS IN THE YEARS TO COME. THE MOMENTS BEFORE THE FIRST SHOT. THE SUDDEN THUNDER, ECHOING OFF THE WALLS. THE THINGS HE COULD HAVE DONE, HAD HE KNOWN **HOW.**
BLAM
THE TWO BREATHS BETWEEN THE FIRST AND SECOND SHOT. ALL THE TIME IN THE **WORLD.**
AGAIN AND AGAIN AND **AGAIN.**
AND MOST OF ALL...

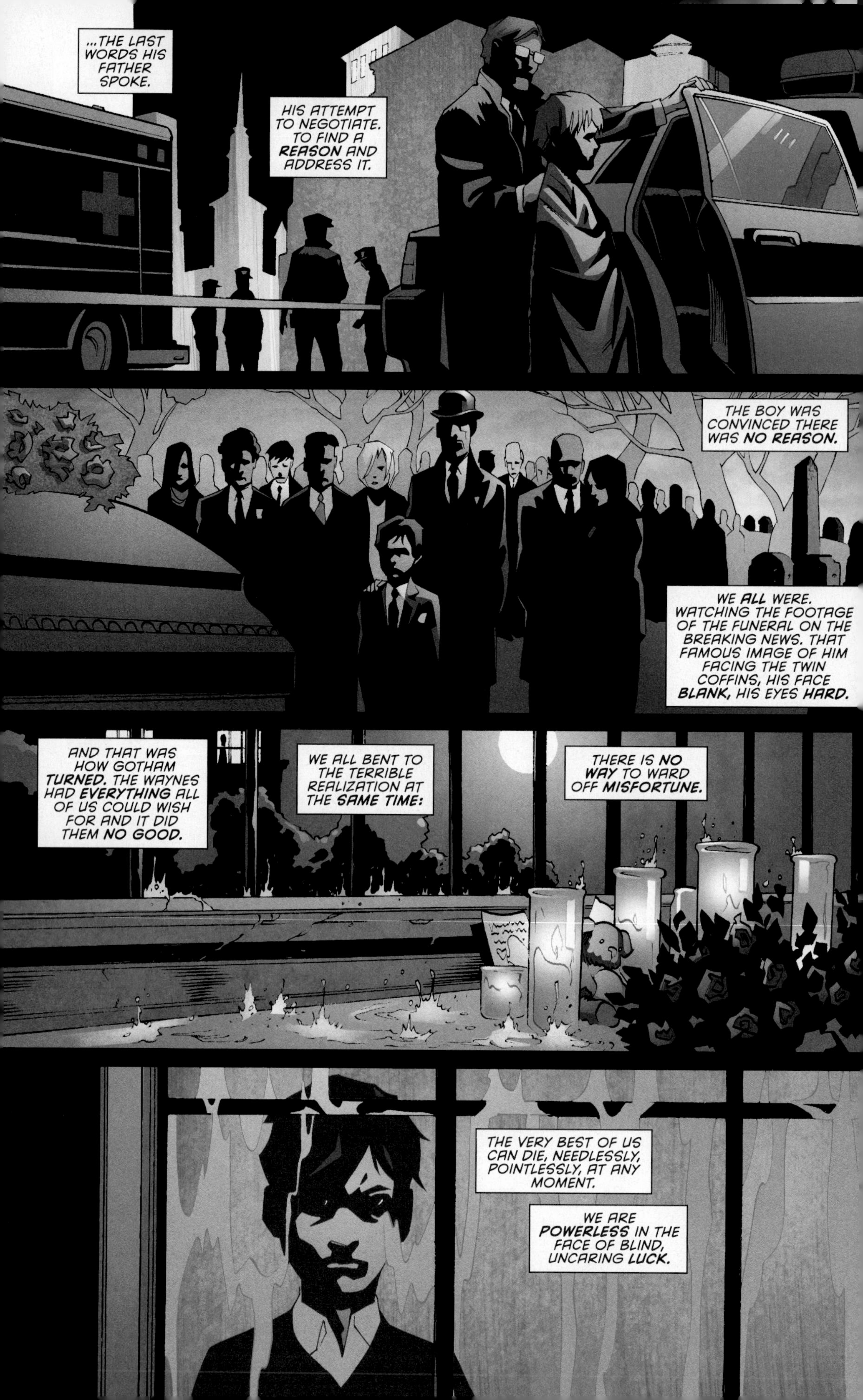
...THE LAST WORDS HIS FATHER SPOKE.
HIS ATTEMPT TO NEGOTIATE. TO FIND A REASON AND ADDRESS IT.
THE BOY WAS CONVINCED THERE WAS NO REASON.
WE ALL WERE. WATCHING THE FOOTAGE OF THE FUNERAL ON THE BREAKING NEWS. THAT FAMOUS IMAGE OF HIM FACING THE TWIN COFFINS, HIS FACE BLANK, HIS EYES HARD.
AND THAT WAS HOW GOTHAM TURNED. THE WAYNES HAD EVERYTHING ALL OF US COULD WISH FOR AND IT DID THEM NO GOOD.
WE ALL BENT TO THE TERRIBLE REALIZATION AT THE SAME TIME:
THERE IS NO WAY TO WARD OFF MISFORTUNE.
THE VERY BEST OF US CAN DIE, NEEDLESSLY, POINTLESSLY, AT ANY MOMENT.
WE ARE POWERLESS IN THE FACE OF BLIND, UNCARING LUCK.

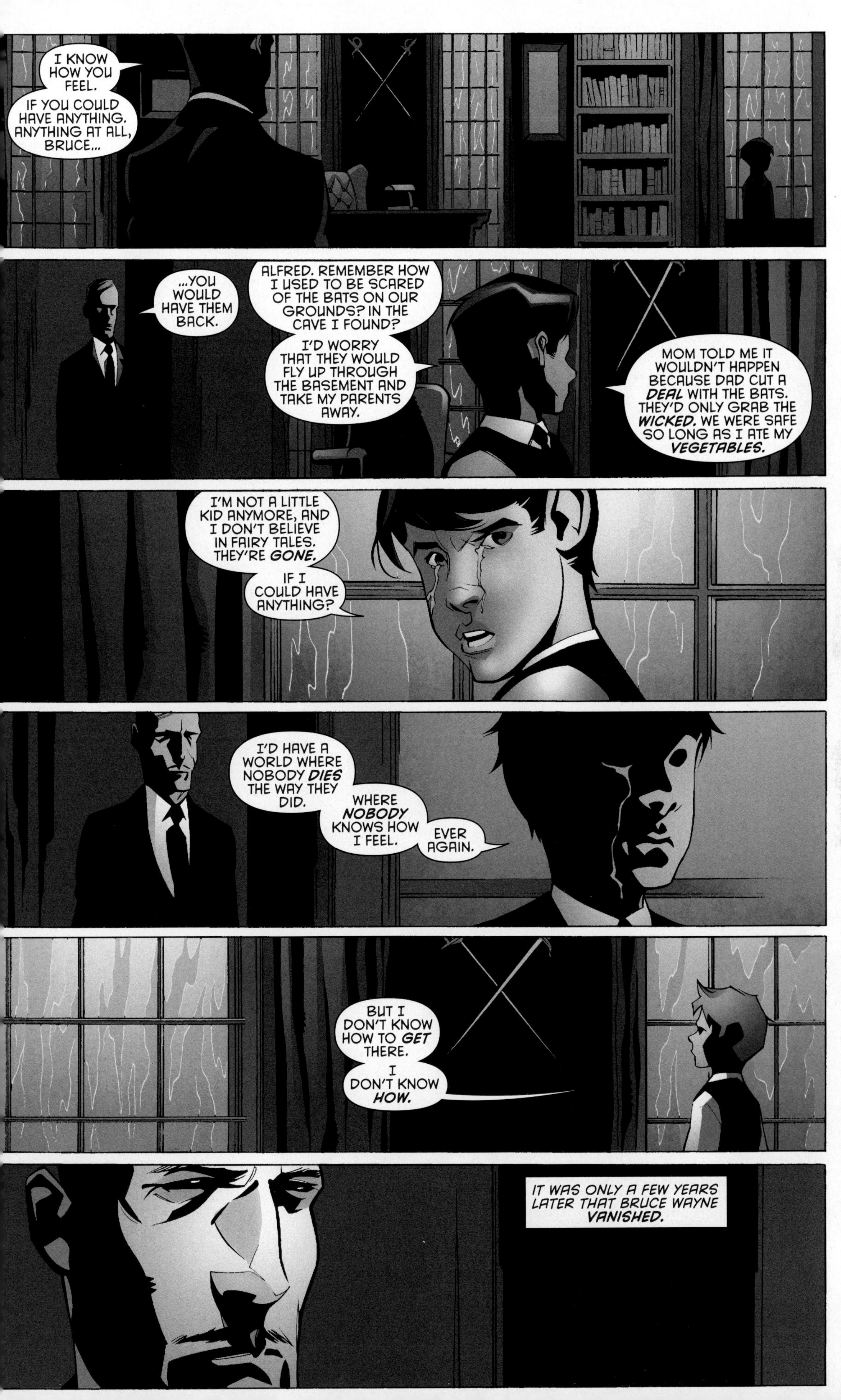
I KNOW HOW YOU FEEL.
IF YOU COULD HAVE ANYTHING. ANYTHING AT ALL, BRUCE...
...YOU WOULD HAVE THEM BACK.
ALFRED. REMEMBER HOW I USED TO BE SCARED OF THE BATS ON OUR GROUNDS? IN THE CAVE I FOUND?
I'D WORRY THAT THEY WOULD FLY UP THROUGH THE BASEMENT AND TAKE MY PARENTS AWAY.
MOM TOLD ME IT WOULDN'T HAPPEN BECAUSE DAD CUT A DEAL WITH THE BATS. THEY'D ONLY GRAB THE WICKED. WE WERE SAFE SO LONG AS I ATE MY VEGETABLES.
I'M NOT A LITTLE KID ANYMORE, AND I DON'T BELIEVE IN FAIRY TALES. THEY'RE GONE.
IF I COULD HAVE ANYTHING?
I'D HAVE A WORLD WHERE NOBODY DIES THE WAY THEY DID.
WHERE NOBODY KNOWS HOW I FEEL.
EVER AGAIN.
BUT I DON'T KNOW HOW TO GET THERE.
I DON'T KNOW HOW.
IT WAS ONLY A FEW YEARS LATER THAT BRUCE WAYNE VANISHED.

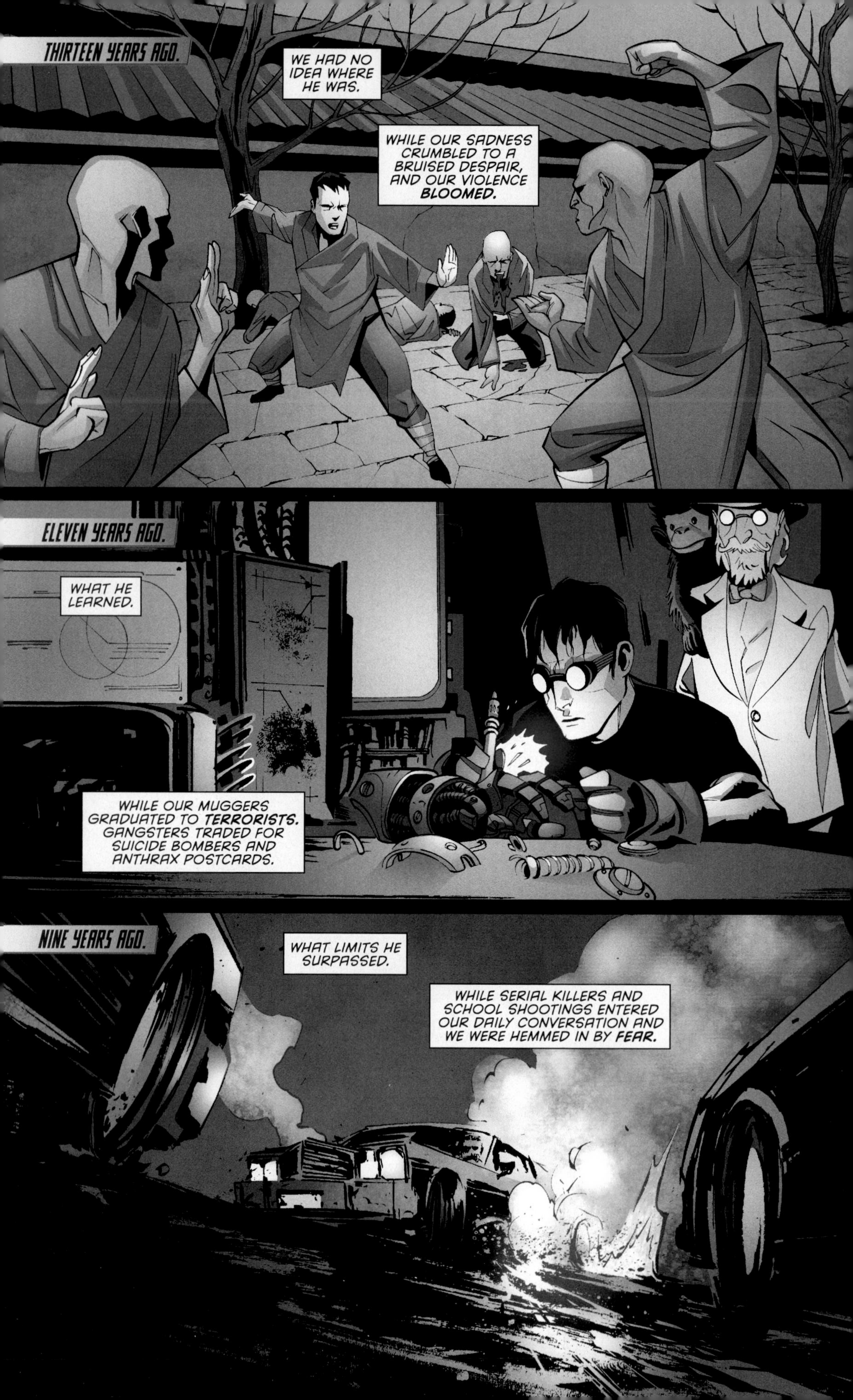
THIRTEEN YEARS AGO.
WE HAD NO IDEA WHERE HE WAS.
WHILE OUR SADNESS CRUMBLED TO A BRUISED DESPAIR, AND OUR VIOLENCE BLOOMED.
ELEVEN YEARS AGO.
WHAT HE LEARNED.
WHILE OUR MUGGERS GRADUATED TO TERRORISTS. GANGSTERS TRADED FOR SUICIDE BOMBERS AND ANTHRAX POSTCARDS.
NINE YEARS AGO.
WHAT LIMITS HE SURPASSED.
WHILE SERIAL KILLERS AND SCHOOL SHOOTINGS ENTERED OUR DAILY CONVERSATION AND WE WERE HEMMED IN BY FEAR.

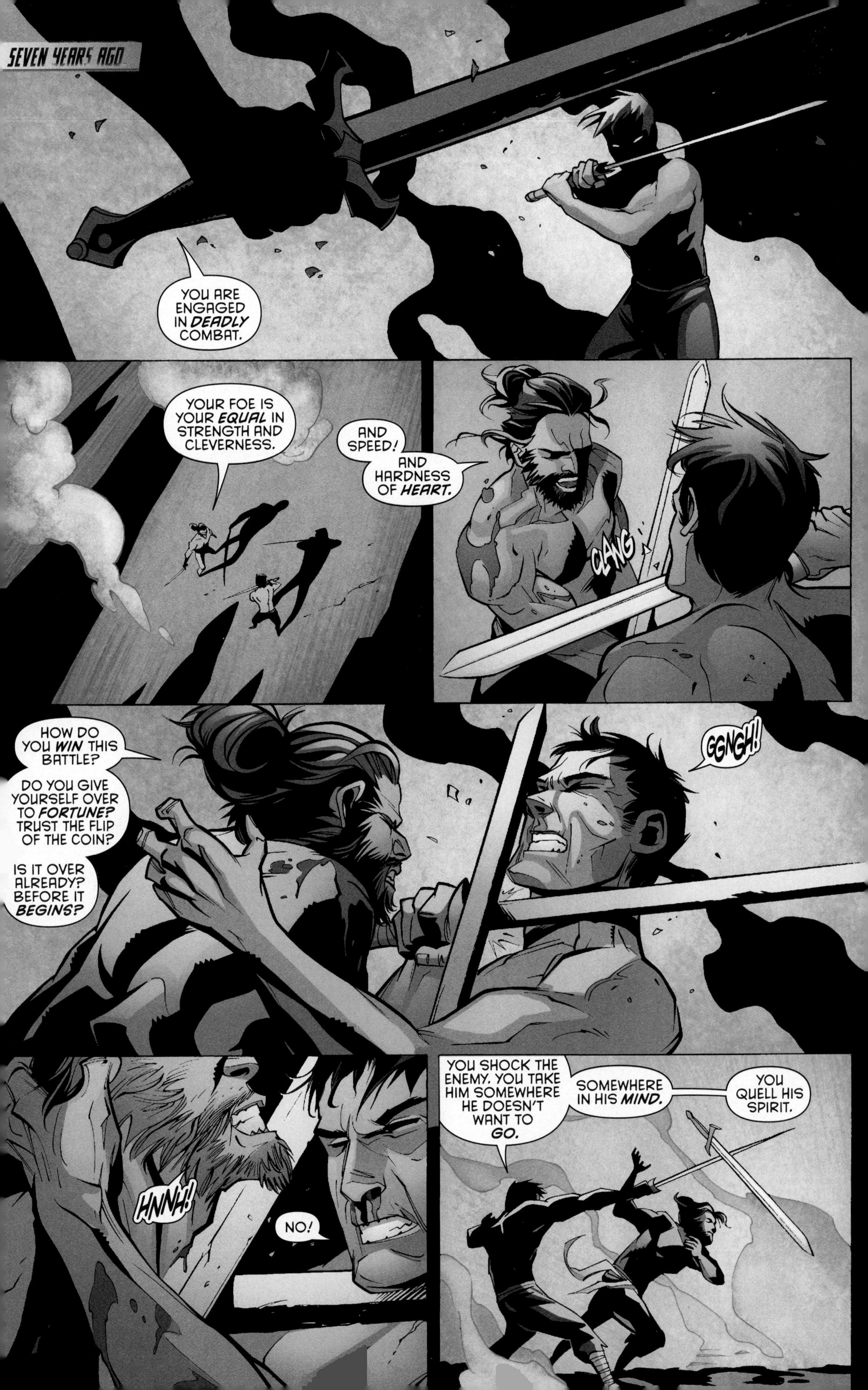
SEVEN YEARS AGO
YOU ARE ENGAGED IN DEADLY COMBAT.
YOUR FOE IS YOUR EQUAL IN STRENGTH AND CLEVERNESS.
AND SPEED!
AND HARDNESS OF HEART.
CLANG
HOW DO YOU WIN THIS BATTLE?
DO YOU GIVE YOURSELF OVER TO FORTUNE? TRUST THE FLIP OF THE COIN?
IS IT OVER ALREADY? BEFORE IT BEGINS?
GGNGH!
HNNH!
NO!
YOU SHOCK THE ENEMY. YOU TAKE HIM SOMEWHERE HE DOESN'T WANT TO GO.
SOMEWHERE IN HIS MIND.
YOU QUELL HIS SPIRIT.

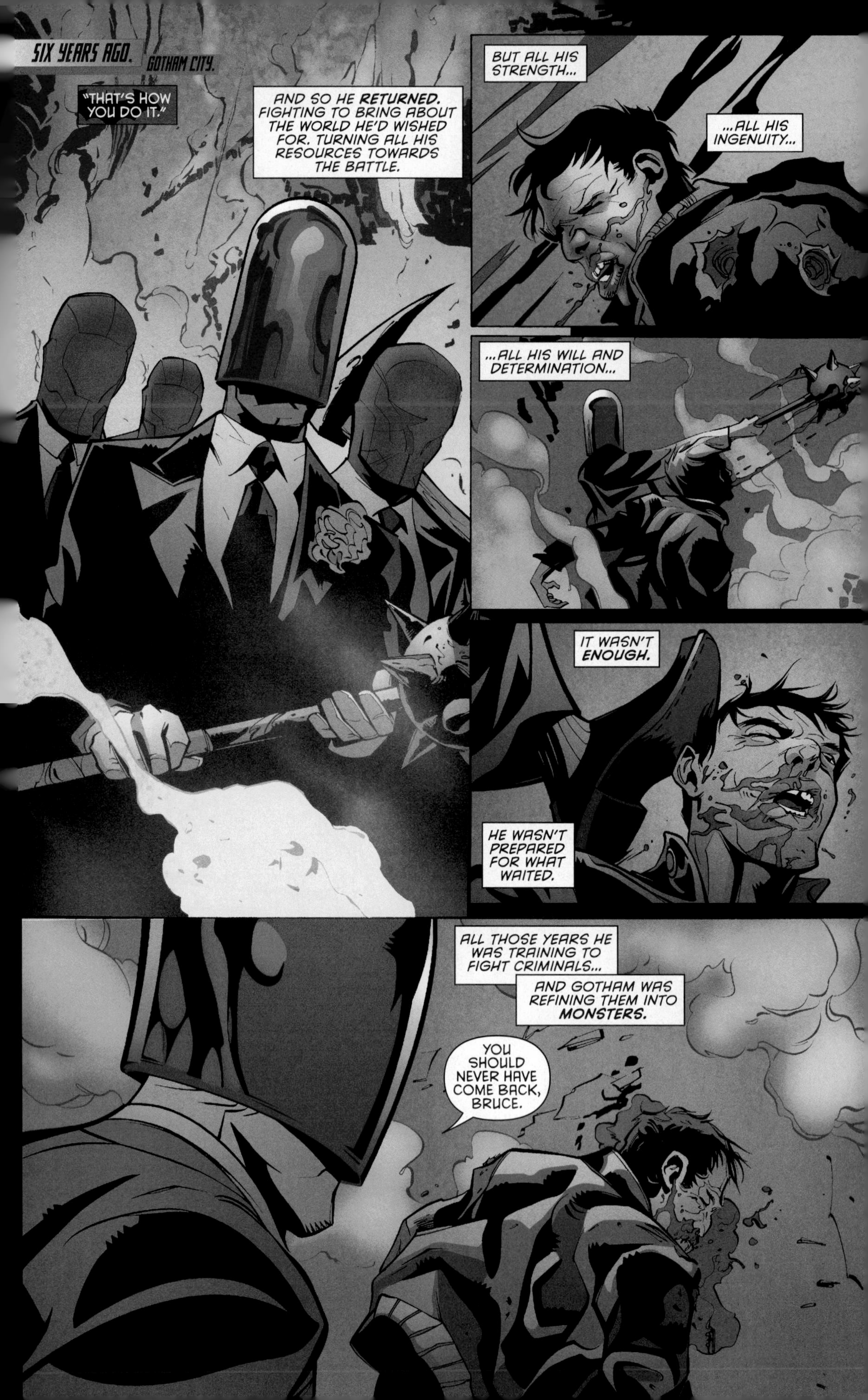
SIX YEARS AGO.
GOTHAM CITY.
"THAT'S HOW YOU DO IT."
AND SO HE RETURNED. FIGHTING TO BRING ABOUT THE WORLD HE'D WISHED FOR. TURNING ALL HIS RESOURCES TOWARDS THE BATTLE.
BUT ALL HIS STRENGTH...
...ALL HIS INGENUITY...
...ALL HIS WILL AND DETERMINATION...
IT WASN'T ENOUGH.
HE WASN'T PREPARED FOR WHAT WAITED.
ALL THOSE YEARS HE WAS TRAINING TO FIGHT CRIMINALS...
AND GOTHAM WAS REFINING THEM INTO MONSTERS.
YOU SHOULD NEVER HAVE COME BACK, BRUCE.

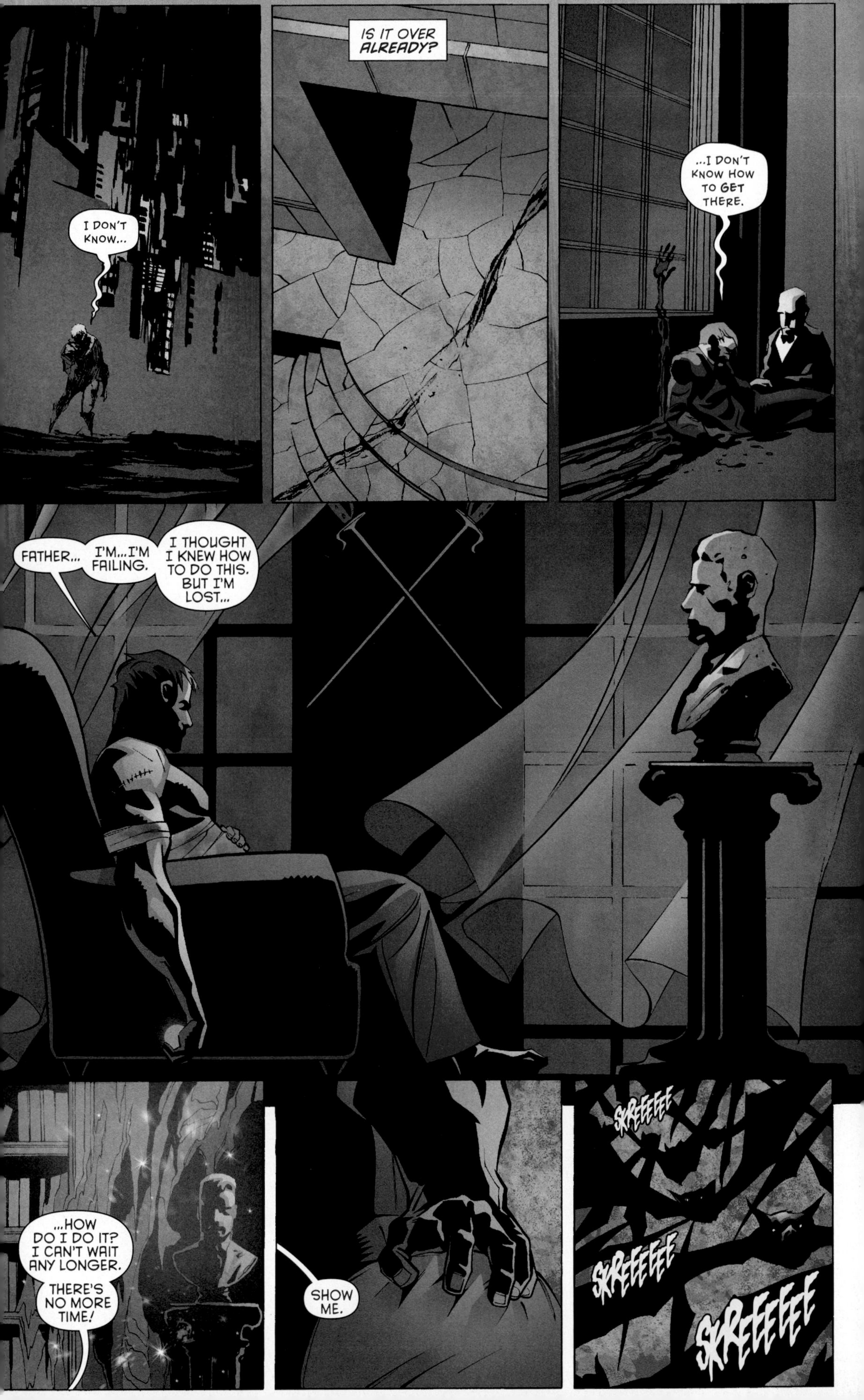
I DON'T KNOW...
IS IT OVER ALREADY?
...I DON'T KNOW HOW TO GET THERE.
FATHER...
I'M...I'M FAILING.
I THOUGHT I KNEW HOW TO DO THIS. BUT I'M LOST...
...HOW DO I DO IT? I CAN'T WAIT ANY LONGER.
THERE'S NO MORE TIME!
SHOW ME.
SKREEEEE
SKREEEEEE
SKREEEEEE

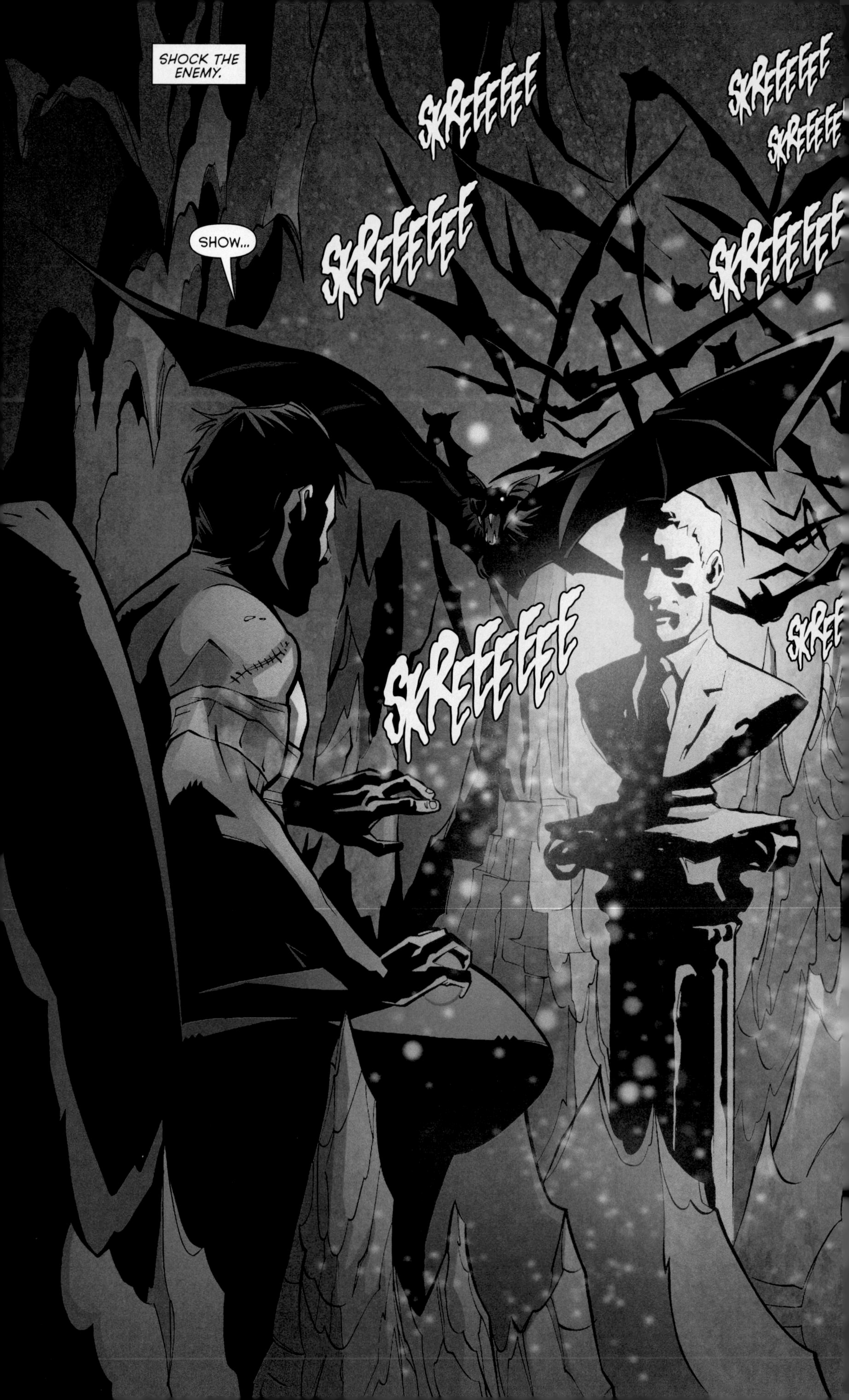
SHOCK THE ENEMY.
SHOW...
SKREEEEEE
SKREEEEEE
SKREEEEEE
SKREEEEE
SKREEEEEE
SKREEEEEE
SKREE

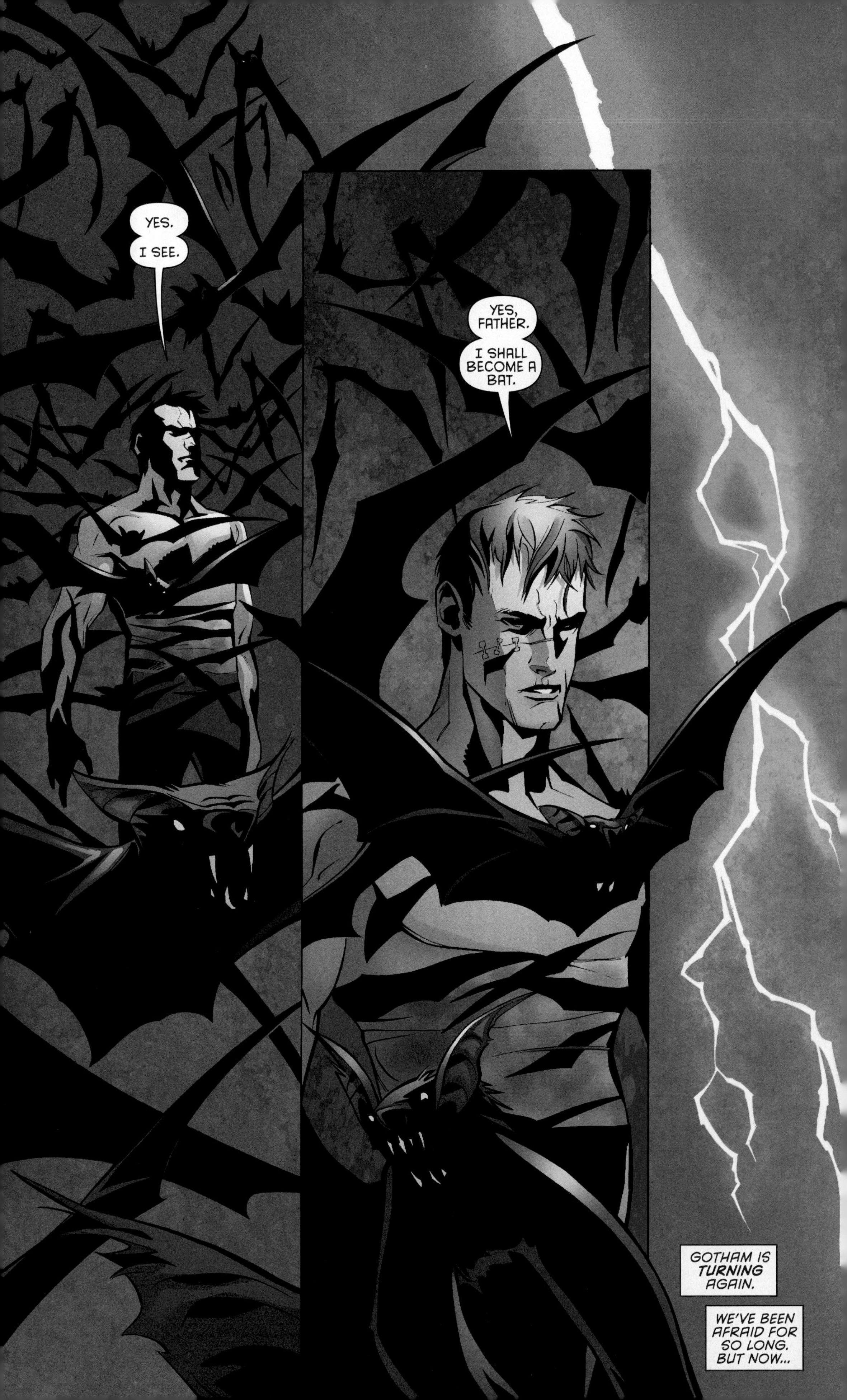
YES.
I SEE.
YES, FATHER.
I SHALL BECOME A BAT.
GOTHAM IS TURNING AGAIN.
WE'VE BEEN AFRAID FOR SO LONG. BUT NOW...

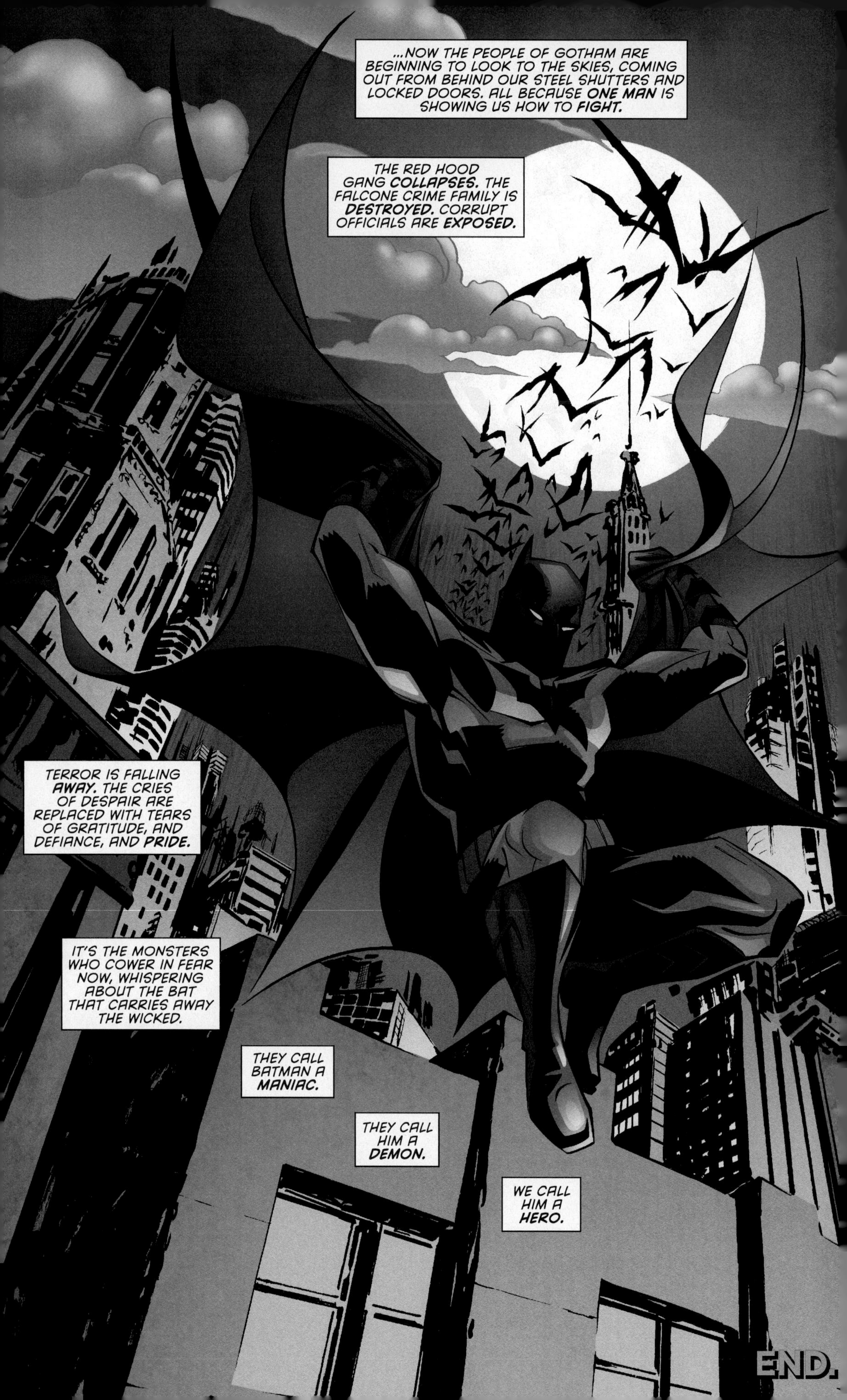
...NOW THE PEOPLE OF GOTHAM ARE BEGINNING TO LOOK TO THE SKIES, COMING OUT FROM BEHIND OUR STEEL SHUTTERS AND LOCKED DOORS. ALL BECAUSE ONE MAN IS SHOWING US HOW TO FIGHT.
THE RED HOOD GANG COLLAPSES. THE FALCONE CRIME FAMILY IS DESTROYED. CORRUPT OFFICIALS ARE EXPOSED.
TERROR IS FALLING AWAY. THE CRIES OF DESPAIR ARE REPLACED WITH TEARS OF GRATITUDE, AND DEFIANCE, AND PRIDE.
IT'S THE MONSTERS WHO COWER IN FEAR NOW, WHISPERING ABOUT THE BAT THAT CARRIES AWAY THE WICKED.
THEY CALL BATMAN A MANIAC.
THEY CALL HIM A DEMON.
WE CALL HIM A HERO.
END.

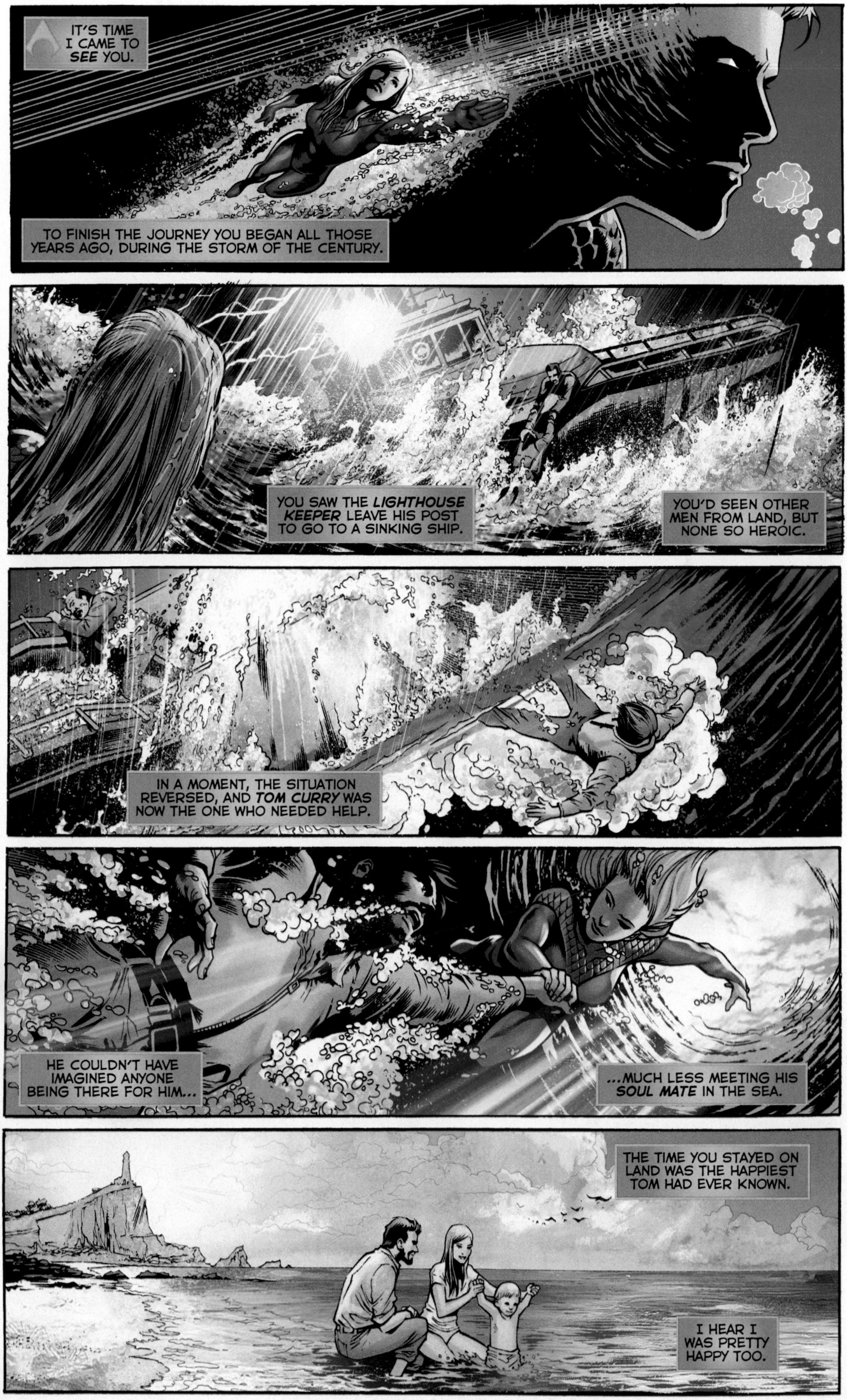
IT'S TIME I CAME TO SEE YOU.
TO FINISH THE JOURNEY YOU BEGAN ALL THOSE YEARS AGO, DURING THE STORM OF THE CENTURY.
YOU SAW THE LIGHTHOUSE KEEPER LEAVE HIS POST TO GO TO A SINKING SHIP.
YOU'D SEEN OTHER MEN FROM LAND, BUT NONE SO HEROIC.
IN A MOMENT, THE SITUATION REVERSED, AND TOM CURRY WAS NOW THE ONE WHO NEEDED HELP.
HE COULDN'T HAVE IMAGINED ANYONE BEING THERE FOR HIM...
...MUCH LESS MEETING HIS SOUL MATE IN THE SEA.
THE TIME YOU STAYED ON LAND WAS THE HAPPIEST TOM HAD EVER KNOWN.
I HEAR I WAS PRETTY HAPPY TOO.

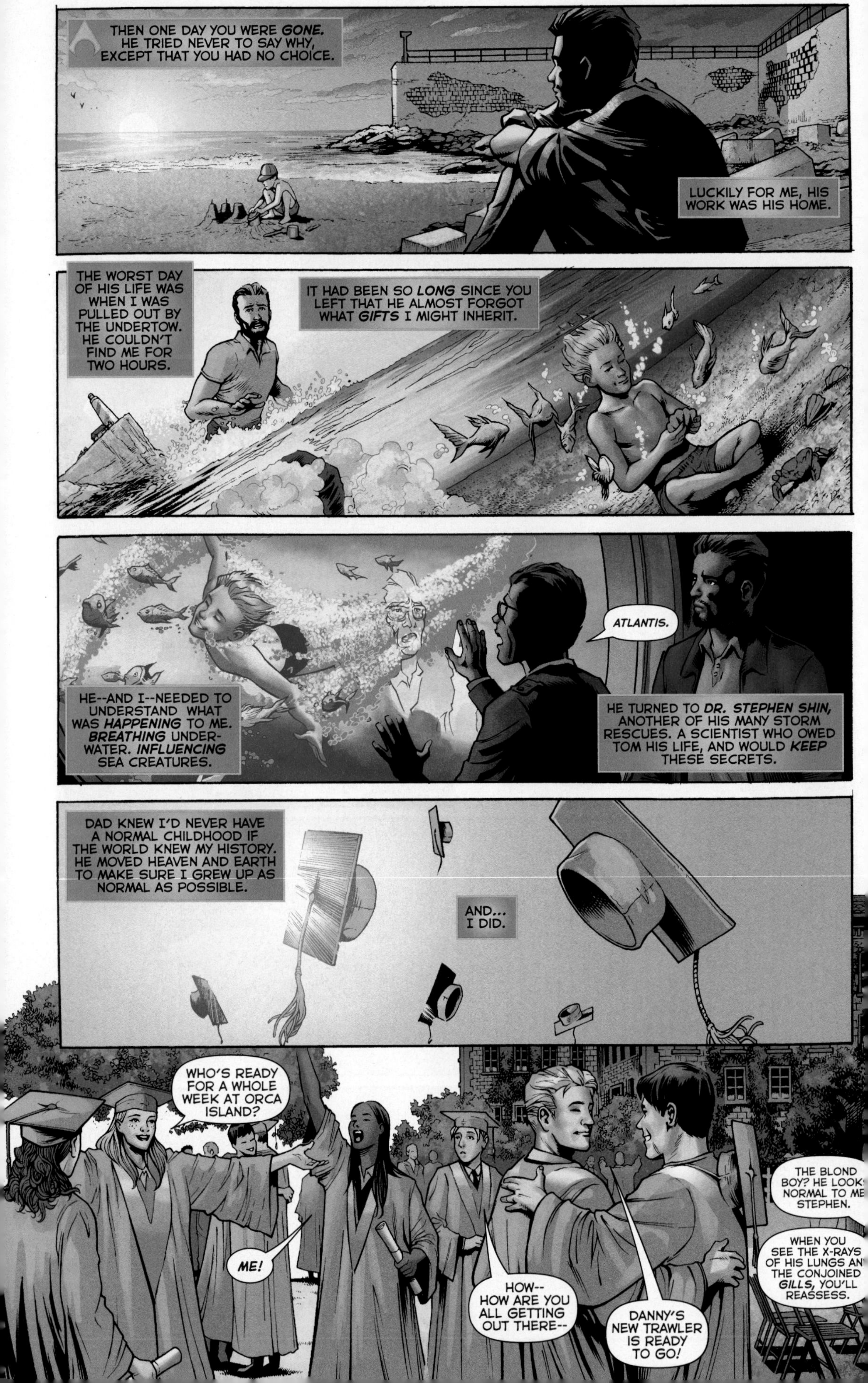
THEN ONE DAY YOU WERE GONE. HE TRIED NEVER TO SAY WHY, EXCEPT THAT YOU HAD NO CHOICE.
LUCKILY FOR ME, HIS WORK WAS HIS HOME.
THE WORST DAY OF HIS LIFE WAS WHEN I WAS PULLED OUT BY THE UNDERTOW. HE COULDN'T FIND ME FOR TWO HOURS.
IT HAD BEEN SO LONG SINCE YOU LEFT THAT HE ALMOST FORGOT WHAT GIFTS I MIGHT INHERIT.
HE--AND I--NEEDED TO UNDERSTAND WHAT WAS HAPPENING TO ME. BREATHING UNDER-WATER. INFLUENCING SEA CREATURES.
ATLANTIS.
HE TURNED TO DR. STEPHEN SHIN, ANOTHER OF HIS MANY STORM RESCUES. A SCIENTIST WHO OWED TOM HIS LIFE, AND WOULD KEEP THESE SECRETS.
DAD KNEW I'D NEVER HAVE A NORMAL CHILDHOOD IF THE WORLD KNEW MY HISTORY. HE MOVED HEAVEN AND EARTH TO MAKE SURE I GREW UP AS NORMAL AS POSSIBLE.
AND... I DID.
WHO'S READY FOR A WHOLE WEEK AT ORCA ISLAND?
ME!
HOW-- HOW ARE YOU ALL GETTING OUT THERE--
DANNY'S NEW TRAWLER IS READY TO GO!
THE BLOND BOY? HE LOOKS NORMAL TO ME STEPHEN.
WHEN YOU SEE THE X-RAYS OF HIS LUNGS AN THE CONJOINED GILLS, YOU'LL REASSESS.

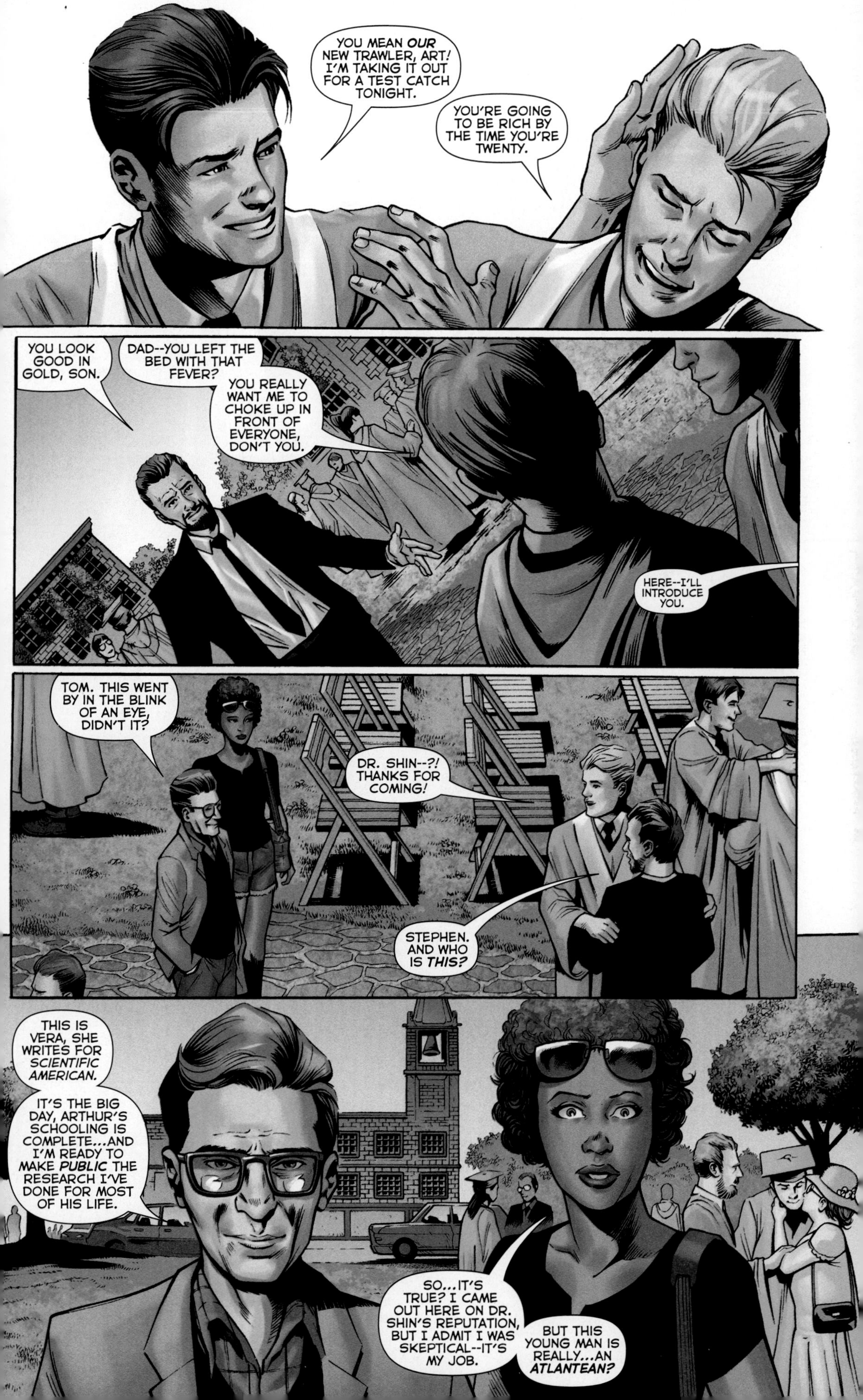
YOU MEAN *OUR* NEW TRAWLER, ART! I'M TAKING IT OUT FOR A TEST CATCH TONIGHT.
YOU'RE GOING TO BE RICH BY THE TIME YOU'RE TWENTY.
YOU LOOK GOOD IN GOLD, SON.
DAD--YOU LEFT THE BED WITH THAT FEVER?
YOU REALLY WANT ME TO CHOKE UP IN FRONT OF EVERYONE, DON'T YOU.
HERE--I'LL INTRODUCE YOU.
TOM. THIS WENT BY IN THE BLINK OF AN EYE, DIDN'T IT?
DR. SHIN--?! THANKS FOR COMING!
STEPHEN. AND WHO IS *THIS?*
THIS IS VERA, SHE WRITES FOR *SCIENTIFIC AMERICAN.*
IT'S THE BIG DAY, ARTHUR'S SCHOOLING IS COMPLETE...AND I'M READY TO MAKE *PUBLIC* THE RESEARCH I'VE DONE FOR MOST OF HIS LIFE.
SO...IT'S TRUE? I CAME OUT HERE ON DR. SHIN'S REPUTATION, BUT I ADMIT I WAS SKEPTICAL--IT'S MY JOB.
BUT THIS YOUNG MAN IS REALLY...AN *ATLANTEAN?*

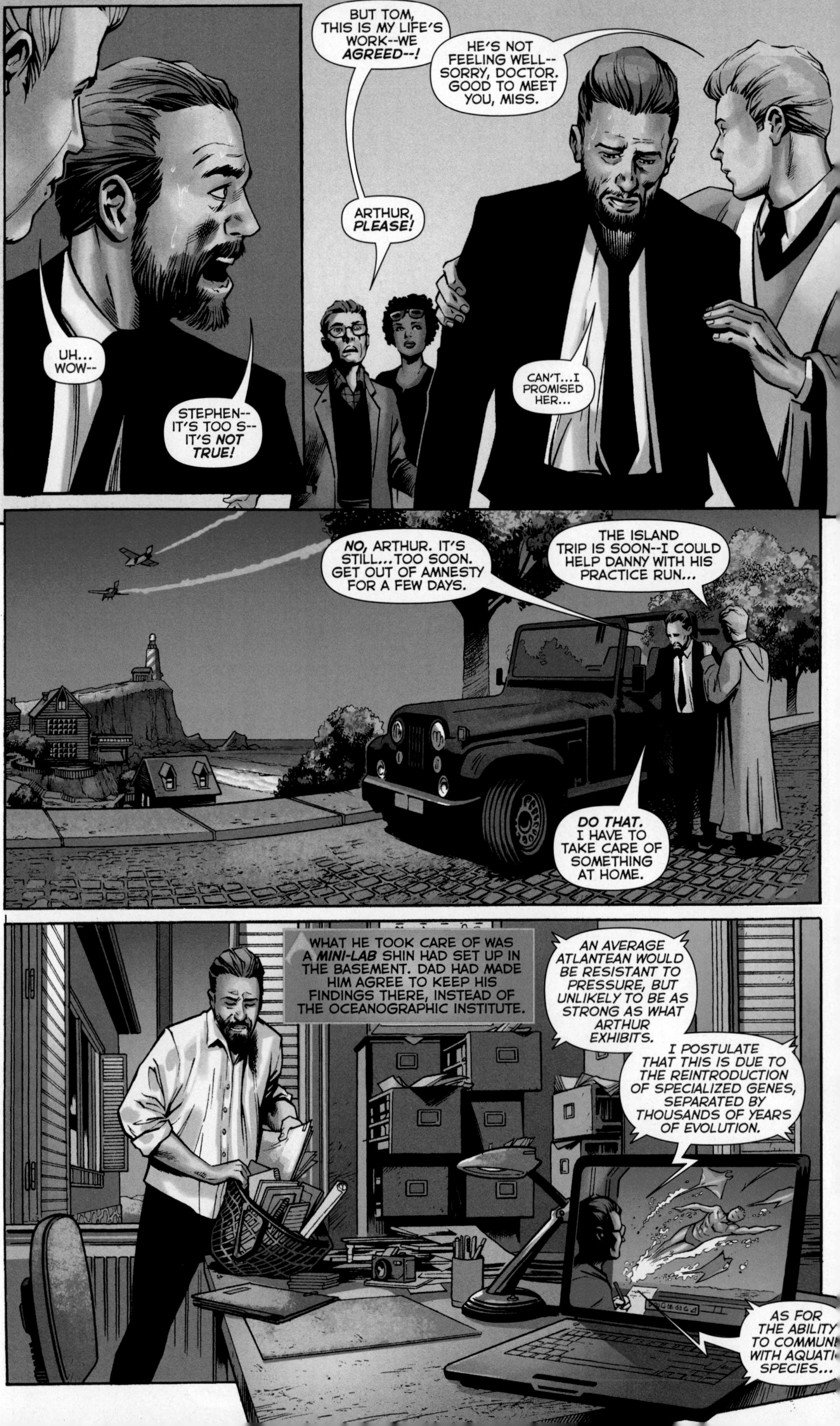
BUT TOM, THIS IS MY LIFE'S WORK--WE AGREED--!
HE'S NOT FEELING WELL-- SORRY, DOCTOR. GOOD TO MEET YOU, MISS.
ARTHUR, PLEASE!
UH... WOW--
STEPHEN-- IT'S TOO S-- IT'S NOT TRUE!
CAN'T...I PROMISED HER...
NO, ARTHUR. IT'S STILL...TOO SOON. GET OUT OF AMNESTY FOR A FEW DAYS.
THE ISLAND TRIP IS SOON--I COULD HELP DANNY WITH HIS PRACTICE RUN...
DO THAT. I HAVE TO TAKE CARE OF SOMETHING AT HOME.
WHAT HE TOOK CARE OF WAS A MINI-LAB SHIN HAD SET UP IN THE BASEMENT. DAD HAD MADE HIM AGREE TO KEEP HIS FINDINGS THERE, INSTEAD OF THE OCEANOGRAPHIC INSTITUTE.
AN AVERAGE ATLANTEAN WOULD BE RESISTANT TO PRESSURE, BUT UNLIKELY TO BE AS STRONG AS WHAT ARTHUR EXHIBITS.
I POSTULATE THAT THIS IS DUE TO THE REINTRODUCTION OF SPECIALIZED GENES, SEPARATED BY THOUSANDS OF YEARS OF EVOLUTION.
AS FOR THE ABILITY TO COMMUNI WITH AQUATI SPECIES...

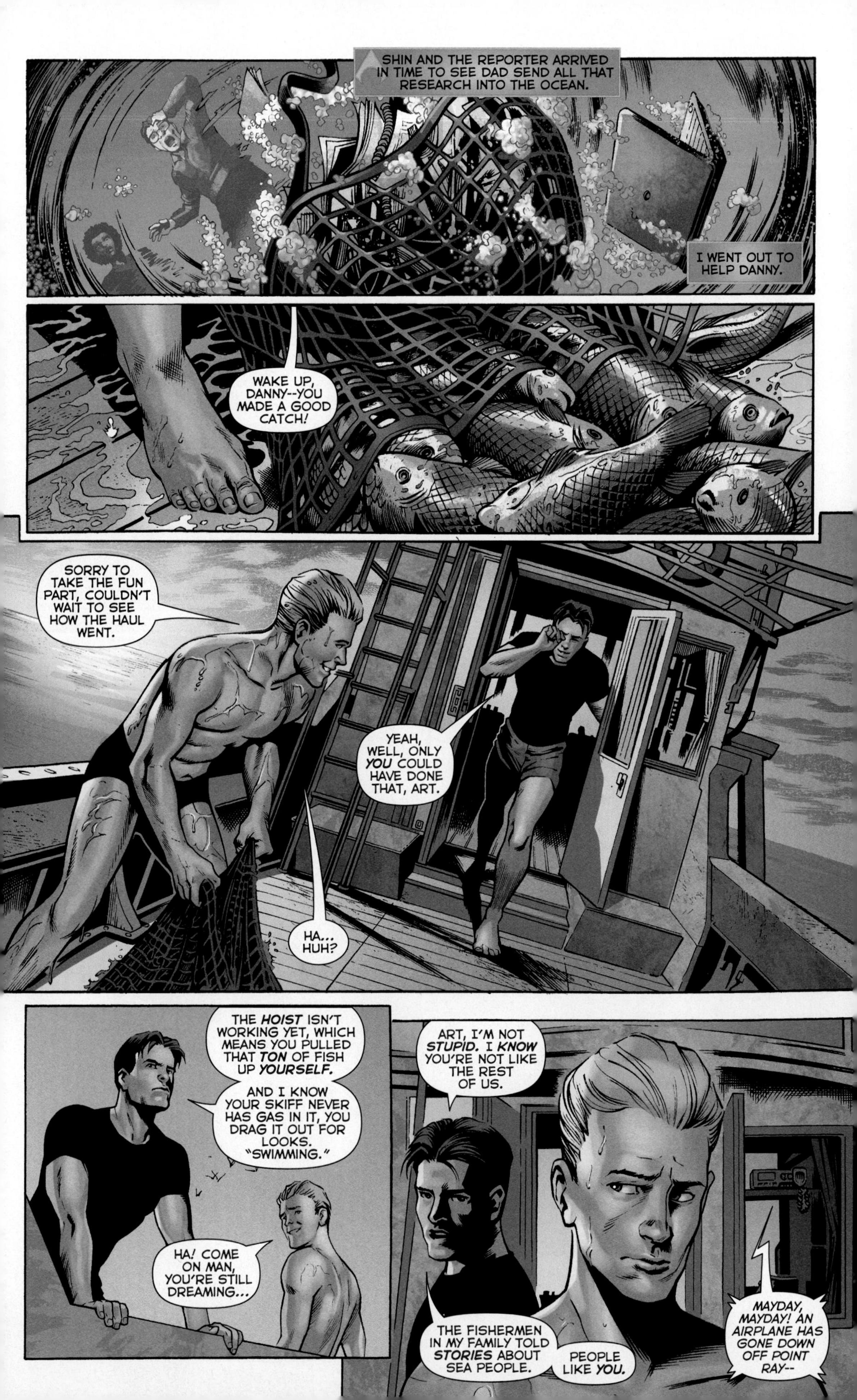
SHIN AND THE REPORTER ARRIVED IN TIME TO SEE DAD SEND ALL THAT RESEARCH INTO THE OCEAN.
I WENT OUT TO HELP DANNY.
WAKE UP, DANNY--YOU MADE A GOOD CATCH!
SORRY TO TAKE THE FUN PART, COULDN'T WAIT TO SEE HOW THE HAUL WENT.
YEAH, WELL, ONLY YOU COULD HAVE DONE THAT, ART.
HA... HUH?
THE HOIST ISN'T WORKING YET, WHICH MEANS YOU PULLED THAT TON OF FISH UP YOURSELF.
AND I KNOW YOUR SKIFF NEVER HAS GAS IN IT, YOU DRAG IT OUT FOR LOOKS. "SWIMMING."
HA! COME ON MAN, YOU'RE STILL DREAMING...
ART, I'M NOT STUPID. I KNOW YOU'RE NOT LIKE THE REST OF US.
THE FISHERMEN IN MY FAMILY TOLD STORIES ABOUT SEA PEOPLE.
PEOPLE LIKE YOU.
MAYDAY, MAYDAY! AN AIRPLANE HAS GONE DOWN OFF POINT RAY--

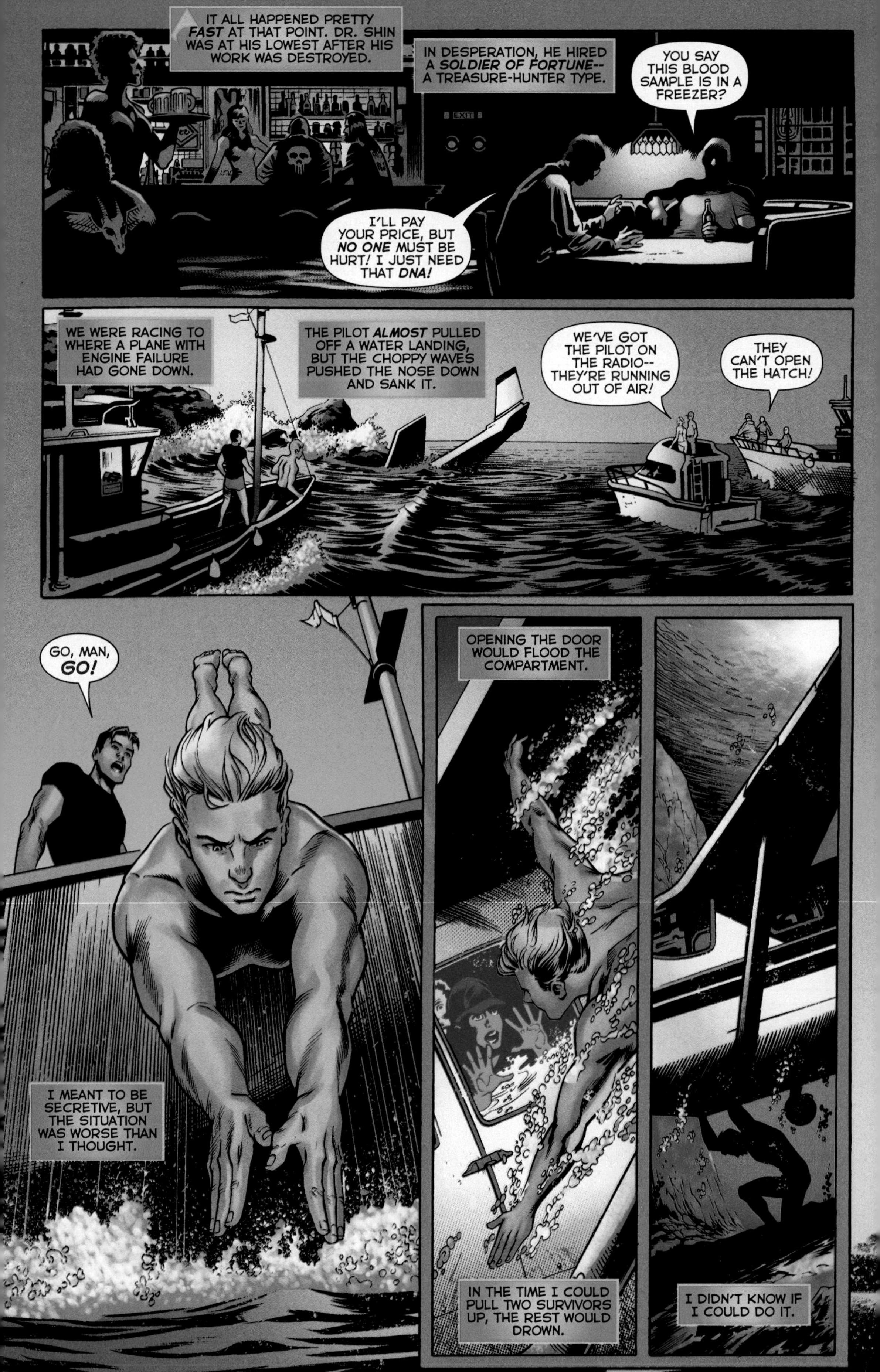

IT ALL HAPPENED PRETTY FAST AT THAT POINT. DR. SHIN WAS AT HIS LOWEST AFTER HIS WORK WAS DESTROYED.
IN DESPERATION, HE HIRED A SOLDIER OF FORTUNE-- A TREASURE-HUNTER TYPE.
YOU SAY THIS BLOOD SAMPLE IS IN A FREEZER?
I'LL PAY YOUR PRICE, BUT NO ONE MUST BE HURT! I JUST NEED THAT DNA!
EXIT
WE WERE RACING TO WHERE A PLANE WITH ENGINE FAILURE HAD GONE DOWN.
THE PILOT ALMOST PULLED OFF A WATER LANDING, BUT THE CHOPPY WAVES PUSHED THE NOSE DOWN AND SANK IT.
WE'VE GOT THE PILOT ON THE RADIO-- THEY'RE RUNNING OUT OF AIR!
THEY CAN'T OPEN THE HATCH!
GO, MAN, GO!
I MEANT TO BE SECRETIVE, BUT THE SITUATION WAS WORSE THAN I THOUGHT.
OPENING THE DOOR WOULD FLOOD THE COMPARTMENT.
IN THE TIME I COULD PULL TWO SURVIVORS UP, THE REST WOULD DROWN.
I DIDN'T KNOW IF I COULD DO IT.

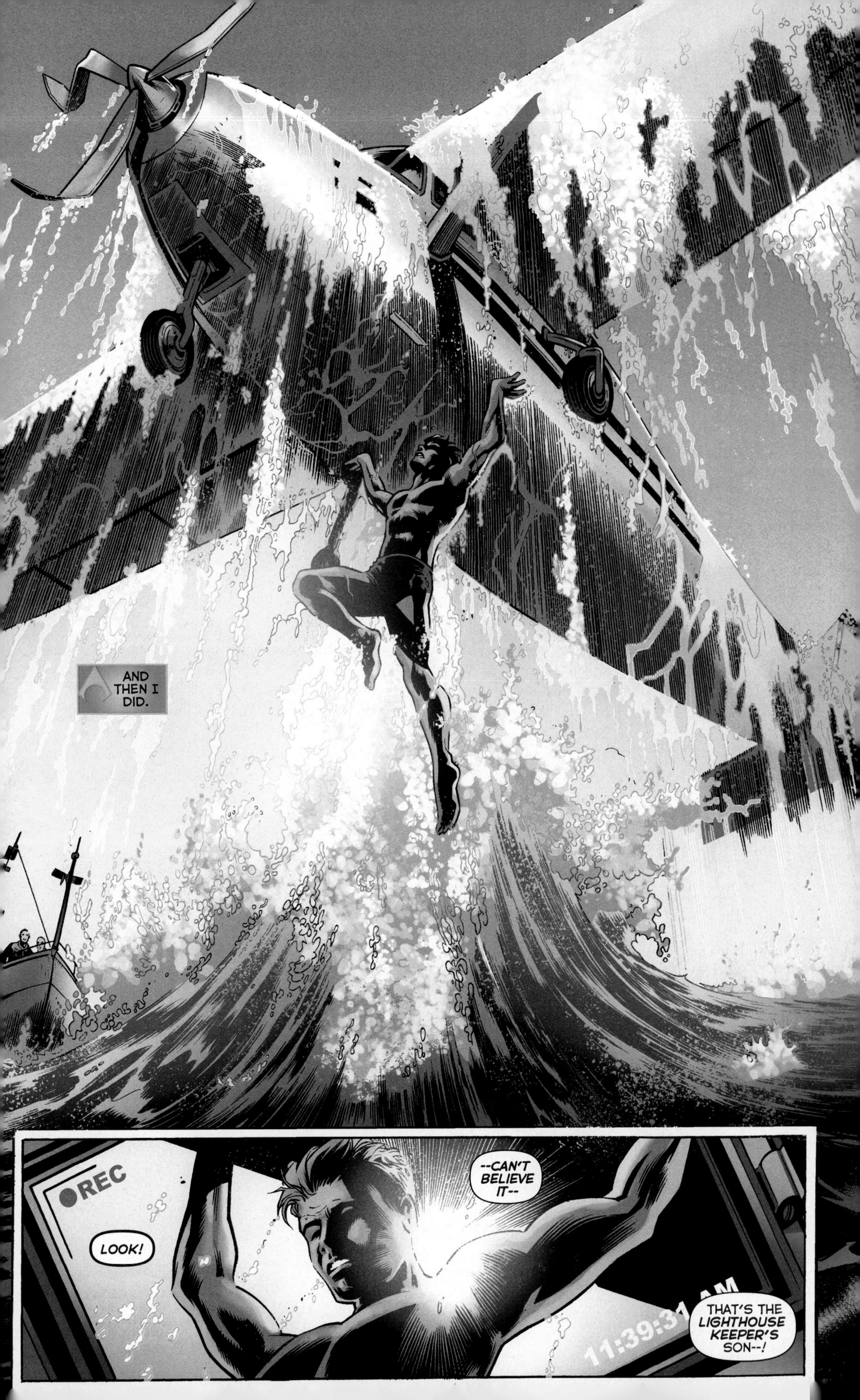
AND THEN I DID.
REC
--CAN'T BELIEVE IT--
LOOK!
11:39:31 AM
THAT'S THE LIGHTHOUSE KEEPER'S SON--!

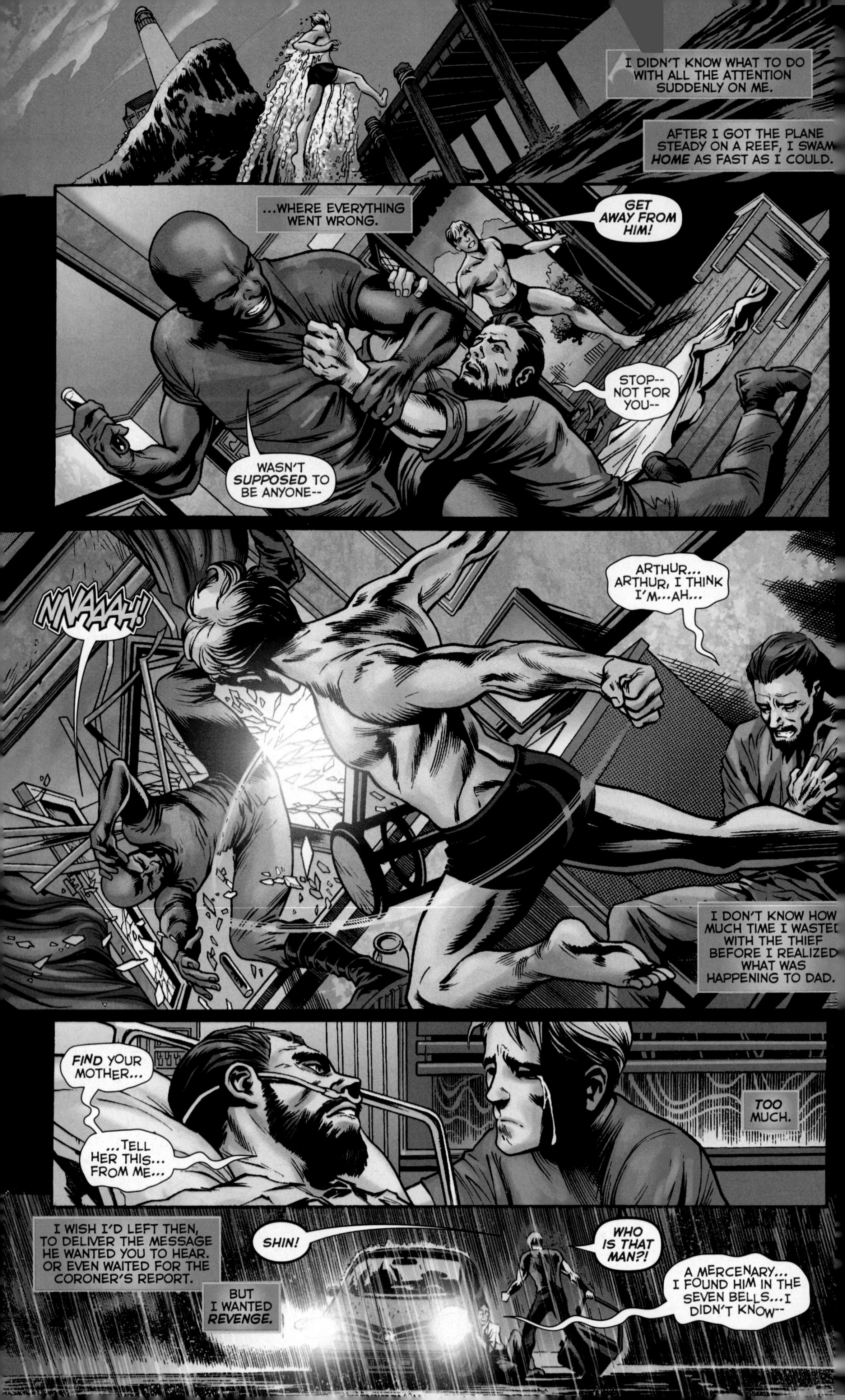
I DIDN'T KNOW WHAT TO DO WITH ALL THE ATTENTION SUDDENLY ON ME.
AFTER I GOT THE PLANE STEADY ON A REEF, I SWAM HOME AS FAST AS I COULD.
...WHERE EVERYTHING WENT WRONG.
GET AWAY FROM HIM!
STOP-- NOT FOR YOU--
WASN'T SUPPOSED TO BE ANYONE--
NNAAAH!
ARTHUR... ARTHUR, I THINK I'M...AH...
I DON'T KNOW HOW MUCH TIME I WASTED WITH THE THIEF BEFORE I REALIZED WHAT WAS HAPPENING TO DAD.
FIND YOUR MOTHER...
...TELL HER THIS... FROM ME...
TOO MUCH.
I WISH I'D LEFT THEN, TO DELIVER THE MESSAGE HE WANTED YOU TO HEAR. OR EVEN WAITED FOR THE CORONER'S REPORT.
BUT I WANTED REVENGE.
SHIN!
WHO IS THAT MAN?!
A MERCENARY... I FOUND HIM IN THE SEVEN BELLS...I DIDN'T KNOW--

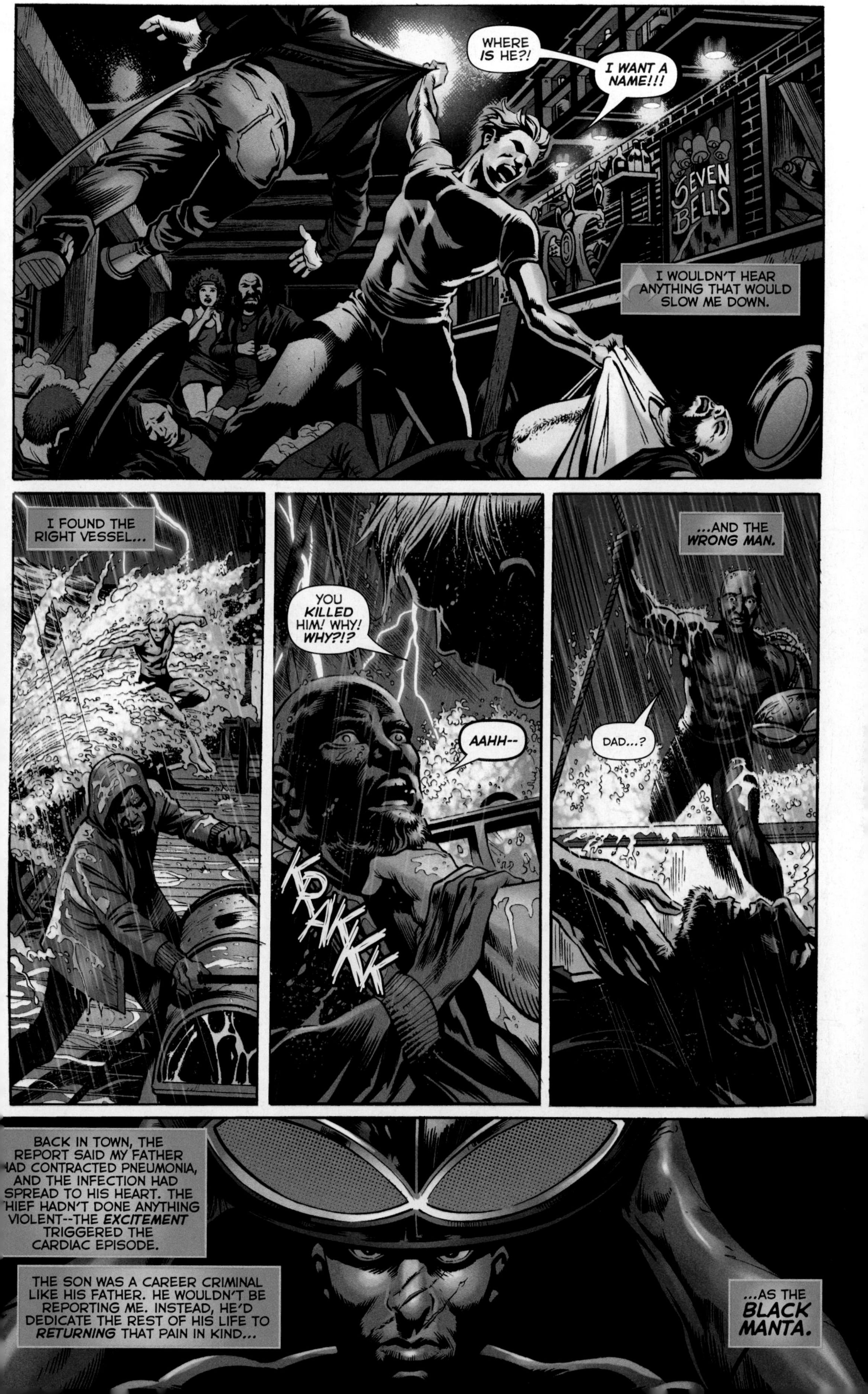

WHERE IS HE?!
I WANT A NAME!!!
I WOULDN'T HEAR ANYTHING THAT WOULD SLOW ME DOWN.
SEVEN BELLS
I FOUND THE RIGHT VESSEL...
YOU KILLED HIM! WHY! WHY?!?
AAHH--
KRAKKKK
...AND THE WRONG MAN.
DAD...?
BACK IN TOWN, THE REPORT SAID MY FATHER HAD CONTRACTED PNEUMONIA, AND THE INFECTION HAD SPREAD TO HIS HEART. THE THIEF HADN'T DONE ANYTHING VIOLENT--THE EXCITEMENT TRIGGERED THE CARDIAC EPISODE.
THE SON WAS A CAREER CRIMINAL LIKE HIS FATHER. HE WOULDN'T BE REPORTING ME. INSTEAD, HE'D DEDICATE THE REST OF HIS LIFE TO RETURNING THAT PAIN IN KIND...
...AS THE BLACK MANTA.

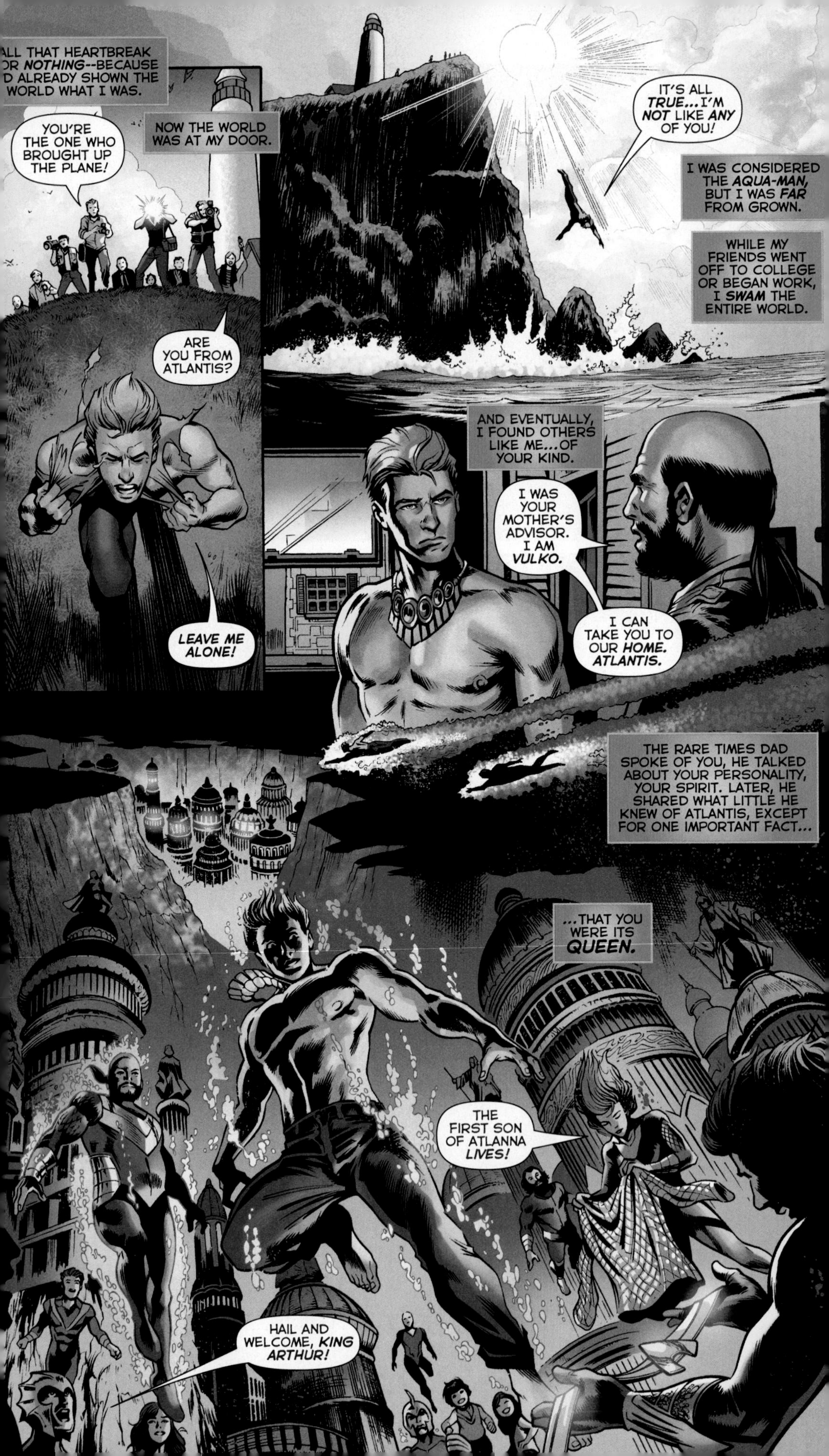
ALL THAT HEARTBREAK FOR NOTHING--BECAUSE I'D ALREADY SHOWN THE WORLD WHAT I WAS.
NOW THE WORLD WAS AT MY DOOR.
YOU'RE THE ONE WHO BROUGHT UP THE PLANE!
ARE YOU FROM ATLANTIS?
LEAVE ME ALONE!
IT'S ALL TRUE...I'M NOT LIKE ANY OF YOU!
I WAS CONSIDERED THE AQUA-MAN, BUT I WAS FAR FROM GROWN.
WHILE MY FRIENDS WENT OFF TO COLLEGE OR BEGAN WORK, I SWAM THE ENTIRE WORLD.
AND EVENTUALLY, I FOUND OTHERS LIKE ME...OF YOUR KIND.
I WAS YOUR MOTHER'S ADVISOR. I AM VULKO.
I CAN TAKE YOU TO OUR HOME. ATLANTIS.
THE RARE TIMES DAD SPOKE OF YOU, HE TALKED ABOUT YOUR PERSONALITY, YOUR SPIRIT. LATER, HE SHARED WHAT LITTLE HE KNEW OF ATLANTIS, EXCEPT FOR ONE IMPORTANT FACT...
...THAT YOU WERE ITS QUEEN.
THE FIRST SON OF ATLANNA LIVES!
HAIL AND WELCOME, KING ARTHUR!

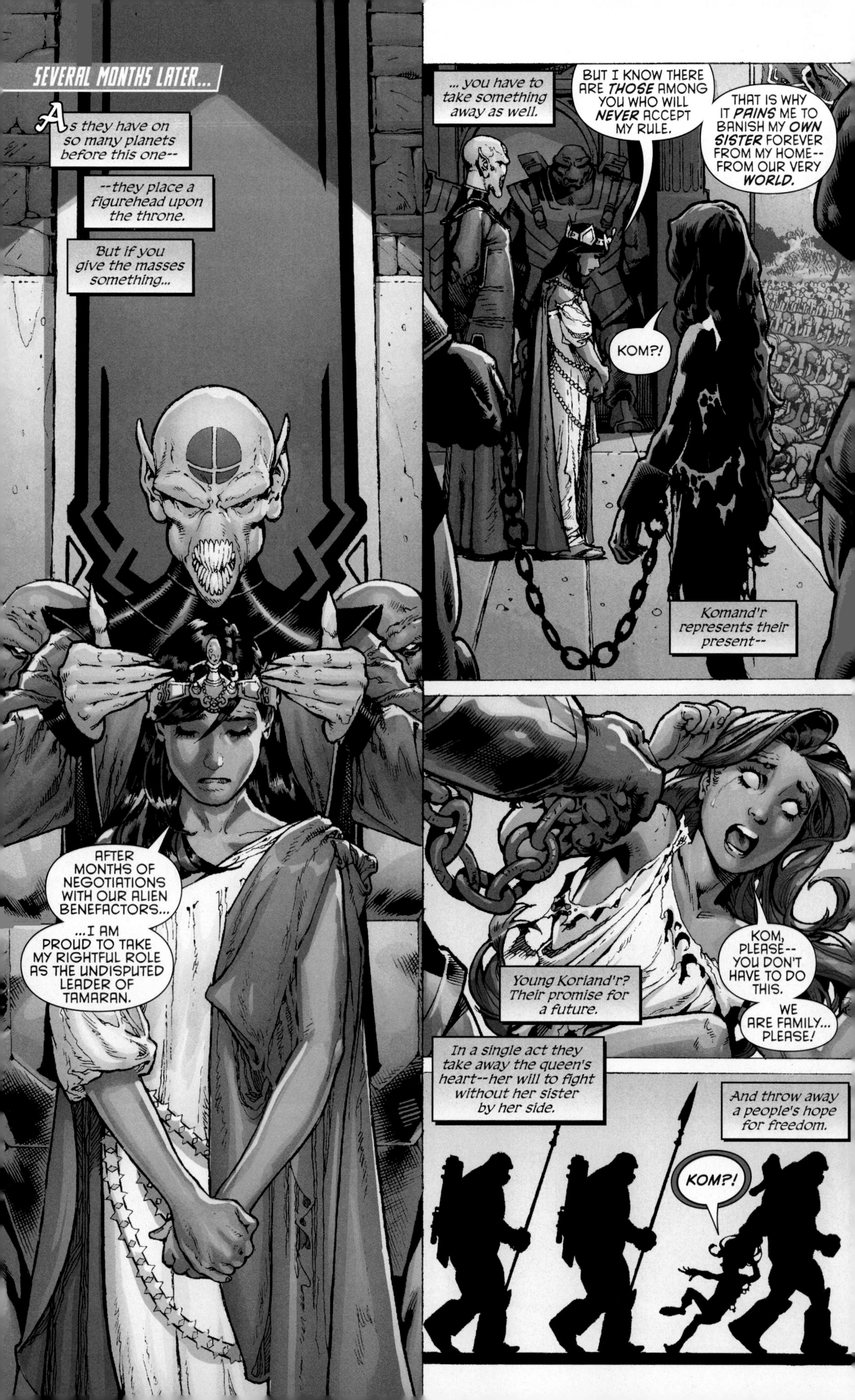
SEVERAL MONTHS LATER...
As they have on so many planets before this one--
--they place a figurehead upon the throne.
But if you give the masses something...
AFTER MONTHS OF NEGOTIATIONS WITH OUR ALIEN BENEFACTORS...
...I AM PROUD TO TAKE MY RIGHTFUL ROLE AS THE UNDISPUTED LEADER OF TAMARAN.
...you have to take something away as well.
BUT I KNOW THERE ARE THOSE AMONG YOU WHO WILL NEVER ACCEPT MY RULE.
THAT IS WHY IT PAINS ME TO BANISH MY OWN SISTER FOREVER FROM MY HOME--FROM OUR VERY WORLD.
KOM?!
Komand'r represents their present--
Young Koriand'r? Their promise for a future.
KOM, PLEASE-- YOU DON'T HAVE TO DO THIS.
WE ARE FAMILY... PLEASE!
In a single act they take away the queen's heart--her will to fight without her sister by her side.
And throw away a people's hope for freedom.
KOM?!

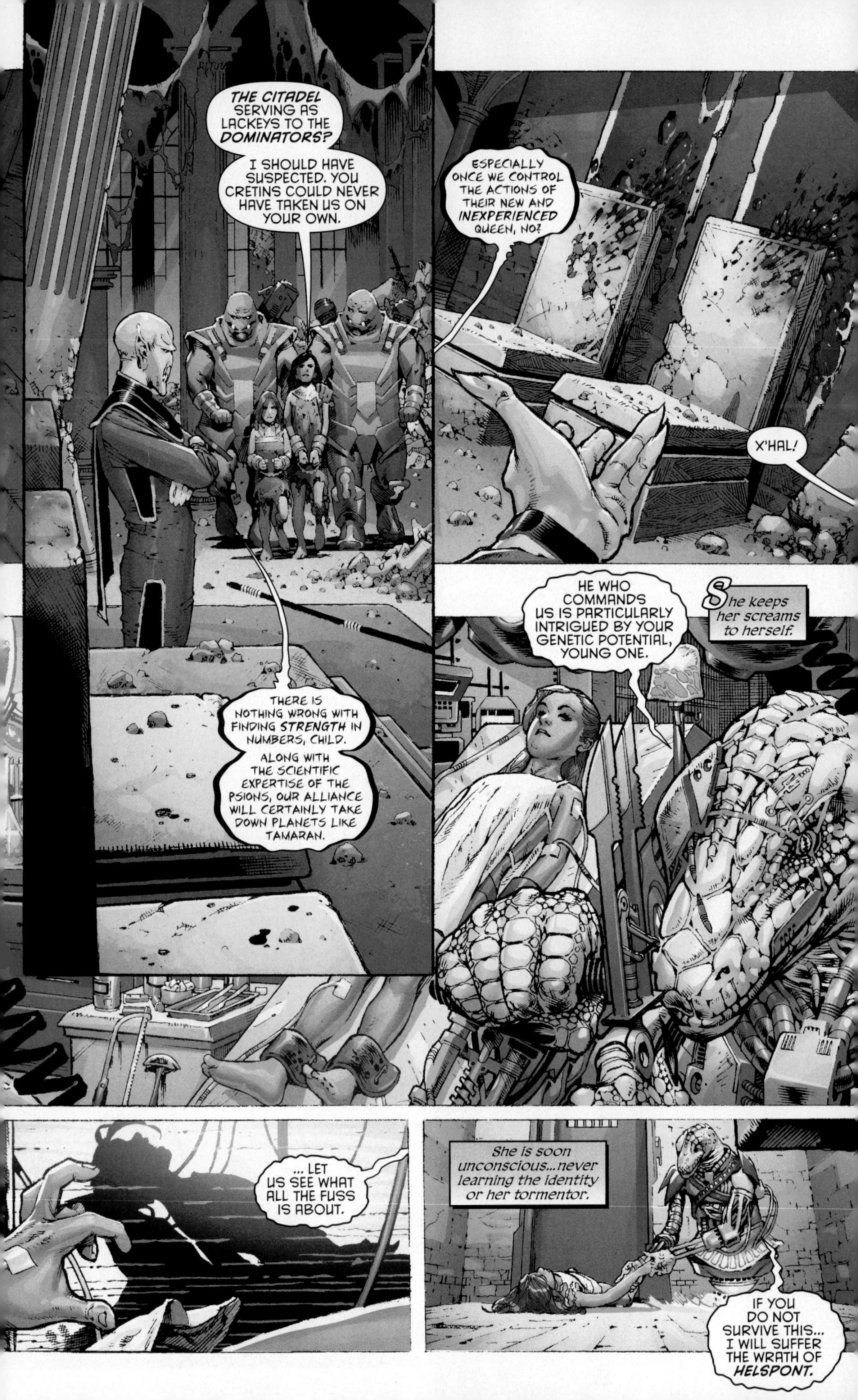
THE CITADEL SERVING AS LACKEYS TO THE DOMINATORS?
I SHOULD HAVE SUSPECTED. YOU CRETINS COULD NEVER HAVE TAKEN US ON YOUR OWN.
THERE IS NOTHING WRONG WITH FINDING STRENGTH IN NUMBERS, CHILD.
ALONG WITH THE SCIENTIFIC EXPERTISE OF THE PSIONS, OUR ALLIANCE WILL CERTAINLY TAKE DOWN PLANETS LIKE TAMARAN.
ESPECIALLY ONCE WE CONTROL THE ACTIONS OF THEIR NEW AND INEXPERIENCED QUEEN, NO?
X'HAL!
HE WHO COMMANDS US IS PARTICULARLY INTRIGUED BY YOUR GENETIC POTENTIAL, YOUNG ONE.
She keeps her screams to herself.
... LET US SEE WHAT ALL THE FUSS IS ABOUT.
She is soon unconscious...never learning the identity or her tormentor.
IF YOU DO NOT SURVIVE THIS... I WILL SUFFER THE WRATH OF HELSPONT.

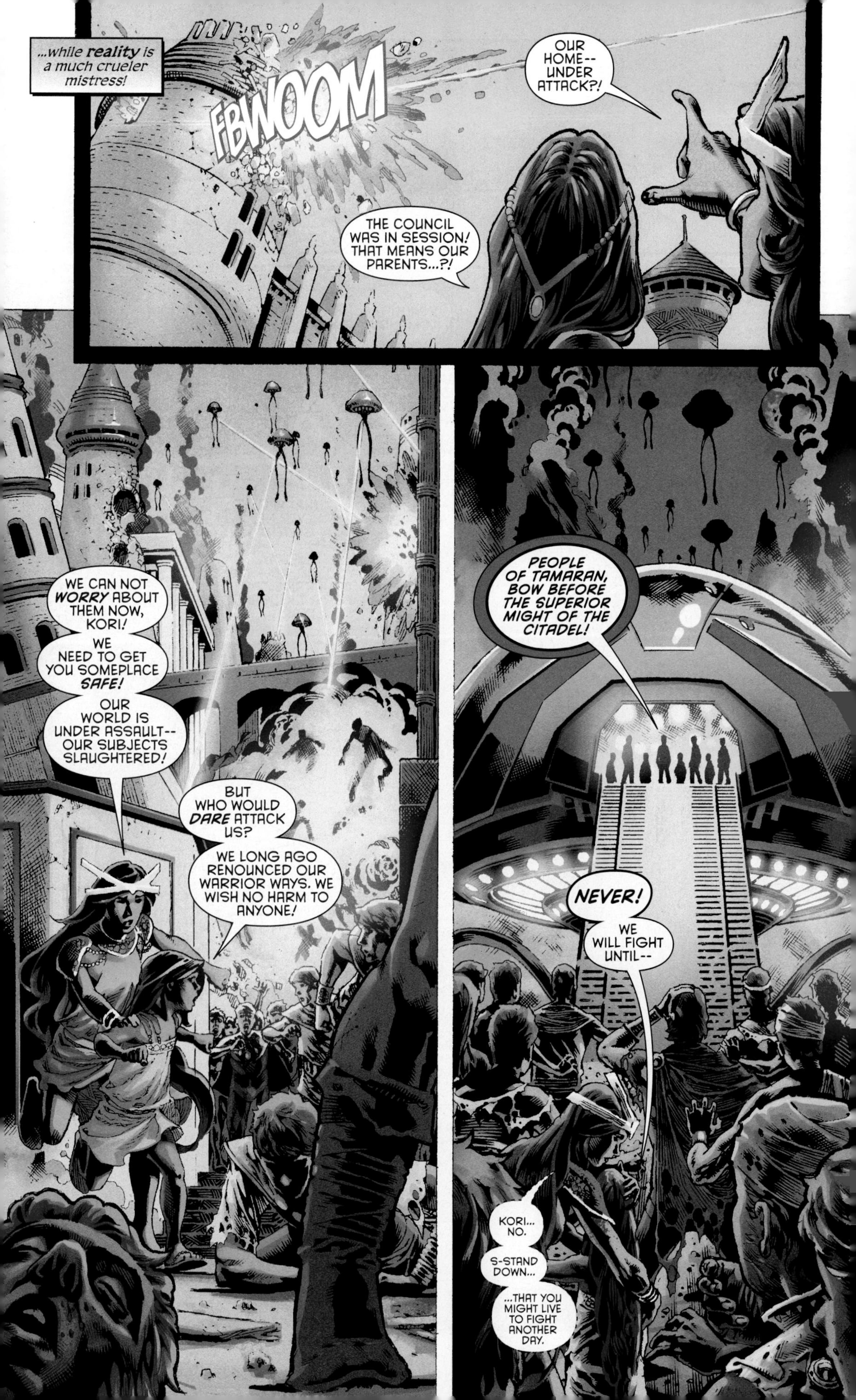
...while reality is a much crueler mistress!
FBWOOM
OUR HOME-- UNDER ATTACK?!
THE COUNCIL WAS IN SESSION! THAT MEANS OUR PARENTS...?!
WE CAN NOT WORRY ABOUT THEM NOW, KORI!
WE NEED TO GET YOU SOMEPLACE SAFE!
OUR WORLD IS UNDER ASSAULT-- OUR SUBJECTS SLAUGHTERED!
BUT WHO WOULD DARE ATTACK US?
WE LONG AGO RENOUNCED OUR WARRIOR WAYS. WE WISH NO HARM TO ANYONE!
PEOPLE OF TAMARAN, BOW BEFORE THE SUPERIOR MIGHT OF THE CITADEL!
NEVER!
WE WILL FIGHT UNTIL--
KORI... NO.
S-STAND DOWN...
...THAT YOU MIGHT LIVE TO FIGHT ANOTHER DAY.

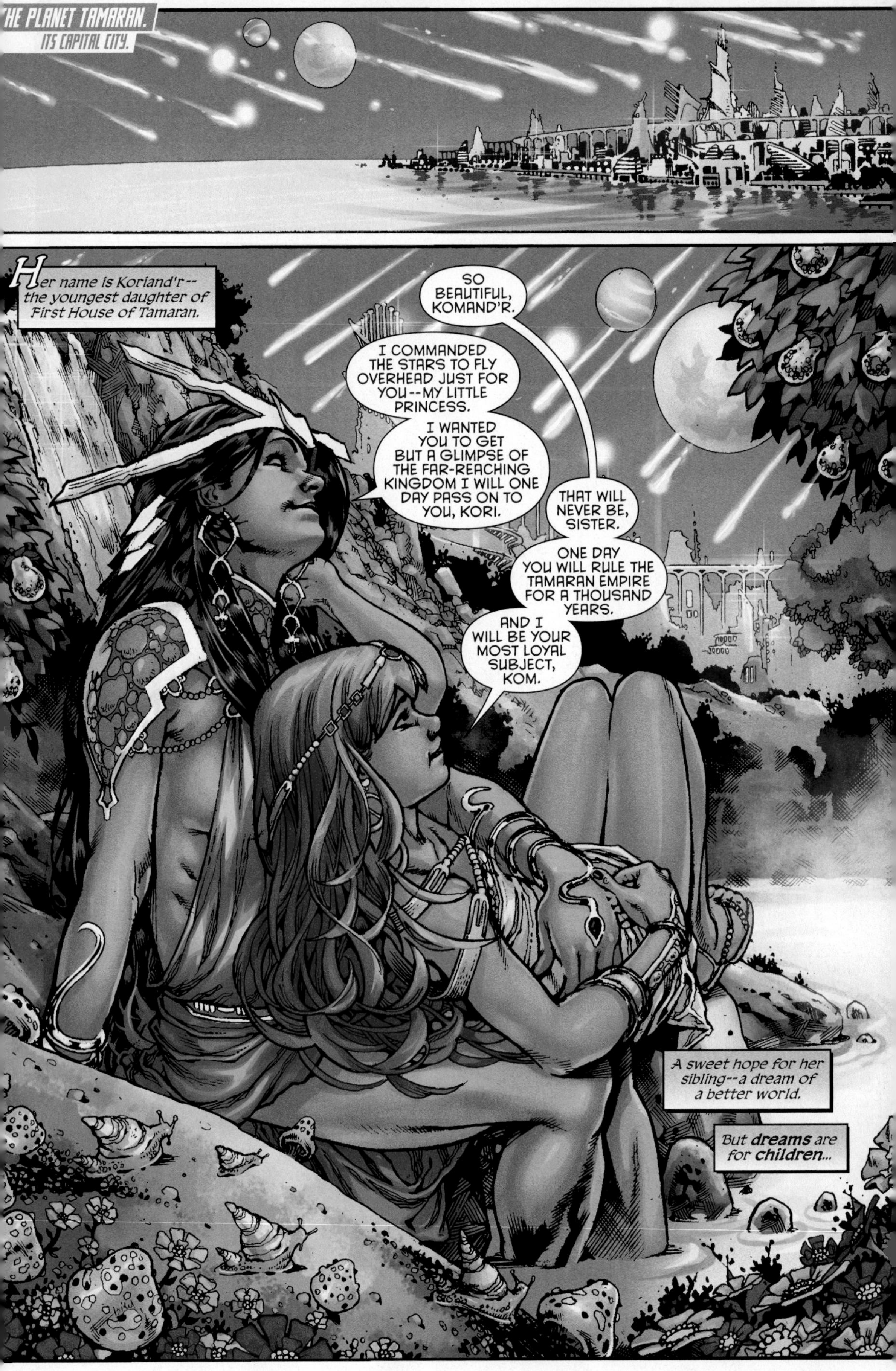
THE PLANET TAMARAN.
ITS CAPITAL CITY.
Her name is Koriand'r-- the youngest daughter of First House of Tamaran.
SO BEAUTIFUL, KOMAND'R.
I COMMANDED THE STARS TO FLY OVERHEAD JUST FOR YOU--MY LITTLE PRINCESS.
I WANTED YOU TO GET BUT A GLIMPSE OF THE FAR-REACHING KINGDOM I WILL ONE DAY PASS ON TO YOU, KORI.
THAT WILL NEVER BE, SISTER.
ONE DAY YOU WILL RULE THE TAMARAN EMPIRE FOR A THOUSAND YEARS.
AND I WILL BE YOUR MOST LOYAL SUBJECT, KOM.
A sweet hope for her sibling--a dream of a better world.
But **dreams** are for **children**...

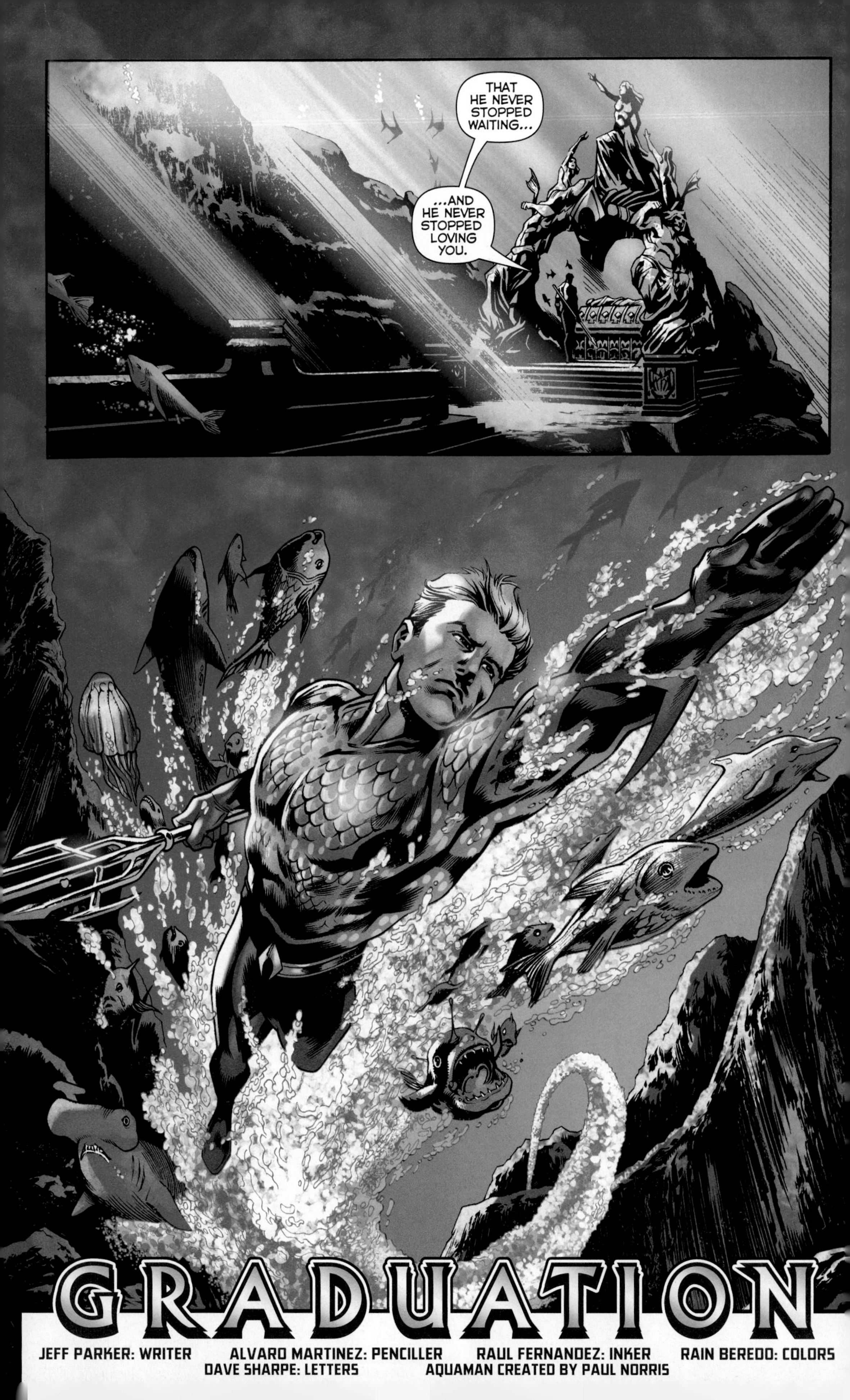
THAT HE NEVER STOPPED WAITING...
...AND HE NEVER STOPPED LOVING YOU.
GRADUATION
JEFF PARKER: WRITER
ALVARO MARTINEZ: PENCILLER
RAUL FERNANDEZ: INKER
RAIN BEREDO: COLORS
DAVE SHARPE: LETTERS
AQUAMAN CREATED BY PAUL NORRIS

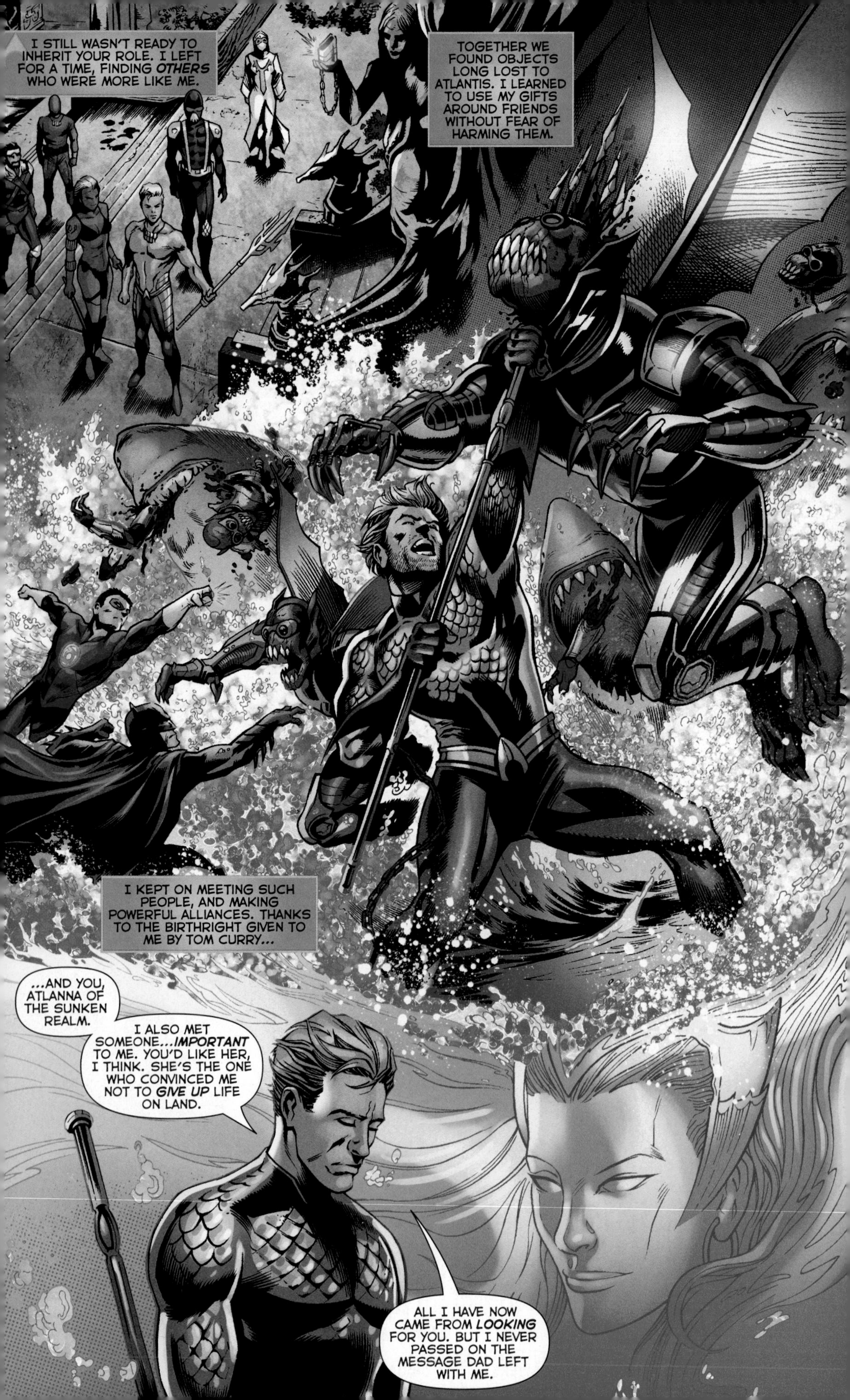
I STILL WASN'T READY TO INHERIT YOUR ROLE. I LEFT FOR A TIME, FINDING *OTHERS* WHO WERE MORE LIKE ME.
TOGETHER WE FOUND OBJECTS LONG LOST TO ATLANTIS. I LEARNED TO USE MY GIFTS AROUND FRIENDS WITHOUT FEAR OF HARMING THEM.
I KEPT ON MEETING SUCH PEOPLE, AND MAKING POWERFUL ALLIANCES. THANKS TO THE BIRTHRIGHT GIVEN TO ME BY TOM CURRY...
...AND YOU, ATLANNA OF THE SUNKEN REALM.
I ALSO MET SOMEONE...*IMPORTANT* TO ME. YOU'D LIKE HER, I THINK. SHE'S THE ONE WHO CONVINCED ME NOT TO *GIVE UP* LIFE ON LAND.
ALL I HAVE NOW CAME FROM *LOOKING* FOR YOU. BUT I NEVER PASSED ON THE MESSAGE DAD LEFT WITH ME.

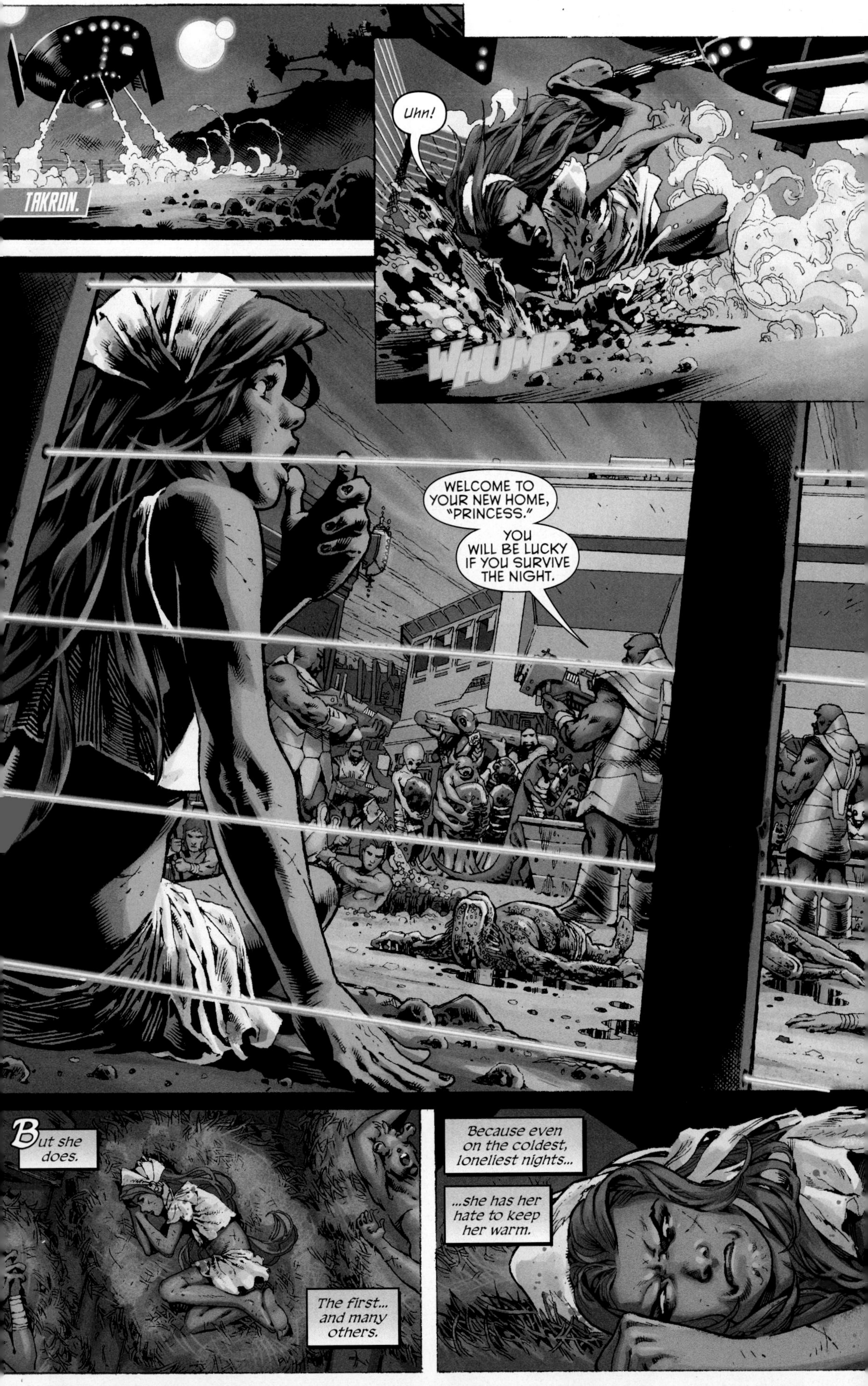
TAKRON.
Uhn!
WHUMP
WELCOME TO YOUR NEW HOME, "PRINCESS."
YOU WILL BE LUCKY IF YOU SURVIVE THE NIGHT.
But she does.
The first... and many others.
Because even on the coldest, loneliest nights...
...she has her hate to keep her warm.

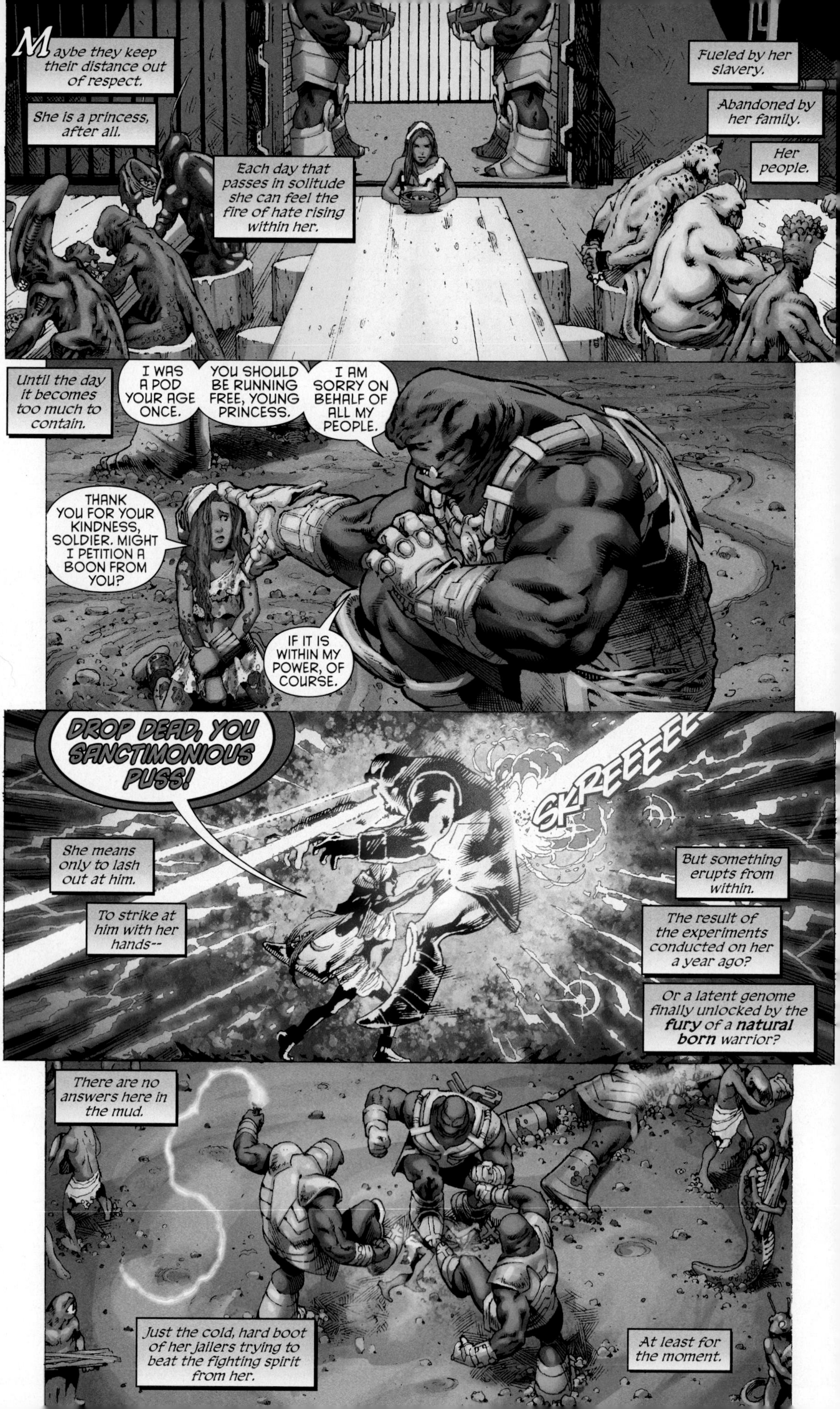

Maybe they keep their distance out of respect.
She is a princess, after all.
Each day that passes in solitude she can feel the fire of hate rising within her.
Fueled by her slavery.
Abandoned by her family.
Her people.
Until the day it becomes too much to contain.
I WAS A POD YOUR AGE ONCE.
YOU SHOULD BE RUNNING FREE, YOUNG PRINCESS.
I AM SORRY ON BEHALF OF ALL MY PEOPLE.
THANK YOU FOR YOUR KINDNESS, SOLDIER. MIGHT I PETITION A BOON FROM YOU?
IF IT IS WITHIN MY POWER, OF COURSE.
DROP DEAD, YOU SANCTIMONIOUS PUSS!
SKREEEEEE
She means only to lash out at him.
To strike at him with her hands--
But something erupts from within.
The result of the experiments conducted on her a year ago?
Or a latent genome finally unlocked by the fury of a natural born warrior?
There are no answers here in the mud.
Just the cold, hard boot of her jailers trying to beat the fighting spirit from her.
At least for the moment.

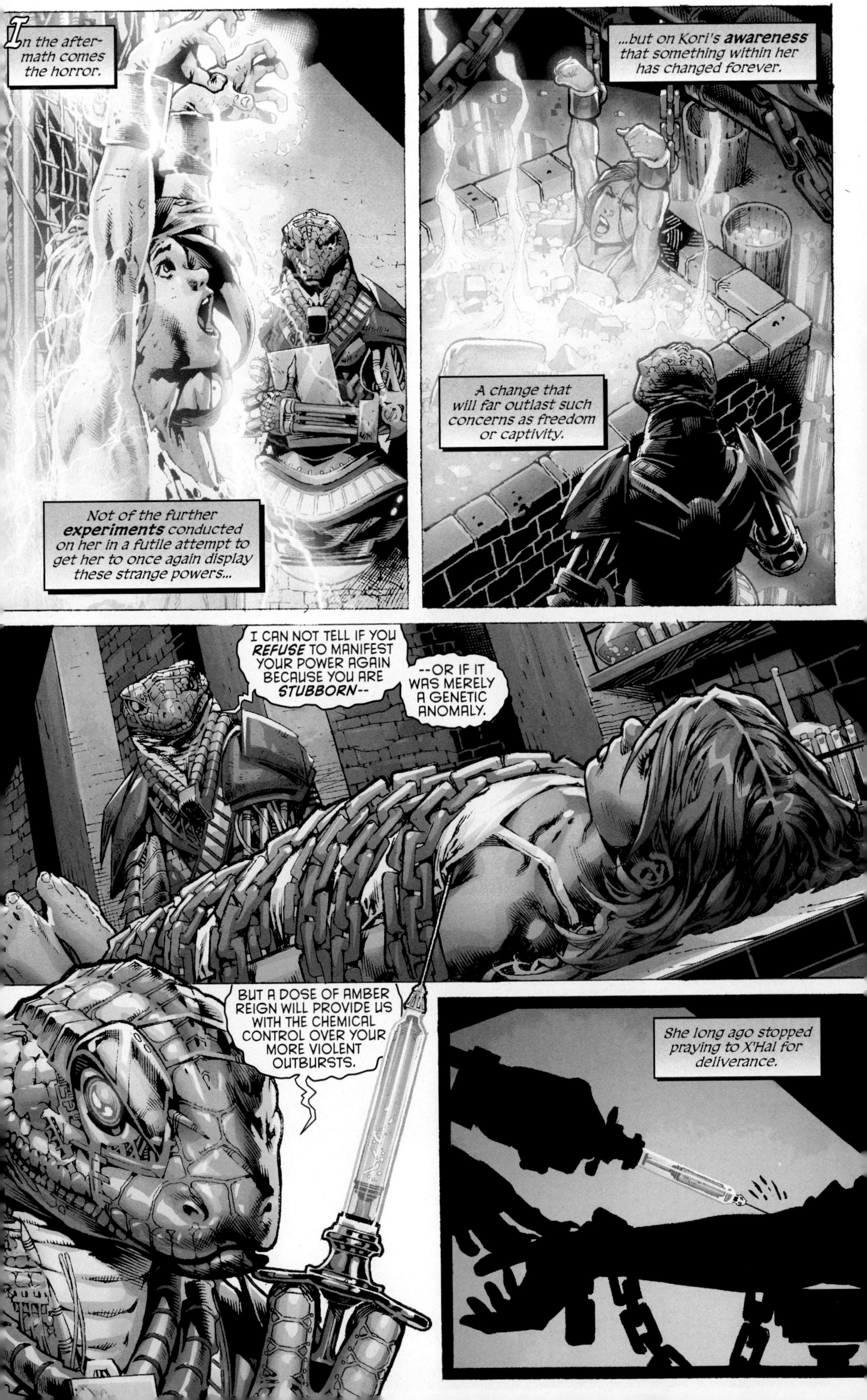
In the aftermath comes the horror.
Not of the further experiments conducted on her in a futile attempt to get her to once again display these strange powers...
...but on Kori's awareness that something within her has changed forever.
A change that will far outlast such concerns as freedom or captivity.
I CAN NOT TELL IF YOU REFUSE TO MANIFEST YOUR POWER AGAIN BECAUSE YOU ARE STUBBORN--
--OR IF IT WAS MERELY A GENETIC ANOMALY.
BUT A DOSE OF AMBER REIGN WILL PROVIDE US WITH THE CHEMICAL CONTROL OVER YOUR MORE VIOLENT OUTBURSTS.
She long ago stopped praying to X'Hal for deliverance.

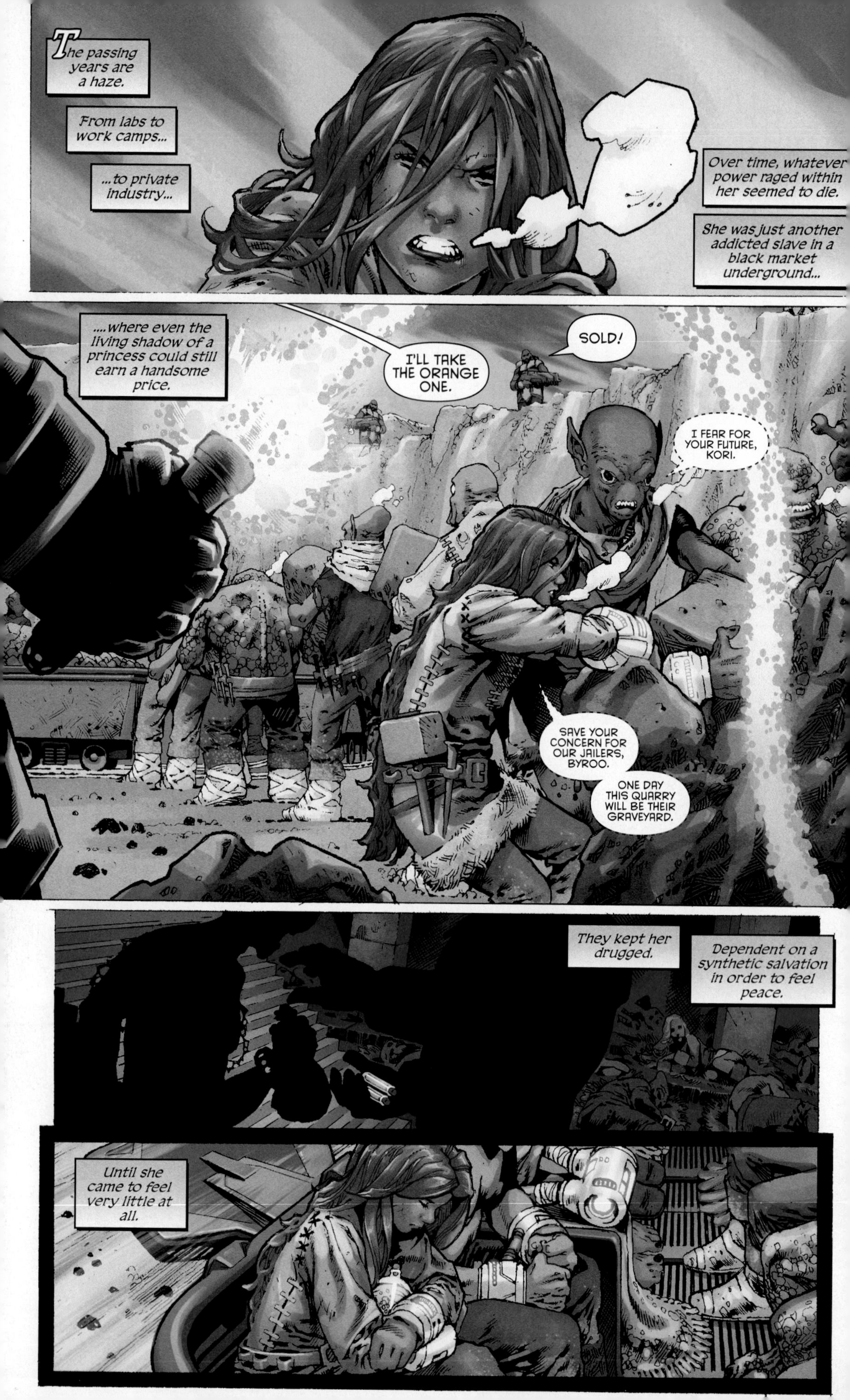
The passing years are a haze.
From labs to work camps...
...to private industry...
Over time, whatever power raged within her seemed to die.
She was just another addicted slave in a black market underground...
....where even the living shadow of a princess could still earn a handsome price.
I'LL TAKE THE ORANGE ONE.
SOLD!
I FEAR FOR YOUR FUTURE, KORI.
SAVE YOUR CONCERN FOR OUR JAILERS, BYROO.
ONE DAY THIS QUARRY WILL BE THEIR GRAVEYARD.
They kept her drugged.
Dependent on a synthetic salvation in order to feel peace.
Until she came to feel very little at all.

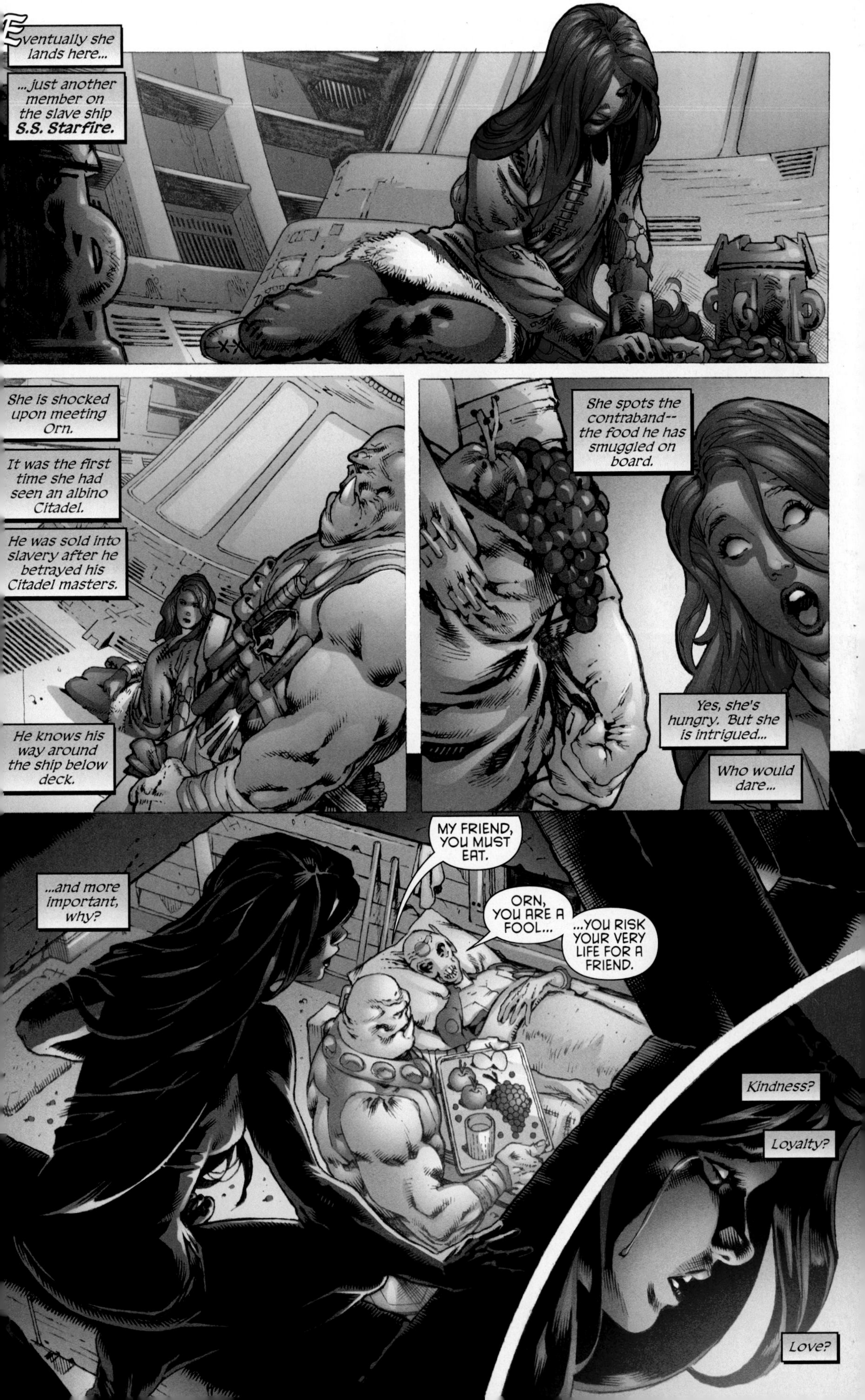
Eventually she lands here...
...just another member on the slave ship S.S. Starfire.
She is shocked upon meeting Orn.
It was the first time she had seen an albino Citadel.
He was sold into slavery after he betrayed his Citadel masters.
He knows his way around the ship below deck.
She spots the contraband-- the food he has smuggled on board.
Yes, she's hungry. But she is intrigued...
Who would dare...
...and more important, why?
MY FRIEND, YOU MUST EAT.
ORN, YOU ARE A FOOL...
...YOU RISK YOUR VERY LIFE FOR A FRIEND.
Kindness?
Loyalty?
Love?

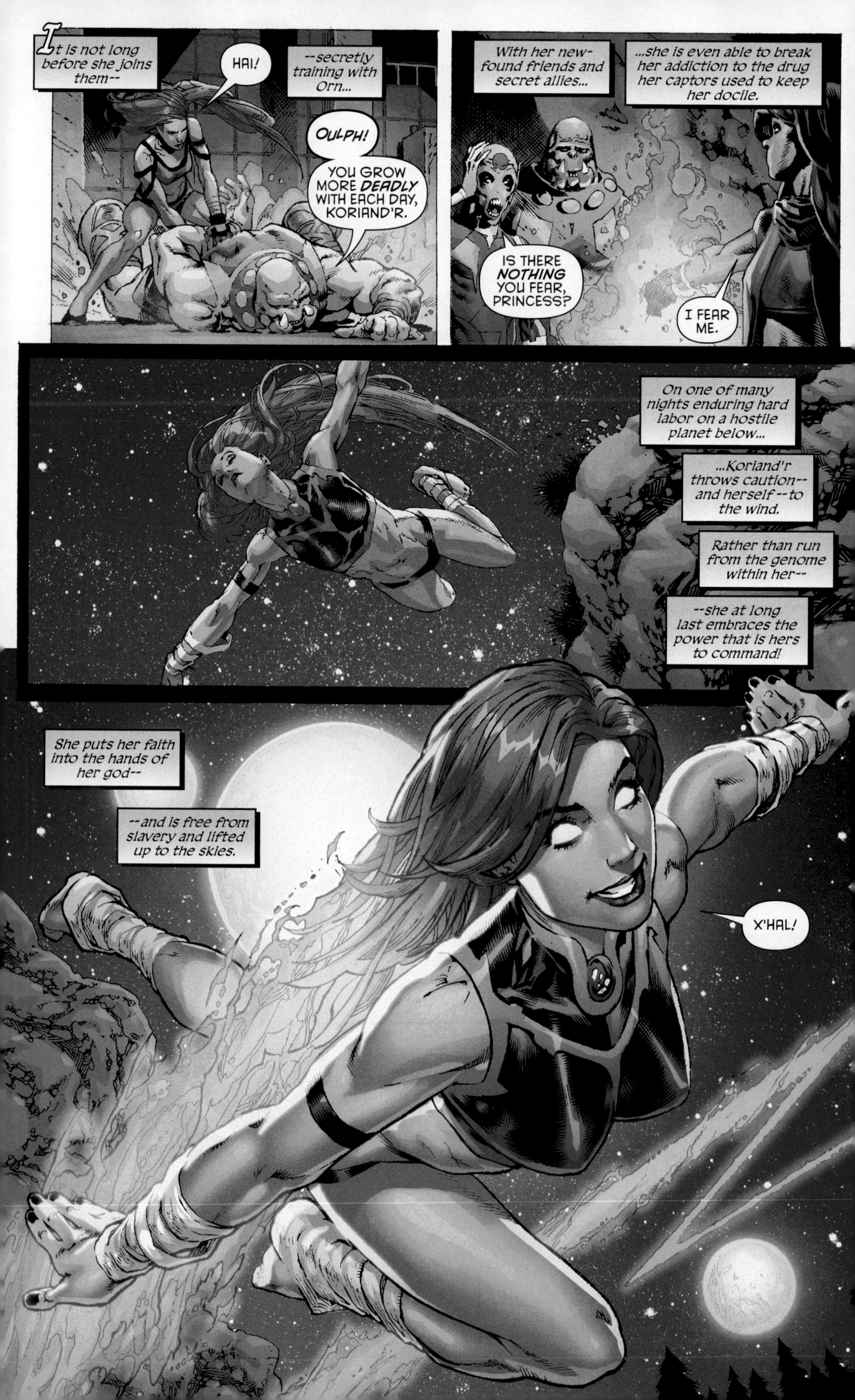
It is not long before she joins them--
HAI!
--secretly training with Orn...
OULPH!
YOU GROW MORE DEADLY WITH EACH DAY, KORIAND'R.
With her new-found friends and secret allies...
...she is even able to break her addiction to the drug her captors used to keep her docile.
IS THERE NOTHING YOU FEAR, PRINCESS?
I FEAR ME.
On one of many nights enduring hard labor on a hostile planet below...
...Koriand'r throws caution--and herself--to the wind.
Rather than run from the genome within her--
--she at long last embraces the power that is hers to command!
She puts her faith into the hands of her god--
--and is free from slavery and lifted up to the skies.
X'HAL!

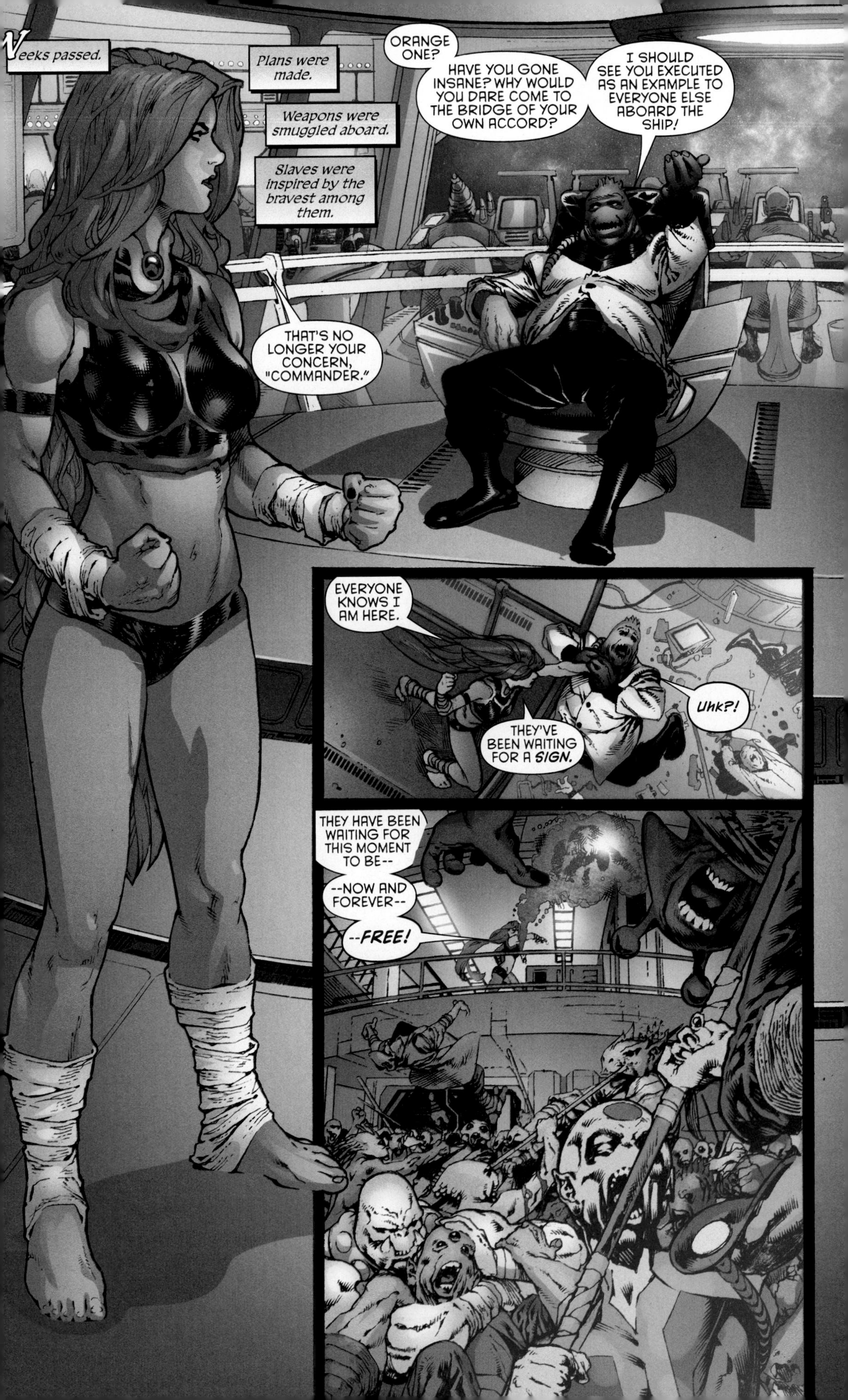
Weeks passed.
Plans were made.
Weapons were smuggled aboard.
Slaves were inspired by the bravest among them.
ORANGE ONE?
HAVE YOU GONE INSANE? WHY WOULD YOU DARE COME TO THE BRIDGE OF YOUR OWN ACCORD?
I SHOULD SEE YOU EXECUTED AS AN EXAMPLE TO EVERYONE ELSE ABOARD THE SHIP!
THAT'S NO LONGER YOUR CONCERN, "COMMANDER."
EVERYONE KNOWS I AM HERE.
UHK?!
THEY'VE BEEN WAITING FOR A SIGN.
THEY HAVE BEEN WAITING FOR THIS MOMENT TO BE--
--NOW AND FOREVER--
--FREE!

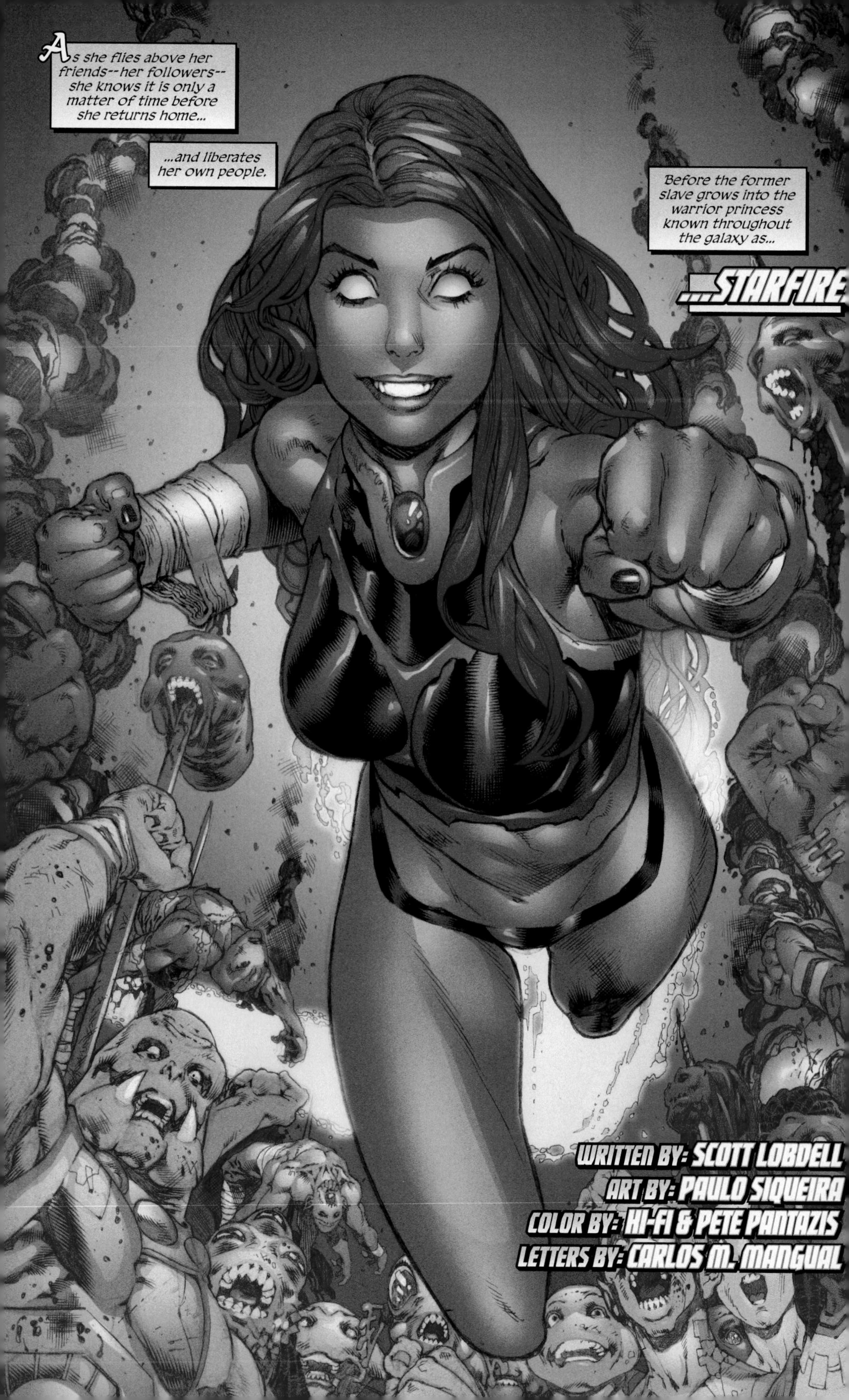
As she flies above her friends--her followers--she knows it is only a matter of time before she returns home...
...and liberates her own people.
Before the former slave grows into the warrior princess known throughout the galaxy as...
...STARFIRE
WRITTEN BY: SCOTT LOBDELL
ART BY: PAULO SIQUEIRA
COLOR BY: HI-FI & PETE PANTAZIS
LETTERS BY: CARLOS M. MANGUAL

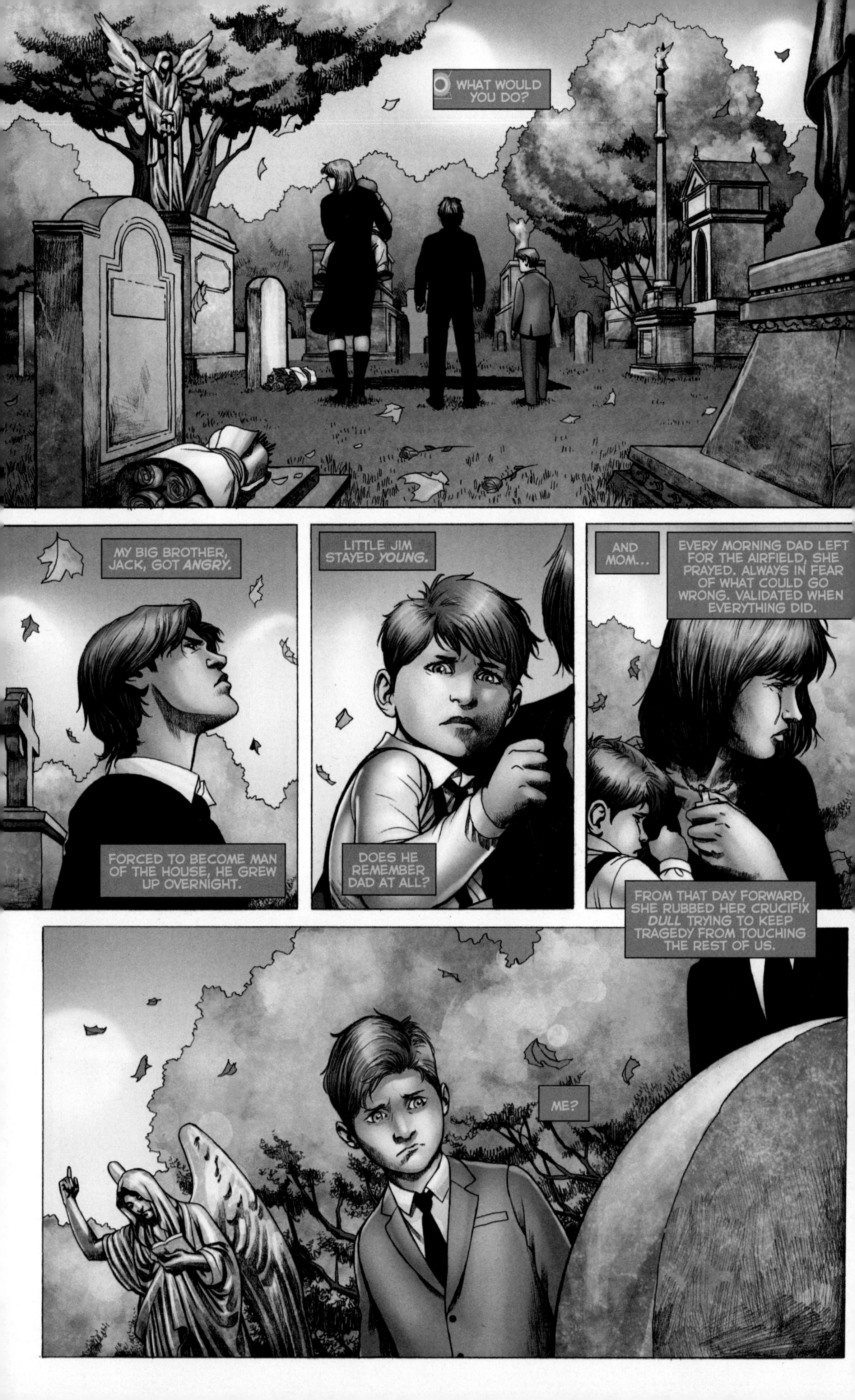
WHAT WOULD YOU DO?
MY BIG BROTHER, JACK, GOT ANGRY.
FORCED TO BECOME MAN OF THE HOUSE, HE GREW UP OVERNIGHT.
LITTLE JIM STAYED YOUNG.
DOES HE REMEMBER DAD AT ALL?
AND MOM...
EVERY MORNING DAD LEFT FOR THE AIRFIELD, SHE PRAYED. ALWAYS IN FEAR OF WHAT COULD GO WRONG. VALIDATED WHEN EVERYTHING DID.
FROM THAT DAY FORWARD, SHE RUBBED HER CRUCIFIX DULL TRYING TO KEEP TRAGEDY FROM TOUCHING THE REST OF US.
ME?

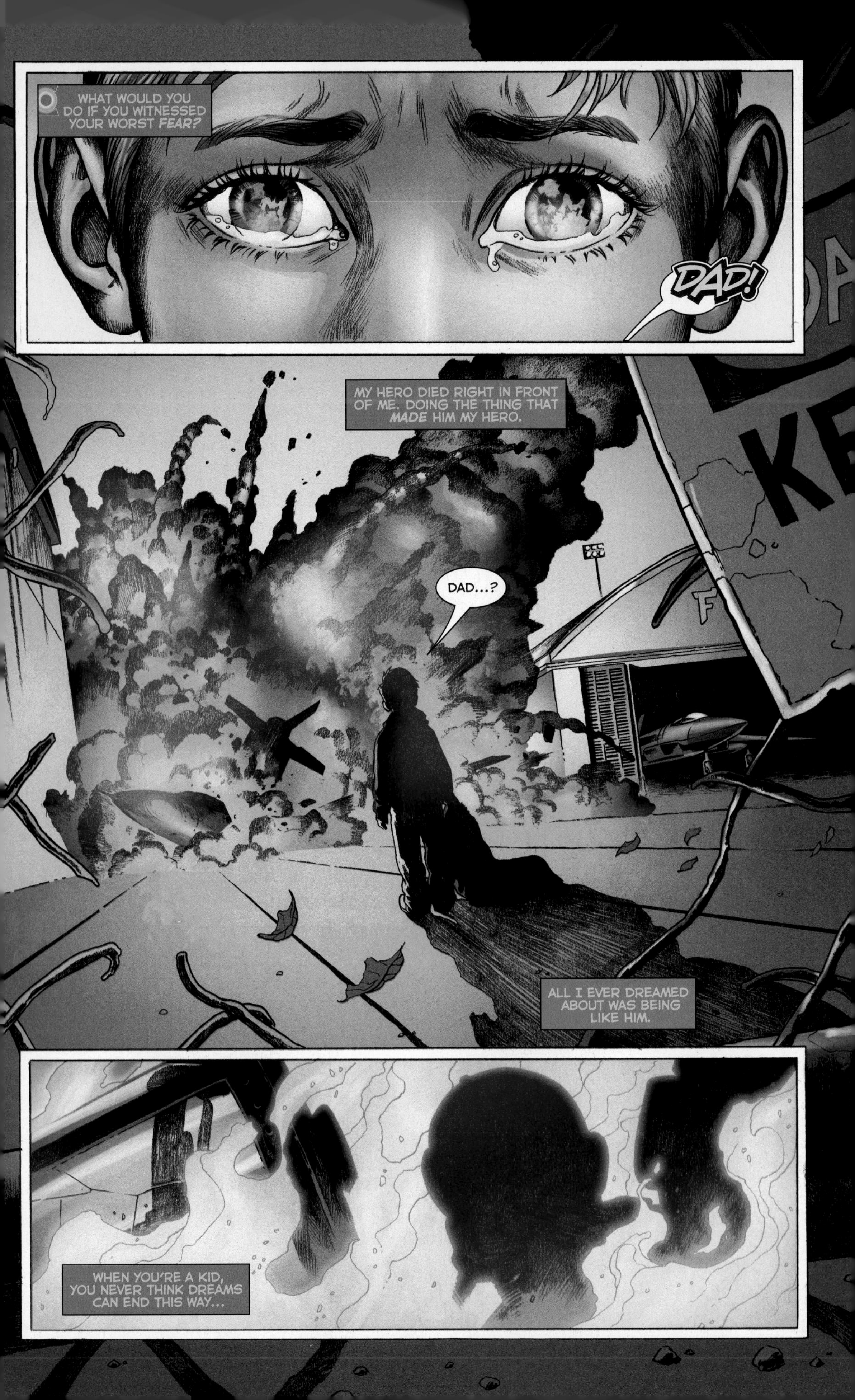
WHAT WOULD YOU DO IF YOU WITNESSED YOUR WORST FEAR?
DAD!
MY HERO DIED RIGHT IN FRONT OF ME. DOING THE THING THAT MADE HIM MY HERO.
DAD...?
ALL I EVER DREAMED ABOUT WAS BEING LIKE HIM.
WHEN YOU'RE A KID, YOU NEVER THINK DREAMS CAN END THIS WAY...

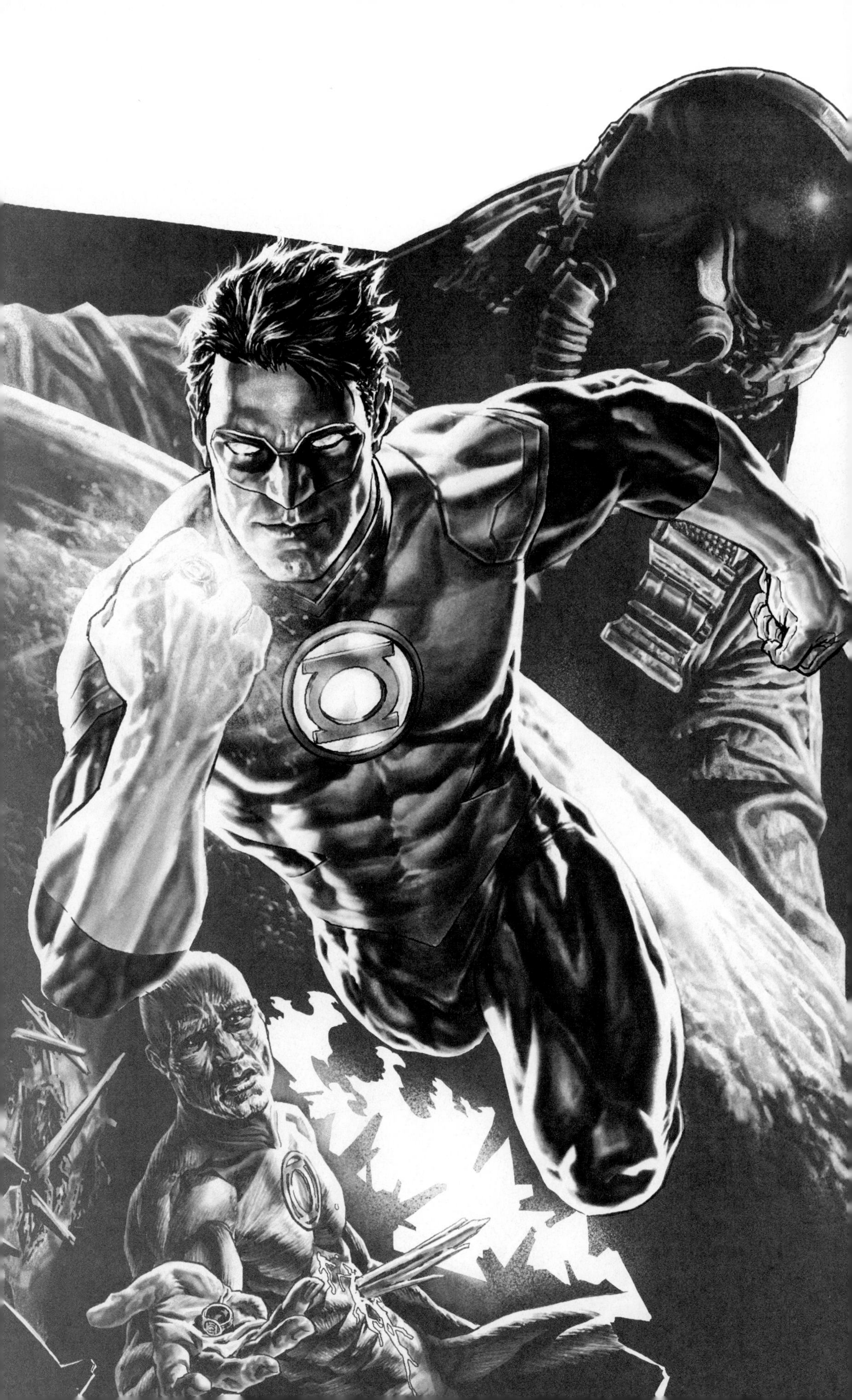

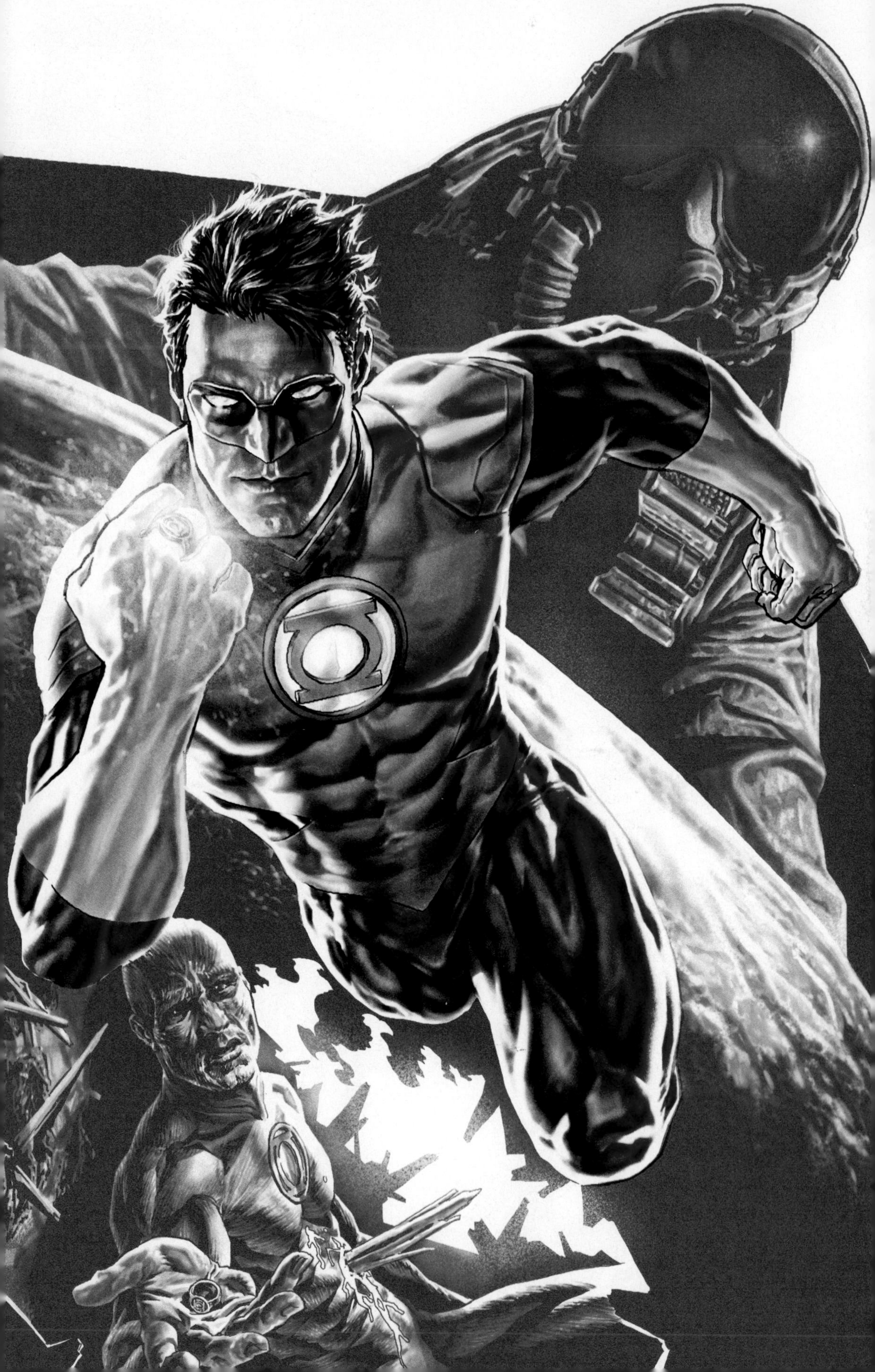

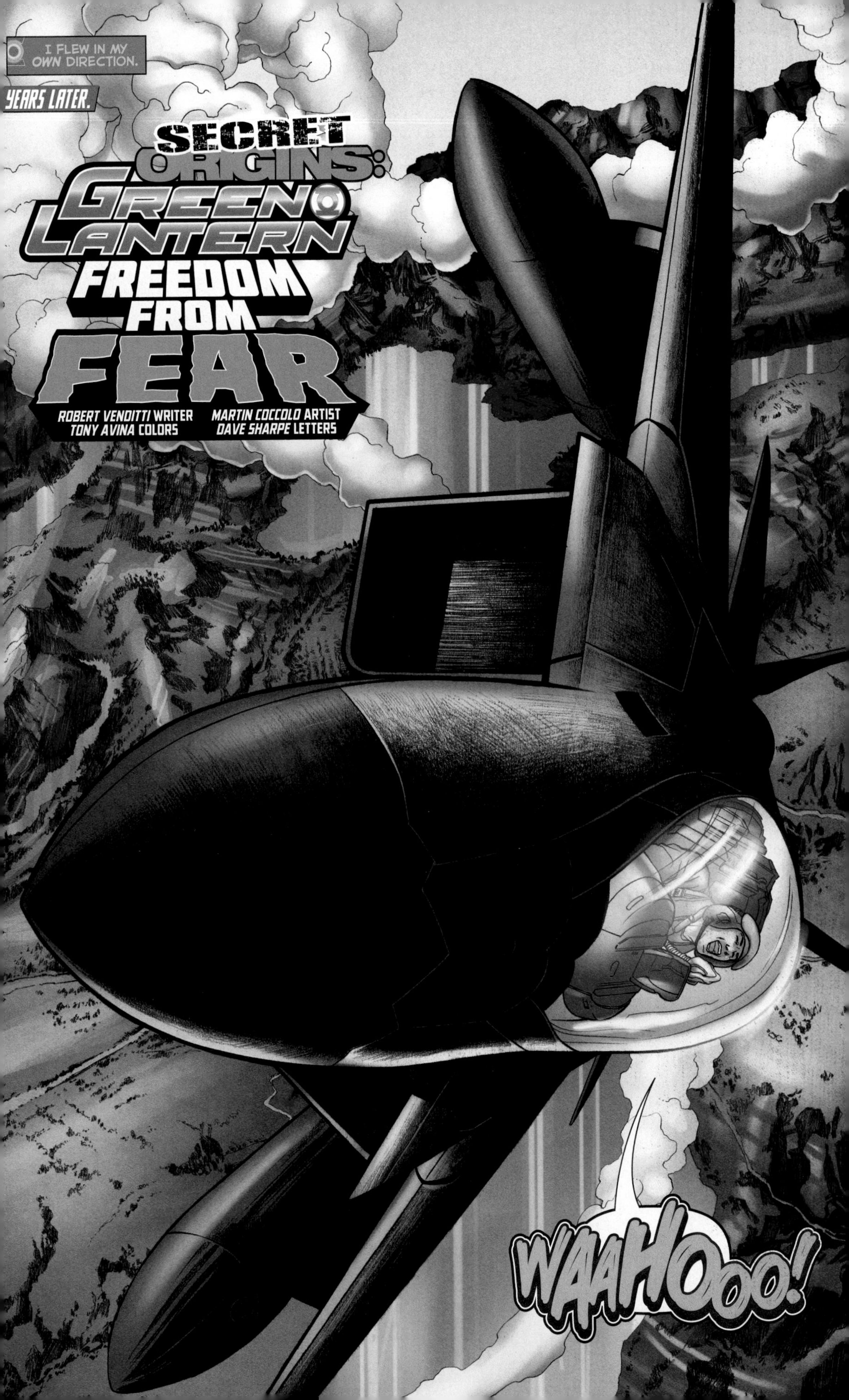

I FLEW IN MY OWN DIRECTION.
YEARS LATER.
SECRET ORIGINS: GREEN LANTERN
FREEDOM FROM FEAR
ROBERT VENDITTI WRITER
MARTIN COCCOLO ARTIST
TONY AVINA COLORS
DAVE SHARPE LETTERS
WAAHOOO!

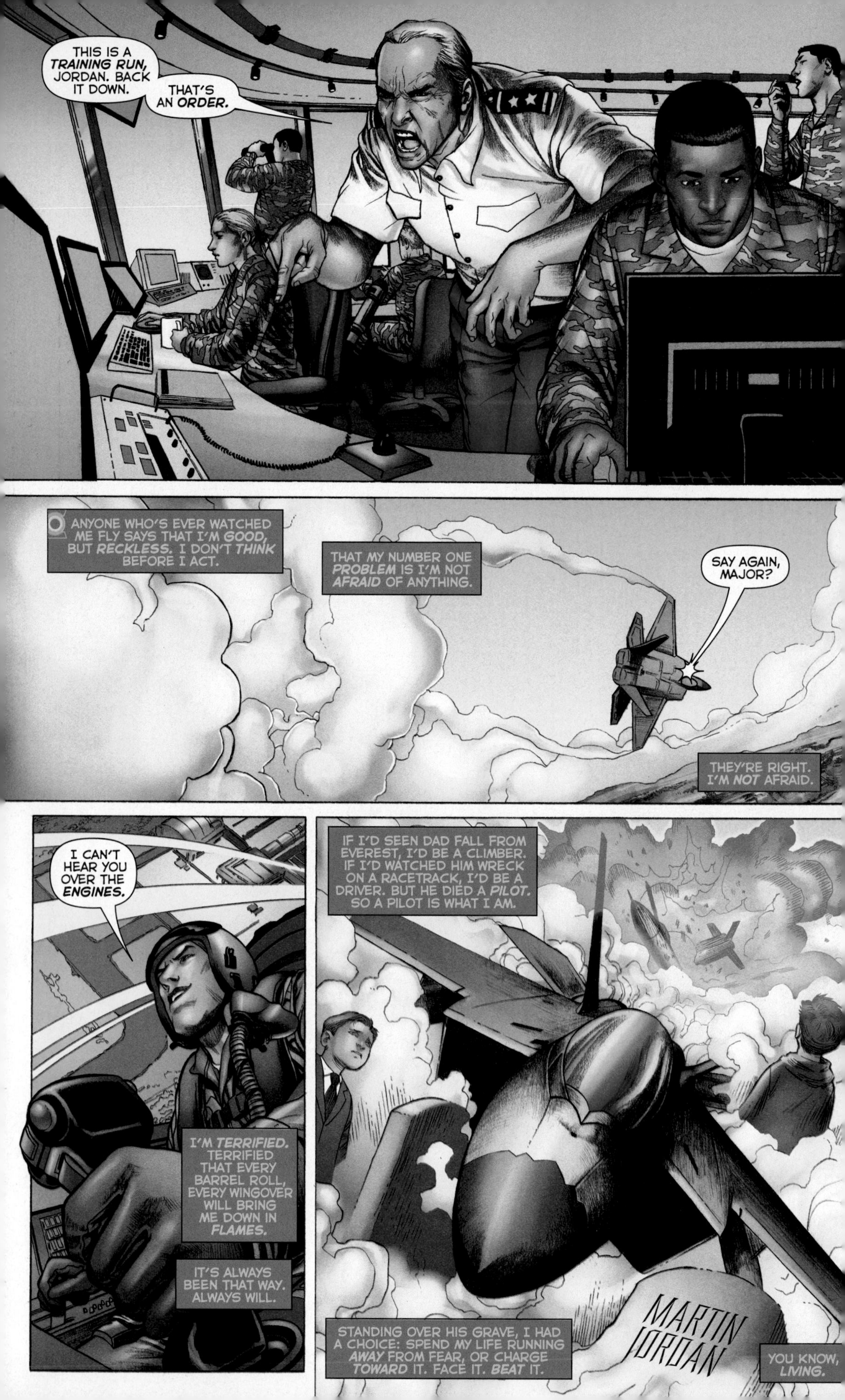
THIS IS A TRAINING RUN, JORDAN. BACK IT DOWN.
THAT'S AN ORDER.
ANYONE WHO'S EVER WATCHED ME FLY SAYS THAT I'M GOOD, BUT RECKLESS. I DON'T THINK BEFORE I ACT.
THAT MY NUMBER ONE PROBLEM IS I'M NOT AFRAID OF ANYTHING.
SAY AGAIN, MAJOR?
THEY'RE RIGHT. I'M NOT AFRAID.
I CAN'T HEAR YOU OVER THE ENGINES.
I'M TERRIFIED. TERRIFIED THAT EVERY BARREL ROLL, EVERY WINGOVER WILL BRING ME DOWN IN FLAMES.
IT'S ALWAYS BEEN THAT WAY. ALWAYS WILL.
IF I'D SEEN DAD FALL FROM EVEREST, I'D BE A CLIMBER. IF I'D WATCHED HIM WRECK ON A RACETRACK, I'D BE A DRIVER. BUT HE DIED A PILOT. SO A PILOT IS WHAT I AM.
MARTIN JORDAN
STANDING OVER HIS GRAVE, I HAD A CHOICE: SPEND MY LIFE RUNNING AWAY FROM FEAR, OR CHARGE TOWARD IT. FACE IT. BEAT IT.
YOU KNOW, LIVING.

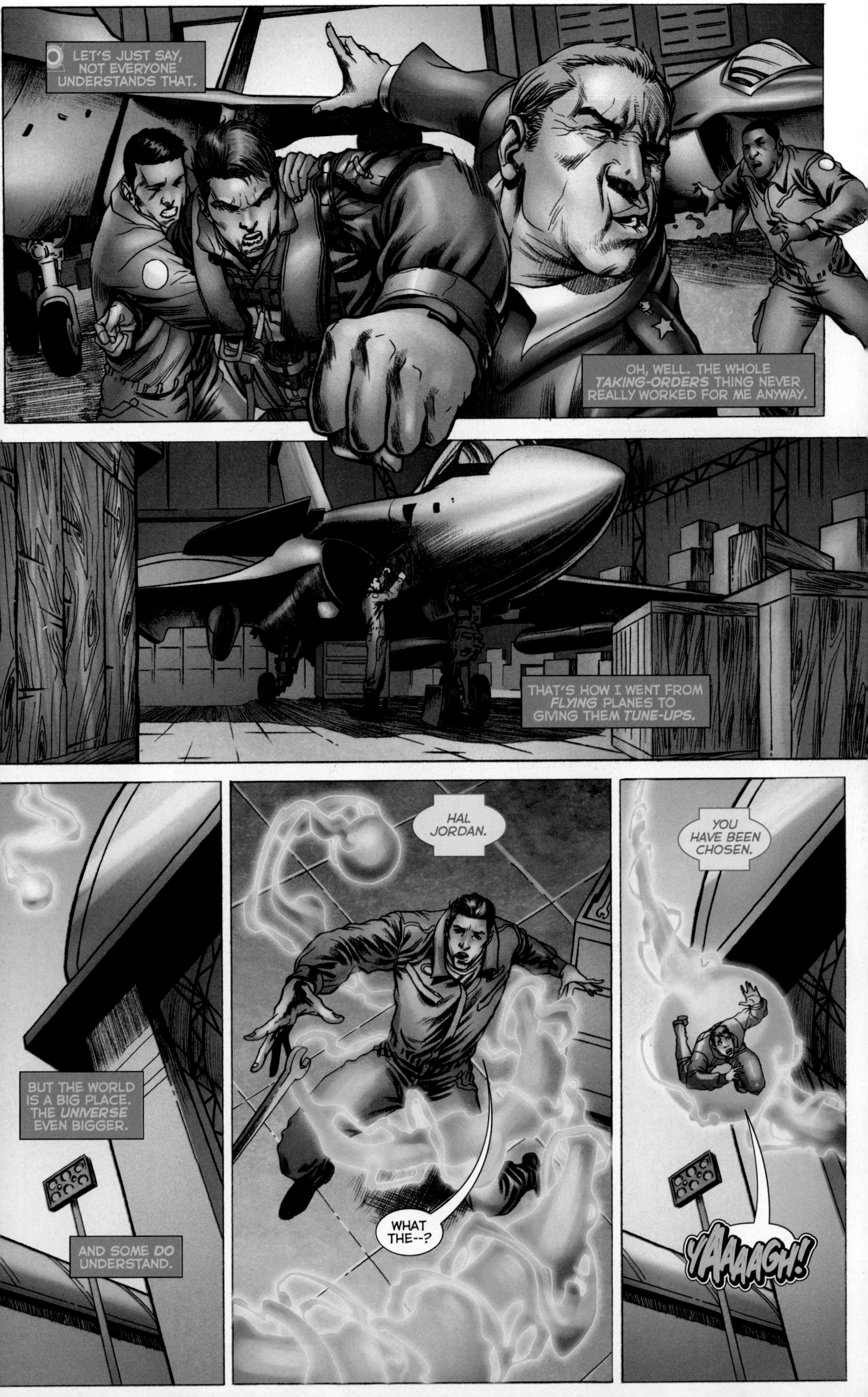
LET'S JUST SAY, NOT EVERYONE UNDERSTANDS THAT.
OH, WELL. THE WHOLE TAKING-ORDERS THING NEVER REALLY WORKED FOR ME ANYWAY.
THAT'S HOW I WENT FROM FLYING PLANES TO GIVING THEM TUNE-UPS.
BUT THE WORLD IS A BIG PLACE. THE UNIVERSE EVEN BIGGER.
AND SOME DO UNDERSTAND.
HAL JORDAN.
WHAT THE--?
YOU HAVE BEEN CHOSEN.
YAAAAGH!

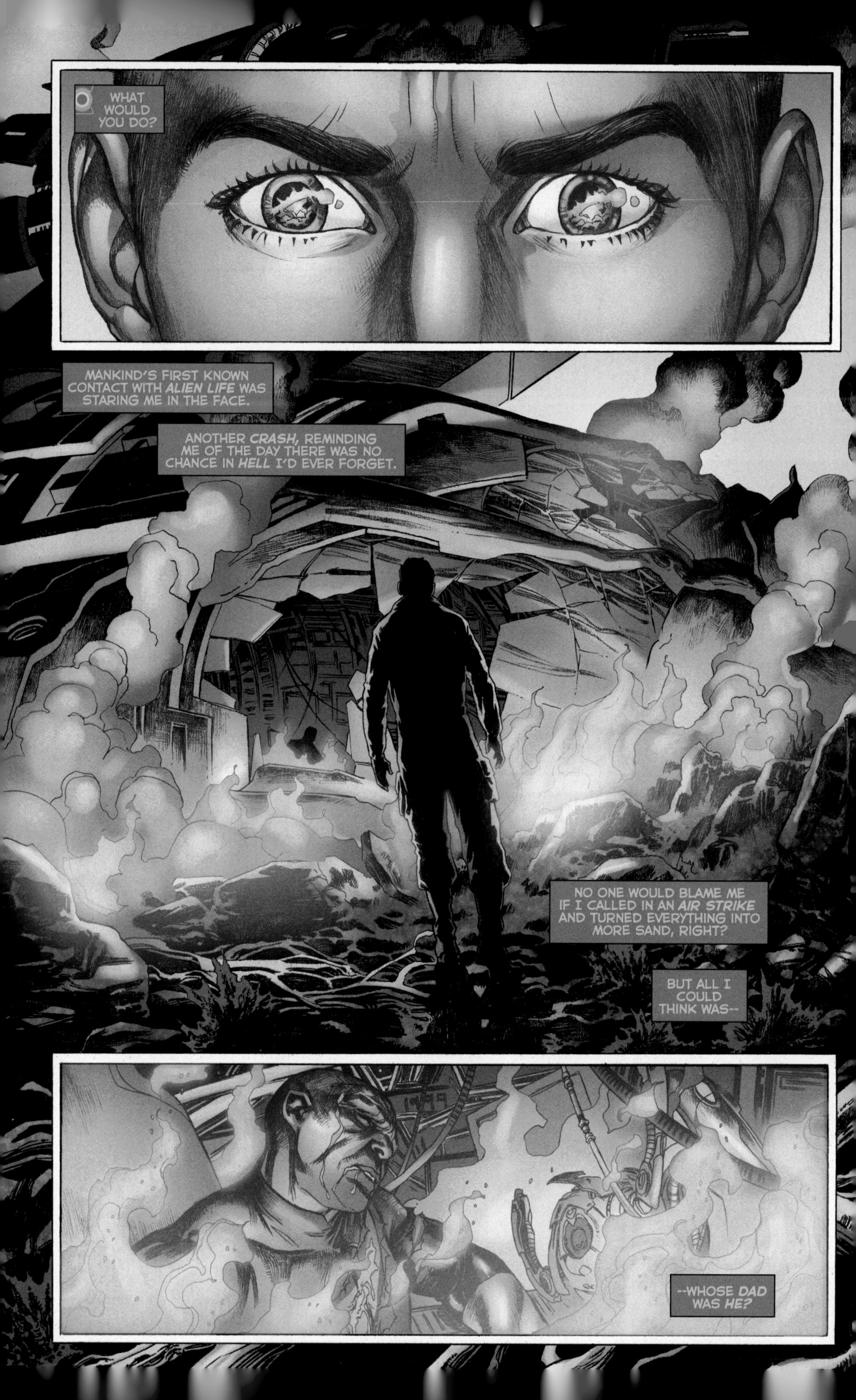
WHAT WOULD YOU DO?
MANKIND'S FIRST KNOWN CONTACT WITH ALIEN LIFE WAS STARING ME IN THE FACE.
ANOTHER CRASH, REMINDING ME OF THE DAY THERE WAS NO CHANCE IN HELL I'D EVER FORGET.
NO ONE WOULD BLAME ME IF I CALLED IN AN AIR STRIKE AND TURNED EVERYTHING INTO MORE SAND, RIGHT?
BUT ALL I COULD THINK WAS--
--WHOSE DAD WAS HE?

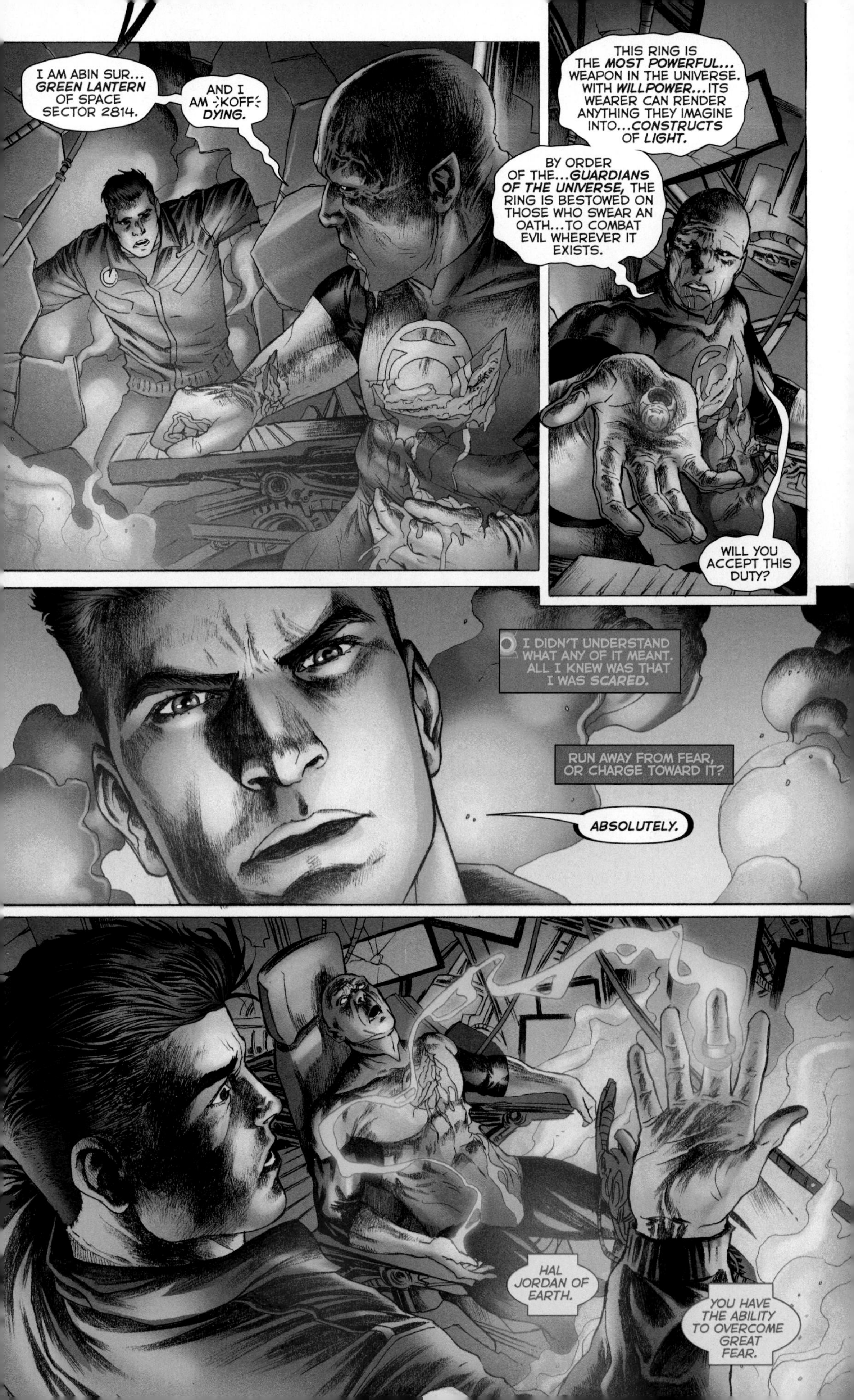

I AM ABIN SUR... GREEN LANTERN OF SPACE SECTOR 2814.
AND I AM KOFF DYING.
THIS RING IS THE MOST POWERFUL... WEAPON IN THE UNIVERSE. WITH WILLPOWER... ITS WEARER CAN RENDER ANYTHING THEY IMAGINE INTO... CONSTRUCTS OF LIGHT.
BY ORDER OF THE... GUARDIANS OF THE UNIVERSE, THE RING IS BESTOWED ON THOSE WHO SWEAR AN OATH... TO COMBAT EVIL WHEREVER IT EXISTS.
WILL YOU ACCEPT THIS DUTY?
I DIDN'T UNDERSTAND WHAT ANY OF IT MEANT. ALL I KNEW WAS THAT I WAS SCARED.
RUN AWAY FROM FEAR, OR CHARGE TOWARD IT?
ABSOLUTELY.
HAL JORDAN OF EARTH.
YOU HAVE THE ABILITY TO OVERCOME GREAT FEAR.

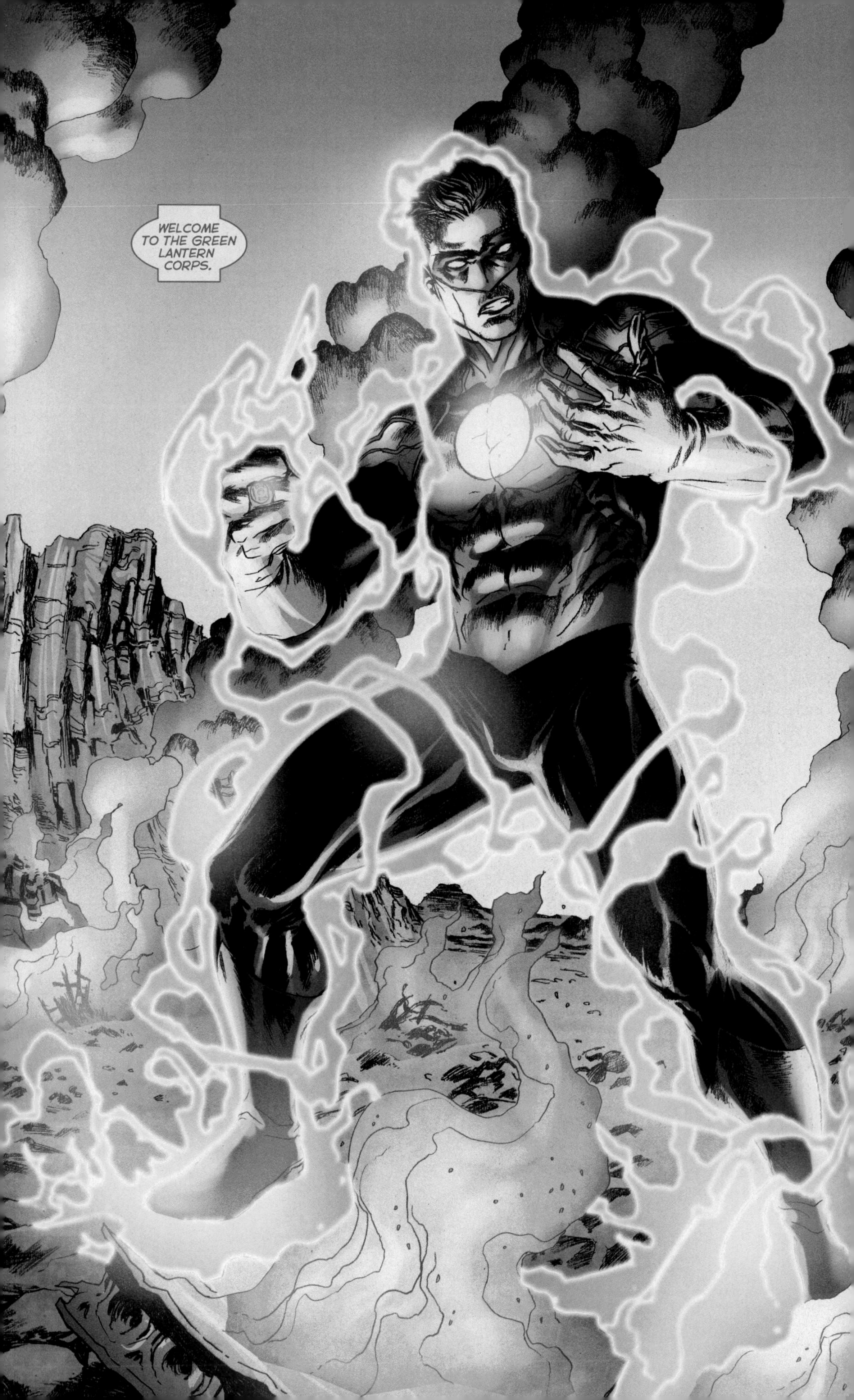
WELCOME TO THE GREEN LANTERN CORPS.

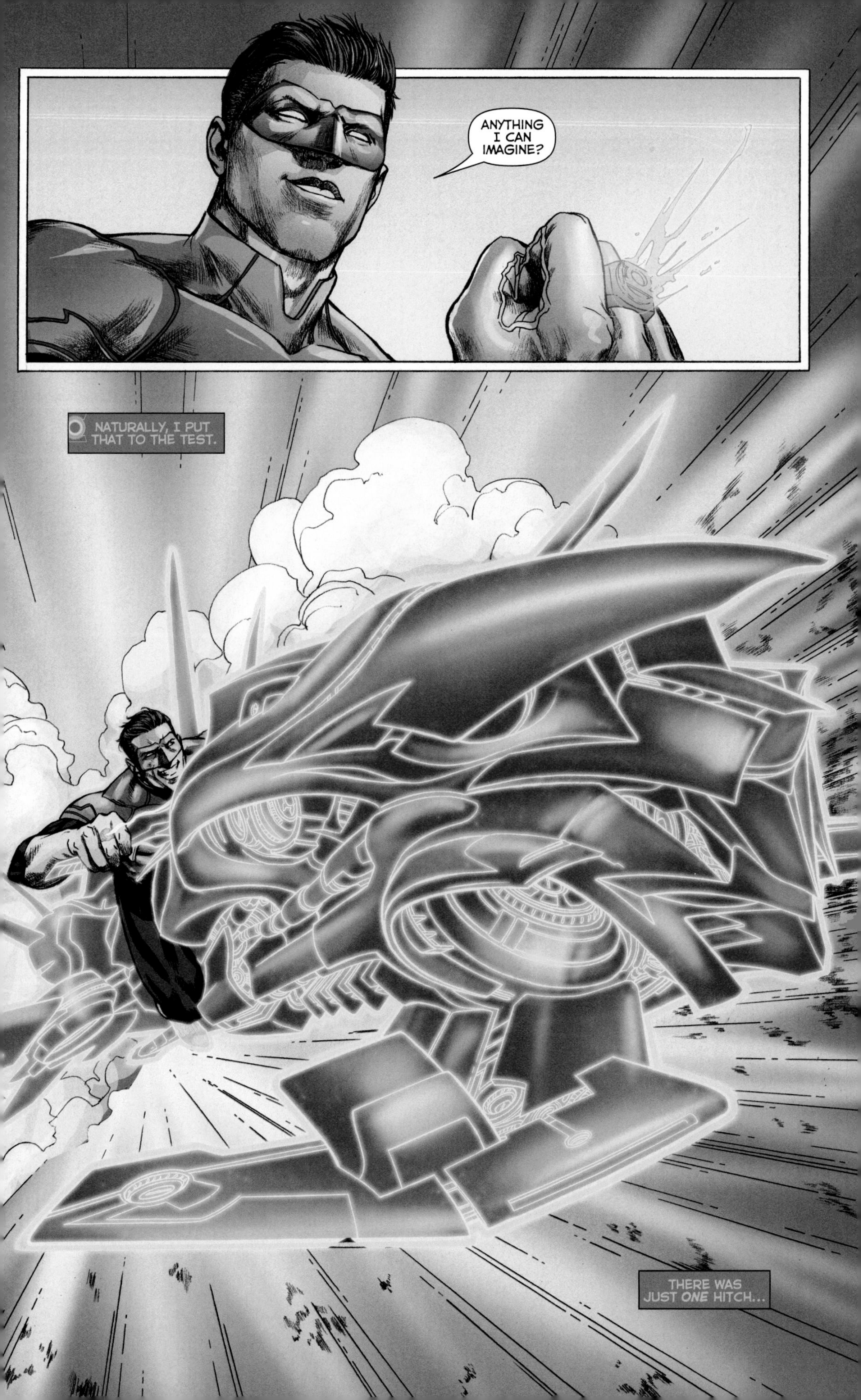
ANYTHING I CAN IMAGINE?
NATURALLY, I PUT THAT TO THE TEST.
THERE WAS JUST *ONE* HITCH...

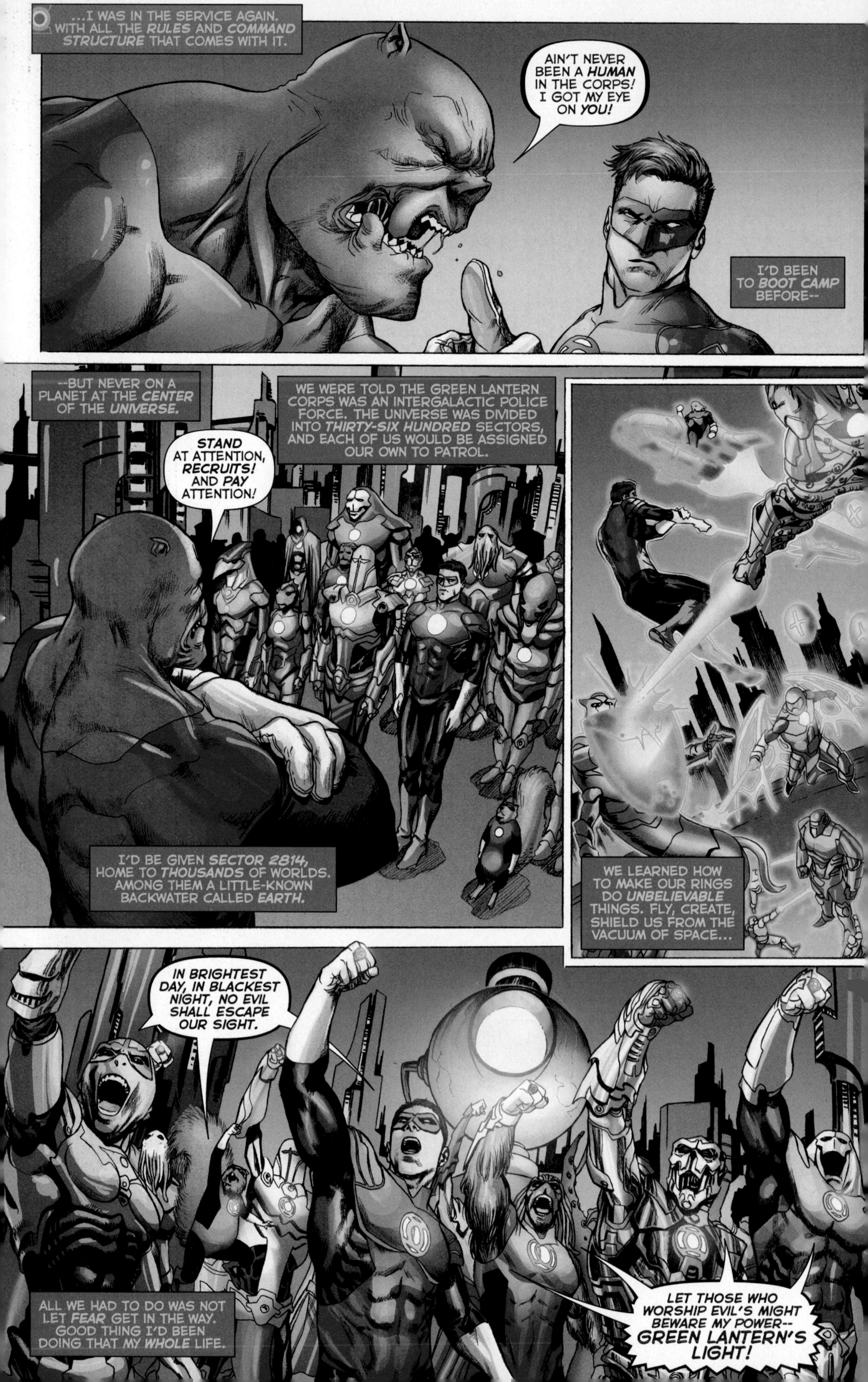
...I WAS IN THE SERVICE AGAIN. WITH ALL THE RULES AND COMMAND STRUCTURE THAT COMES WITH IT.
AIN'T NEVER BEEN A HUMAN IN THE CORPS! I GOT MY EYE ON YOU!
I'D BEEN TO BOOT CAMP BEFORE--
--BUT NEVER ON A PLANET AT THE CENTER OF THE UNIVERSE.
WE WERE TOLD THE GREEN LANTERN CORPS WAS AN INTERGALACTIC POLICE FORCE. THE UNIVERSE WAS DIVIDED INTO THIRTY-SIX HUNDRED SECTORS, AND EACH OF US WOULD BE ASSIGNED OUR OWN TO PATROL.
STAND AT ATTENTION, RECRUITS! AND PAY ATTENTION!
I'D BE GIVEN SECTOR 2814, HOME TO THOUSANDS OF WORLDS. AMONG THEM A LITTLE-KNOWN BACKWATER CALLED EARTH.
WE LEARNED HOW TO MAKE OUR RINGS DO UNBELIEVABLE THINGS. FLY, CREATE, SHIELD US FROM THE VACUUM OF SPACE...
IN BRIGHTEST DAY, IN BLACKEST NIGHT, NO EVIL SHALL ESCAPE OUR SIGHT.
ALL WE HAD TO DO WAS NOT LET FEAR GET IN THE WAY. GOOD THING I'D BEEN DOING THAT MY WHOLE LIFE.
LET THOSE WHO WORSHIP EVIL'S MIGHT BEWARE MY POWER-- GREEN LANTERN'S LIGHT!

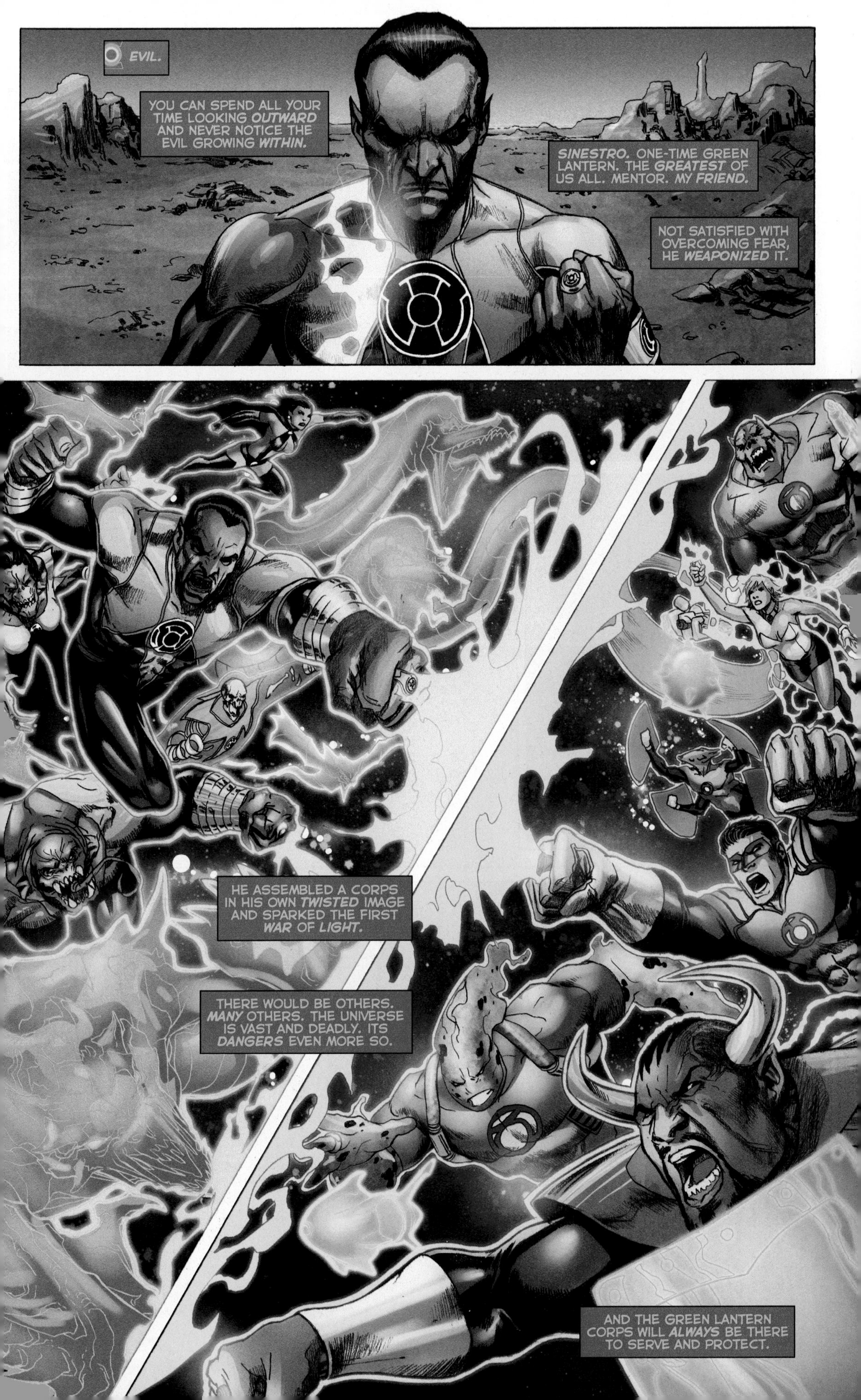
EVIL.
YOU CAN SPEND ALL YOUR TIME LOOKING OUTWARD AND NEVER NOTICE THE EVIL GROWING WITHIN.
SINESTRO. ONE-TIME GREEN LANTERN. THE GREATEST OF US ALL. MENTOR. MY FRIEND.
NOT SATISFIED WITH OVERCOMING FEAR, HE WEAPONIZED IT.
HE ASSEMBLED A CORPS IN HIS OWN TWISTED IMAGE AND SPARKED THE FIRST WAR OF LIGHT.
THERE WOULD BE OTHERS. MANY OTHERS. THE UNIVERSE IS VAST AND DEADLY. ITS DANGERS EVEN MORE SO.
AND THE GREEN LANTERN CORPS WILL ALWAYS BE THERE TO SERVE AND PROTECT.

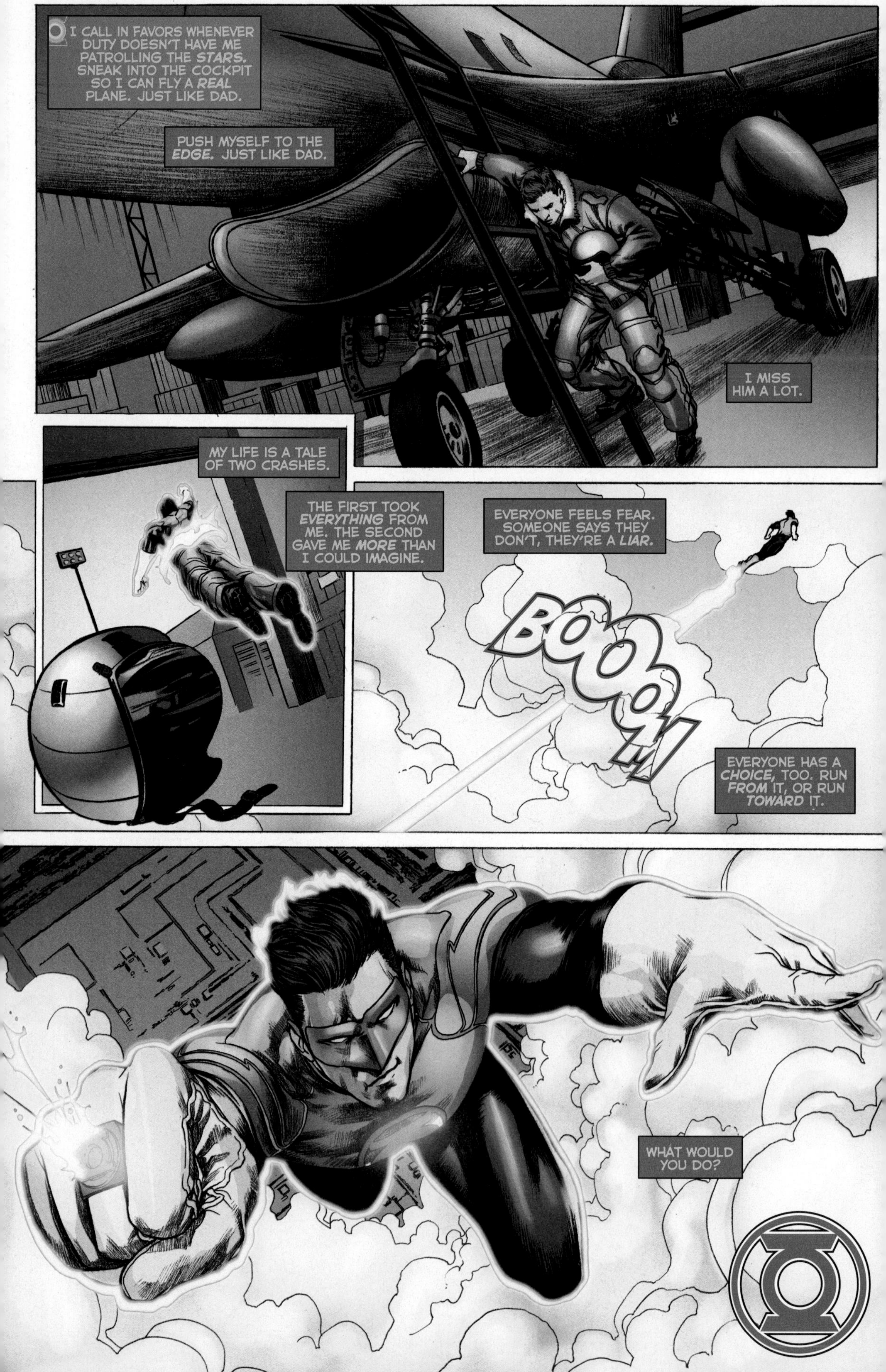
I CALL IN FAVORS WHENEVER DUTY DOESN'T HAVE ME PATROLLING THE STARS. SNEAK INTO THE COCKPIT SO I CAN FLY A REAL PLANE. JUST LIKE DAD.
PUSH MYSELF TO THE EDGE. JUST LIKE DAD.
I MISS HIM A LOT.
MY LIFE IS A TALE OF TWO CRASHES.
THE FIRST TOOK EVERYTHING FROM ME. THE SECOND GAVE ME MORE THAN I COULD IMAGINE.
EVERYONE FEELS FEAR. SOMEONE SAYS THEY DON'T, THEY'RE A LIAR.
BOOOOM
EVERYONE HAS A CHOICE, TOO. RUN FROM IT, OR RUN TOWARD IT.
WHAT WOULD YOU DO?

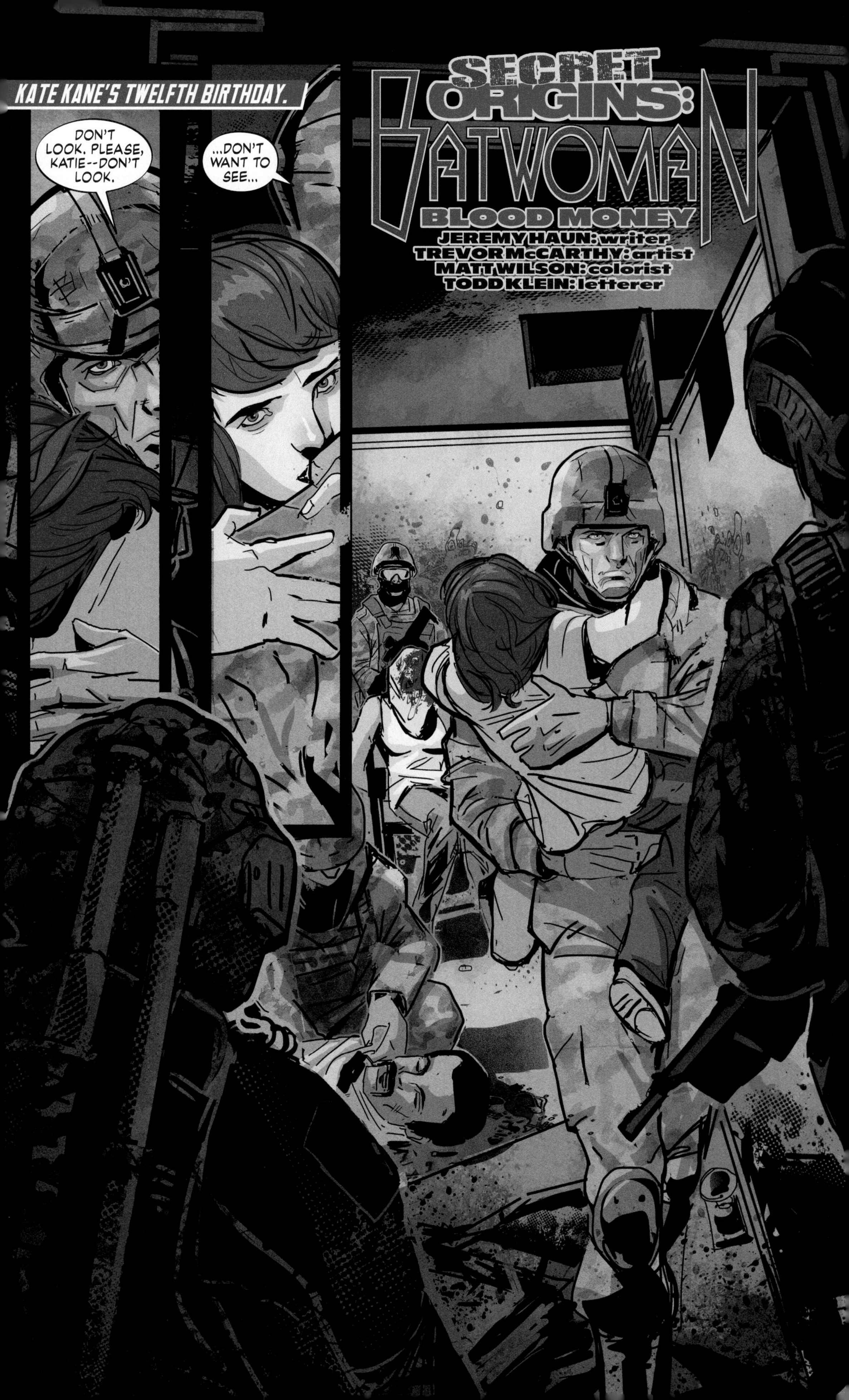
KATE KANE'S TWELFTH BIRTHDAY.
DON'T LOOK. PLEASE, KATIE--DON'T LOOK.
...DON'T WANT TO SEE...
SECRET ORIGINS: BATWOMAN
BLOOD MONEY
JEREMY HAUN: writer
TREVOR McCARTHY: artist
MATT WILSON: colorist
TODD KLEIN: letterer

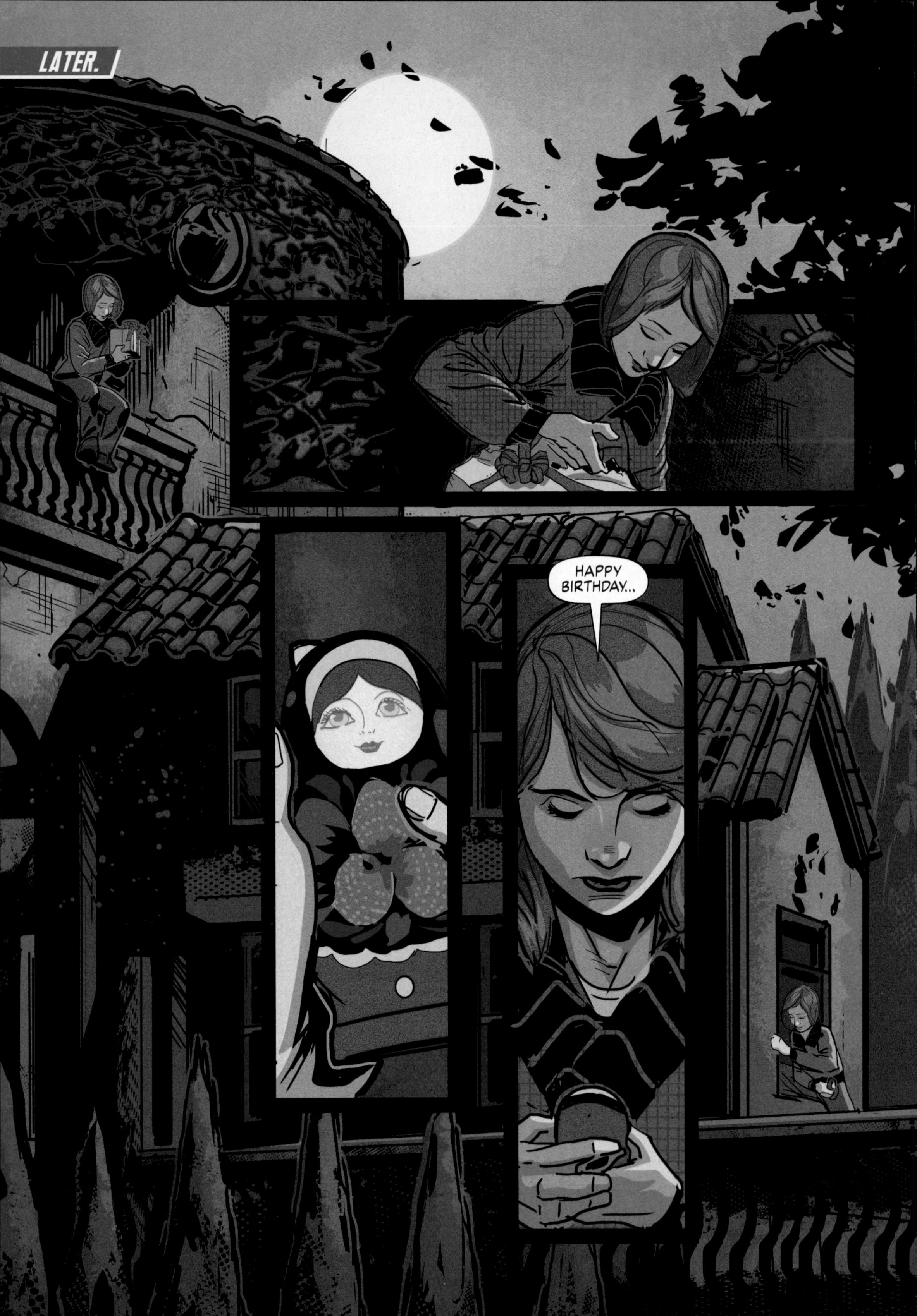
LATER.
HAPPY BIRTHDAY...

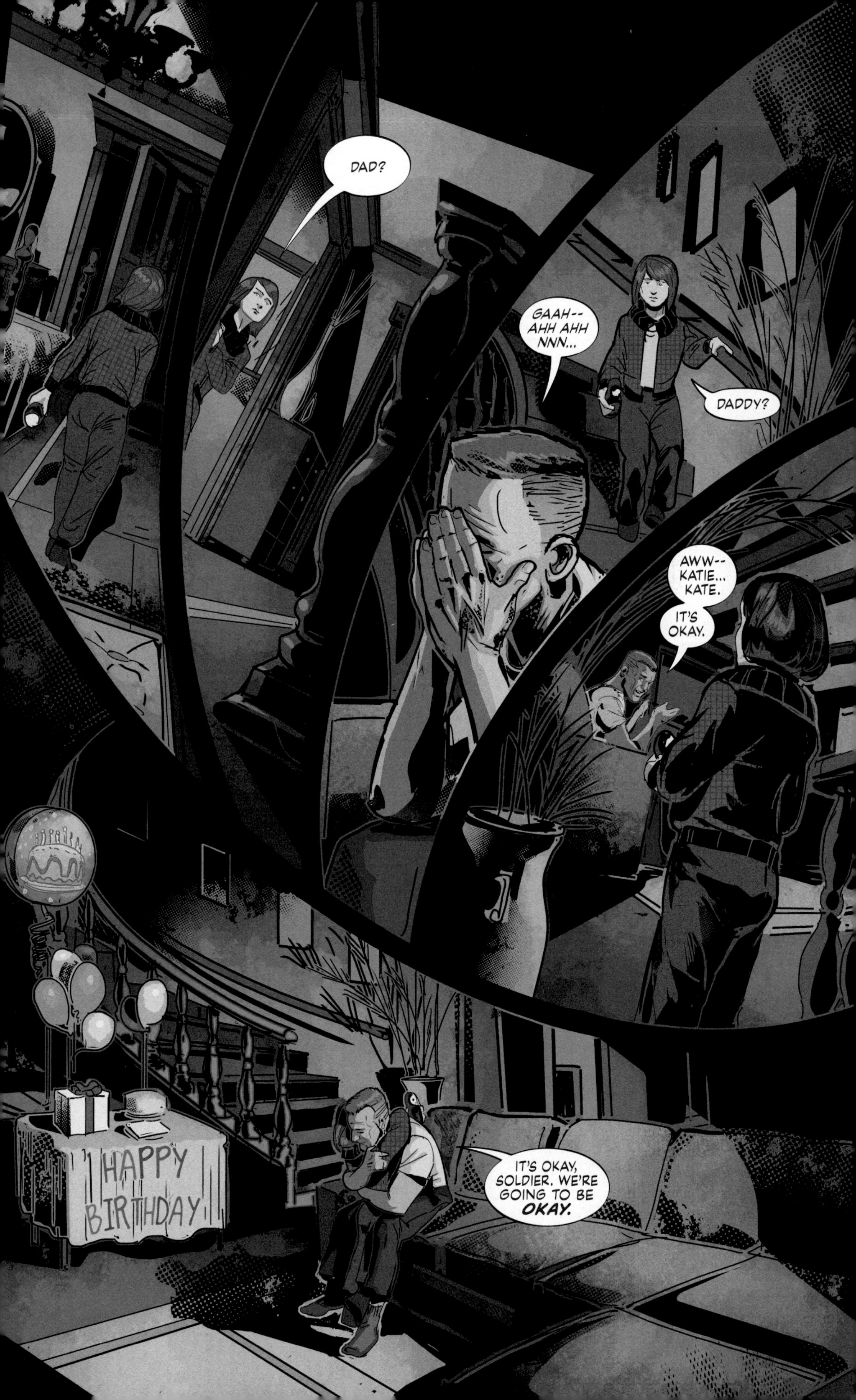

DAD?
GAAH--
AHH AHH
NNN...
DADDY?
AWW--
KATIE...
KATE.
IT'S
OKAY.
HAPPY
BIRTHDAY
IT'S OKAY, SOLDIER. WE'RE GOING TO BE **OKAY.**

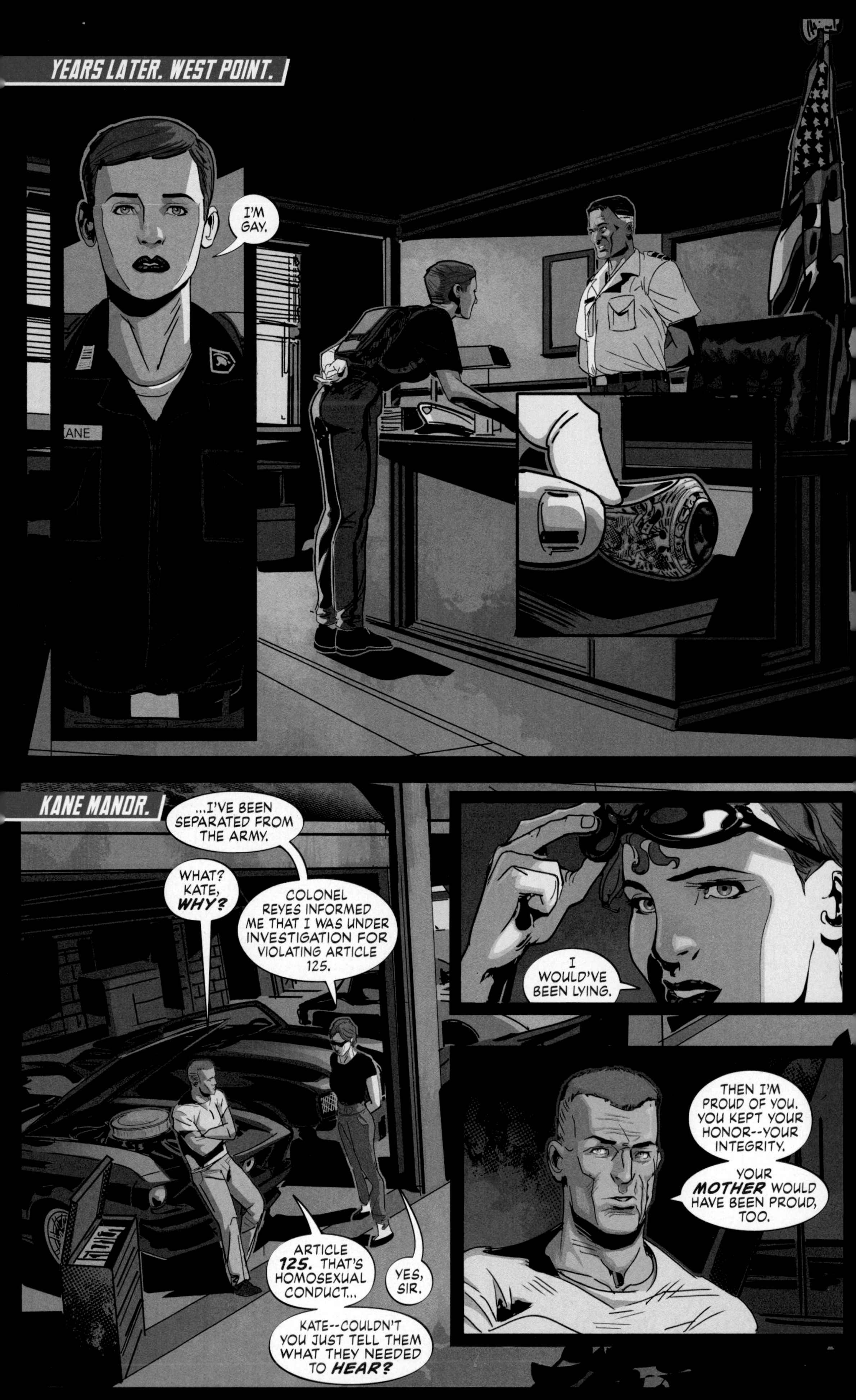
YEARS LATER. WEST POINT.
I'M GAY.
KANE
KANE MANOR.
...I'VE BEEN SEPARATED FROM THE ARMY.
WHAT? KATE, WHY?
COLONEL REYES INFORMED ME THAT I WAS UNDER INVESTIGATION FOR VIOLATING ARTICLE 125.
ARTICLE 125. THAT'S HOMOSEXUAL CONDUCT...
YES, SIR.
KATE--COULDN'T YOU JUST TELL THEM WHAT THEY NEEDED TO HEAR?
I WOULD'VE BEEN LYING.
THEN I'M PROUD OF YOU. YOU KEPT YOUR HONOR--YOUR INTEGRITY.
YOUR MOTHER WOULD HAVE BEEN PROUD, TOO.

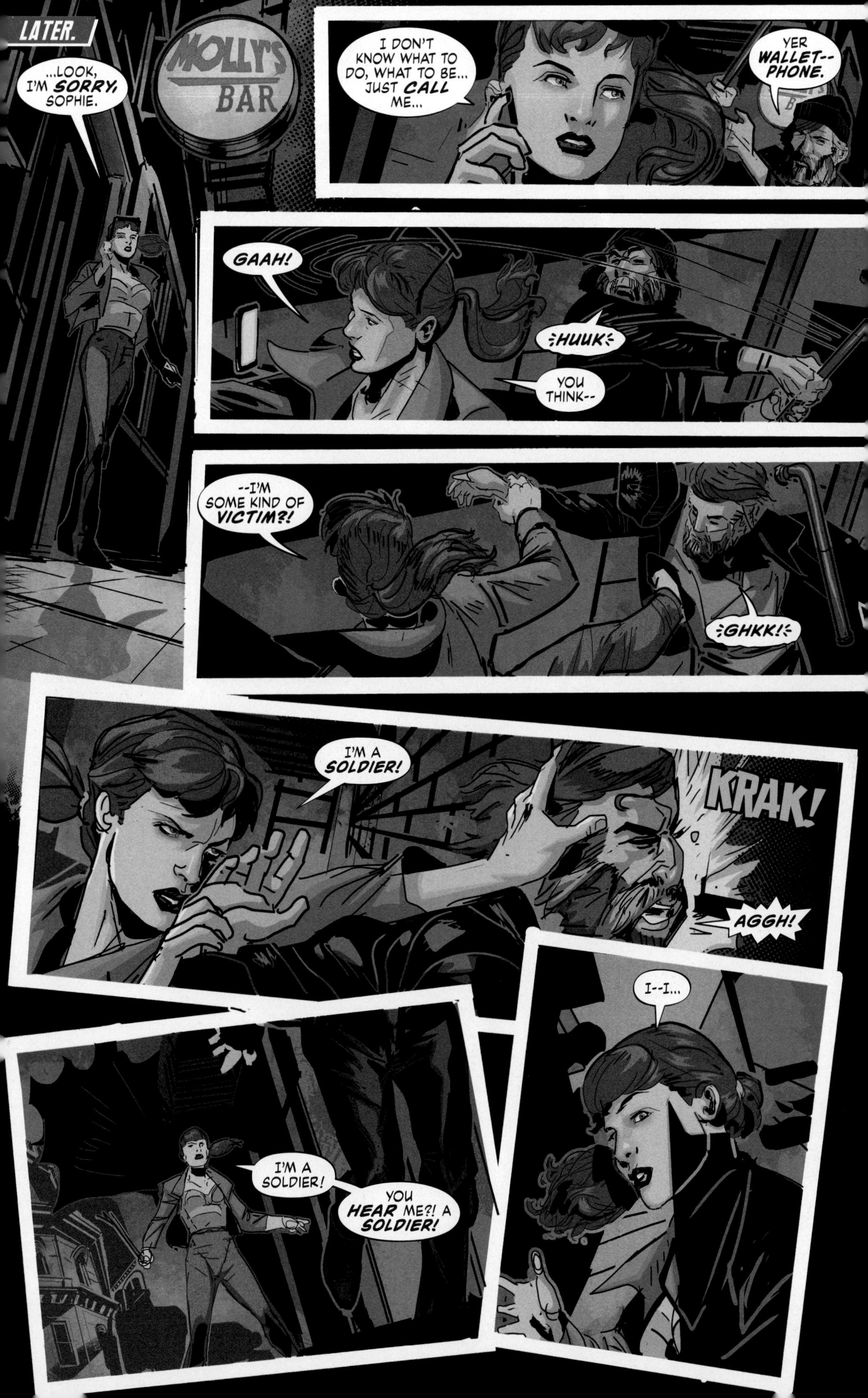
LATER.
MOLLY'S BAR
...LOOK, I'M SORRY, SOPHIE.
I DON'T KNOW WHAT TO DO, WHAT TO BE... JUST CALL ME...
YER WALLET--PHONE.
GAAH!
HUUK
YOU THINK--
--I'M SOME KIND OF VICTIM?!
GHKK!
I'M A SOLDIER!
KRAK!
AGGH!
I'M A SOLDIER!
YOU HEAR ME?! A SOLDIER!
I--I...

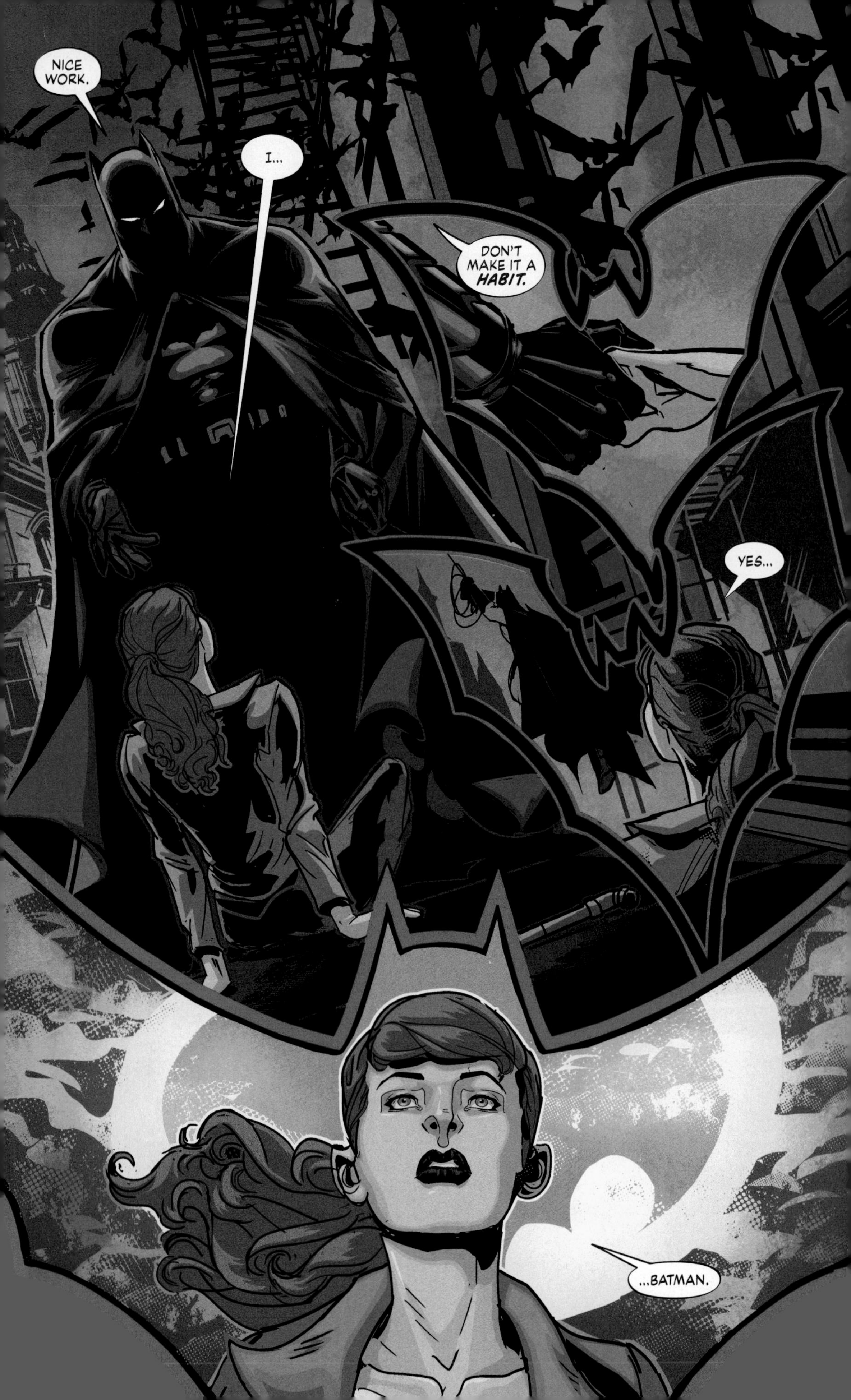
NICE WORK.
I...
DON'T MAKE IT A HABIT.
YES...
...BATMAN.

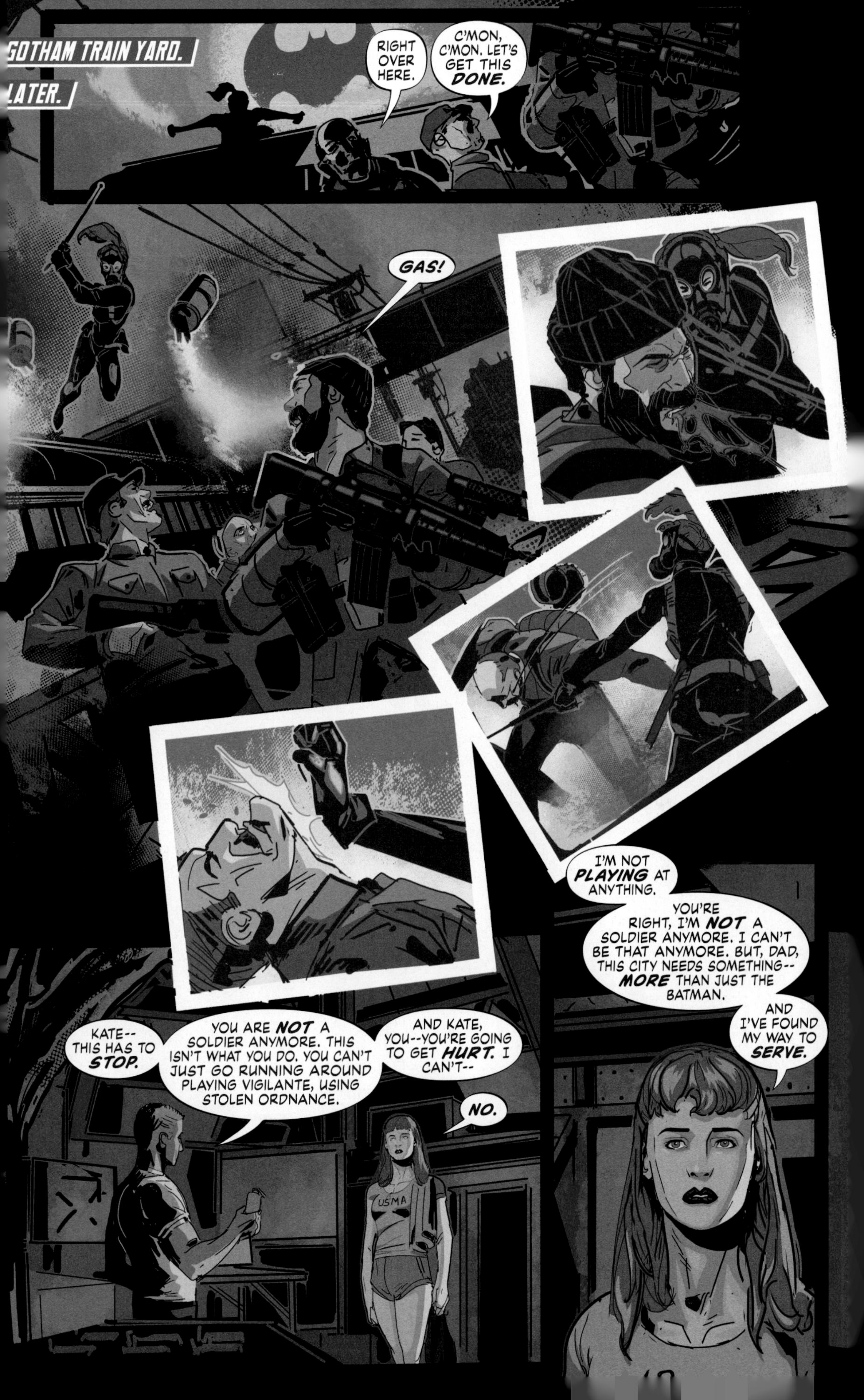

GOTHAM TRAIN YARD.
LATER.
RIGHT OVER HERE.
C'MON, C'MON. LET'S GET THIS DONE.
GAS!
KATE-- THIS HAS TO STOP.
YOU ARE NOT A SOLDIER ANYMORE. THIS ISN'T WHAT YOU DO. YOU CAN'T JUST GO RUNNING AROUND PLAYING VIGILANTE, USING STOLEN ORDNANCE.
AND KATE, YOU--YOU'RE GOING TO GET HURT. I CAN'T--
NO.
I'M NOT PLAYING AT ANYTHING.
YOU'RE RIGHT, I'M NOT A SOLDIER ANYMORE. I CAN'T BE THAT ANYMORE. BUT, DAD, THIS CITY NEEDS SOMETHING-- MORE THAN JUST THE BATMAN.
AND I'VE FOUND MY WAY TO SERVE.

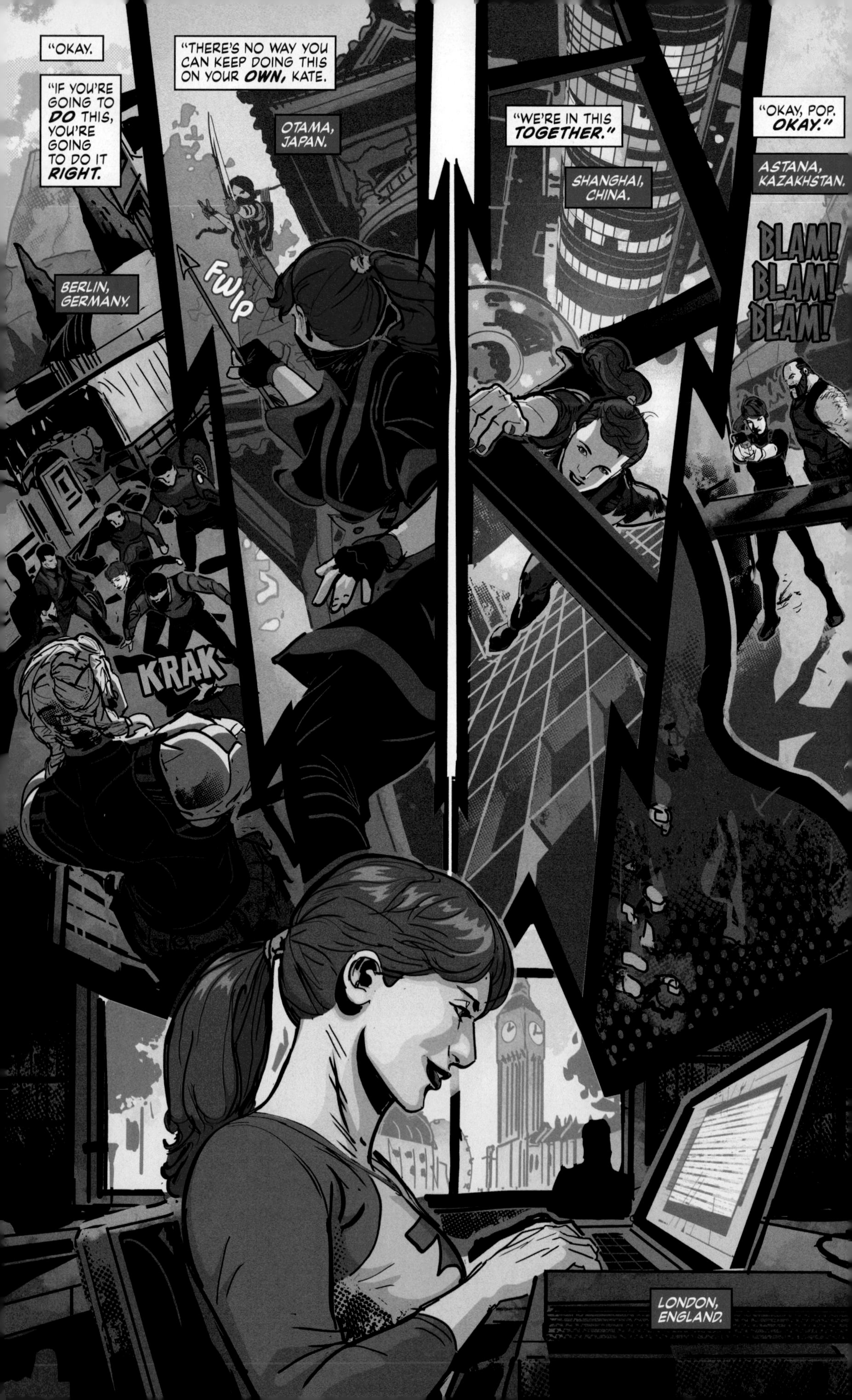
"OKAY.
"IF YOU'RE GOING TO DO THIS, YOU'RE GOING TO DO IT RIGHT.
BERLIN, GERMANY.
KRAK
"THERE'S NO WAY YOU CAN KEEP DOING THIS ON YOUR OWN, KATE.
OTAMA, JAPAN.
FWIP
"WE'RE IN THIS TOGETHER."
SHANGHAI, CHINA.
"OKAY, POP. OKAY."
ASTANA, KAZAKHSTAN.
BLAM! BLAM! BLAM!
LONDON, ENGLAND.

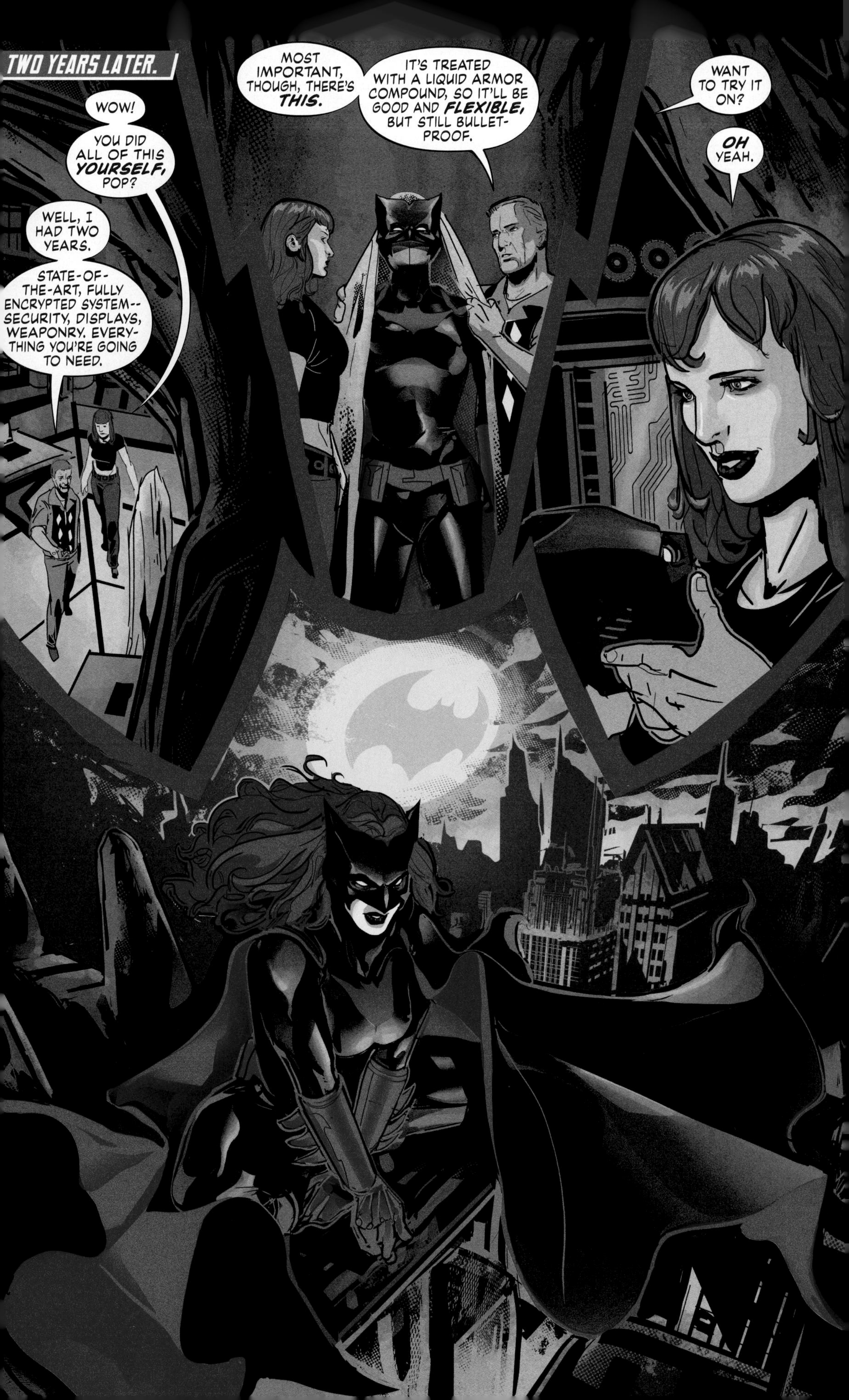
TWO YEARS LATER.
WOW!
YOU DID ALL OF THIS YOURSELF, POP?
WELL, I HAD TWO YEARS.
STATE-OF-THE-ART, FULLY ENCRYPTED SYSTEM--SECURITY, DISPLAYS, WEAPONRY. EVERYTHING YOU'RE GOING TO NEED.
MOST IMPORTANT, THOUGH, THERE'S THIS.
IT'S TREATED WITH A LIQUID ARMOR COMPOUND, SO IT'LL BE GOOD AND FLEXIBLE, BUT STILL BULLET-PROOF.
WANT TO TRY IT ON?
OH YEAH.

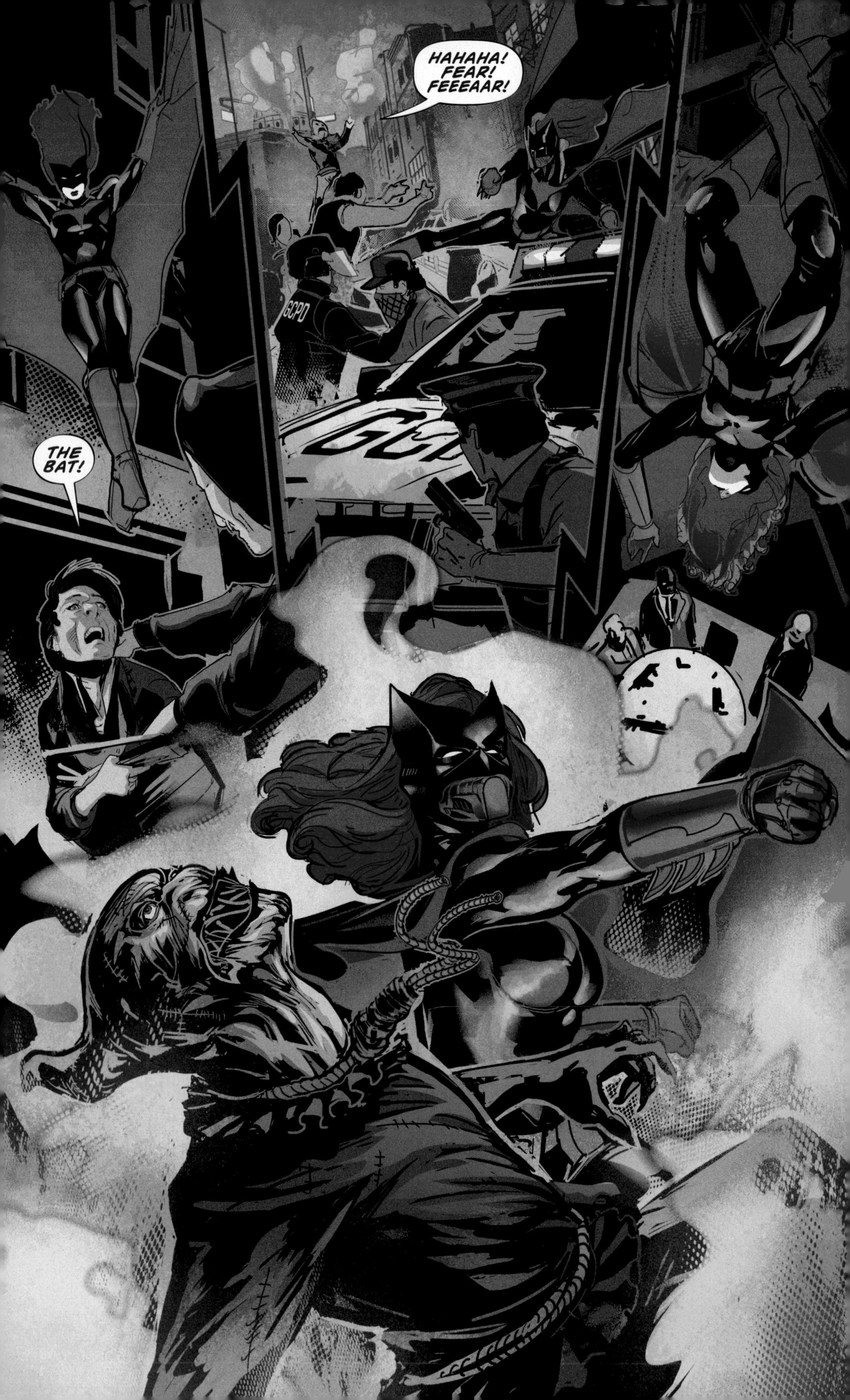
HAHAHA! FEAR! FEEEAAR!
THE BAT!

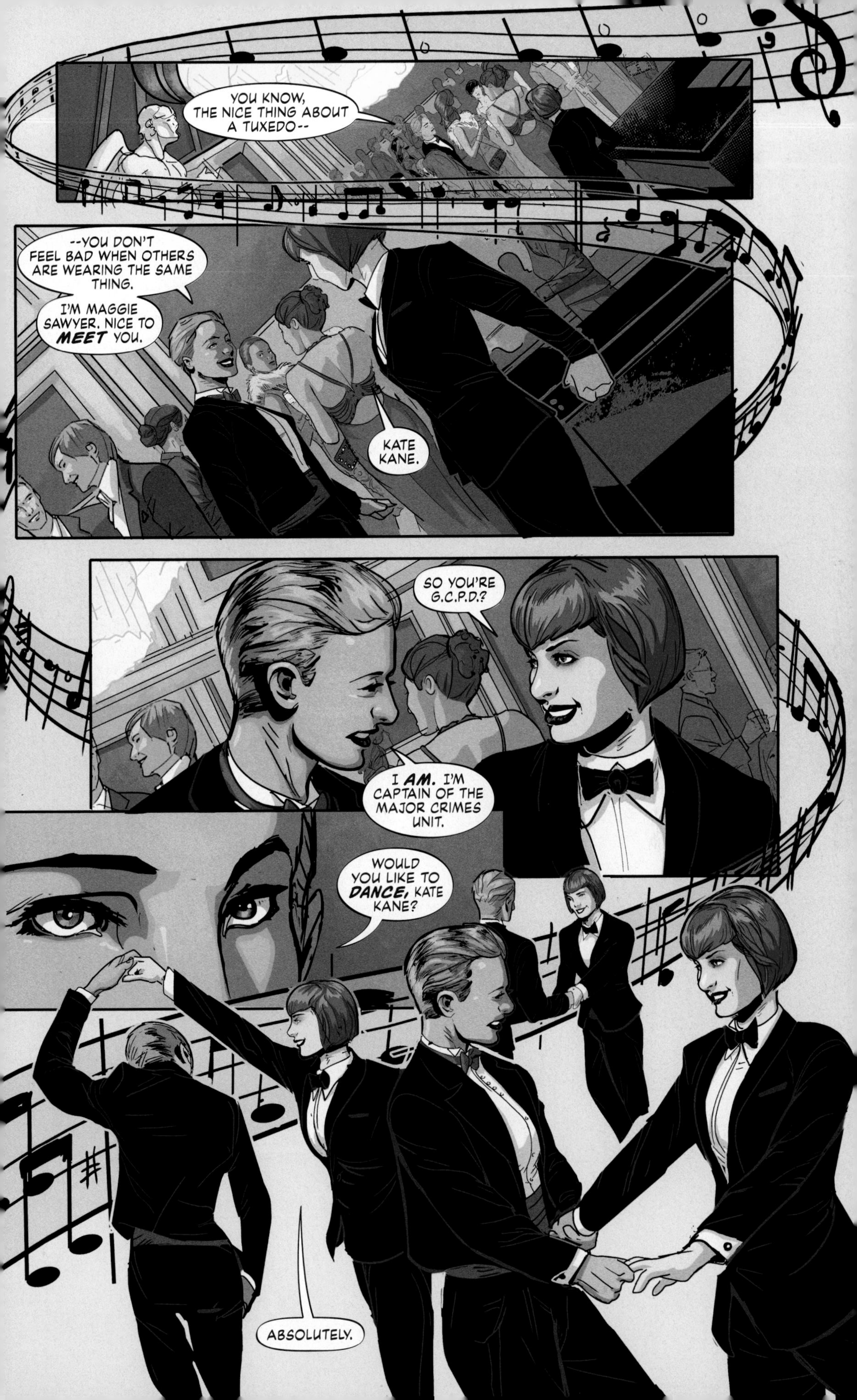
YOU KNOW, THE NICE THING ABOUT A TUXEDO--
--YOU DON'T FEEL BAD WHEN OTHERS ARE WEARING THE SAME THING.
I'M MAGGIE SAWYER. NICE TO **MEET** YOU.
KATE KANE.
SO YOU'RE G.C.P.D.?
I **AM.** I'M CAPTAIN OF THE MAJOR CRIMES UNIT.
WOULD YOU LIKE TO **DANCE,** KATE KANE?
ABSOLUTELY.

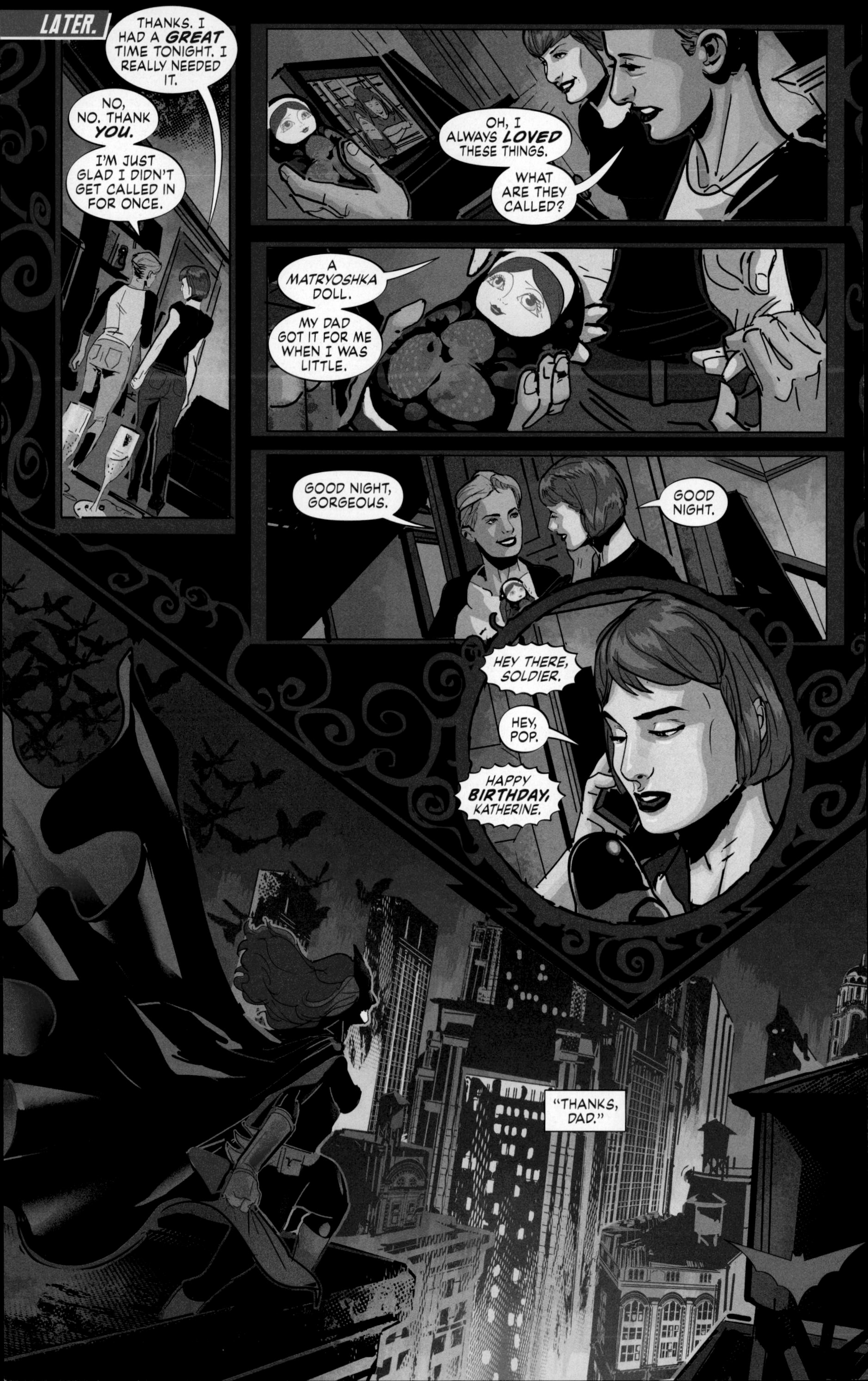
LATER.
THANKS. I HAD A GREAT TIME TONIGHT. I REALLY NEEDED IT.
NO, NO. THANK YOU.
I'M JUST GLAD I DIDN'T GET CALLED IN FOR ONCE.
OH, I ALWAYS LOVED THESE THINGS.
WHAT ARE THEY CALLED?
A MATRYOSHKA DOLL.
MY DAD GOT IT FOR ME WHEN I WAS LITTLE.
GOOD NIGHT, GORGEOUS.
GOOD NIGHT.
HEY THERE, SOLDIER.
HEY, POP.
HAPPY BIRTHDAY, KATHERINE.
"THANKS, DAD."

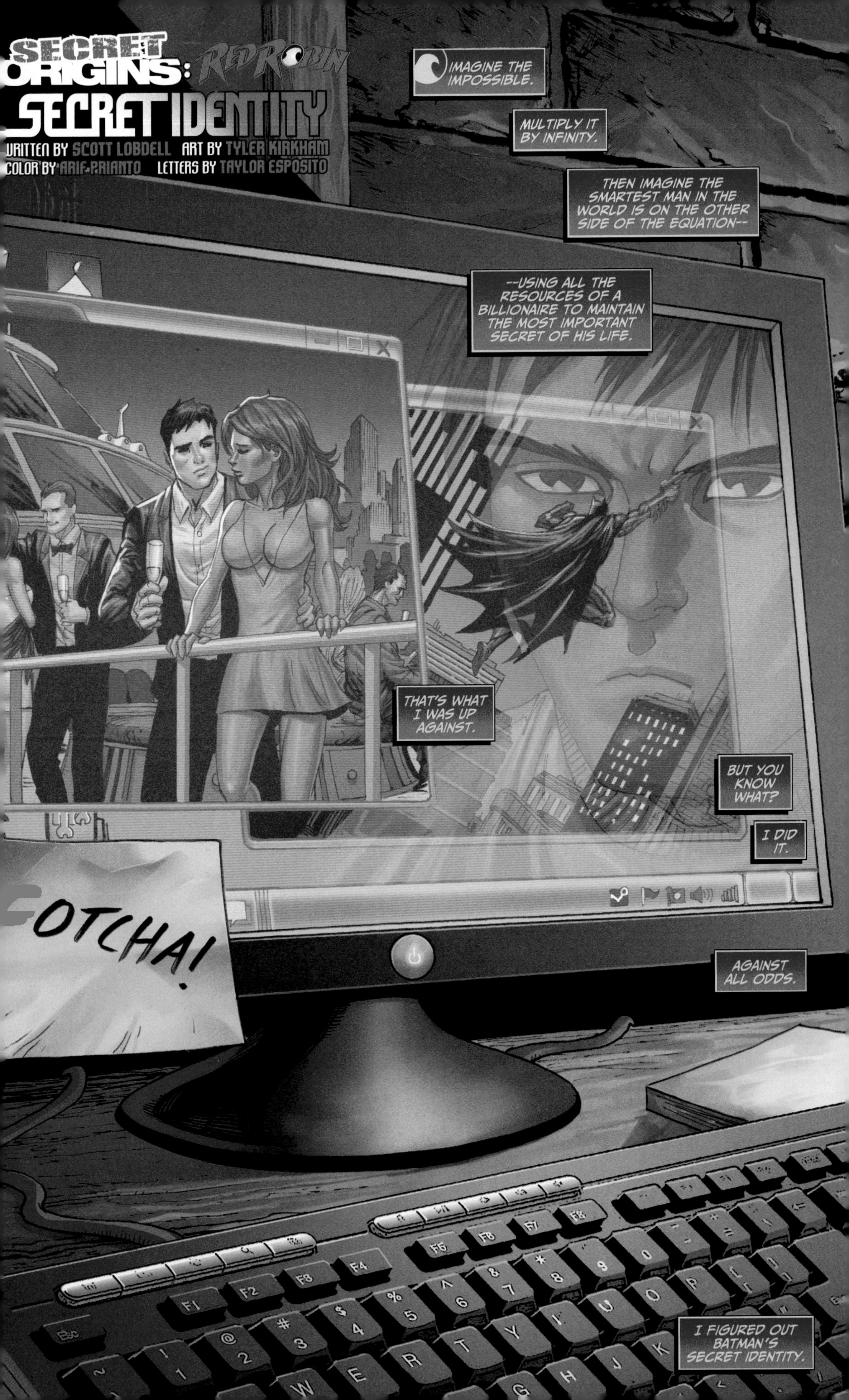
SECRET ORIGINS: RED ROBIN
SECRET IDENTITY
WRITTEN BY SCOTT LOBDELL ART BY TYLER KIRKHAM
COLOR BY ARIF PRIANTO LETTERS BY TAYLOR ESPOSITO
IMAGINE THE IMPOSSIBLE.
MULTIPLY IT BY INFINITY.
THEN IMAGINE THE SMARTEST MAN IN THE WORLD IS ON THE OTHER SIDE OF THE EQUATION--
--USING ALL THE RESOURCES OF A BILLIONAIRE TO MAINTAIN THE MOST IMPORTANT SECRET OF HIS LIFE.
THAT'S WHAT I WAS UP AGAINST.
BUT YOU KNOW WHAT?
I DID IT.
OTCHA!
AGAINST ALL ODDS.
I FIGURED OUT BATMAN'S SECRET IDENTITY.

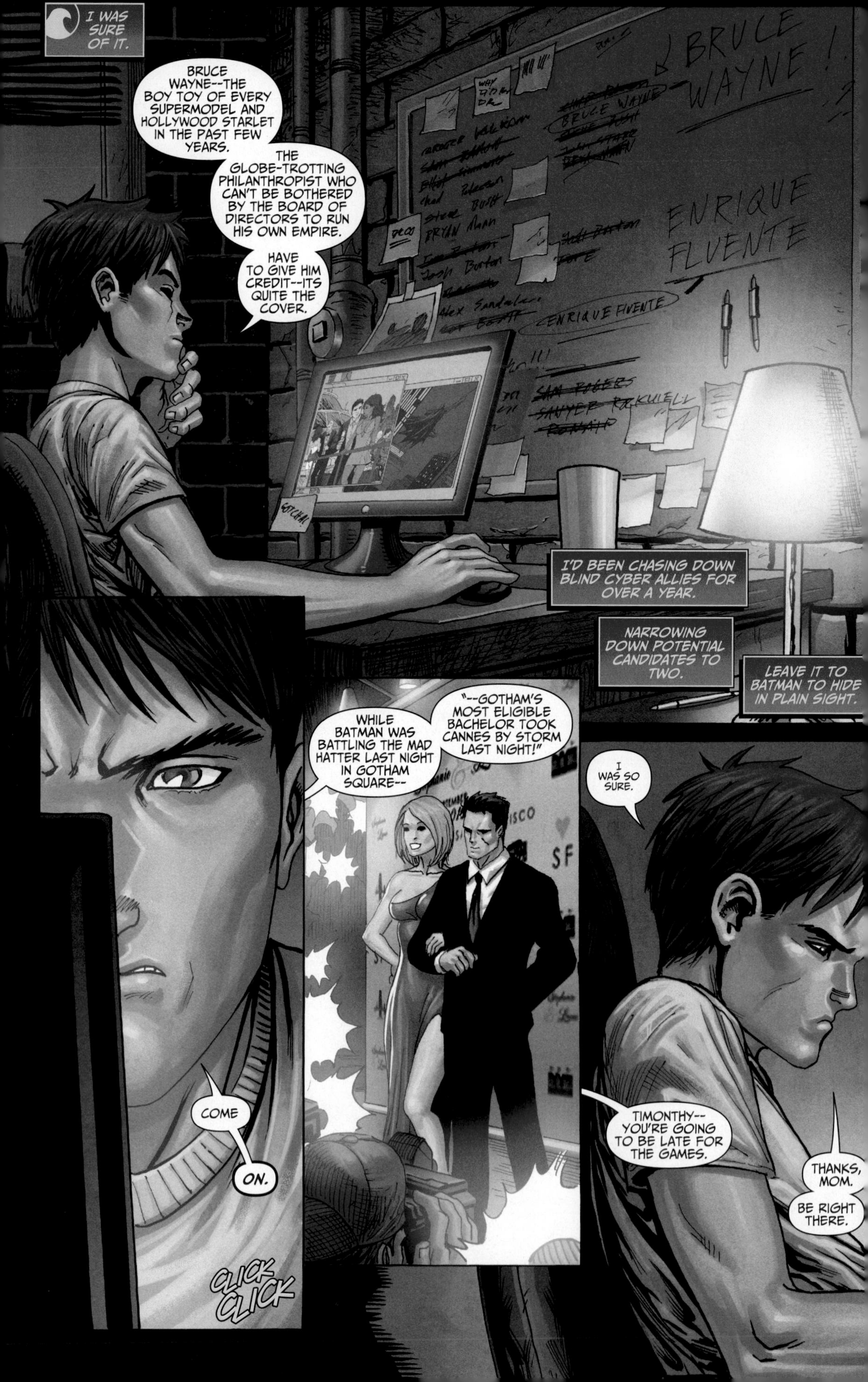
I WAS SURE OF IT.
BRUCE WAYNE--THE BOY TOY OF EVERY SUPERMODEL AND HOLLYWOOD STARLET IN THE PAST FEW YEARS.
THE GLOBE-TROTTING PHILANTHROPIST WHO CAN'T BE BOTHERED BY THE BOARD OF DIRECTORS TO RUN HIS OWN EMPIRE.
HAVE TO GIVE HIM CREDIT--ITS QUITE THE COVER.
BRUCE WAYNE!
ENRIQUE FLUENTE
ENRIQUE FUENTE
GOTCHA!
I'D BEEN CHASING DOWN BLIND CYBER ALLIES FOR OVER A YEAR.
NARROWING DOWN POTENTIAL CANDIDATES TO TWO.
LEAVE IT TO BATMAN TO HIDE IN PLAIN SIGHT.
COME
ON.
CLICK CLICK
WHILE BATMAN WAS BATTLING THE MAD HATTER LAST NIGHT IN GOTHAM SQUARE--
"--GOTHAM'S MOST ELIGIBLE BACHELOR TOOK CANNES BY STORM LAST NIGHT!"
I WAS SO SURE.
TIMONTHY--YOU'RE GOING TO BE LATE FOR THE GAMES.
THANKS, MOM.
BE RIGHT THERE.

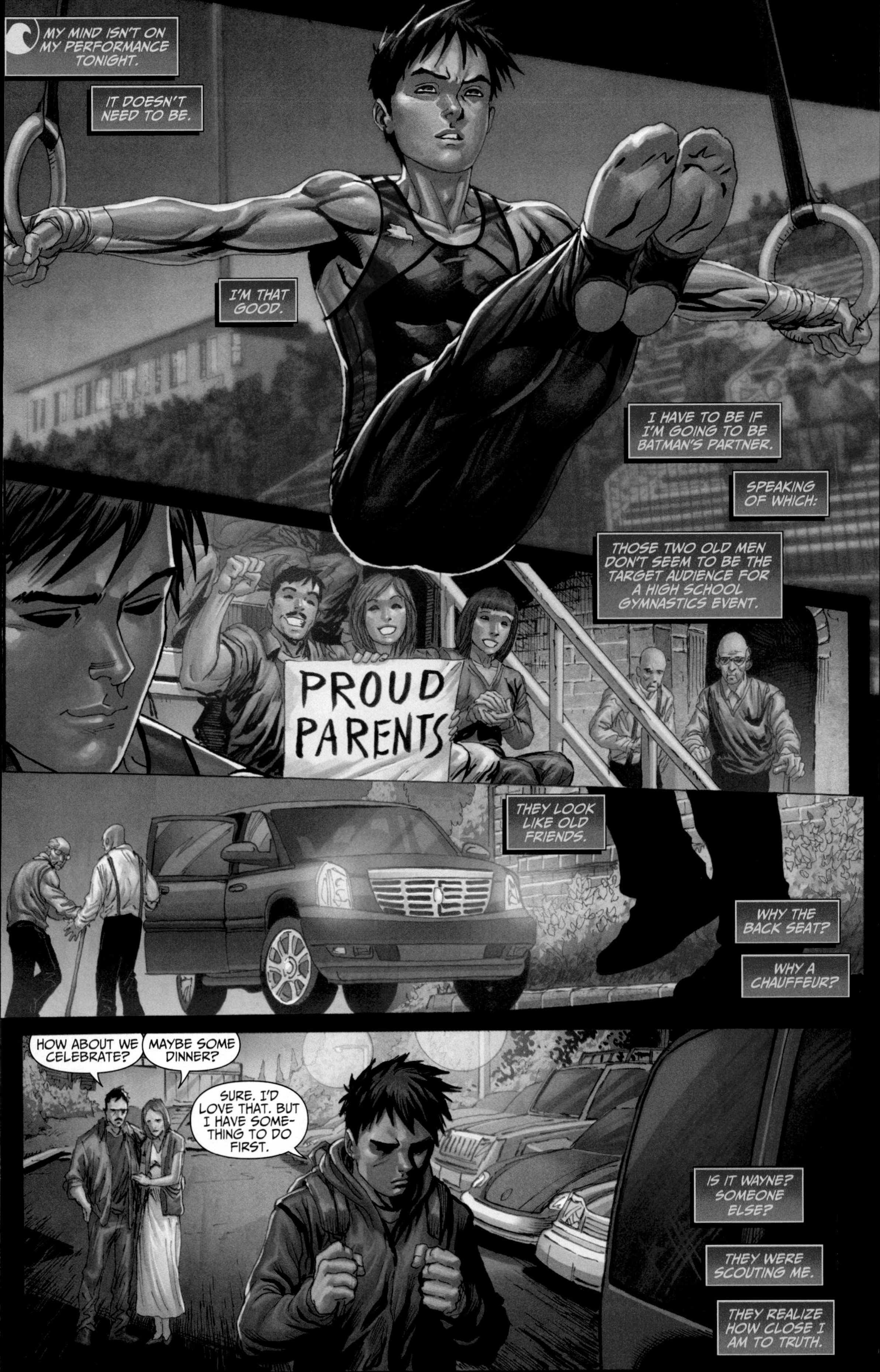
MY MIND ISN'T ON MY PERFORMANCE TONIGHT.
IT DOESN'T NEED TO BE.
I'M THAT GOOD.
I HAVE TO BE IF I'M GOING TO BE BATMAN'S PARTNER.
SPEAKING OF WHICH:
THOSE TWO OLD MEN DON'T SEEM TO BE THE TARGET AUDIENCE FOR A HIGH SCHOOL GYMNASTICS EVENT.
PROUD PARENTS
THEY LOOK LIKE OLD FRIENDS.
WHY THE BACK SEAT?
WHY A CHAUFFEUR?
HOW ABOUT WE CELEBRATE?
MAYBE SOME DINNER?
SURE. I'D LOVE THAT. BUT I HAVE SOMETHING TO DO FIRST.
IS IT WAYNE? SOMEONE ELSE?
THEY WERE SCOUTING ME.
THEY REALIZE HOW CLOSE I AM TO TRUTH.

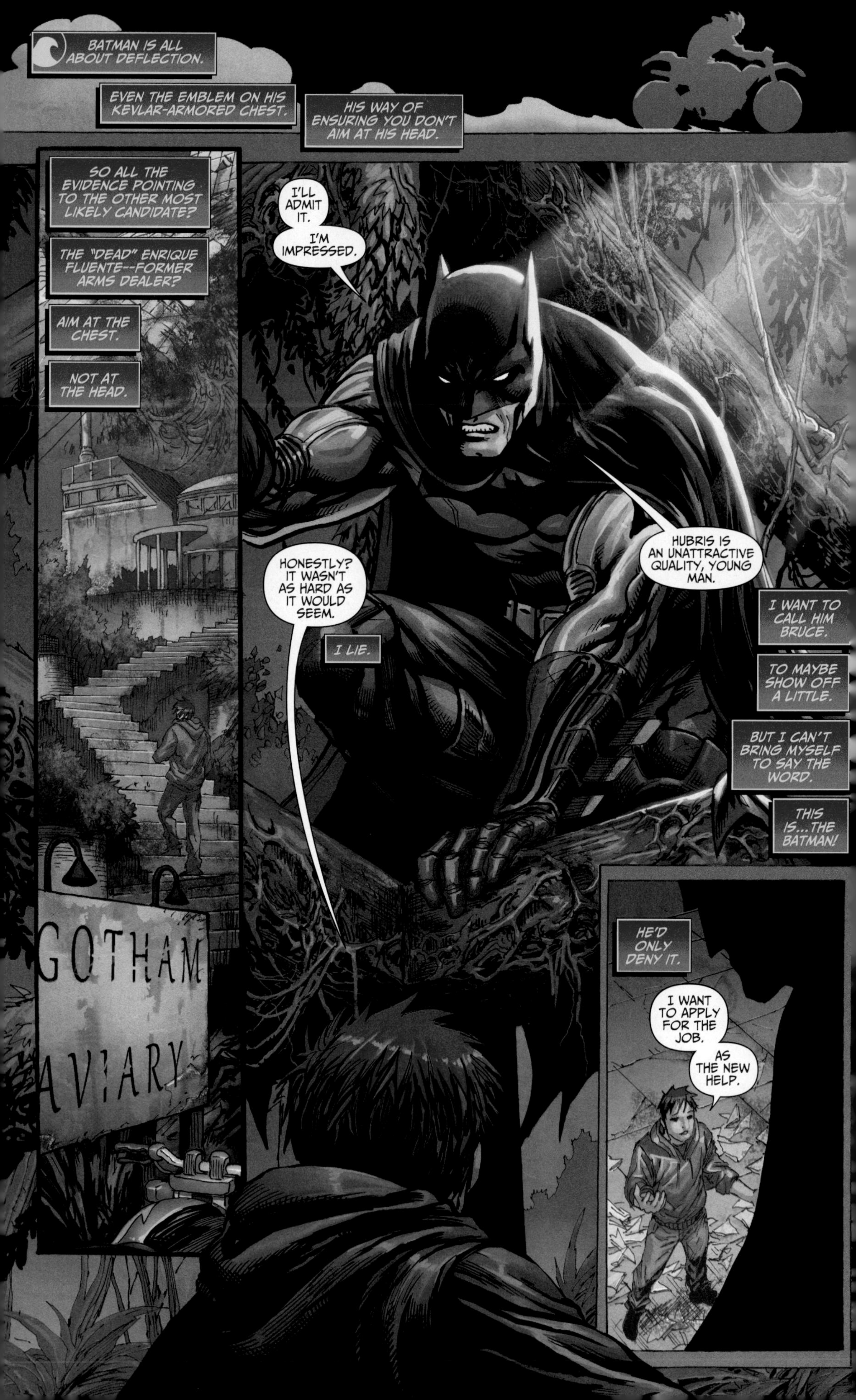
BATMAN IS ALL ABOUT DEFLECTION.
EVEN THE EMBLEM ON HIS KEVLAR-ARMORED CHEST.
HIS WAY OF ENSURING YOU DON'T AIM AT HIS HEAD.
SO ALL THE EVIDENCE POINTING TO THE OTHER MOST LIKELY CANDIDATE?
THE "DEAD" ENRIQUE FLUENTE--FORMER ARMS DEALER?
AIM AT THE CHEST.
NOT AT THE HEAD.
GOTHAM AVIARY
I'LL ADMIT IT.
I'M IMPRESSED.
HONESTLY? IT WASN'T AS HARD AS IT WOULD SEEM.
I LIE.
HUBRIS IS AN UNATTRACTIVE QUALITY, YOUNG MAN.
I WANT TO CALL HIM BRUCE.
TO MAYBE SHOW OFF A LITTLE.
BUT I CAN'T BRING MYSELF TO SAY THE WORD.
THIS IS...THE BATMAN!
HE'D ONLY DENY IT.
I WANT TO APPLY FOR THE JOB.
AS THE NEW HELP.

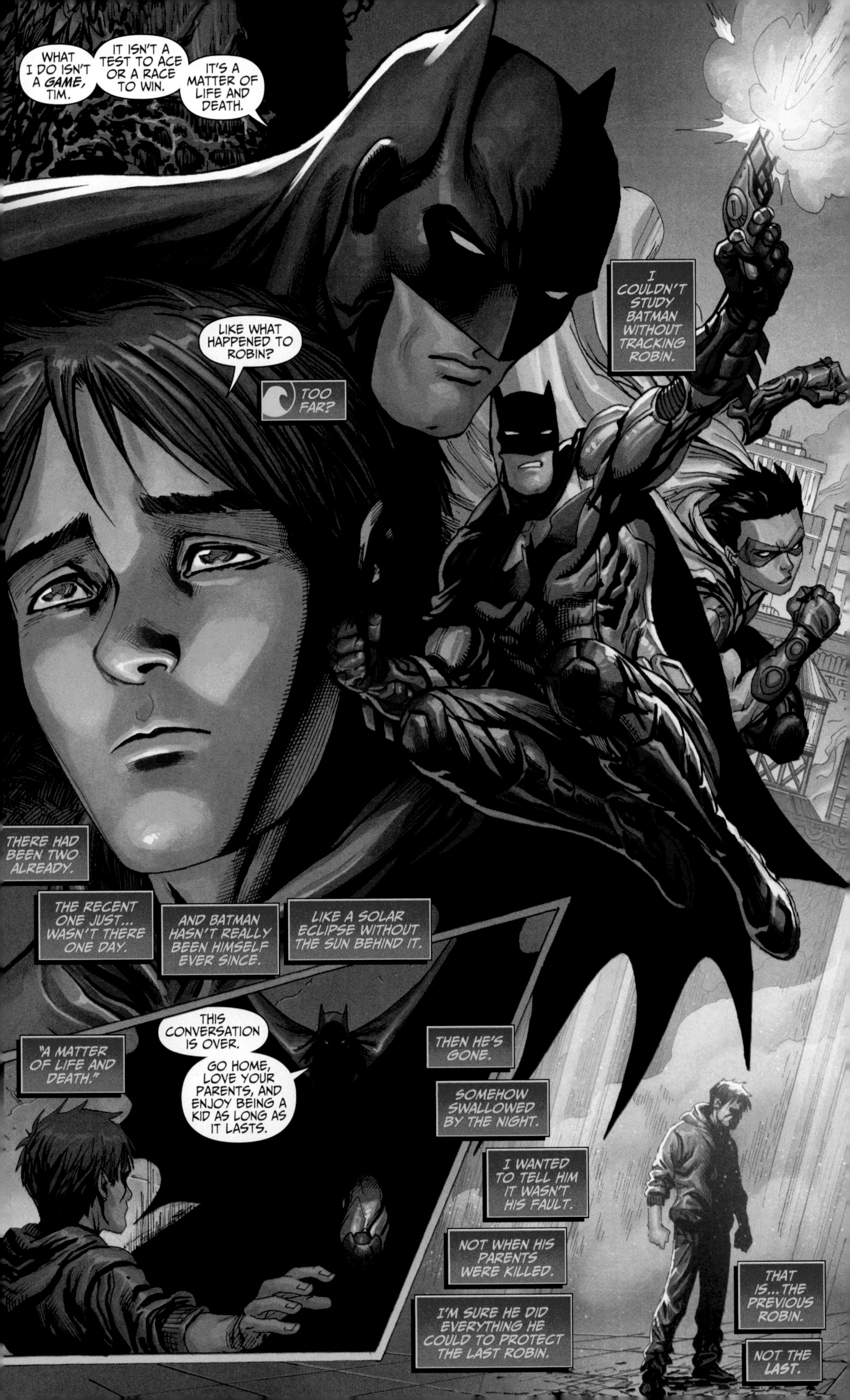

WHAT I DO ISN'T A GAME, TIM.
IT ISN'T A TEST TO ACE OR A RACE TO WIN.
IT'S A MATTER OF LIFE AND DEATH.
LIKE WHAT HAPPENED TO ROBIN?
TOO FAR?
I COULDN'T STUDY BATMAN WITHOUT TRACKING ROBIN.
THERE HAD BEEN TWO ALREADY.
THE RECENT ONE JUST... WASN'T THERE ONE DAY.
AND BATMAN HASN'T REALLY BEEN HIMSELF EVER SINCE.
LIKE A SOLAR ECLIPSE WITHOUT THE SUN BEHIND IT.
"A MATTER OF LIFE AND DEATH."
THIS CONVERSATION IS OVER.
GO HOME, LOVE YOUR PARENTS, AND ENJOY BEING A KID AS LONG AS IT LASTS.
THEN HE'S GONE.
SOMEHOW SWALLOWED BY THE NIGHT.
I WANTED TO TELL HIM IT WASN'T HIS FAULT.
NOT WHEN HIS PARENTS WERE KILLED.
I'M SURE HE DID EVERYTHING HE COULD TO PROTECT THE LAST ROBIN.
THAT IS...THE PREVIOUS ROBIN.
NOT THE LAST.

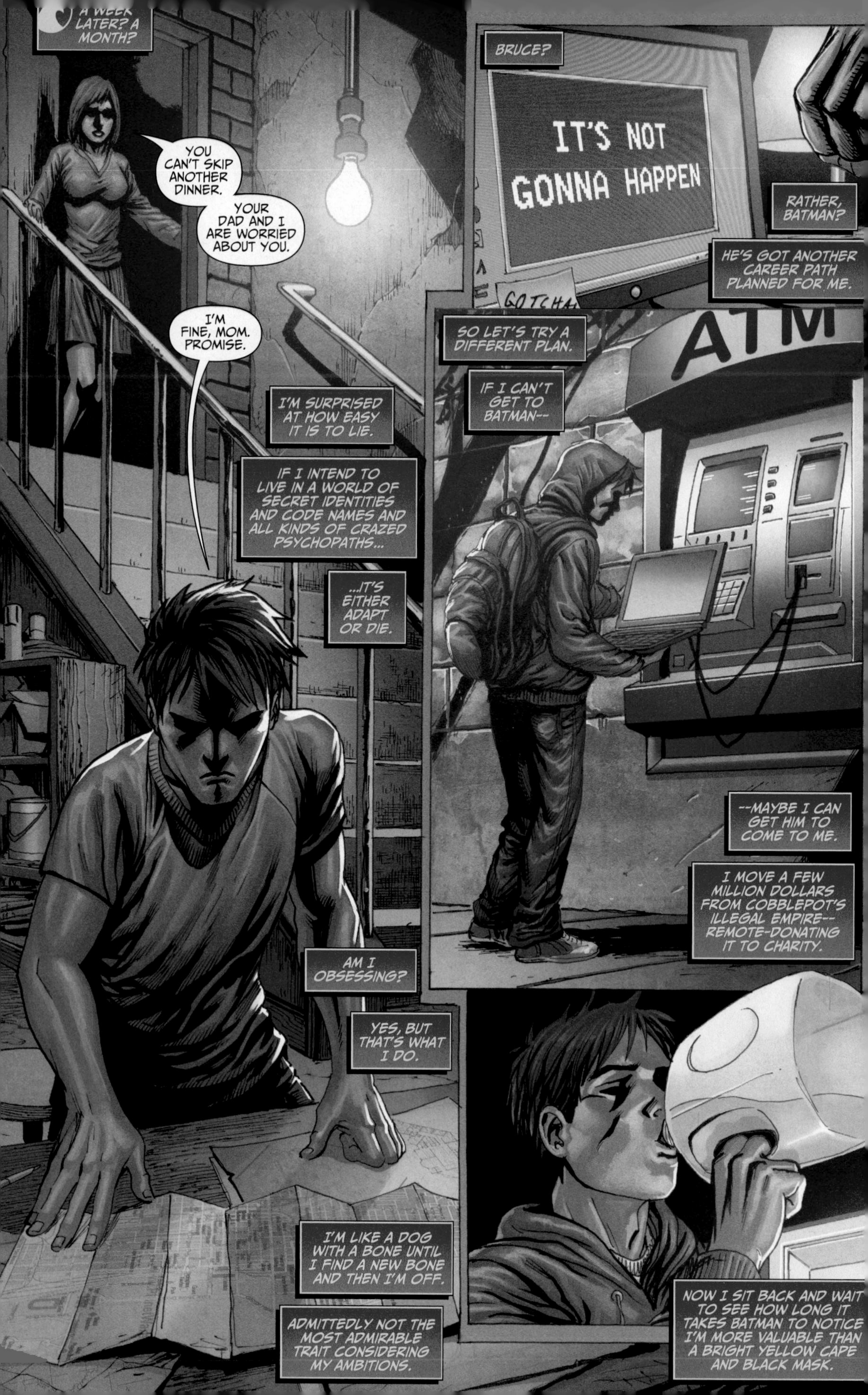
A WEEK LATER? A MONTH?
YOU CAN'T SKIP ANOTHER DINNER.
YOUR DAD AND I ARE WORRIED ABOUT YOU.
I'M FINE, MOM. PROMISE.
I'M SURPRISED AT HOW EASY IT IS TO LIE.
IF I INTEND TO LIVE IN A WORLD OF SECRET IDENTITIES AND CODE NAMES AND ALL KINDS OF CRAZED PSYCHOPATHS...
...IT'S EITHER ADAPT OR DIE.
AM I OBSESSING?
YES, BUT THAT'S WHAT I DO.
I'M LIKE A DOG WITH A BONE UNTIL I FIND A NEW BONE AND THEN I'M OFF.
ADMITTEDLY NOT THE MOST ADMIRABLE TRAIT CONSIDERING MY AMBITIONS.
BRUCE?
IT'S NOT GONNA HAPPEN
RATHER, BATMAN?
HE'S GOT ANOTHER CAREER PATH PLANNED FOR ME.
SO LET'S TRY A DIFFERENT PLAN.
IF I CAN'T GET TO BATMAN--
ATM
--MAYBE I CAN GET HIM TO COME TO ME.
I MOVE A FEW MILLION DOLLARS FROM COBBLEPOT'S ILLEGAL EMPIRE--REMOTE-DONATING IT TO CHARITY.
NOW I SIT BACK AND WAIT TO SEE HOW LONG IT TAKES BATMAN TO NOTICE I'M MORE VALUABLE THAN A BRIGHT YELLOW CAPE AND BLACK MASK.

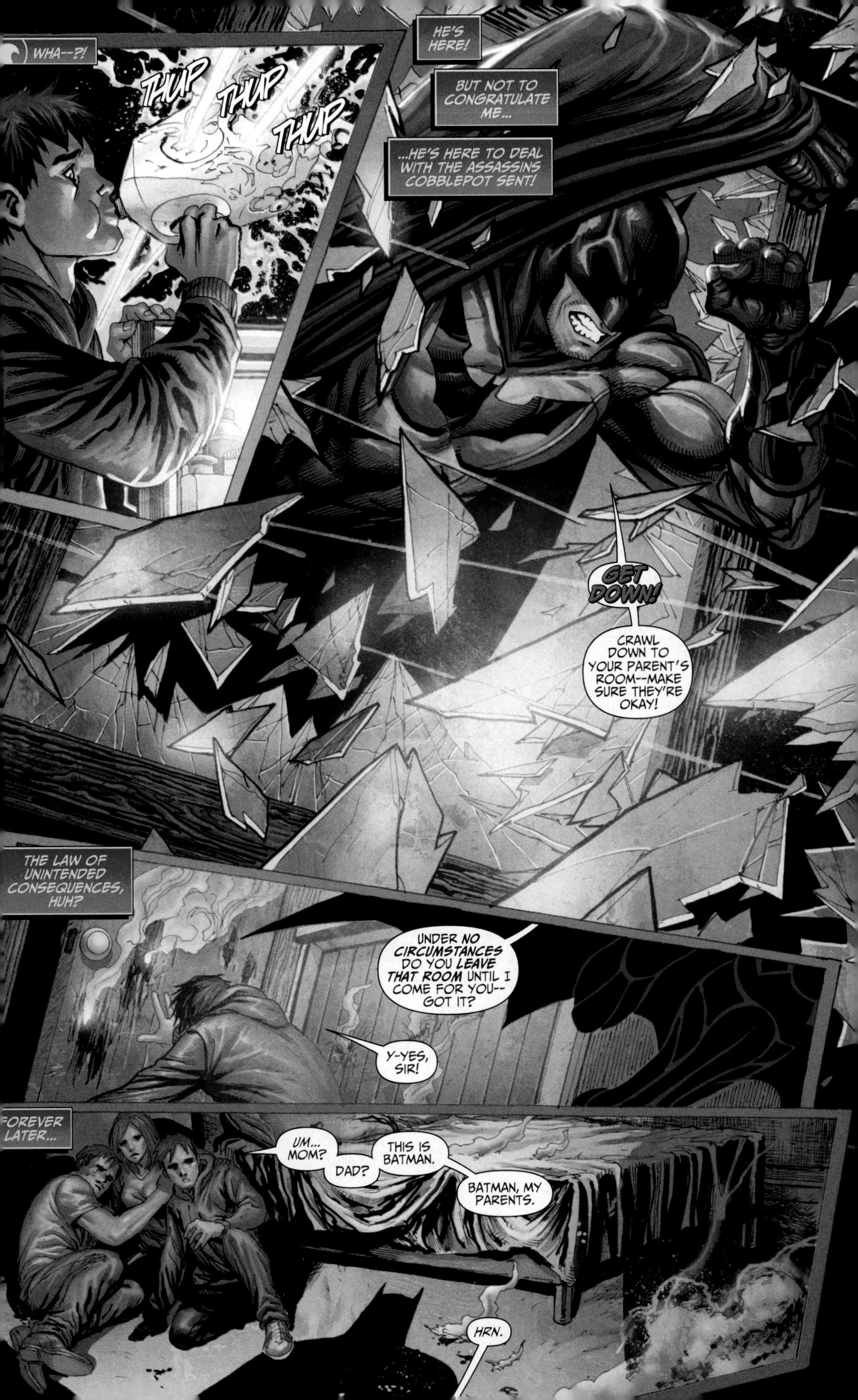
WHA--?!
THUP
THUP
THUP
HE'S HERE!
BUT NOT TO CONGRATULATE ME...
...HE'S HERE TO DEAL WITH THE ASSASSINS COBBLEPOT SENT!
GET DOWN!
CRAWL DOWN TO YOUR PARENT'S ROOM--MAKE SURE THEY'RE OKAY!
THE LAW OF UNINTENDED CONSEQUENCES, HUH?
UNDER NO CIRCUMSTANCES DO YOU LEAVE THAT ROOM UNTIL I COME FOR YOU--GOT IT?
Y-YES, SIR!
FOREVER LATER...
UM... MOM?
DAD?
THIS IS BATMAN.
BATMAN, MY PARENTS.
HRN.

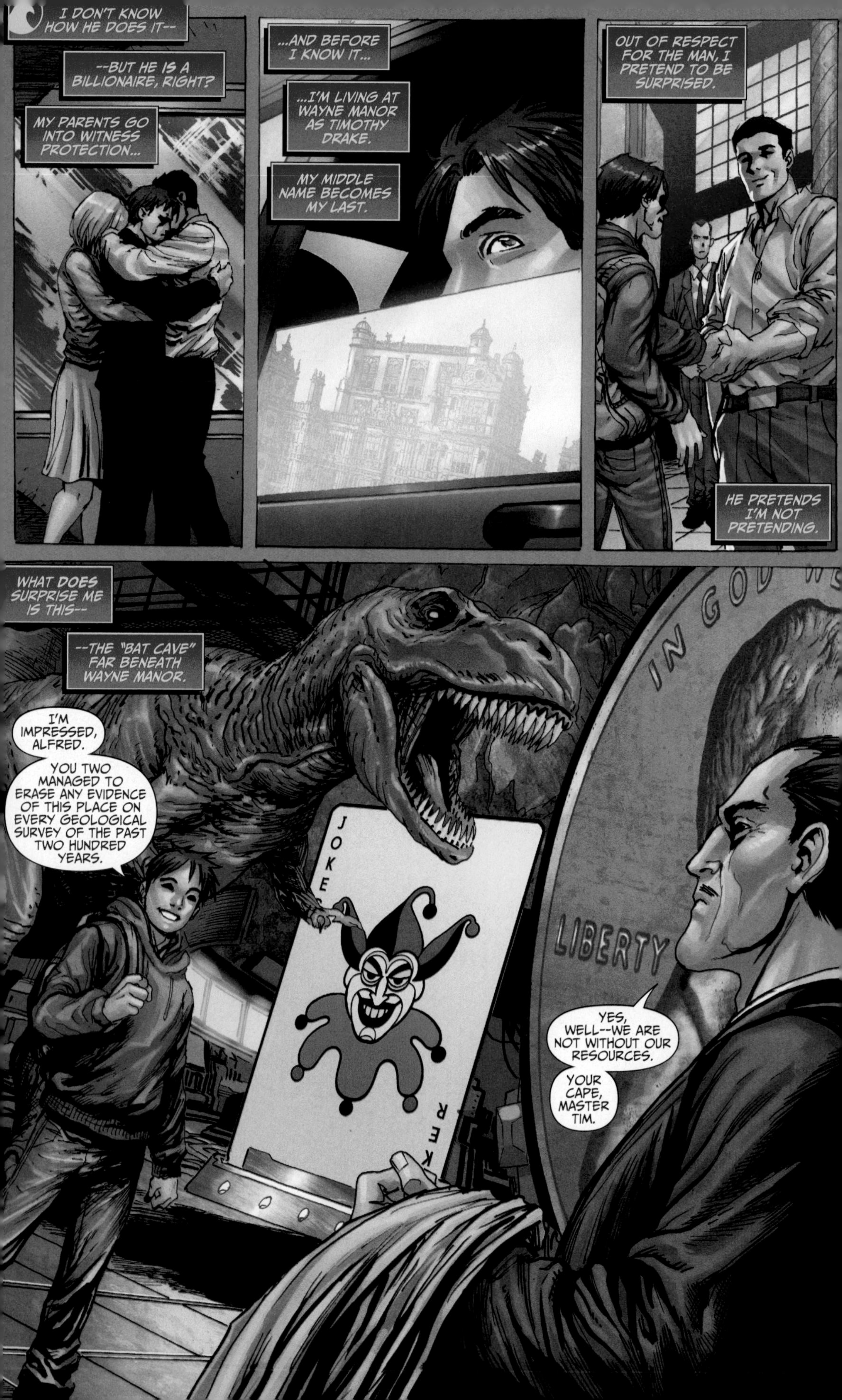
I DON'T KNOW HOW HE DOES IT--
--BUT HE IS A BILLIONAIRE, RIGHT?
MY PARENTS GO INTO WITNESS PROTECTION...
...AND BEFORE I KNOW IT...
...I'M LIVING AT WAYNE MANOR AS TIMOTHY DRAKE.
MY MIDDLE NAME BECOMES MY LAST.
OUT OF RESPECT FOR THE MAN, I PRETEND TO BE SURPRISED.
HE PRETENDS I'M NOT PRETENDING.
WHAT DOES SURPRISE ME IS THIS--
--THE "BAT CAVE" FAR BENEATH WAYNE MANOR.
I'M IMPRESSED, ALFRED.
YOU TWO MANAGED TO ERASE ANY EVIDENCE OF THIS PLACE ON EVERY GEOLOGICAL SURVEY OF THE PAST TWO HUNDRED YEARS.
YES, WELL--WE ARE NOT WITHOUT OUR RESOURCES.
YOUR CAPE, MASTER TIM.

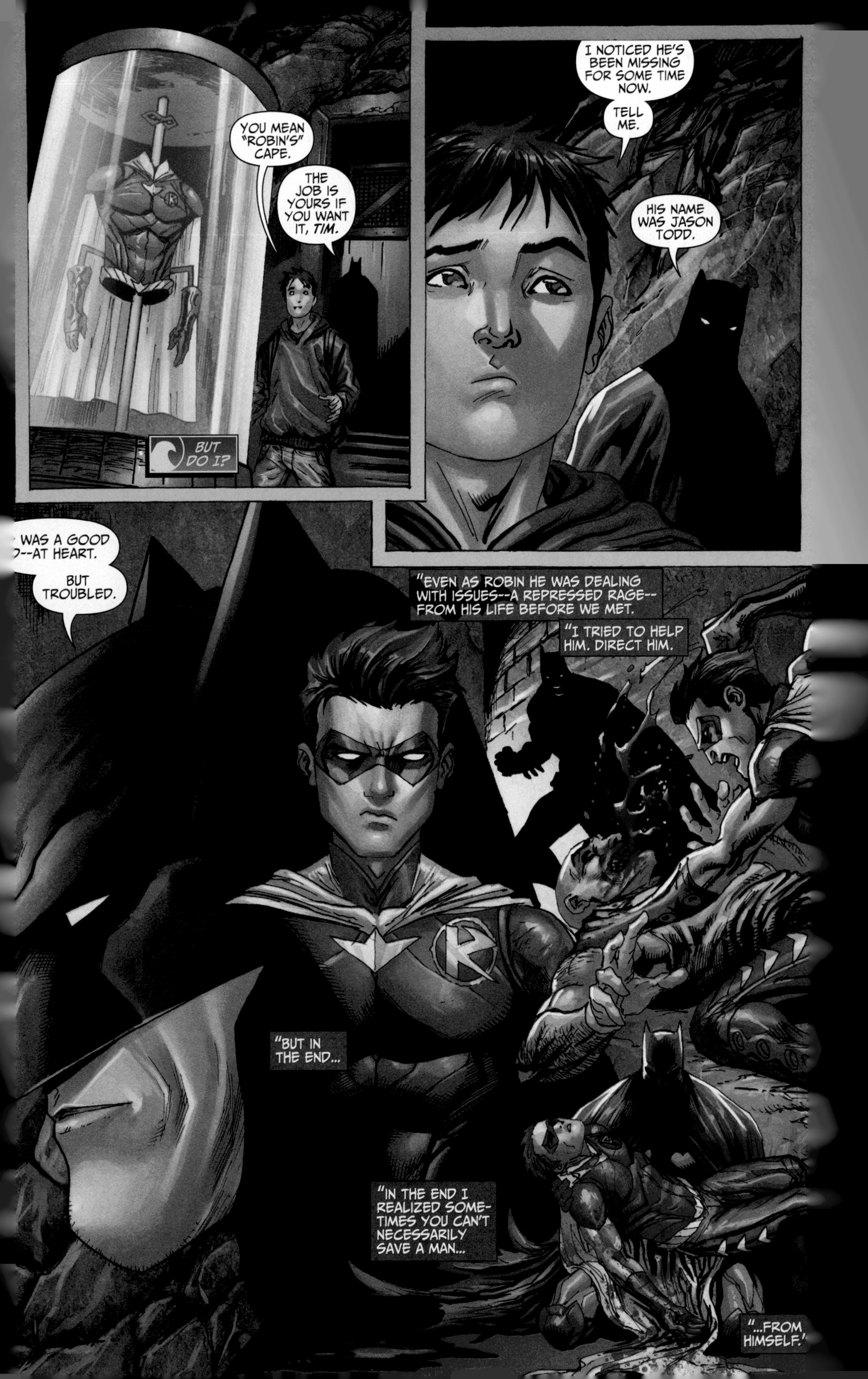
YOU MEAN "ROBIN'S" CAPE.
THE JOB IS YOURS IF YOU WANT IT, *TIM*.
BUT DO I?
I NOTICED HE'S BEEN MISSING FOR SOME TIME NOW.
TELL ME.
HIS NAME WAS JASON TODD.
WAS A GOOD D--AT HEART.
BUT TROUBLED.
"EVEN AS ROBIN HE WAS DEALING WITH ISSUES--A REPRESSED RAGE--FROM HIS LIFE BEFORE WE MET.
"I TRIED TO HELP HIM. DIRECT HIM.
"BUT IN THE END...
"IN THE END I REALIZED SOME-TIMES YOU CAN'T NECESSARILY SAVE A MAN...
"...FROM HIMSELF."

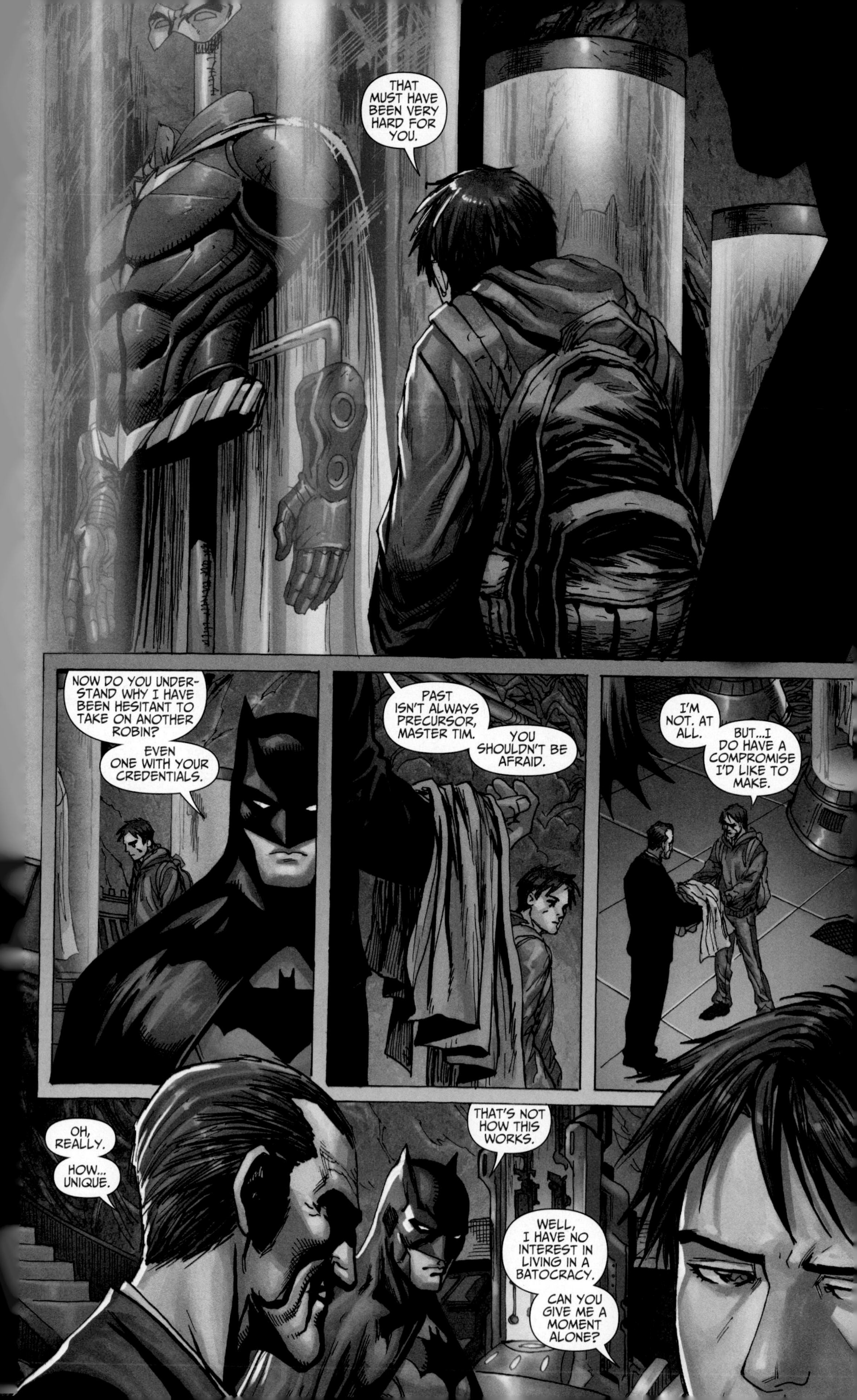
THAT MUST HAVE BEEN VERY HARD FOR YOU.
NOW DO YOU UNDERSTAND WHY I HAVE BEEN HESITANT TO TAKE ON ANOTHER ROBIN?
EVEN ONE WITH YOUR CREDENTIALS.
PAST ISN'T ALWAYS PRECURSOR, MASTER TIM.
YOU SHOULDN'T BE AFRAID.
I'M NOT. AT ALL.
BUT...I DO HAVE A COMPROMISE I'D LIKE TO MAKE.
OH, REALLY.
HOW... UNIQUE.
THAT'S NOT HOW THIS WORKS.
WELL, I HAVE NO INTEREST IN LIVING IN A BATOCRACY.
CAN YOU GIVE ME A MOMENT ALONE?

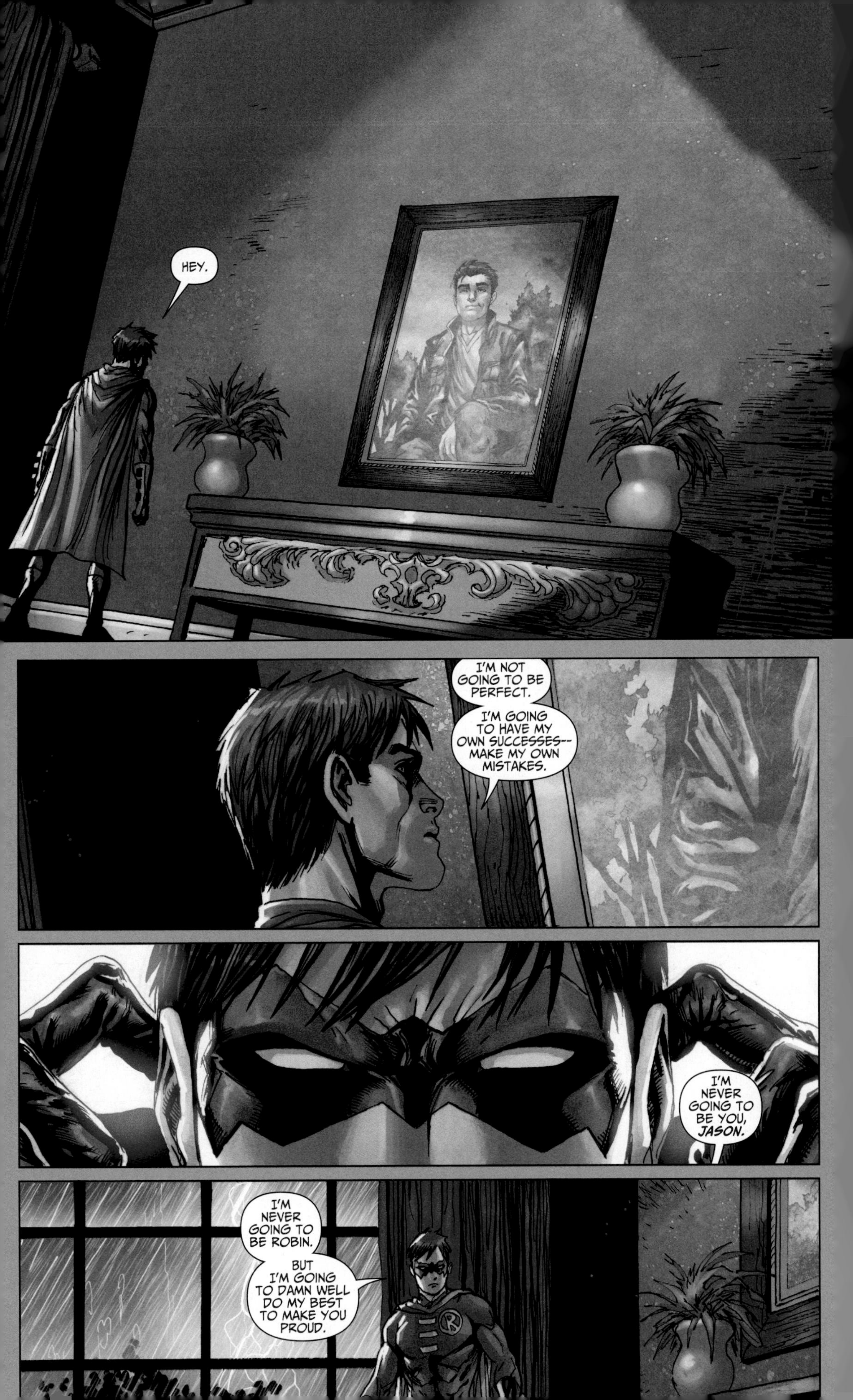
HEY.
I'M NOT GOING TO BE PERFECT.
I'M GOING TO HAVE MY OWN SUCCESSES-- MAKE MY OWN MISTAKES.
I'M NEVER GOING TO BE YOU, JASON.
I'M NEVER GOING TO BE ROBIN.
BUT I'M GOING TO DAMN WELL DO MY BEST TO MAKE YOU PROUD.

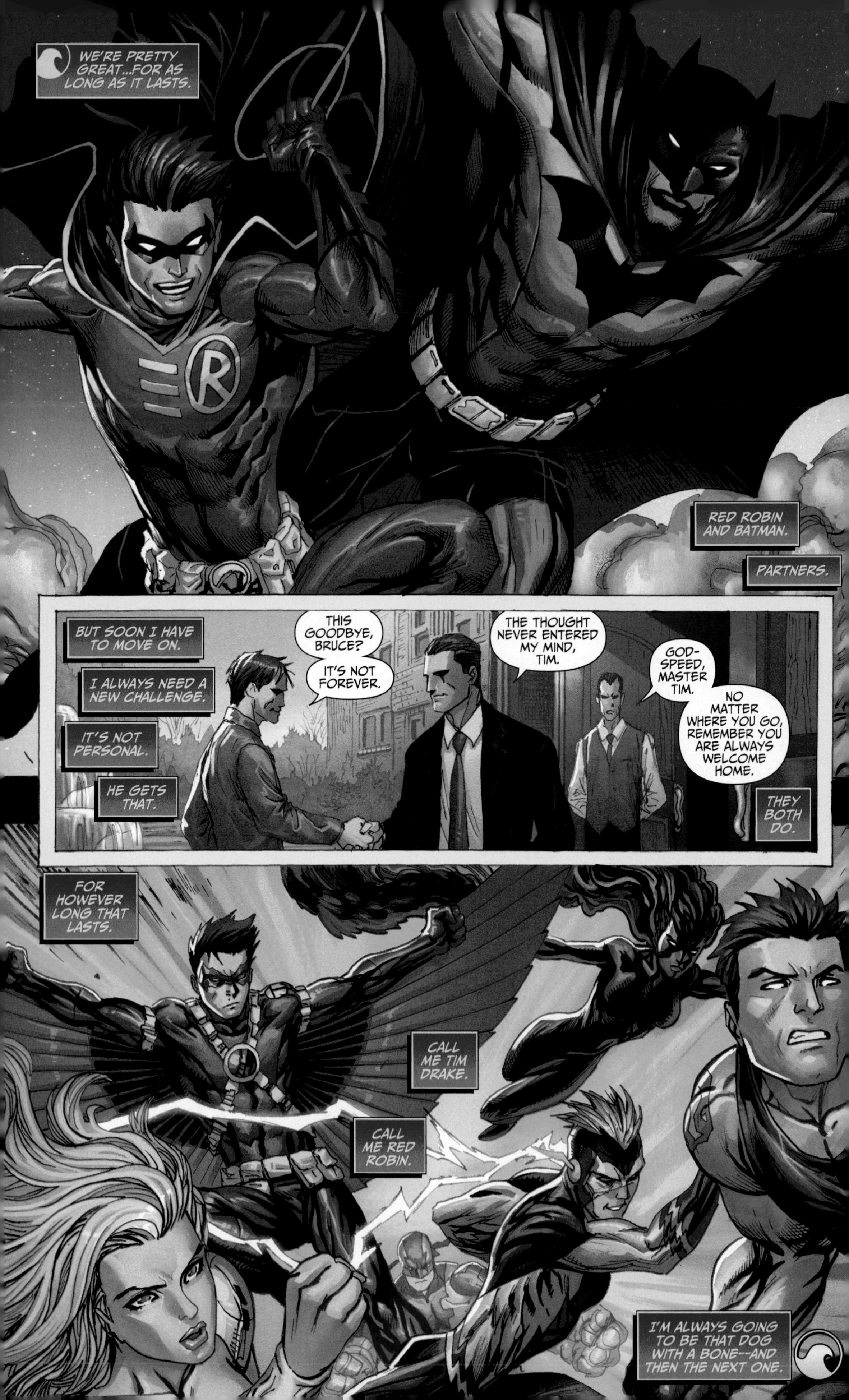
WE'RE PRETTY GREAT...FOR AS LONG AS IT LASTS.
RED ROBIN AND BATMAN.
PARTNERS.
BUT SOON I HAVE TO MOVE ON.
I ALWAYS NEED A NEW CHALLENGE.
IT'S NOT PERSONAL.
HE GETS THAT.
THIS GOODBYE, BRUCE?
IT'S NOT FOREVER.
THE THOUGHT NEVER ENTERED MY MIND, TIM.
GOD-SPEED, MASTER TIM.
NO MATTER WHERE YOU GO, REMEMBER YOU ARE ALWAYS WELCOME HOME.
THEY BOTH DO.
FOR HOWEVER LONG THAT LASTS.
CALL ME TIM DRAKE.
CALL ME RED ROBIN.
I'M ALWAYS GOING TO BE THAT DOG WITH A BONE--AND THEN THE NEXT ONE.

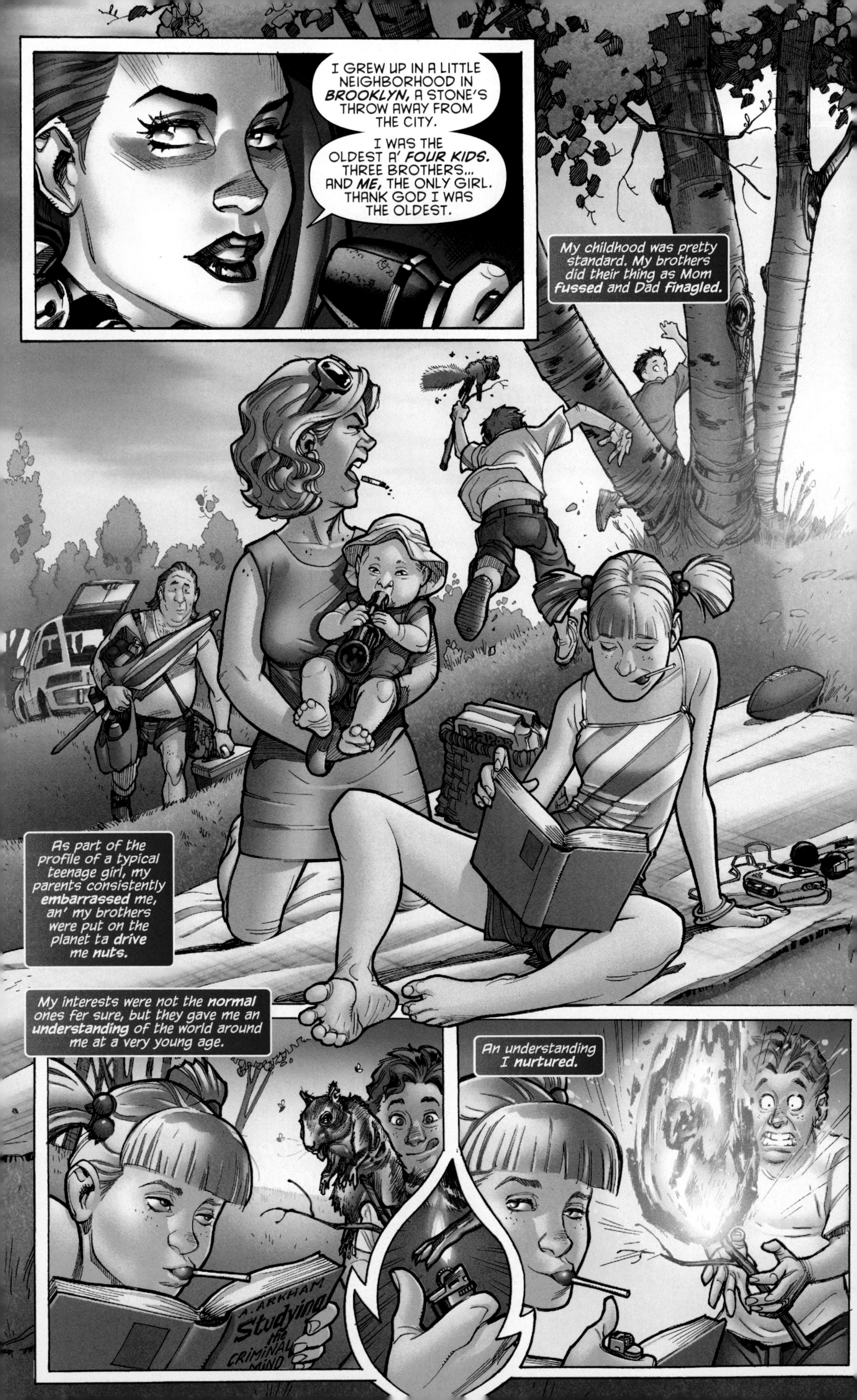
I GREW UP IN A LITTLE NEIGHBORHOOD IN BROOKLYN, A STONE'S THROW AWAY FROM THE CITY.
I WAS THE OLDEST A' FOUR KIDS. THREE BROTHERS... AND ME, THE ONLY GIRL. THANK GOD I WAS THE OLDEST.
My childhood was pretty standard. My brothers did their thing as Mom fussed and Dad finagled.
As part of the profile of a typical teenage girl, my parents consistently embarrassed me, an' my brothers were put on the planet ta drive me nuts.
My interests were not the normal ones fer sure, but they gave me an understanding of the world around me at a very young age.
A. ARKHAM Studying the CRIMINAL MIND
An understanding I nurtured.

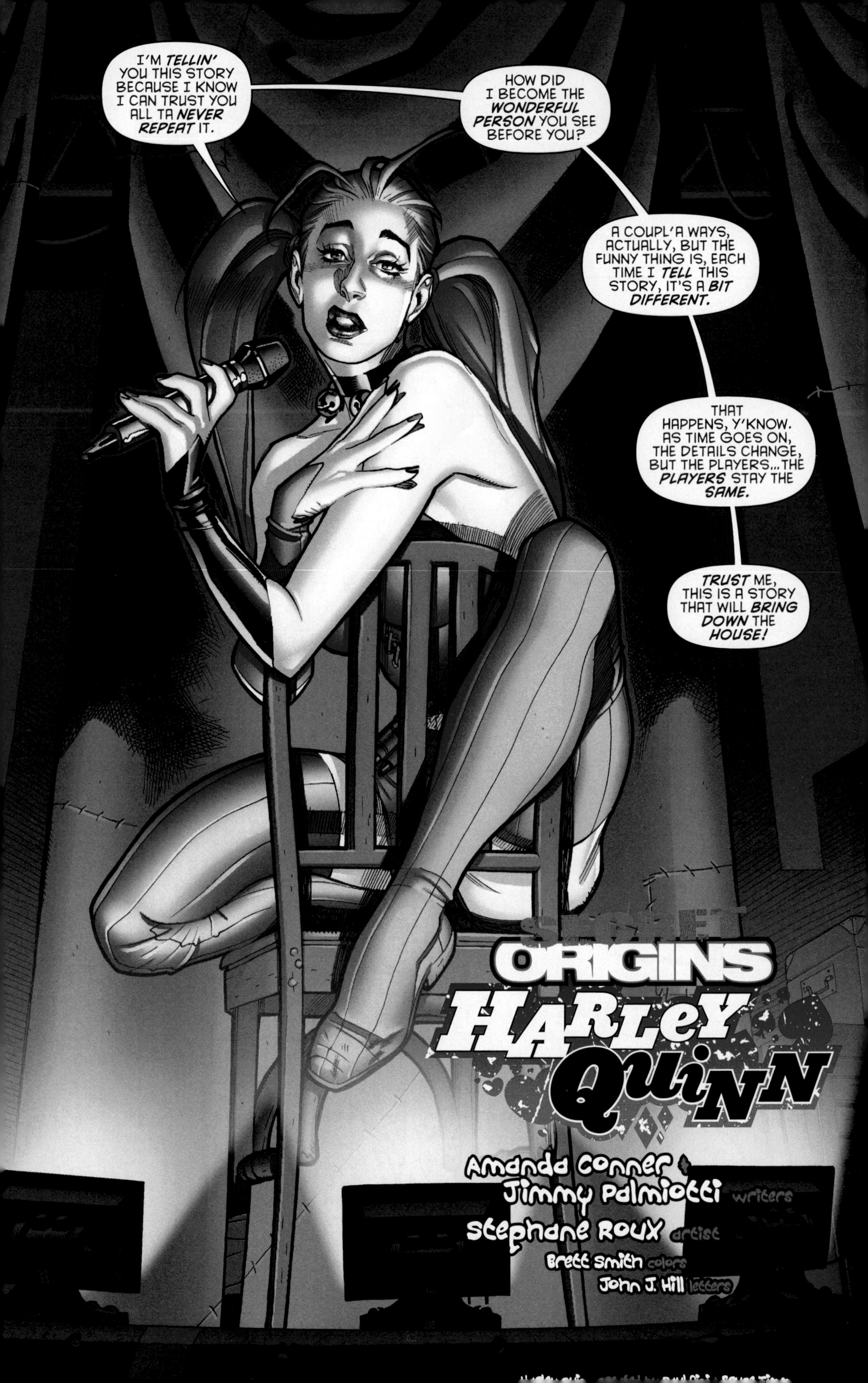
I'M TELLIN' YOU THIS STORY BECAUSE I KNOW I CAN TRUST YOU ALL TA NEVER REPEAT IT.
HOW DID I BECOME THE WONDERFUL PERSON YOU SEE BEFORE YOU?
A COUPL'A WAYS, ACTUALLY, BUT THE FUNNY THING IS, EACH TIME I TELL THIS STORY, IT'S A BIT DIFFERENT.
THAT HAPPENS, Y'KNOW. AS TIME GOES ON, THE DETAILS CHANGE, BUT THE PLAYERS... THE PLAYERS STAY THE SAME.
TRUST ME, THIS IS A STORY THAT WILL BRING DOWN THE HOUSE!
SECRET ORIGINS
HARLEY QUINN
Amanda Conner & Jimmy Palmiotti writers
Stephane Roux artist
Brett Smith colors
John J. Hill letters

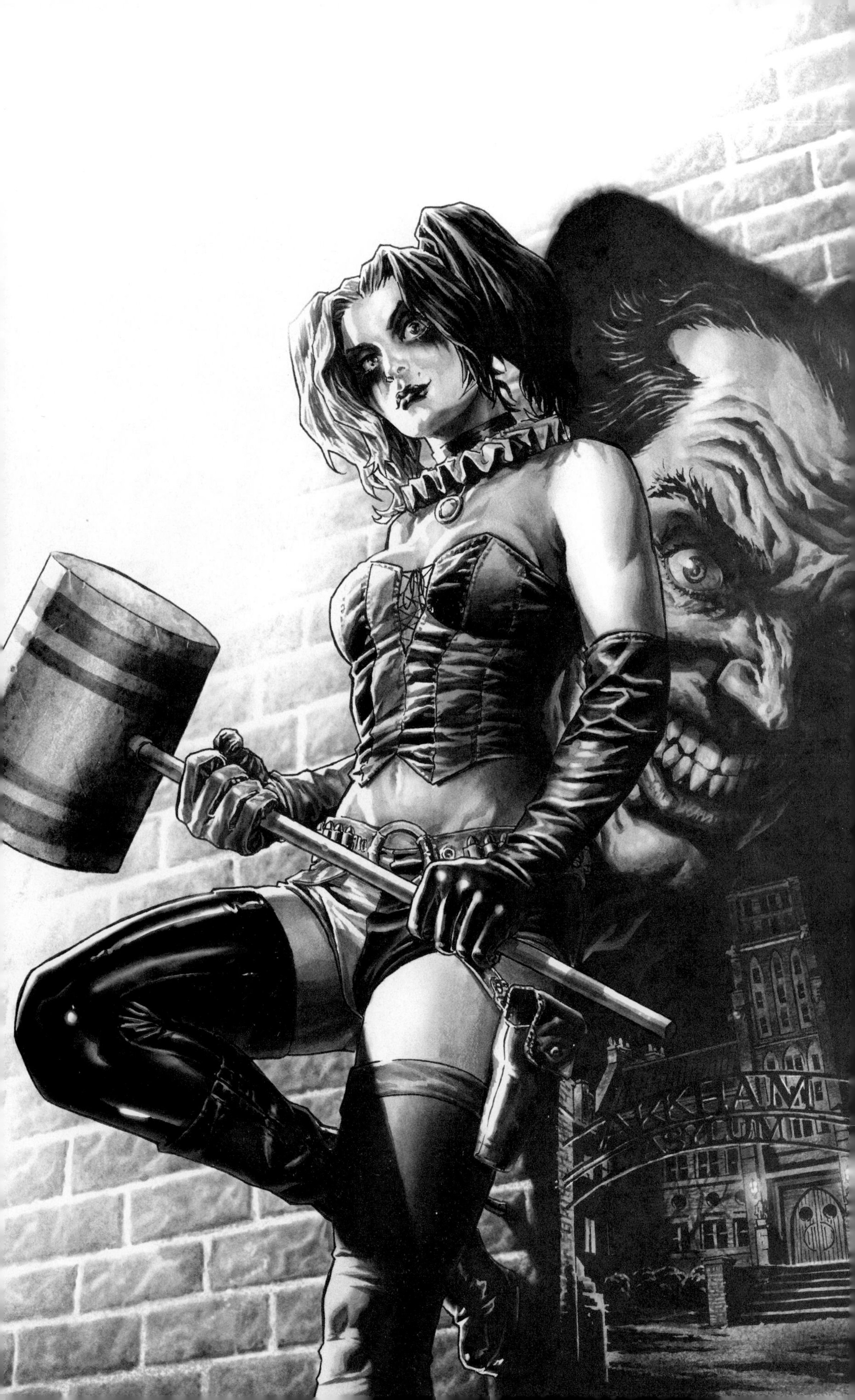

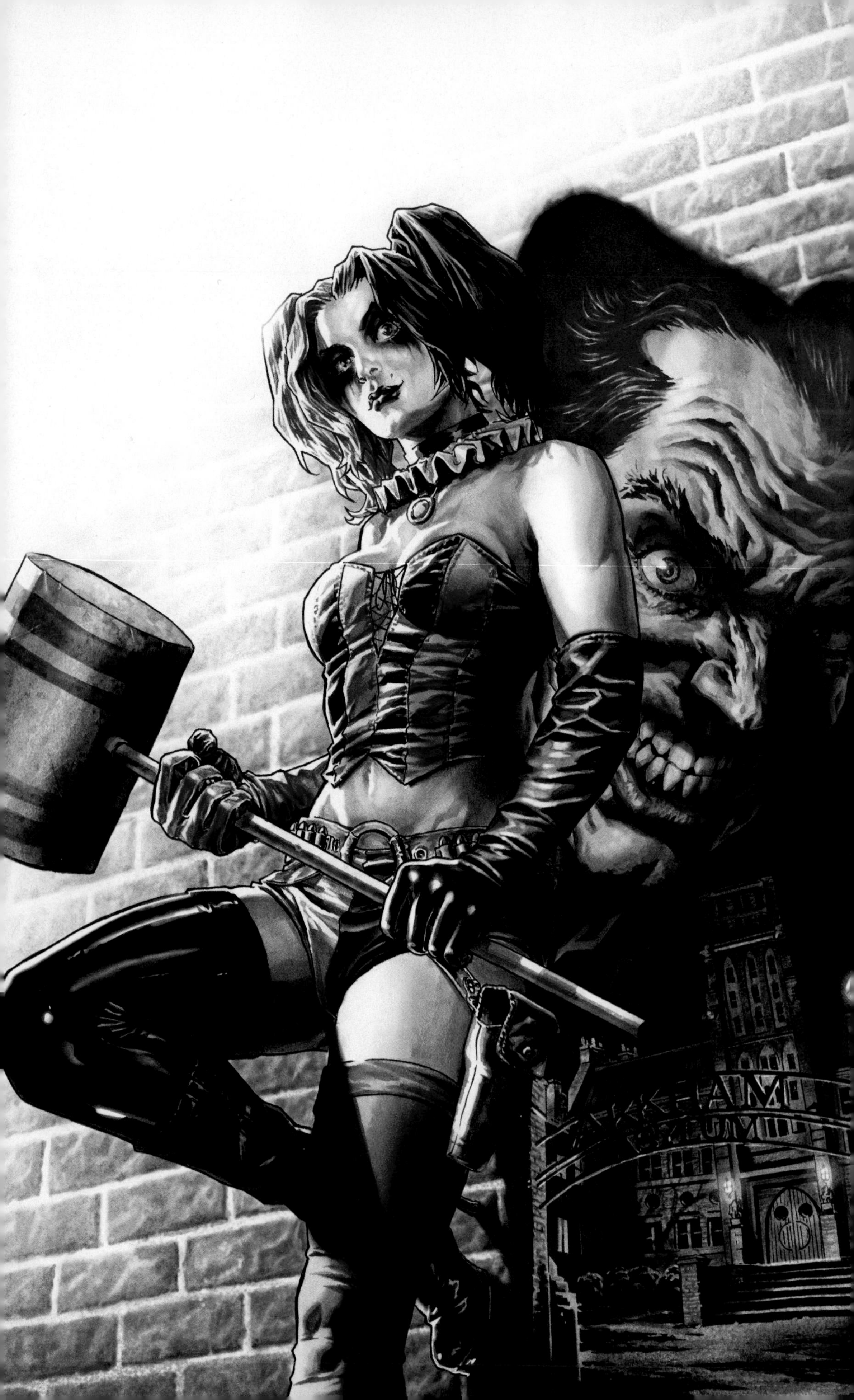

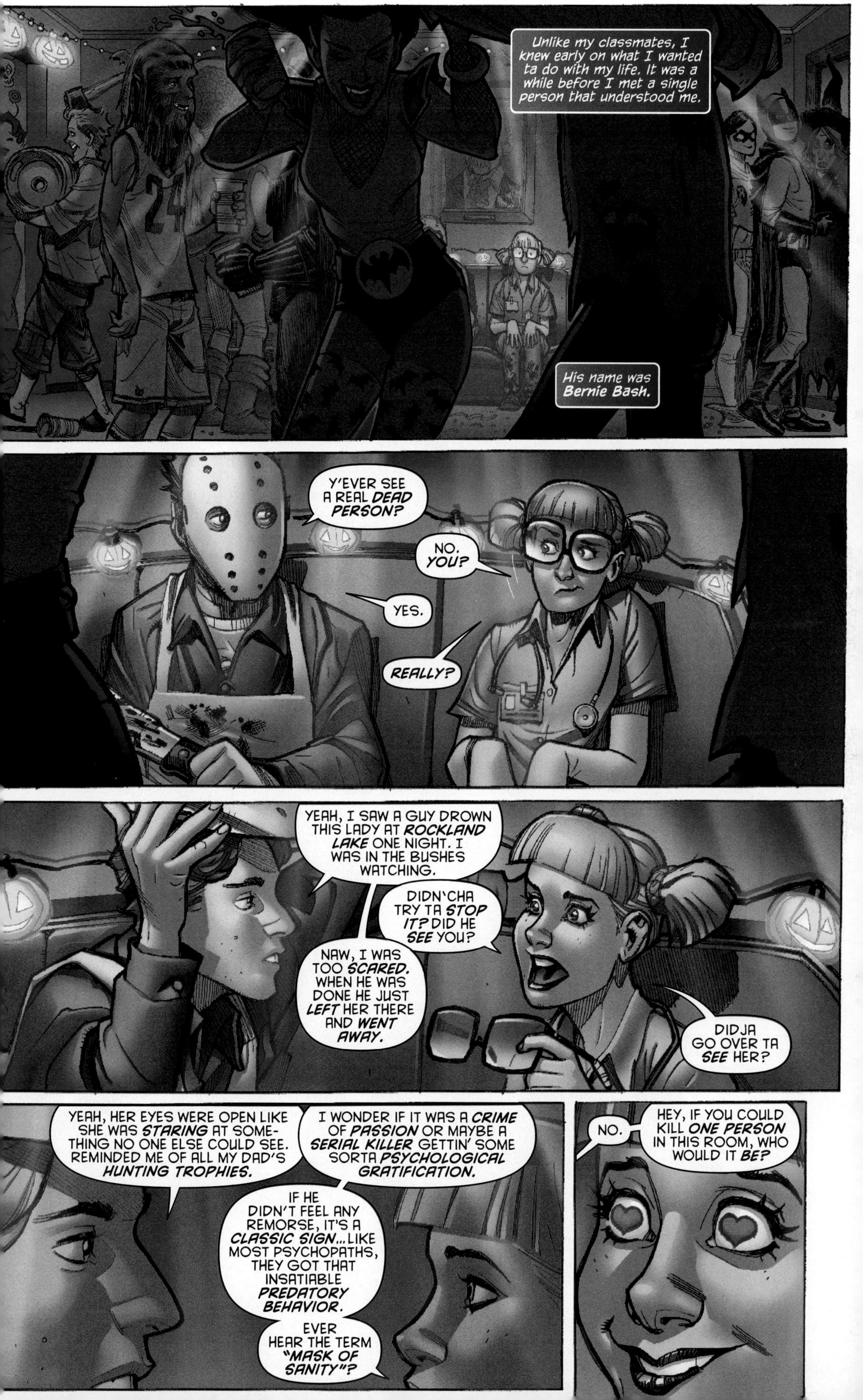
Unlike my classmates, I knew early on what I wanted ta do with my life. It was a while before I met a single person that understood me.
His name was Bernie Bash.
Y'EVER SEE A REAL DEAD PERSON?
NO. YOU?
YES.
REALLY?
YEAH, I SAW A GUY DROWN THIS LADY AT ROCKLAND LAKE ONE NIGHT. I WAS IN THE BUSHES WATCHING.
DIDN'CHA TRY TA STOP IT? DID HE SEE YOU?
NAW, I WAS TOO SCARED. WHEN HE WAS DONE HE JUST LEFT HER THERE AND WENT AWAY.
DIDJA GO OVER TA SEE HER?
YEAH, HER EYES WERE OPEN LIKE SHE WAS STARING AT SOME-THING NO ONE ELSE COULD SEE. REMINDED ME OF ALL MY DAD'S HUNTING TROPHIES.
I WONDER IF IT WAS A CRIME OF PASSION OR MAYBE A SERIAL KILLER GETTIN' SOME SORTA PSYCHOLOGICAL GRATIFICATION.
IF HE DIDN'T FEEL ANY REMORSE, IT'S A CLASSIC SIGN... LIKE MOST PSYCHOPATHS, THEY GOT THAT INSATIABLE PREDATORY BEHAVIOR.
EVER HEAR THE TERM "MASK OF SANITY"?
NO.
HEY, IF YOU COULD KILL ONE PERSON IN THIS ROOM, WHO WOULD IT BE?

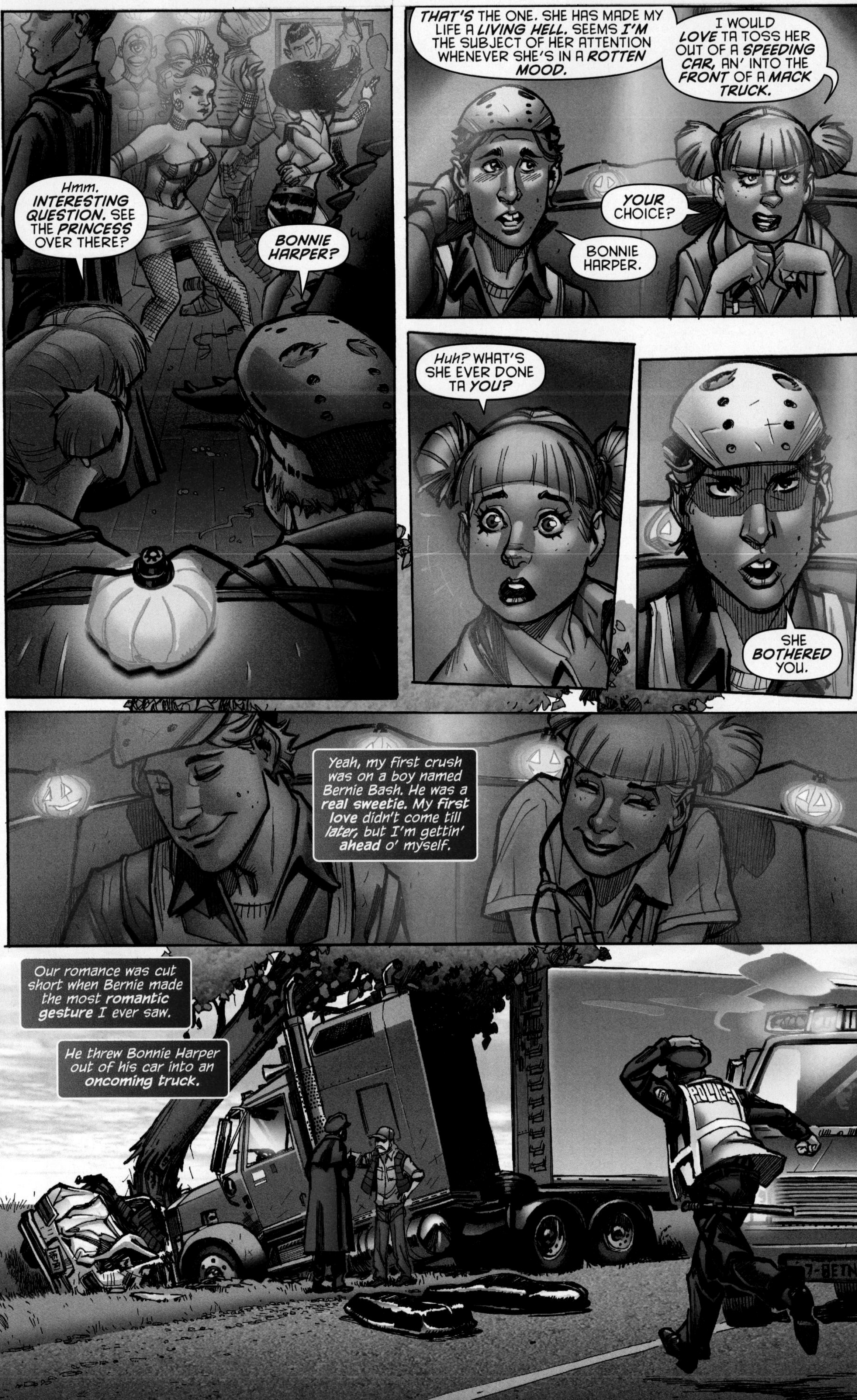

Hmm. INTERESTING QUESTION. SEE THE PRINCESS OVER THERE?
BONNIE HARPER?
THAT'S THE ONE. SHE HAS MADE MY LIFE A LIVING HELL. SEEMS I'M THE SUBJECT OF HER ATTENTION WHENEVER SHE'S IN A ROTTEN MOOD.
I WOULD LOVE TA TOSS HER OUT OF A SPEEDING CAR, AN' INTO THE FRONT OF A MACK TRUCK.
YOUR CHOICE?
BONNIE HARPER.
Huh? WHAT'S SHE EVER DONE TA YOU?
SHE BOTHERED YOU.
Yeah, my first crush was on a boy named Bernie Bash. He was a real sweetie. My first love didn't come till later, but I'm gettin' ahead o' myself.
Our romance was cut short when Bernie made the most romantic gesture I ever saw.
He threw Bonnie Harper out of his car into an oncoming truck.
POLICE

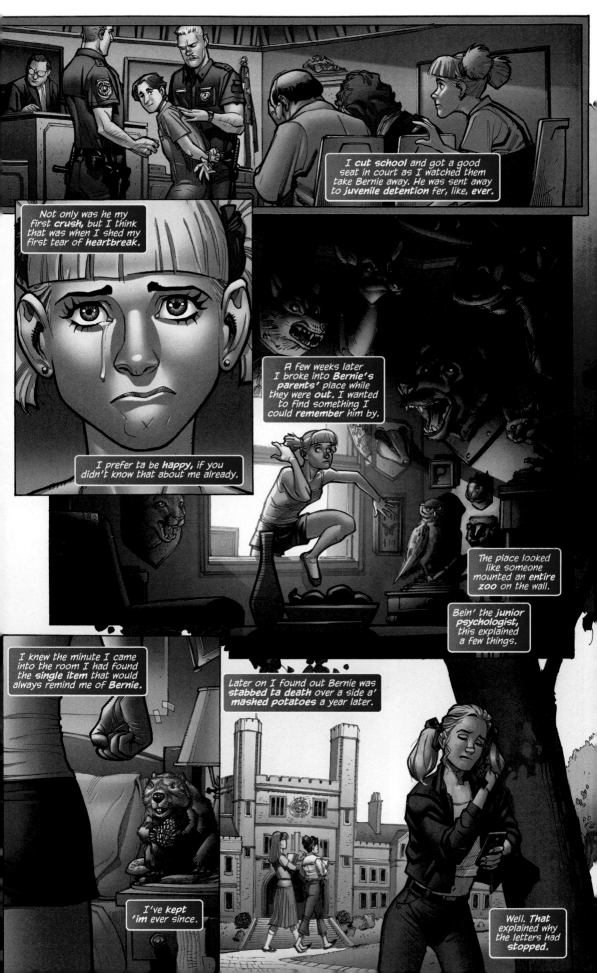

I **cut school** and got a good seat in court as I watched them take Bernie away. He was sent away to **juvenile detention** fer, like, ever.

Not only was he my first **crush**, but I think that was when I shed my first tear of **heartbreak**.

I prefer ta be **happy**, if you didn't know that about me already.

A few weeks later I broke into **Bernie's parents'** place while they were **out**. I wanted to find something I could **remember** him by.

The place looked like someone mounted an entire **zoo** on the wall.

Bein' the junior **psychologist**, this explained a few things.

I knew the minute I came into the room I had found the **single item** that would always remind me of **Bernie**.

Later on I found out Bernie was **stabbed ta death** over a side a' **mashed potatoes** a year later.

I've kept 'im ever since.

Well. **That** explained why the letters had **stopped**.

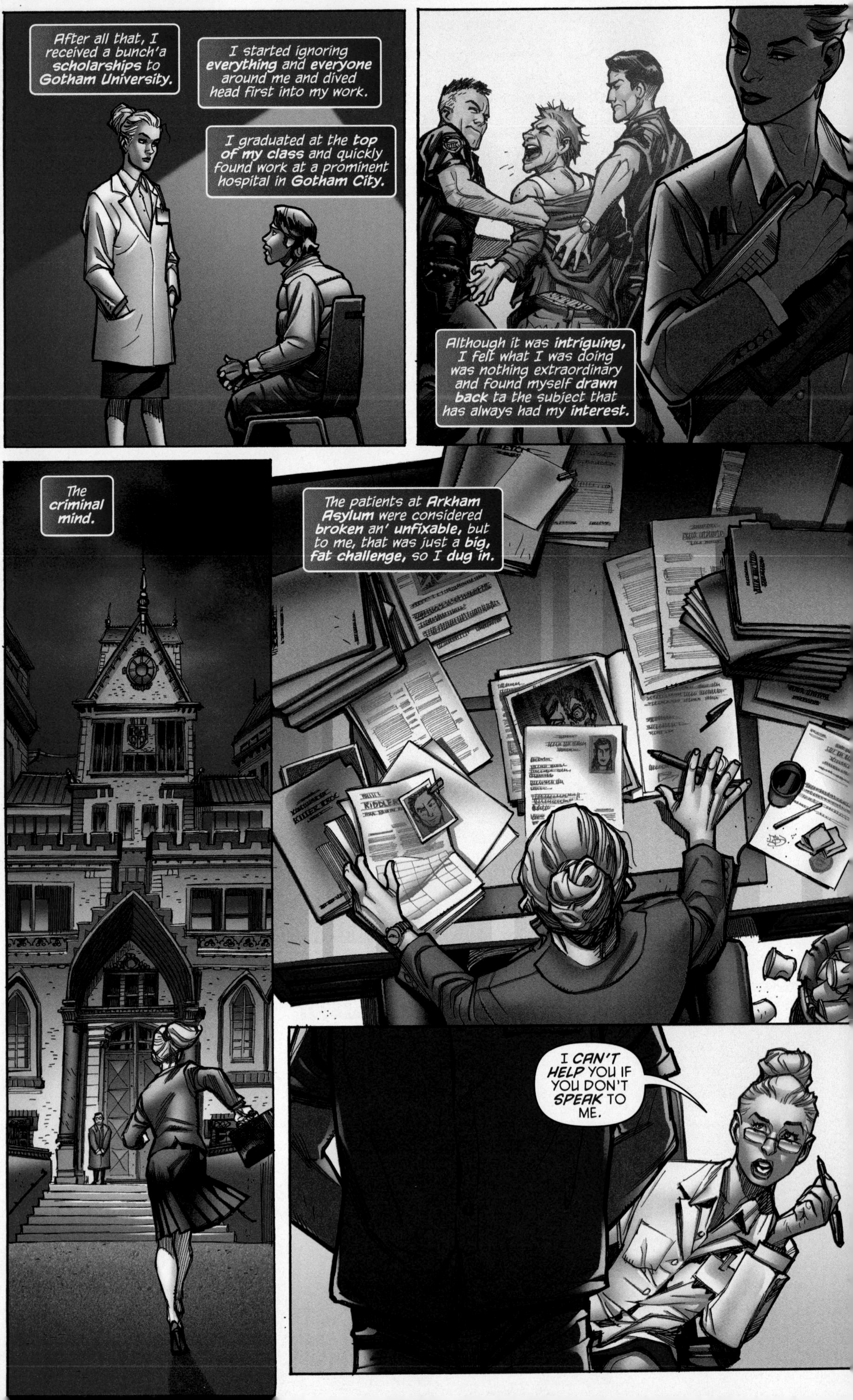
After all that, I received a bunch'a scholarships to Gotham University.
I started ignoring everything and everyone around me and dived head first into my work.
I graduated at the top of my class and quickly found work at a prominent hospital in Gotham City.
Although it was intriguing, I felt what I was doing was nothing extraordinary and found myself drawn back ta the subject that has always had my interest.
The criminal mind.
The patients at Arkham Asylum were considered broken an' unfixable, but to me, that was just a big, fat challenge, so I dug in.
I CAN'T HELP YOU IF YOU DON'T SPEAK TO ME.

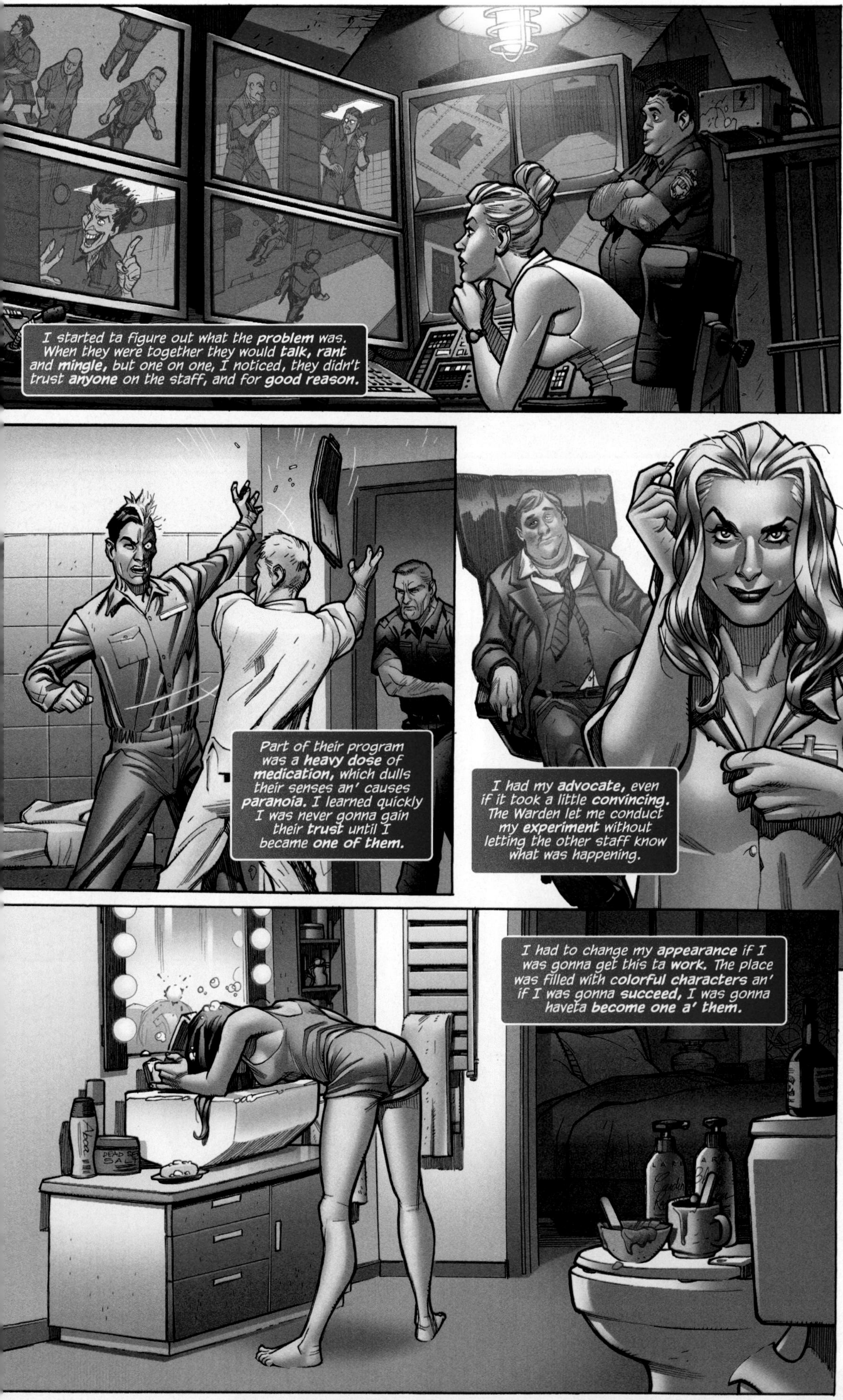
I started ta figure out what the problem was. When they were together they would talk, rant and mingle, but one on one, I noticed, they didn't trust anyone on the staff, and for good reason.
Part of their program was a heavy dose of medication, which dulls their senses an' causes paranoia. I learned quickly I was never gonna gain their trust until I became one of them.
I had my advocate, even if it took a little convincing. The Warden let me conduct my experiment without letting the other staff know what was happening.
I had to change my appearance if I was gonna get this ta work. The place was filled with colorful characters an' if I was gonna succeed, I was gonna haveta become one a' them.

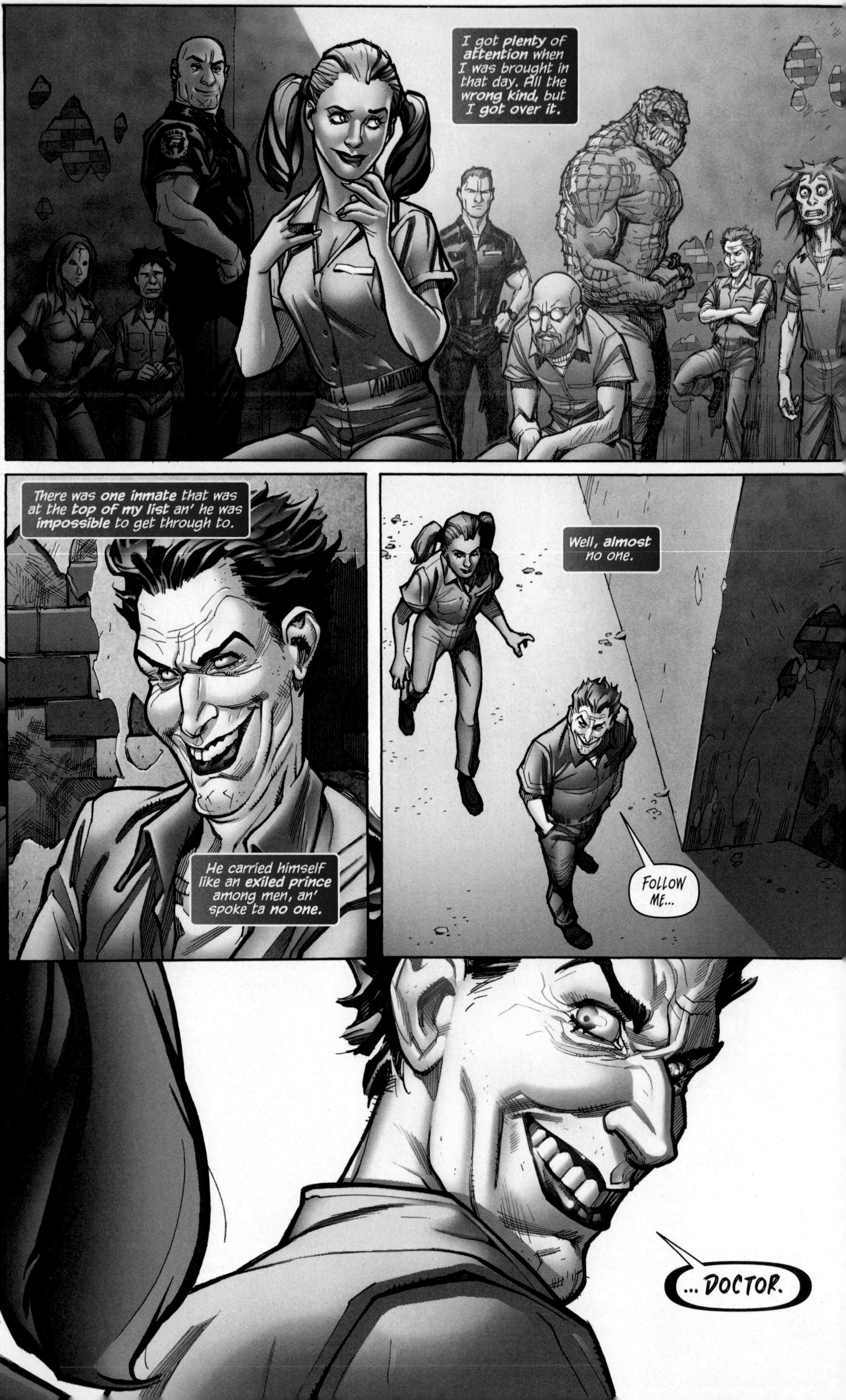
I got plenty of attention when I was brought in that day. All the wrong kind, but I got over it.
There was one inmate that was at the top of my list an' he was impossible to get through to.
He carried himself like an exiled prince among men, an' spoke ta no one.
Well, almost no one.
FOLLOW ME...
...DOCTOR.

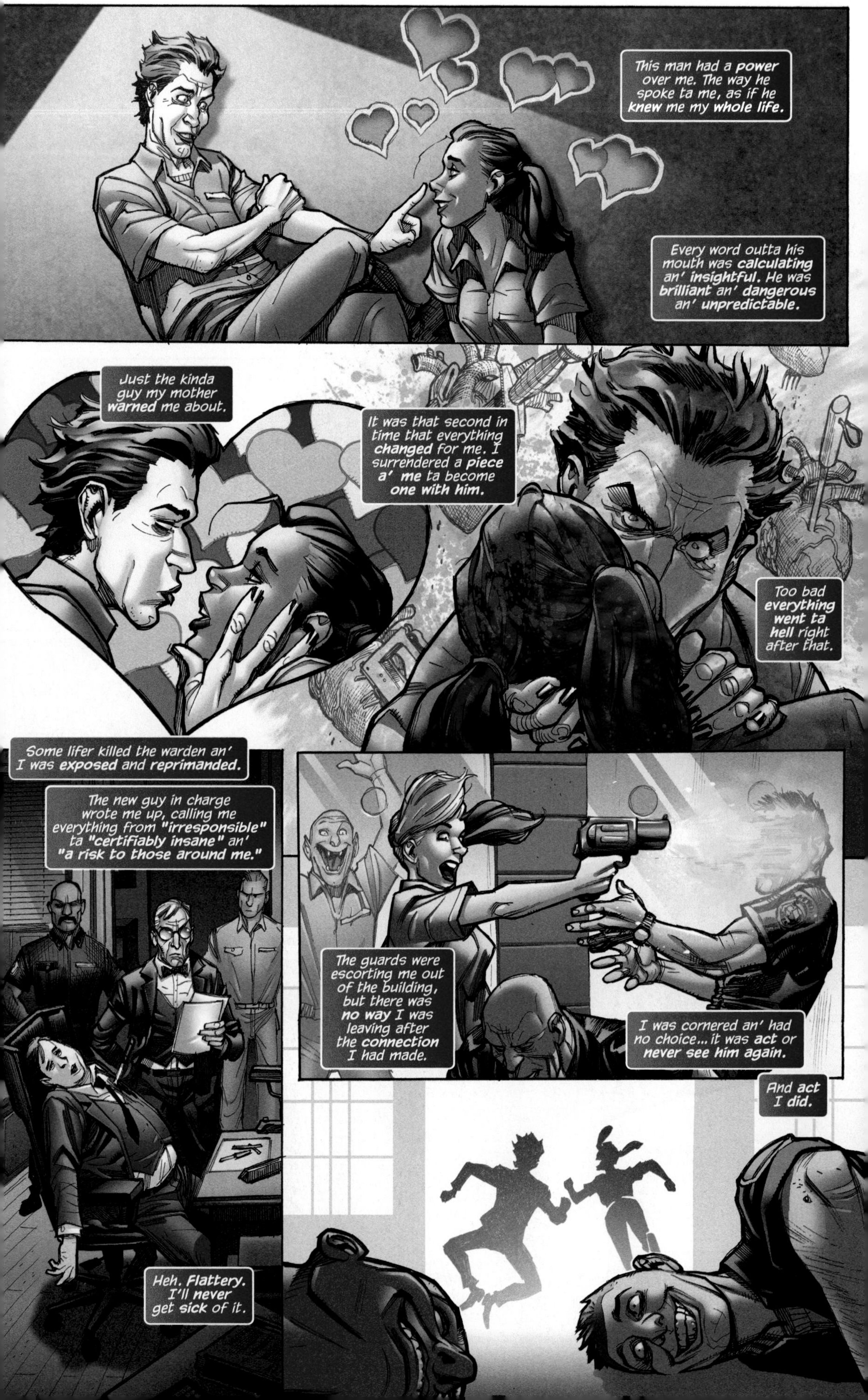
This man had a power over me. The way he spoke ta me, as if he knew me my whole life.
Every word outta his mouth was calculating an' insightful. He was brilliant an' dangerous an' unpredictable.
Just the kinda guy my mother warned me about.
It was that second in time that everything changed for me. I surrendered a piece a' me ta become one with him.
Too bad everything went ta hell right after that.
Some lifer killed the warden an' I was exposed and reprimanded.
The new guy in charge wrote me up, calling me everything from "irresponsible" ta "certifiably insane" an' "a risk to those around me."
Heh. Flattery. I'll never get sick of it.
The guards were escorting me out of the building, but there was no way I was leaving after the connection I had made.
I was cornered an' had no choice... it was act or never see him again.
And act I did.

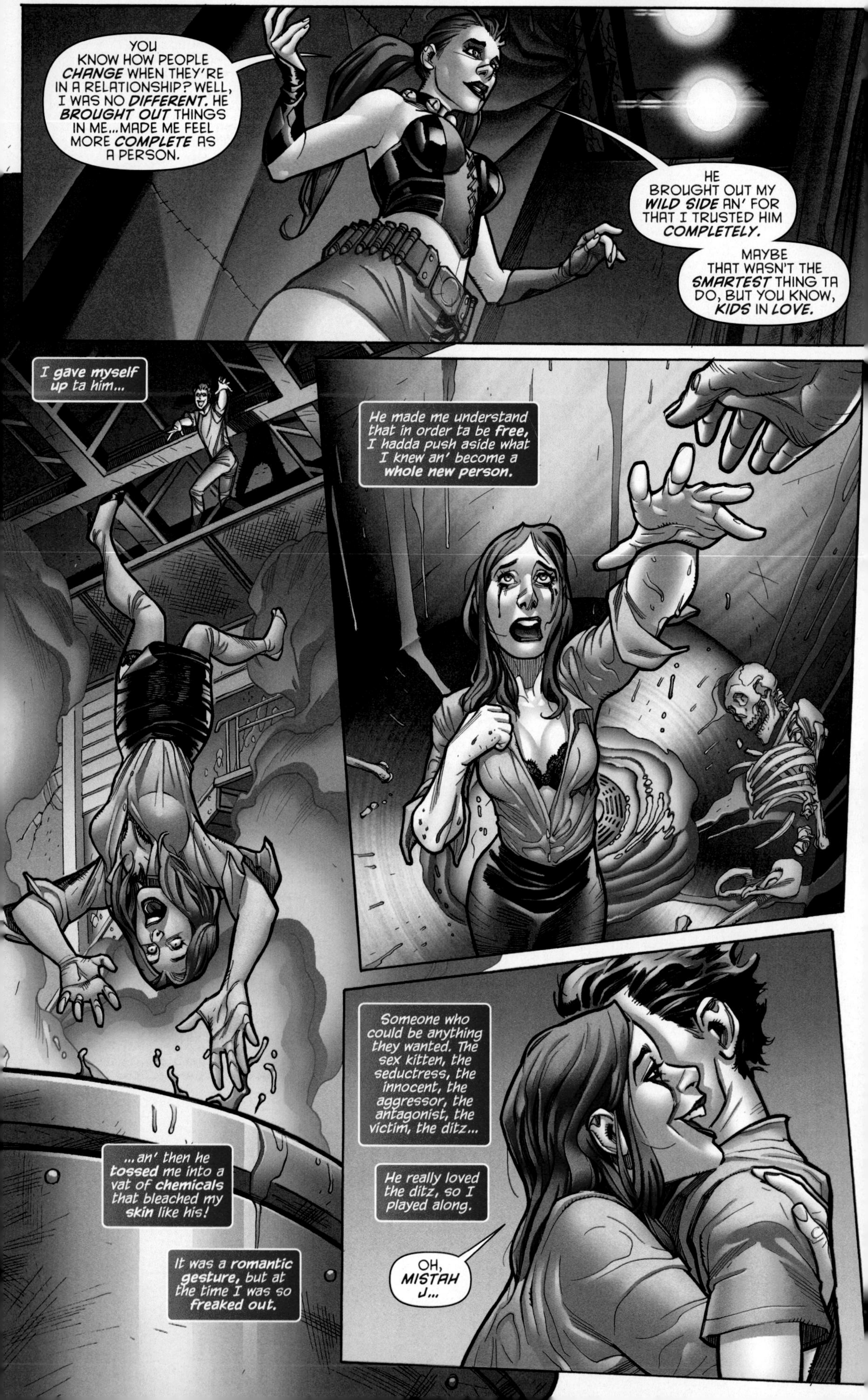
YOU KNOW HOW PEOPLE CHANGE WHEN THEY'RE IN A RELATIONSHIP? WELL, I WAS NO DIFFERENT. HE BROUGHT OUT THINGS IN ME...MADE ME FEEL MORE COMPLETE AS A PERSON.
HE BROUGHT OUT MY WILD SIDE AN' FOR THAT I TRUSTED HIM COMPLETELY.
MAYBE THAT WASN'T THE SMARTEST THING TA DO, BUT YOU KNOW, KIDS IN LOVE.
I gave myself up ta him...
...an' then he tossed me into a vat of chemicals that bleached my skin like his!
It was a romantic gesture, but at the time I was so freaked out.
He made me understand that in order ta be free, I hadda push aside what I knew an' become a whole new person.
Someone who could be anything they wanted. The sex kitten, the seductress, the innocent, the aggressor, the antagonist, the victim, the ditz...
He really loved the ditz, so I played along.
OH, MISTAH J...

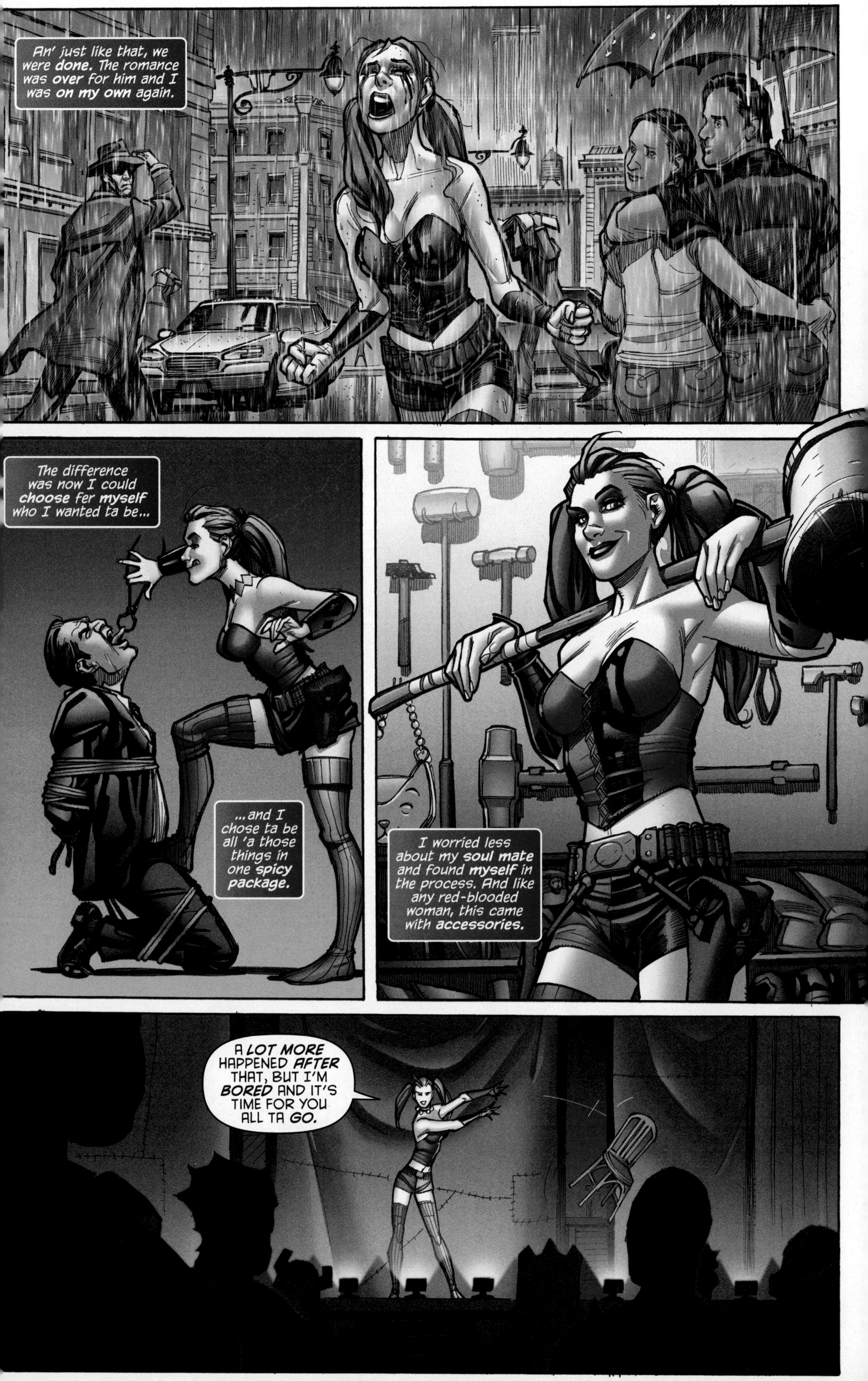
An' just like that, we were done. The romance was over for him and I was on my own again.
The difference was now I could choose fer myself who I wanted ta be...
...and I chose ta be all 'a those things in one spicy package.
I worried less about my soul mate and found myself in the process. And like any red-blooded woman, this came with accessories.
A LOT MORE HAPPENED AFTER THAT, BUT I'M BORED AND IT'S TIME FOR YOU ALL TA GO.

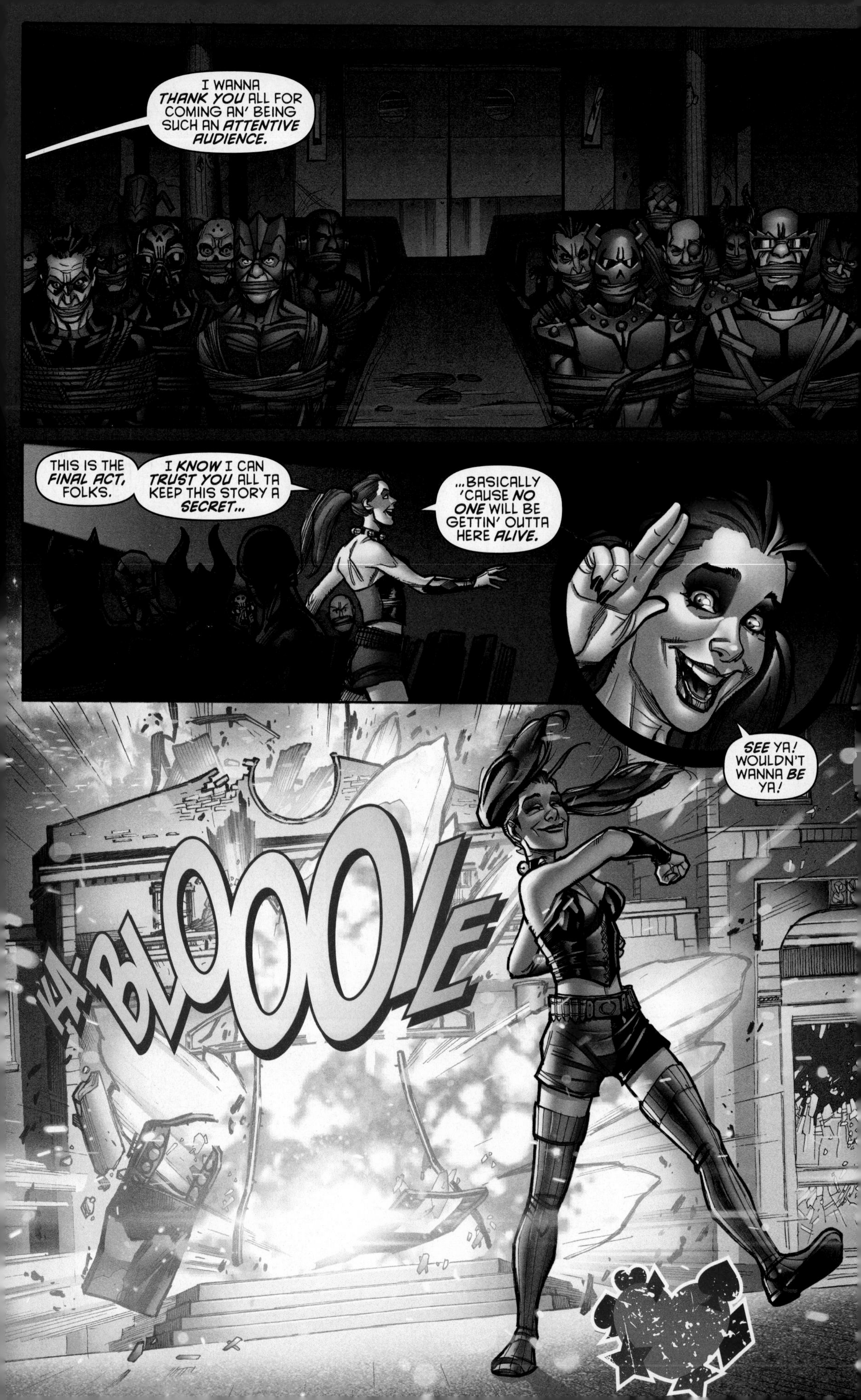
I WANNA THANK YOU ALL FOR COMING AN' BEING SUCH AN ATTENTIVE AUDIENCE.
THIS IS THE FINAL ACT, FOLKS.
I KNOW I CAN TRUST YOU ALL TA KEEP THIS STORY A SECRET...
...BASICALLY 'CAUSE NO ONE WILL BE GETTIN' OUTTA HERE ALIVE.
SEE YA! WOULDN'T WANNA BE YA!
KA-BLOOOIE

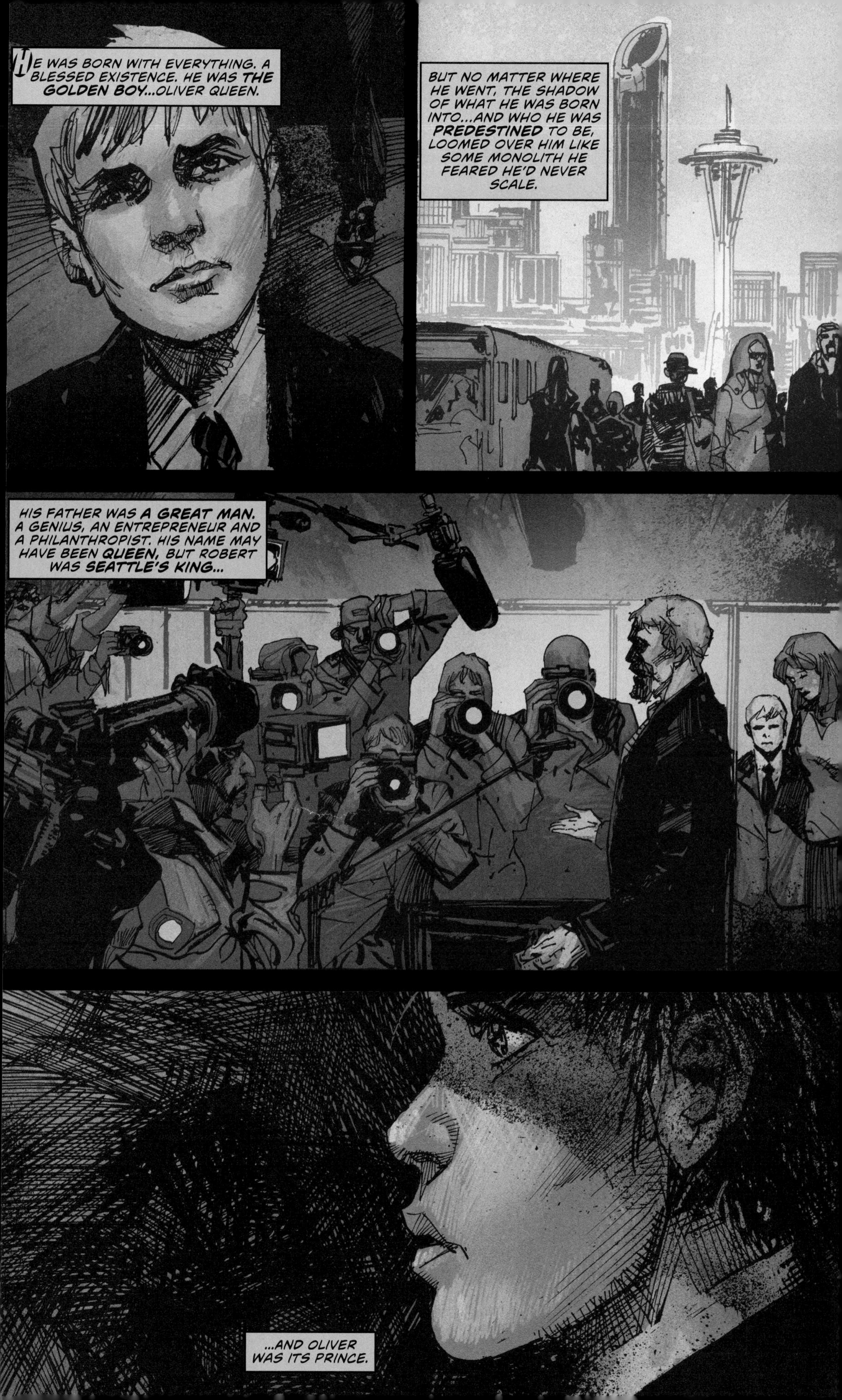
HE WAS BORN WITH EVERYTHING. A BLESSED EXISTENCE. HE WAS THE GOLDEN BOY...OLIVER QUEEN.
BUT NO MATTER WHERE HE WENT, THE SHADOW OF WHAT HE WAS BORN INTO...AND WHO HE WAS PREDESTINED TO BE, LOOMED OVER HIM LIKE SOME MONOLITH HE FEARED HE'D NEVER SCALE.
HIS FATHER WAS A GREAT MAN. A GENIUS, AN ENTREPRENEUR AND A PHILANTHROPIST. HIS NAME MAY HAVE BEEN QUEEN, BUT ROBERT WAS SEATTLE'S KING...
...AND OLIVER WAS ITS PRINCE.

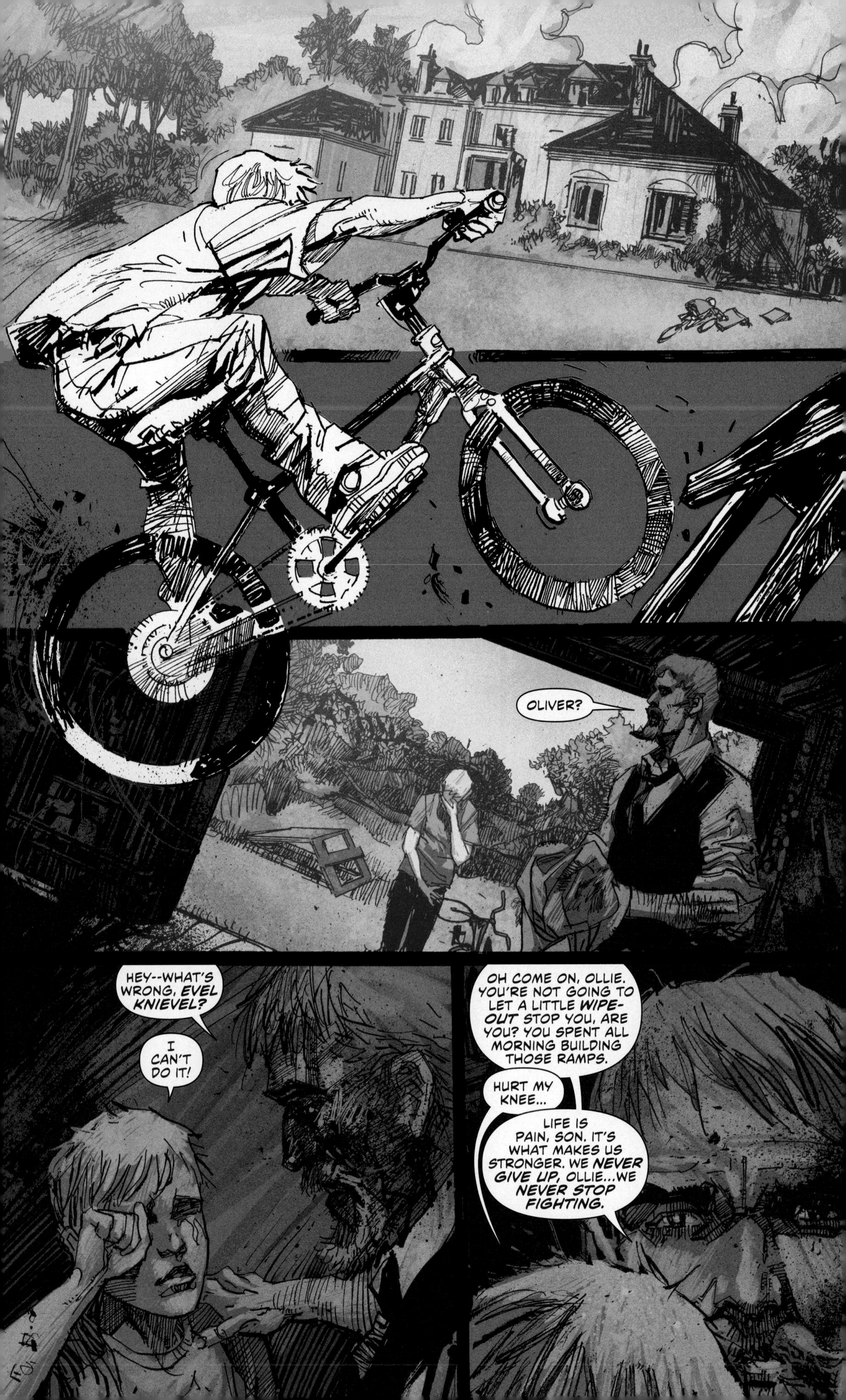
OLIVER?
HEY--WHAT'S WRONG, EVEL KNIEVEL?
I CAN'T DO IT!
OH COME ON, OLLIE. YOU'RE NOT GOING TO LET A LITTLE WIPE-OUT STOP YOU, ARE YOU? YOU SPENT ALL MORNING BUILDING THOSE RAMPS.
HURT MY KNEE...
LIFE IS PAIN, SON. IT'S WHAT MAKES US STRONGER. WE NEVER GIVE UP, OLLIE...WE NEVER STOP FIGHTING.

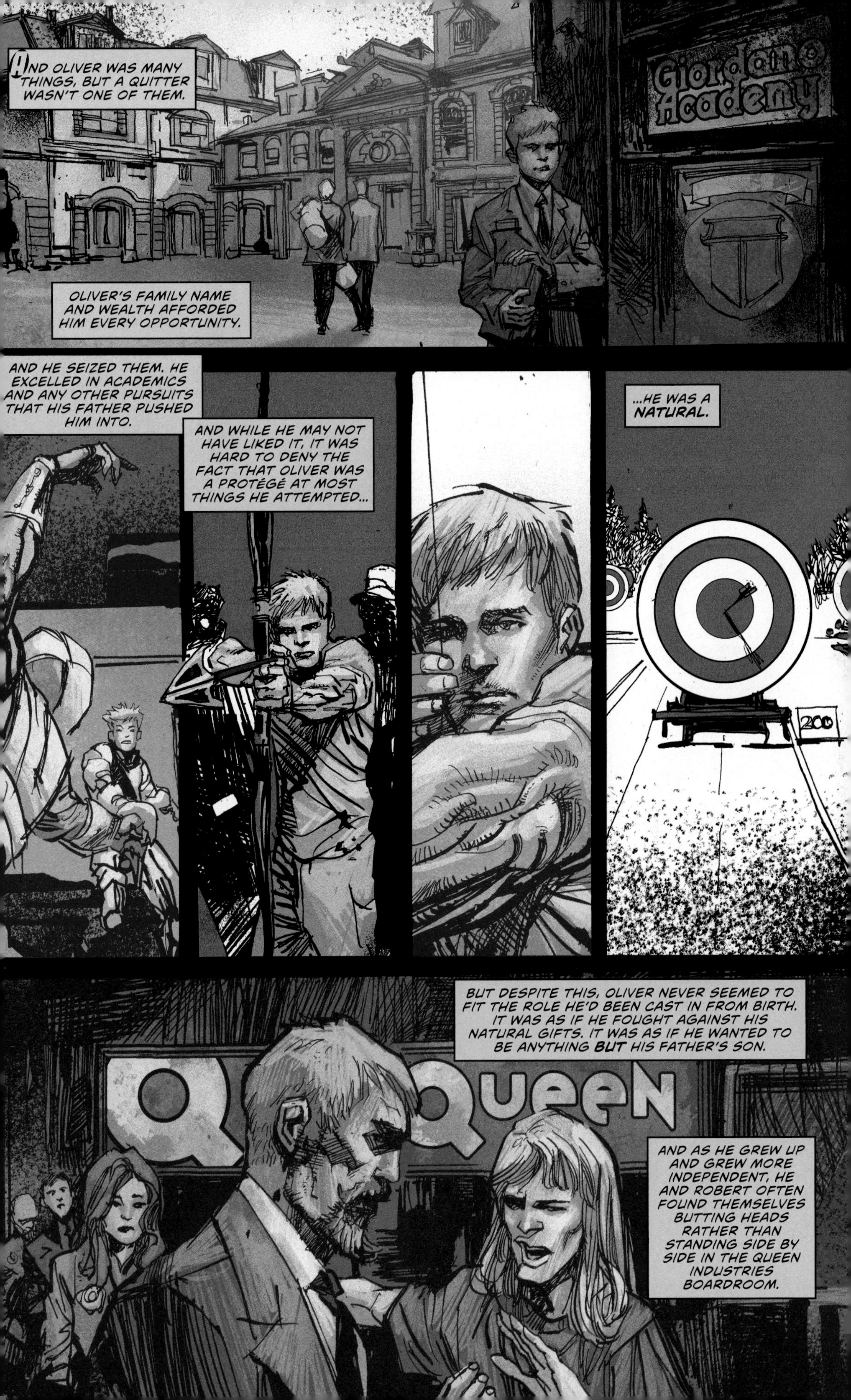
AND OLIVER WAS MANY THINGS, BUT A QUITTER WASN'T ONE OF THEM.
Giordano Academy
OLIVER'S FAMILY NAME AND WEALTH AFFORDED HIM EVERY OPPORTUNITY.
AND HE SEIZED THEM. HE EXCELLED IN ACADEMICS AND ANY OTHER PURSUITS THAT HIS FATHER PUSHED HIM INTO.
AND WHILE HE MAY NOT HAVE LIKED IT, IT WAS HARD TO DENY THE FACT THAT OLIVER WAS A PROTÉGÉ AT MOST THINGS HE ATTEMPTED...
...HE WAS A NATURAL.
200
BUT DESPITE THIS, OLIVER NEVER SEEMED TO FIT THE ROLE HE'D BEEN CAST IN FROM BIRTH. IT WAS AS IF HE FOUGHT AGAINST HIS NATURAL GIFTS. IT WAS AS IF HE WANTED TO BE ANYTHING BUT HIS FATHER'S SON.
Queen
AND AS HE GREW UP AND GREW MORE INDEPENDENT, HE AND ROBERT OFTEN FOUND THEMSELVES BUTTING HEADS RATHER THAN STANDING SIDE BY SIDE IN THE QUEEN INDUSTRIES BOARDROOM.

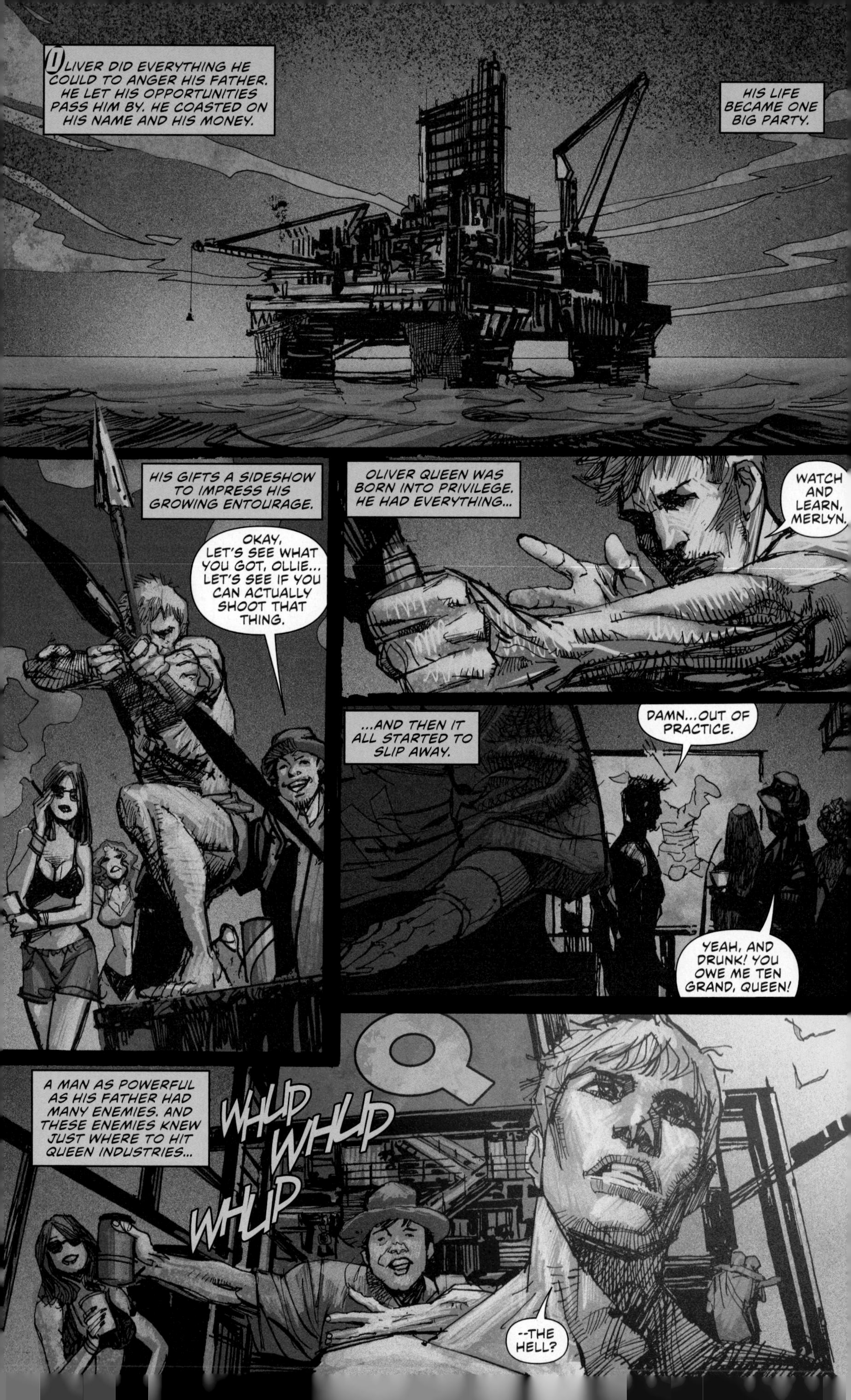
OLIVER DID EVERYTHING HE COULD TO ANGER HIS FATHER. HE LET HIS OPPORTUNITIES PASS HIM BY. HE COASTED ON HIS NAME AND HIS MONEY.
HIS LIFE BECAME ONE BIG PARTY.
HIS GIFTS A SIDESHOW TO IMPRESS HIS GROWING ENTOURAGE.
OKAY, LET'S SEE WHAT YOU GOT, OLLIE... LET'S SEE IF YOU CAN ACTUALLY SHOOT THAT THING.
OLIVER QUEEN WAS BORN INTO PRIVILEGE. HE HAD EVERYTHING...
WATCH AND LEARN, MERLYN.
...AND THEN IT ALL STARTED TO SLIP AWAY.
DAMN...OUT OF PRACTICE.
YEAH, AND DRUNK! YOU OWE ME TEN GRAND, QUEEN!
A MAN AS POWERFUL AS HIS FATHER HAD MANY ENEMIES. AND THESE ENEMIES KNEW JUST WHERE TO HIT QUEEN INDUSTRIES...
WHUP WHUP
WHUP
--THE HELL?

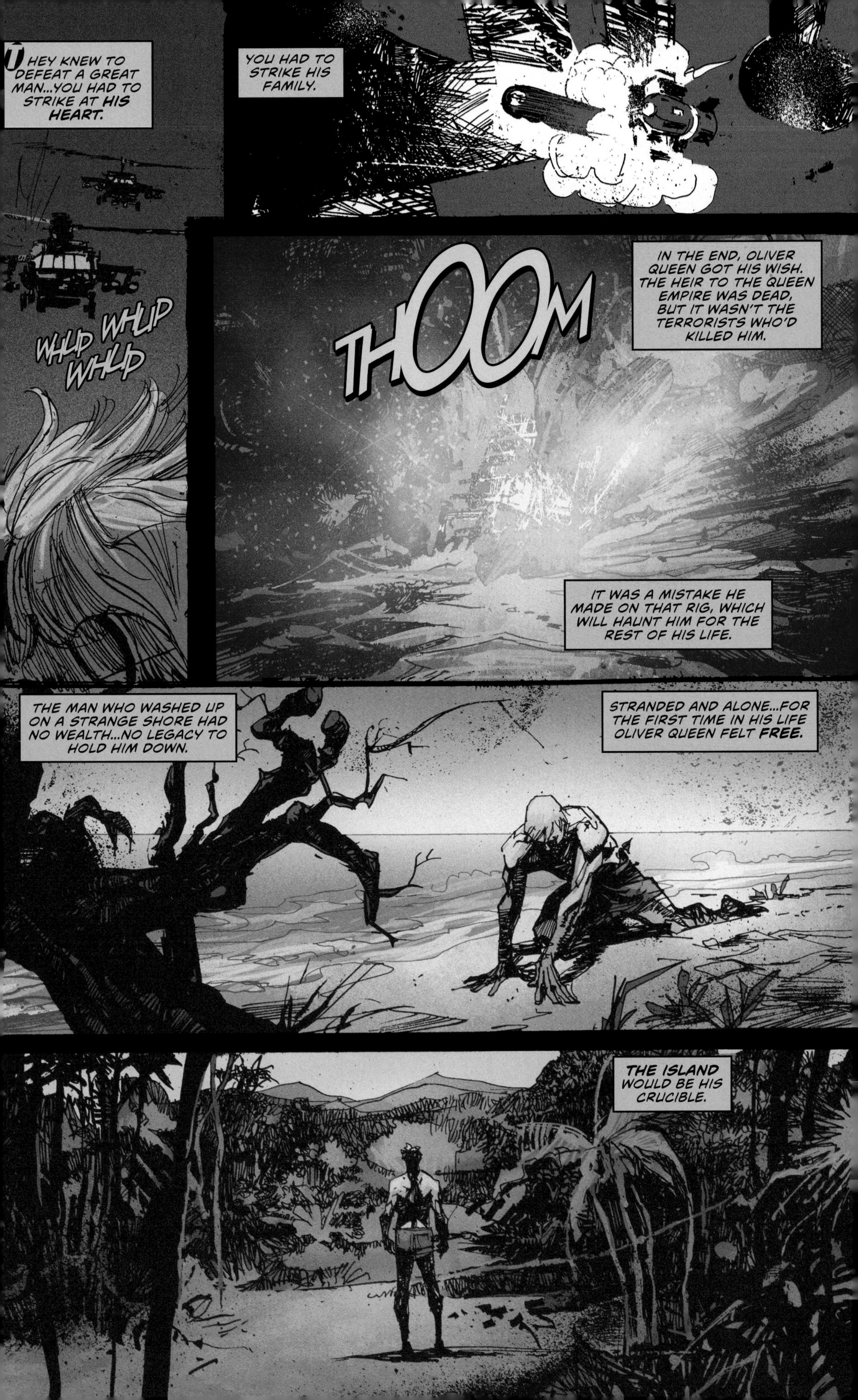
THEY KNEW TO DEFEAT A GREAT MAN...YOU HAD TO STRIKE AT **HIS HEART.**
YOU HAD TO STRIKE HIS FAMILY.
WHUP WHUP WHUP
THOOM
IN THE END, OLIVER QUEEN GOT HIS WISH. THE HEIR TO THE QUEEN EMPIRE WAS DEAD, BUT IT WASN'T THE TERRORISTS WHO'D KILLED HIM.
IT WAS A MISTAKE HE MADE ON THAT RIG, WHICH WILL HAUNT HIM FOR THE REST OF HIS LIFE.
THE MAN WHO WASHED UP ON A STRANGE SHORE HAD NO WEALTH...NO LEGACY TO HOLD HIM DOWN.
STRANDED AND ALONE...FOR THE FIRST TIME IN HIS LIFE OLIVER QUEEN FELT **FREE.**
THE ISLAND WOULD BE HIS CRUCIBLE.

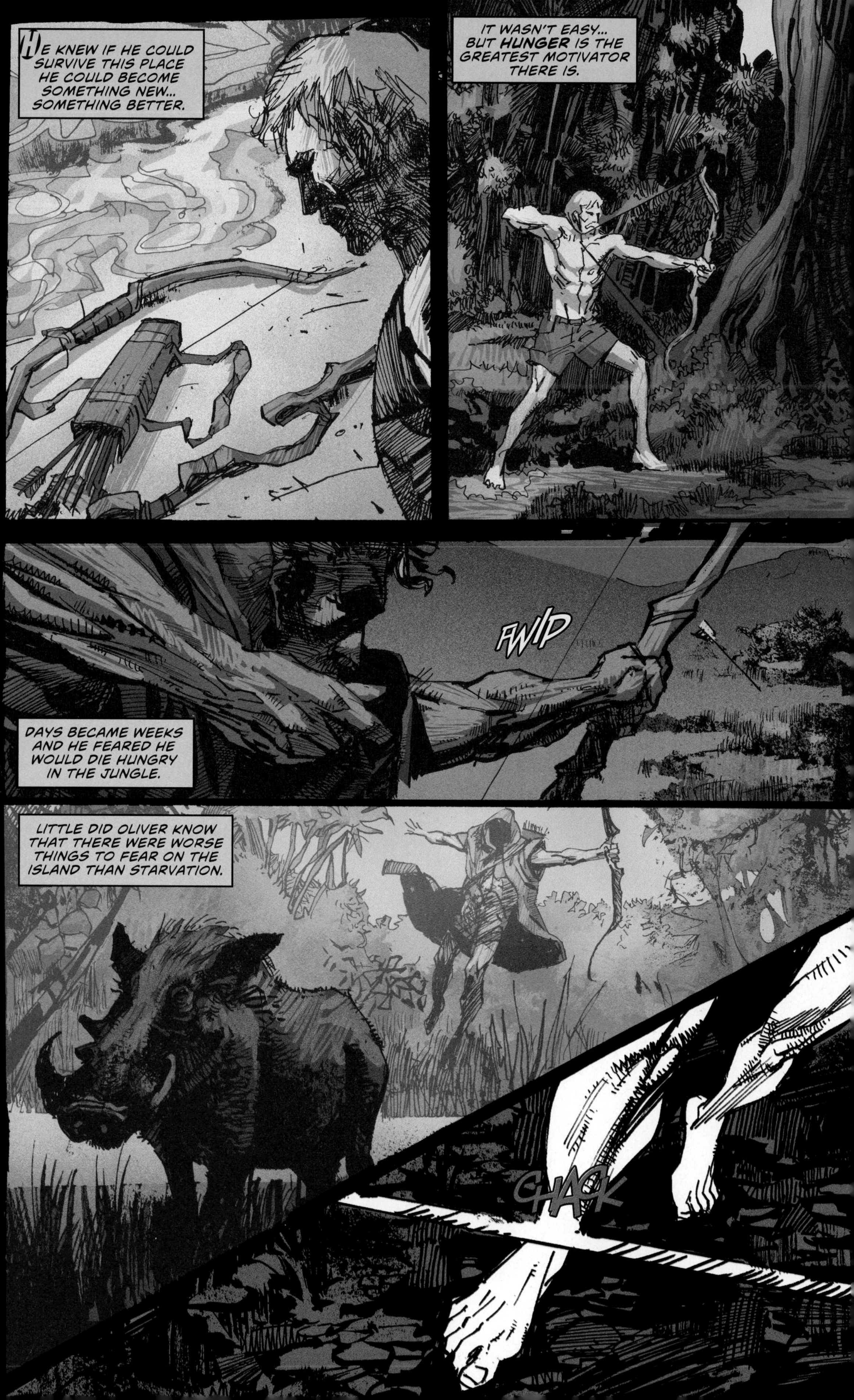
HE KNEW IF HE COULD SURVIVE THIS PLACE HE COULD BECOME SOMETHING NEW... SOMETHING BETTER.
IT WASN'T EASY... BUT **HUNGER** IS THE GREATEST MOTIVATOR THERE IS.
FWIP
DAYS BECAME WEEKS AND HE FEARED HE WOULD DIE HUNGRY IN THE JUNGLE.
LITTLE DID OLIVER KNOW THAT THERE WERE WORSE THINGS TO FEAR ON THE ISLAND THAN STARVATION.
CHACK

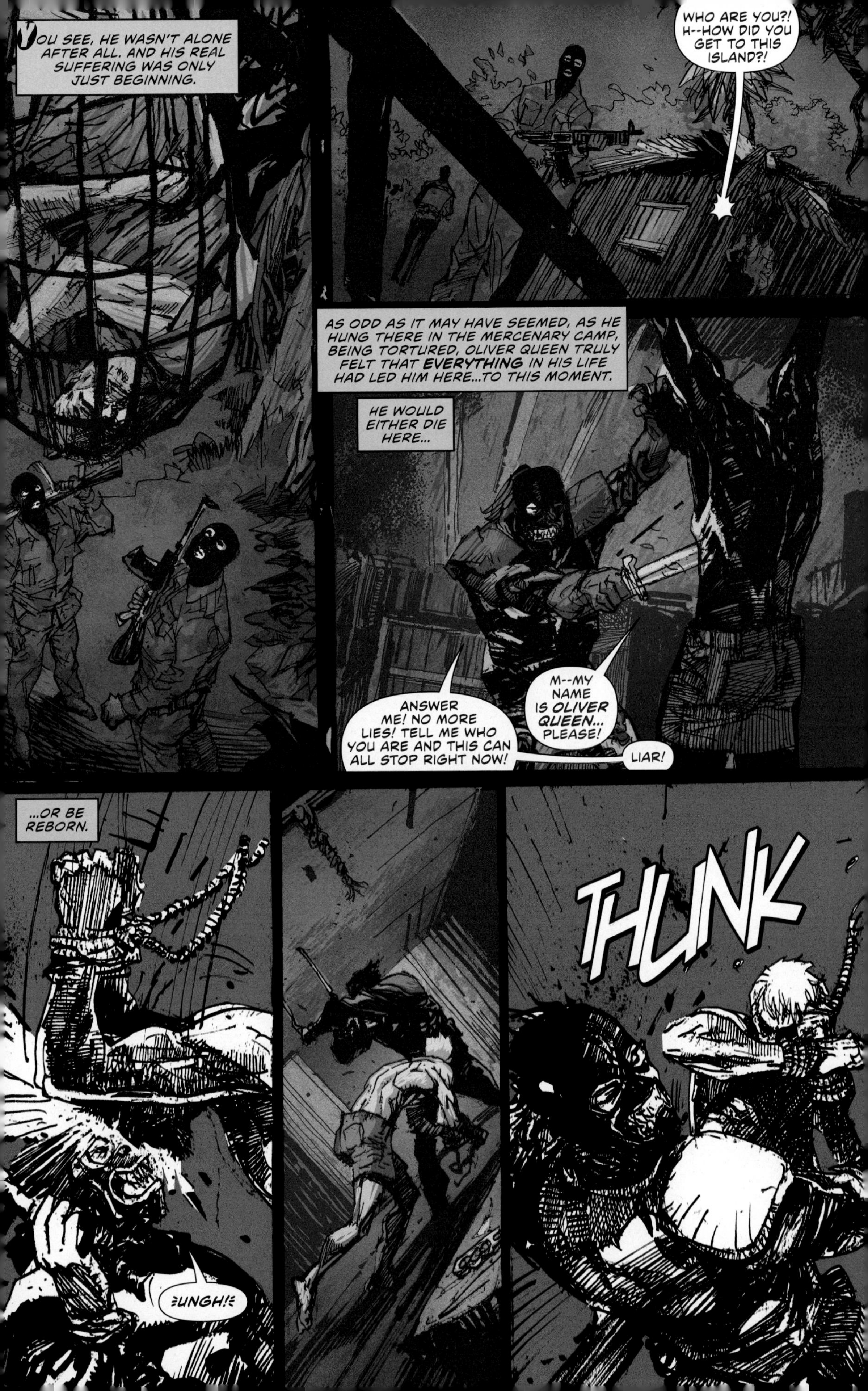
YOU SEE, HE WASN'T ALONE AFTER ALL. AND HIS REAL SUFFERING WAS ONLY JUST BEGINNING.
WHO ARE YOU?! H--HOW DID YOU GET TO THIS ISLAND?!
AS ODD AS IT MAY HAVE SEEMED, AS HE HUNG THERE IN THE MERCENARY CAMP, BEING TORTURED, OLIVER QUEEN TRULY FELT THAT EVERYTHING IN HIS LIFE HAD LED HIM HERE...TO THIS MOMENT.
HE WOULD EITHER DIE HERE...
ANSWER ME! NO MORE LIES! TELL ME WHO YOU ARE AND THIS CAN ALL STOP RIGHT NOW!
M--MY NAME IS OLIVER QUEEN... PLEASE!
LIAR!
...OR BE REBORN.
UNGH!
THUNK

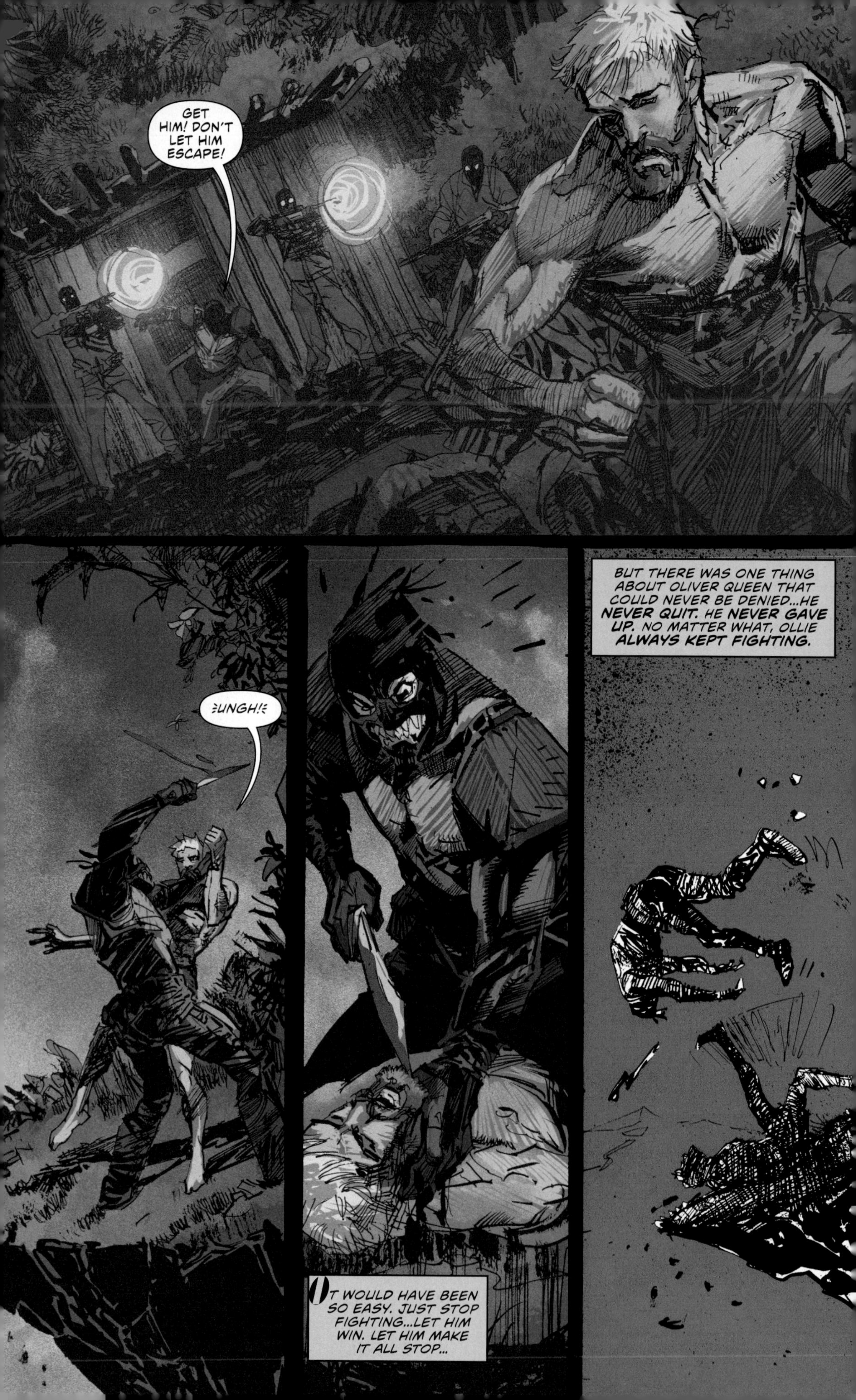
GET HIM! DON'T LET HIM ESCAPE!
UNGH!
IT WOULD HAVE BEEN SO EASY. JUST STOP FIGHTING...LET HIM WIN. LET HIM MAKE IT ALL STOP...
BUT THERE WAS ONE THING ABOUT OLIVER QUEEN THAT COULD NEVER BE DENIED...HE NEVER QUIT. HE NEVER GAVE UP. NO MATTER WHAT, OLLIE ALWAYS KEPT FIGHTING.

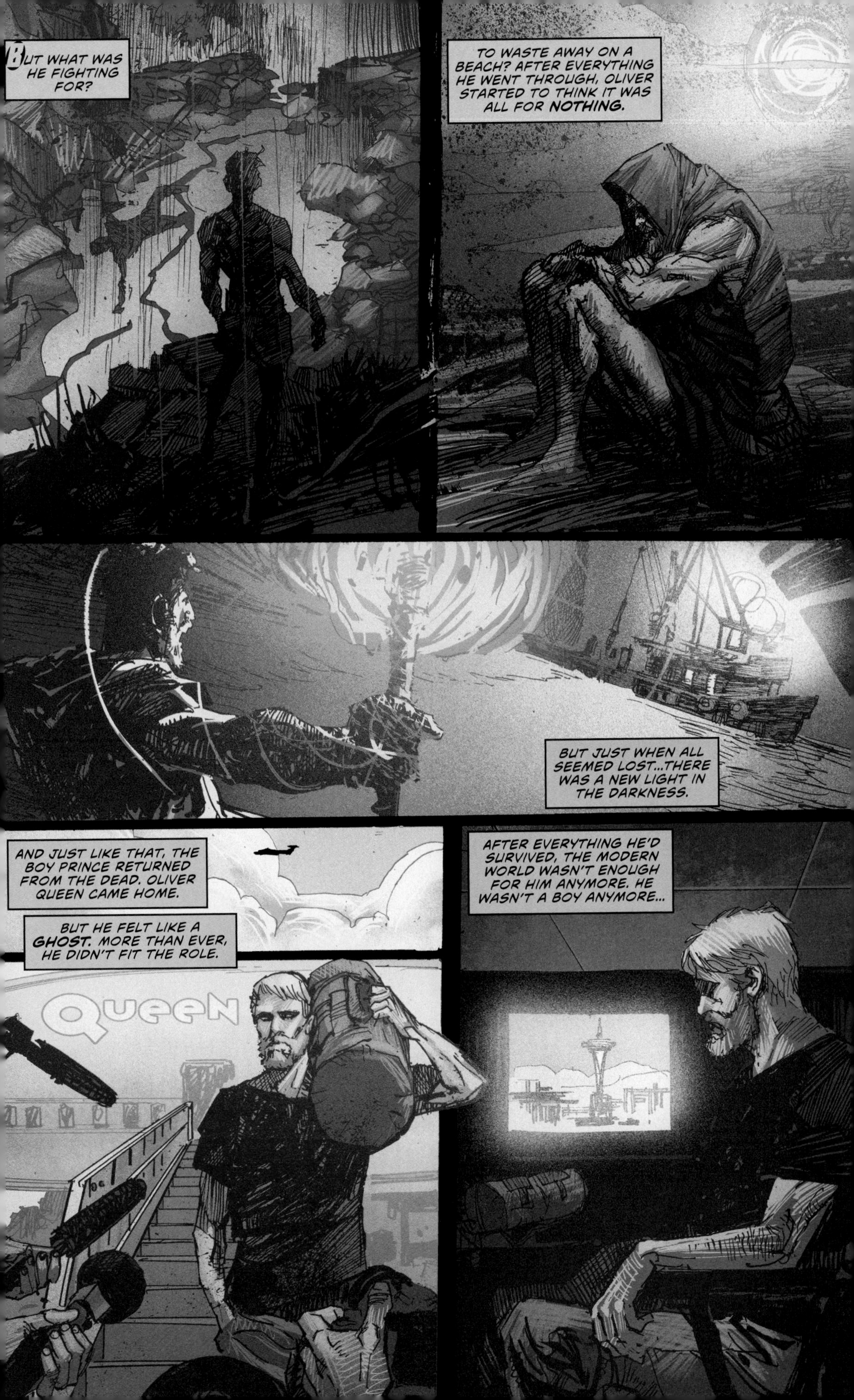
BUT WHAT WAS HE FIGHTING FOR?
TO WASTE AWAY ON A BEACH? AFTER EVERYTHING HE WENT THROUGH, OLIVER STARTED TO THINK IT WAS ALL FOR NOTHING.
BUT JUST WHEN ALL SEEMED LOST...THERE WAS A NEW LIGHT IN THE DARKNESS.
AND JUST LIKE THAT, THE BOY PRINCE RETURNED FROM THE DEAD. OLIVER QUEEN CAME HOME.
BUT HE FELT LIKE A GHOST. MORE THAN EVER, HE DIDN'T FIT THE ROLE.
QUEEN
AFTER EVERYTHING HE'D SURVIVED, THE MODERN WORLD WASN'T ENOUGH FOR HIM ANYMORE. HE WASN'T A BOY ANYMORE...

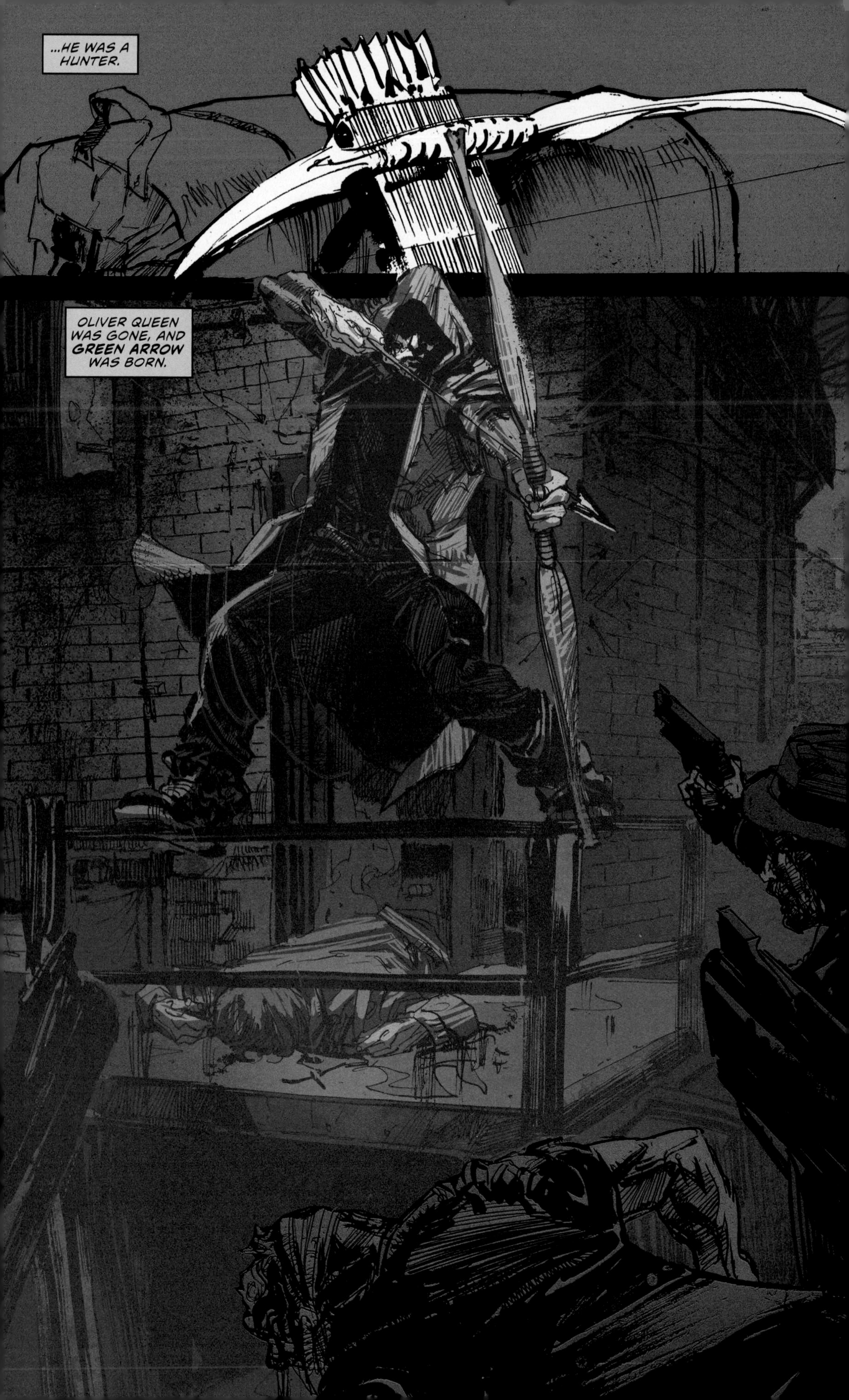
...HE WAS A HUNTER.
OLIVER QUEEN WAS GONE, AND **GREEN ARROW** WAS BORN.

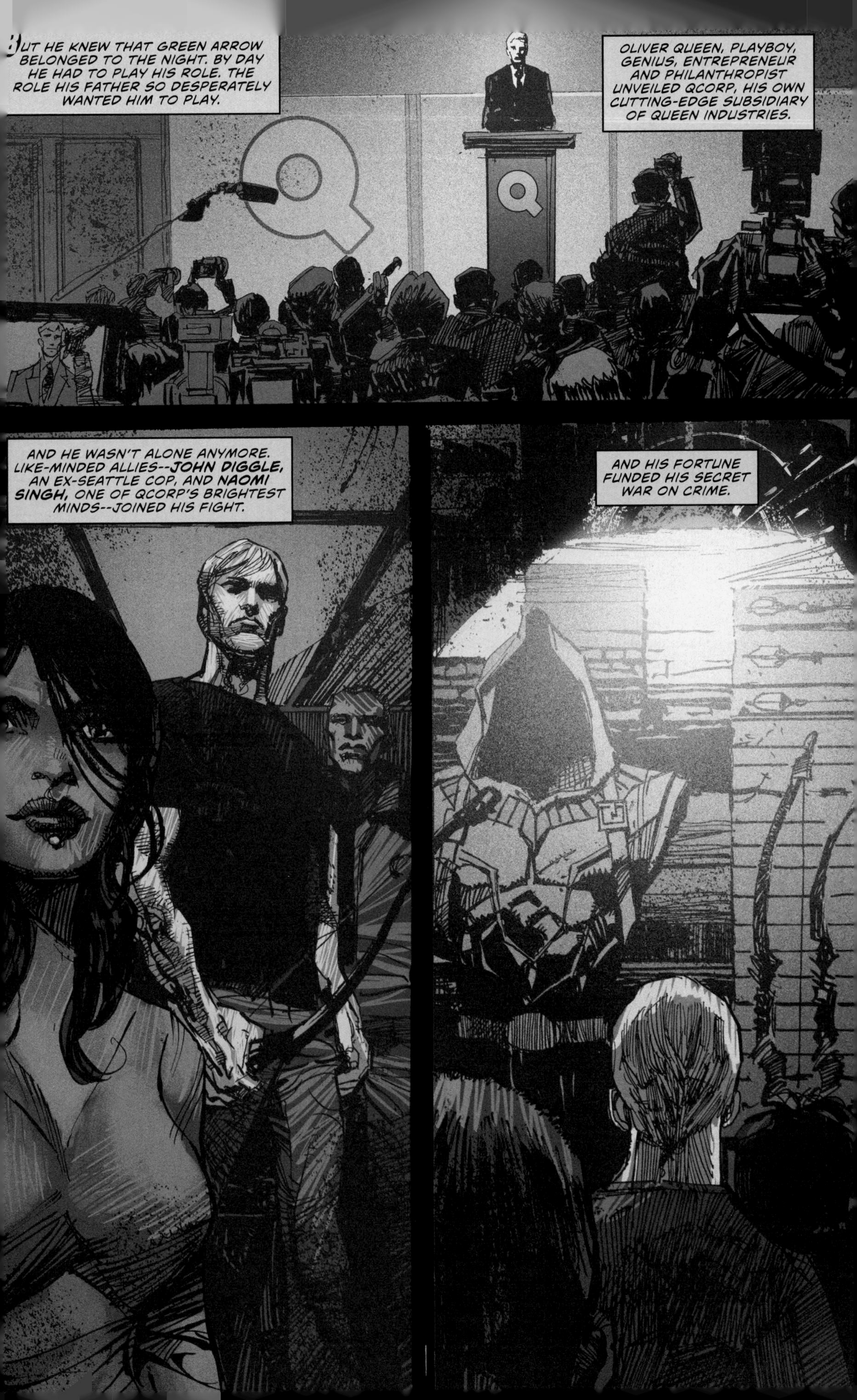
BUT HE KNEW THAT GREEN ARROW BELONGED TO THE NIGHT. BY DAY HE HAD TO PLAY HIS ROLE. THE ROLE HIS FATHER SO DESPERATELY WANTED HIM TO PLAY.
OLIVER QUEEN, PLAYBOY, GENIUS, ENTREPRENEUR AND PHILANTHROPIST UNVEILED QCORP, HIS OWN CUTTING-EDGE SUBSIDIARY OF QUEEN INDUSTRIES.
AND HE WASN'T ALONE ANYMORE. LIKE-MINDED ALLIES--JOHN DIGGLE, AN EX-SEATTLE COP, AND NAOMI SINGH, ONE OF QCORP'S BRIGHTEST MINDS--JOINED HIS FIGHT.
AND HIS FORTUNE FUNDED HIS SECRET WAR ON CRIME.

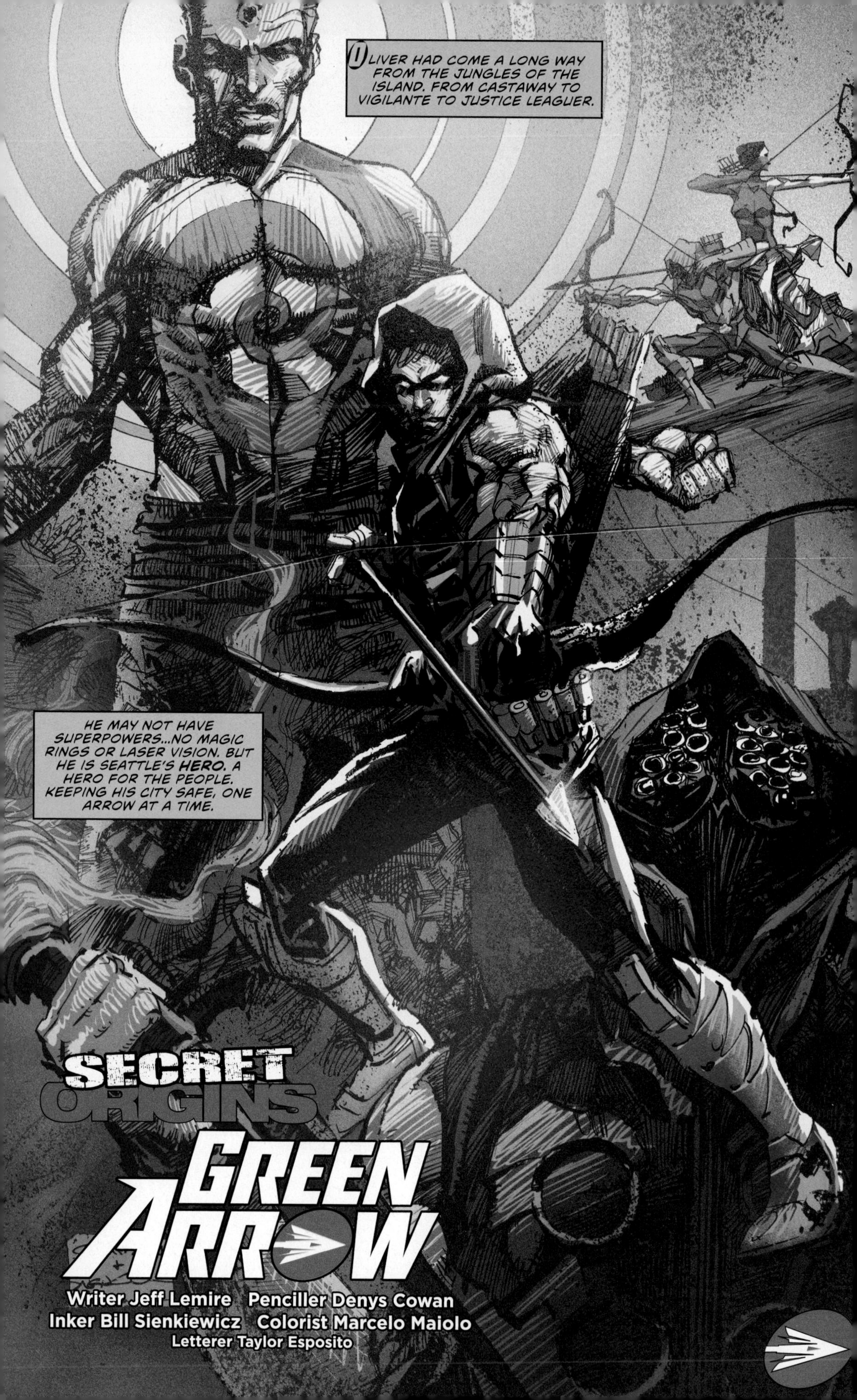
OLIVER HAD COME A LONG WAY FROM THE JUNGLES OF THE ISLAND. FROM CASTAWAY TO VIGILANTE TO JUSTICE LEAGUER.
HE MAY NOT HAVE SUPERPOWERS...NO MAGIC RINGS OR LASER VISION. BUT HE IS SEATTLE'S HERO. A HERO FOR THE PEOPLE. KEEPING HIS CITY SAFE, ONE ARROW AT A TIME.
SECRET ORIGINS
GREEN ARROW
Writer Jeff Lemire Penciller Denys Cowan
Inker Bill Sienkiewicz Colorist Marcelo Maiolo
Letterer Taylor Esposito

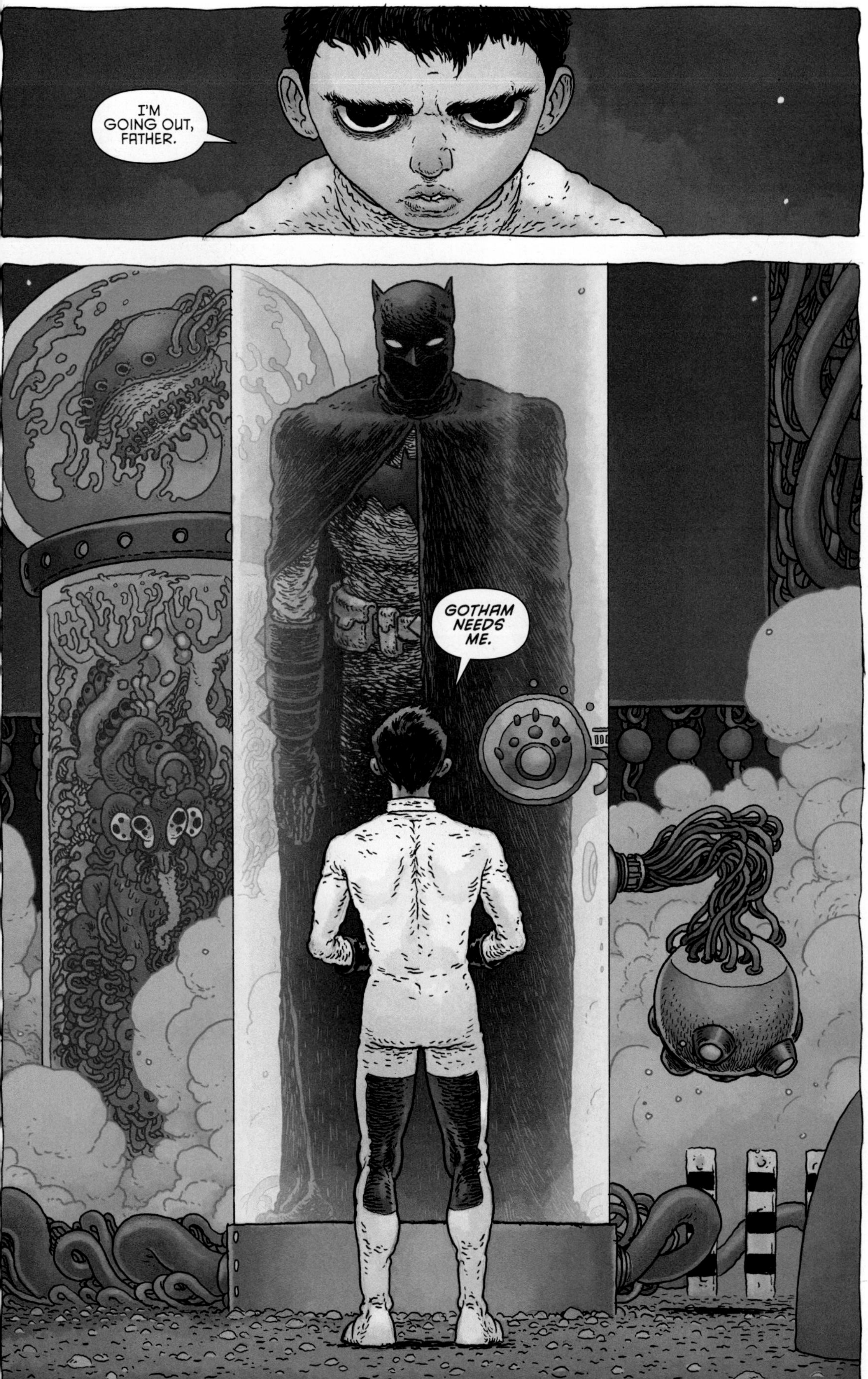
I'M GOING OUT, FATHER.
GOTHAM NEEDS ME.

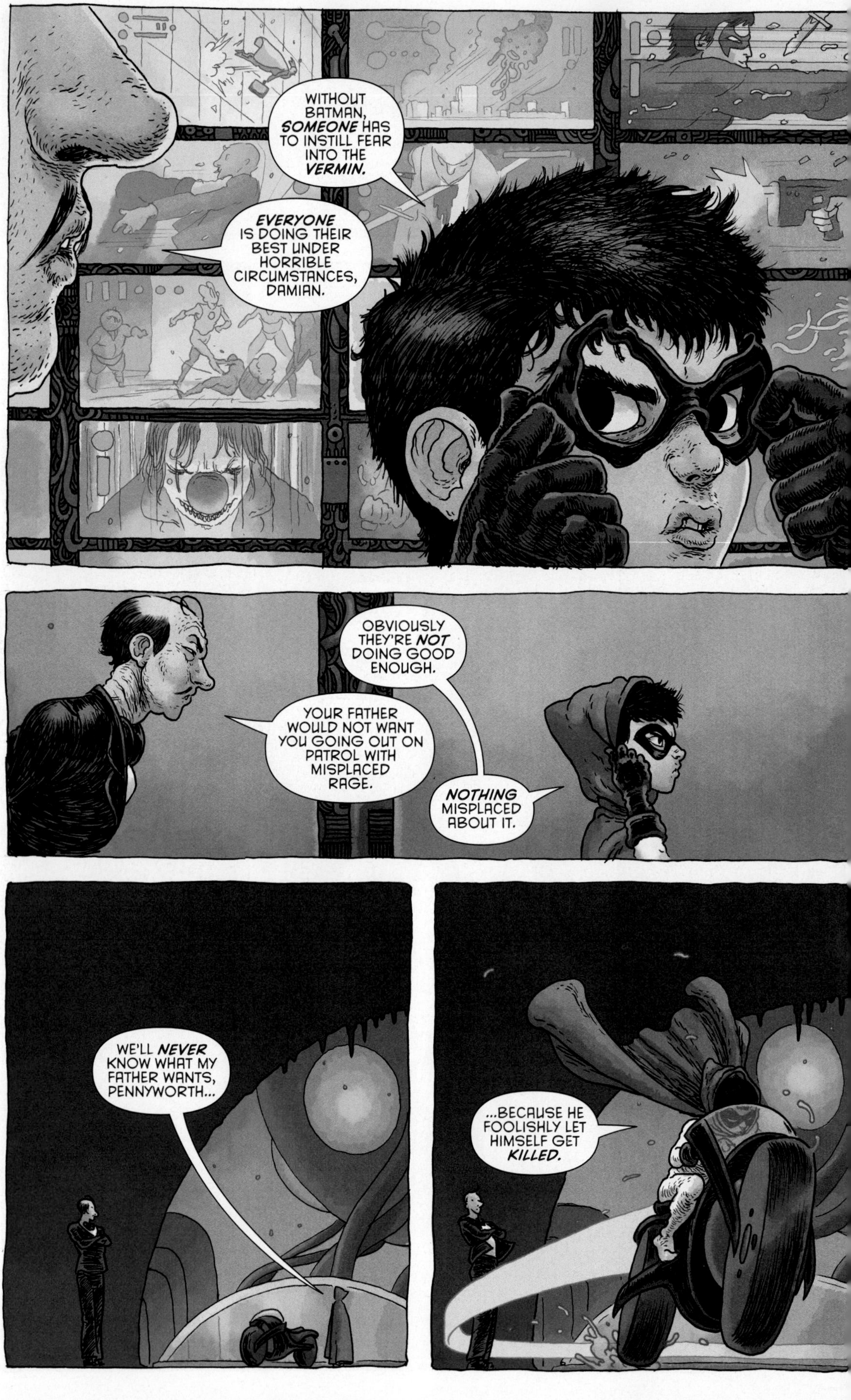
WITHOUT BATMAN, SOMEONE HAS TO INSTILL FEAR INTO THE VERMIN.
EVERYONE IS DOING THEIR BEST UNDER HORRIBLE CIRCUMSTANCES, DAMIAN.
OBVIOUSLY THEY'RE NOT DOING GOOD ENOUGH.
YOUR FATHER WOULD NOT WANT YOU GOING OUT ON PATROL WITH MISPLACED RAGE.
NOTHING MISPLACED ABOUT IT.
WE'LL NEVER KNOW WHAT MY FATHER WANTS, PENNYWORTH...
...BECAUSE HE FOOLISHLY LET HIMSELF GET KILLED.

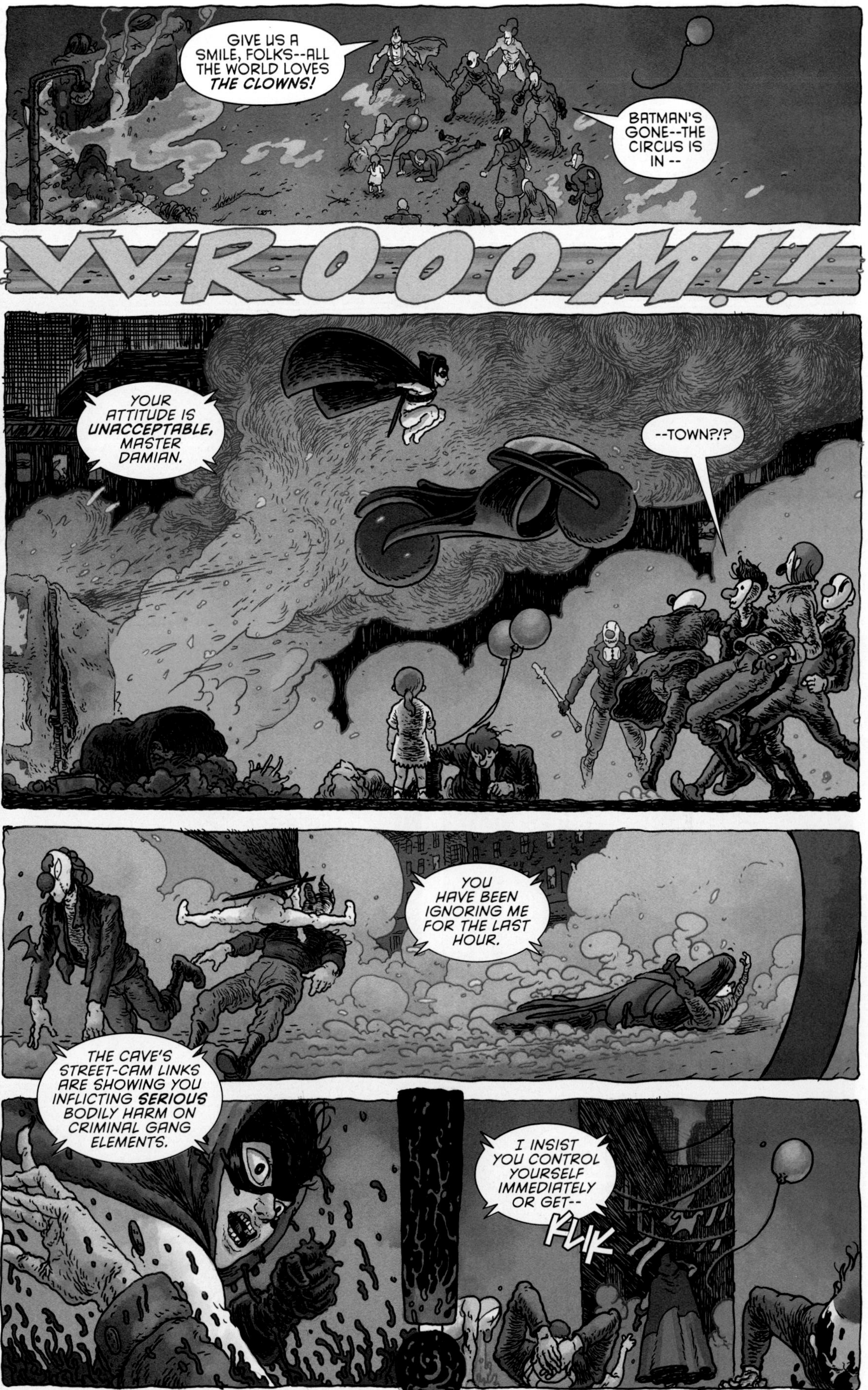
GIVE US A SMILE, FOLKS--ALL THE WORLD LOVES THE CLOWNS!
BATMAN'S GONE--THE CIRCUS IS IN --
VVROOOOM!!
YOUR ATTITUDE IS UNACCEPTABLE, MASTER DAMIAN.
--TOWN?!?
YOU HAVE BEEN IGNORING ME FOR THE LAST HOUR.
THE CAVE'S STREET-CAM LINKS ARE SHOWING YOU INFLICTING SERIOUS BODILY HARM ON CRIMINAL GANG ELEMENTS.
I INSIST YOU CONTROL YOURSELF IMMEDIATELY OR GET--
KLIK

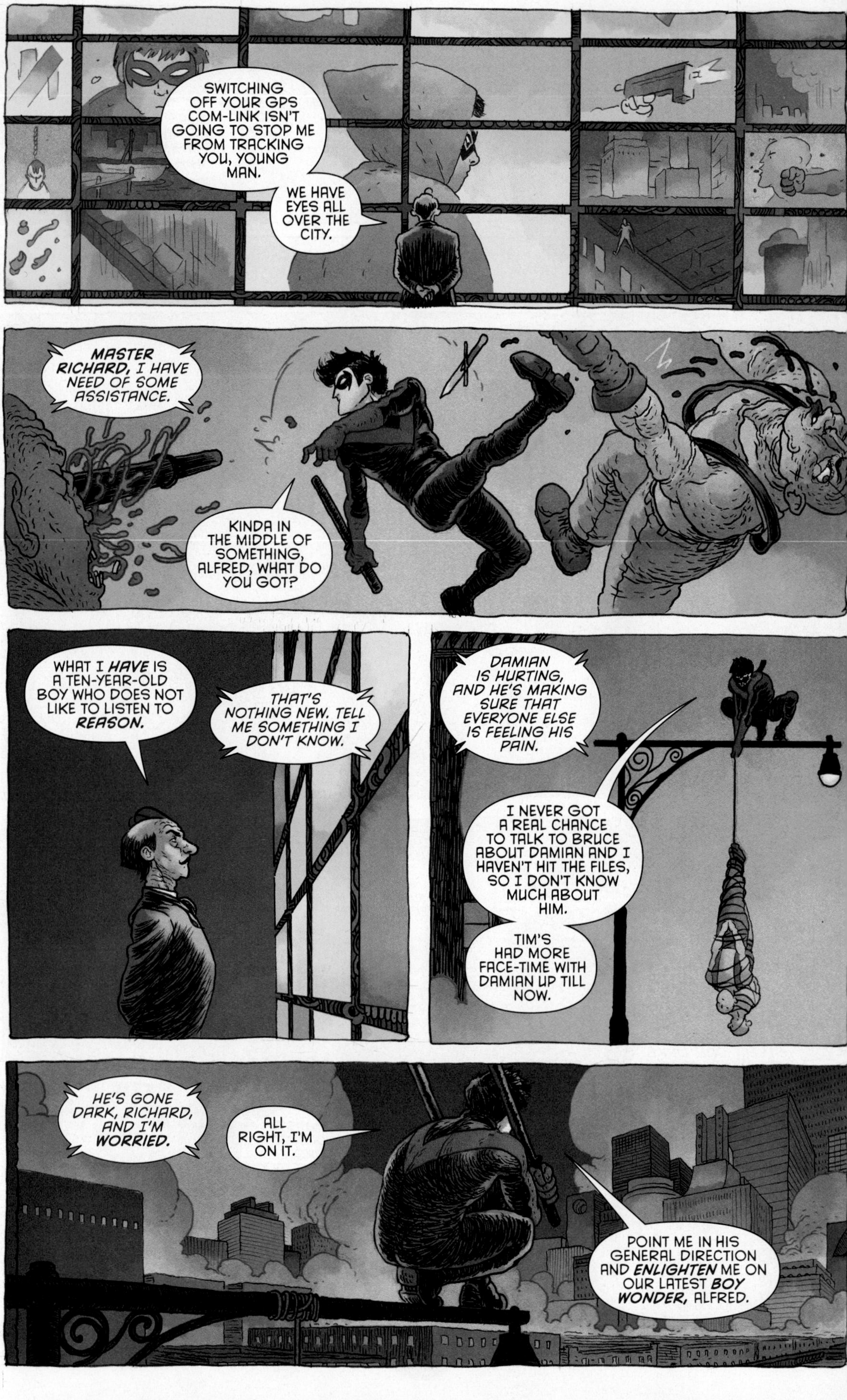
SWITCHING OFF YOUR GPS COM-LINK ISN'T GOING TO STOP ME FROM TRACKING YOU, YOUNG MAN.
WE HAVE EYES ALL OVER THE CITY.
MASTER RICHARD, I HAVE NEED OF SOME ASSISTANCE.
KINDA IN THE MIDDLE OF SOMETHING, ALFRED, WHAT DO YOU GOT?
WHAT I HAVE IS A TEN-YEAR-OLD BOY WHO DOES NOT LIKE TO LISTEN TO REASON.
THAT'S NOTHING NEW. TELL ME SOMETHING I DON'T KNOW.
DAMIAN IS HURTING, AND HE'S MAKING SURE THAT EVERYONE ELSE IS FEELING HIS PAIN.
I NEVER GOT A REAL CHANCE TO TALK TO BRUCE ABOUT DAMIAN AND I HAVEN'T HIT THE FILES, SO I DON'T KNOW MUCH ABOUT HIM.
TIM'S HAD MORE FACE-TIME WITH DAMIAN UP TILL NOW.
HE'S GONE DARK, RICHARD, AND I'M WORRIED.
ALL RIGHT, I'M ON IT.
POINT ME IN HIS GENERAL DIRECTION AND ENLIGHTEN ME ON OUR LATEST BOY WONDER, ALFRED.

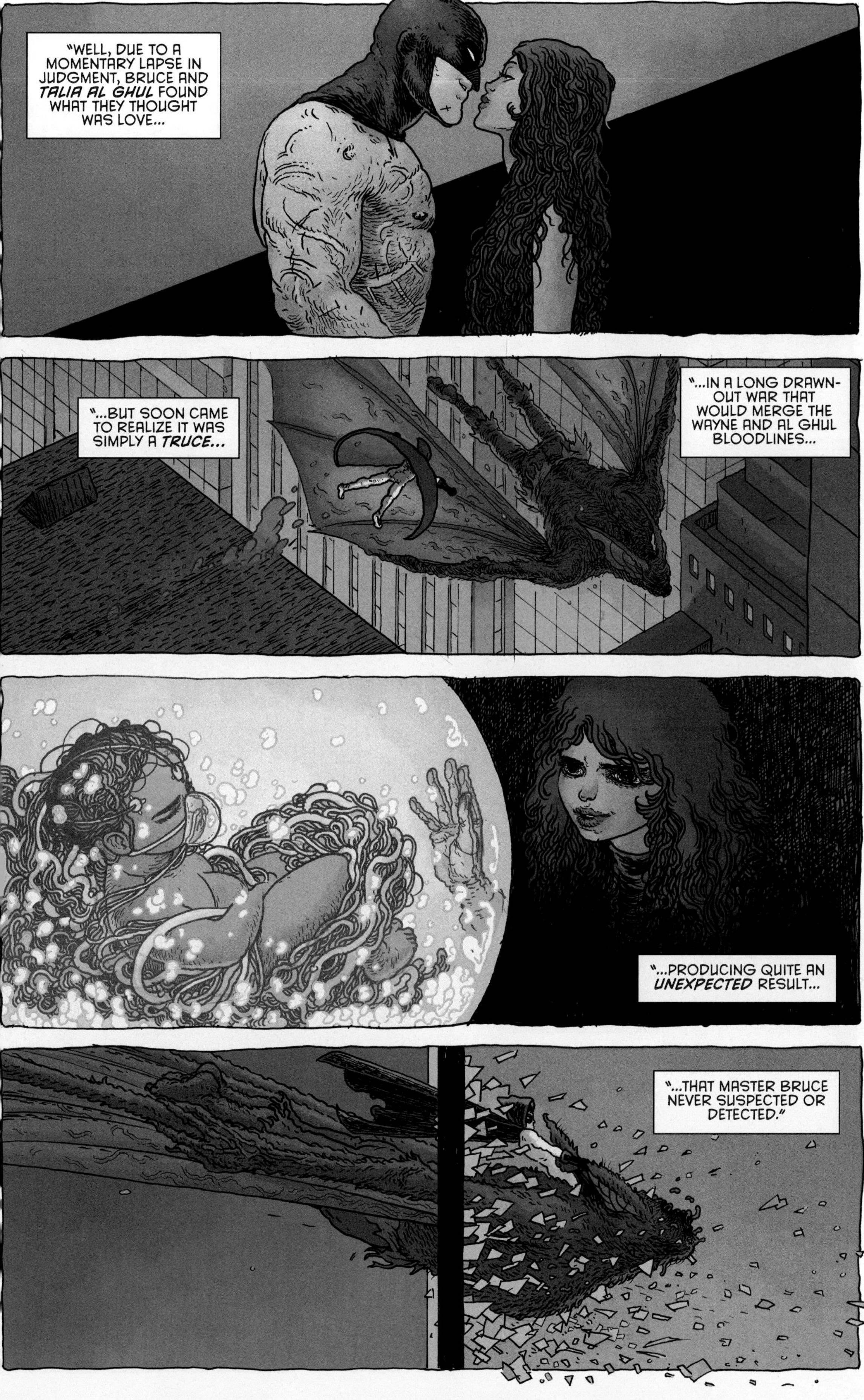
"WELL, DUE TO A MOMENTARY LAPSE IN JUDGMENT, BRUCE AND TALIA AL GHUL FOUND WHAT THEY THOUGHT WAS LOVE...
"...BUT SOON CAME TO REALIZE IT WAS SIMPLY A TRUCE...
"...IN A LONG DRAWN-OUT WAR THAT WOULD MERGE THE WAYNE AND AL GHUL BLOODLINES...
"...PRODUCING QUITE AN UNEXPECTED RESULT...
"...THAT MASTER BRUCE NEVER SUSPECTED OR DETECTED."

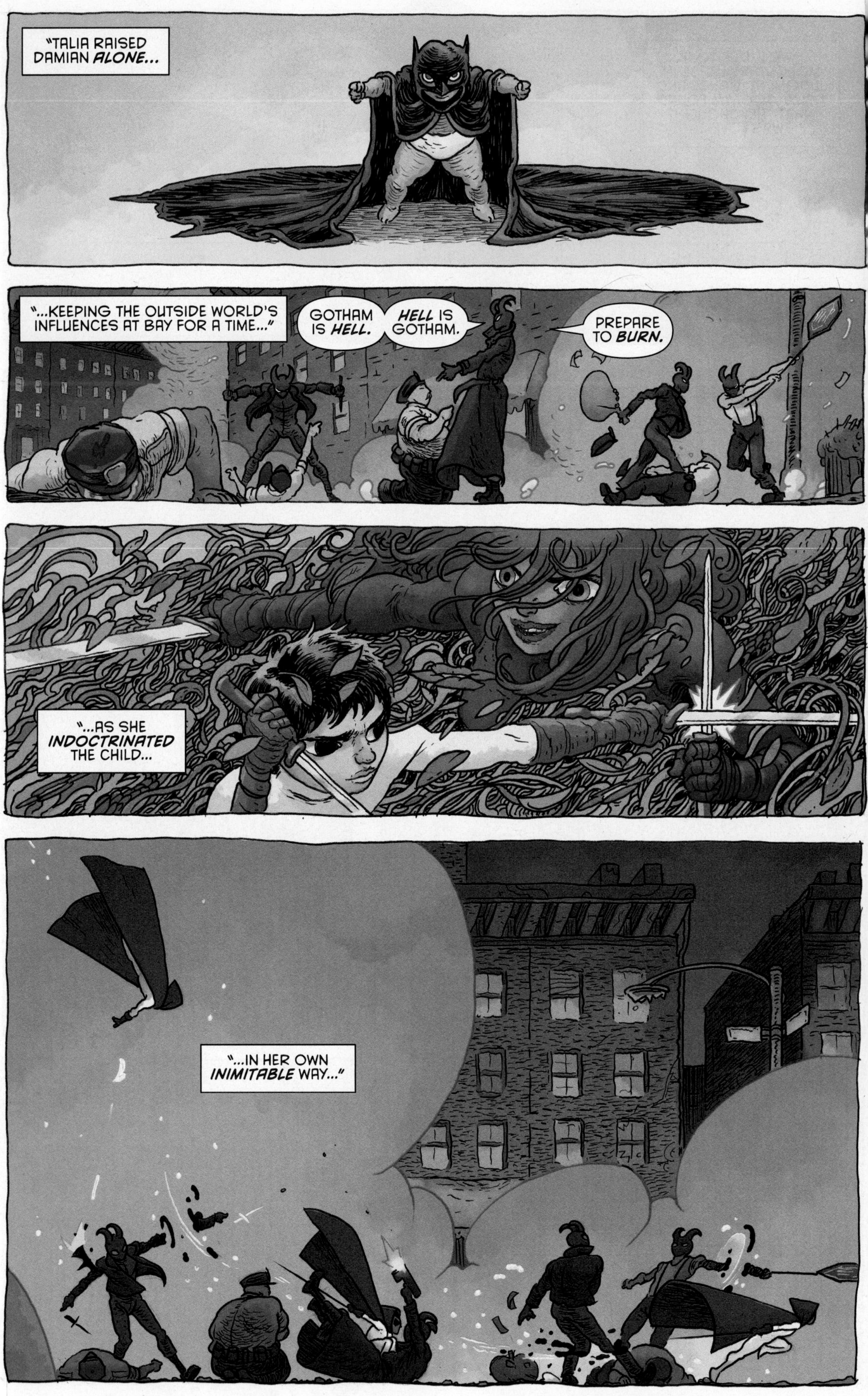
"TALIA RAISED
DAMIAN *ALONE*...
"...KEEPING THE OUTSIDE WORLD'S
INFLUENCES AT BAY FOR A TIME..."
GOTHAM IS *HELL*.
HELL IS GOTHAM.
PREPARE TO *BURN*.
"...AS SHE
INDOCTRINATED
THE CHILD...
"...IN HER OWN
INIMITABLE WAY..."

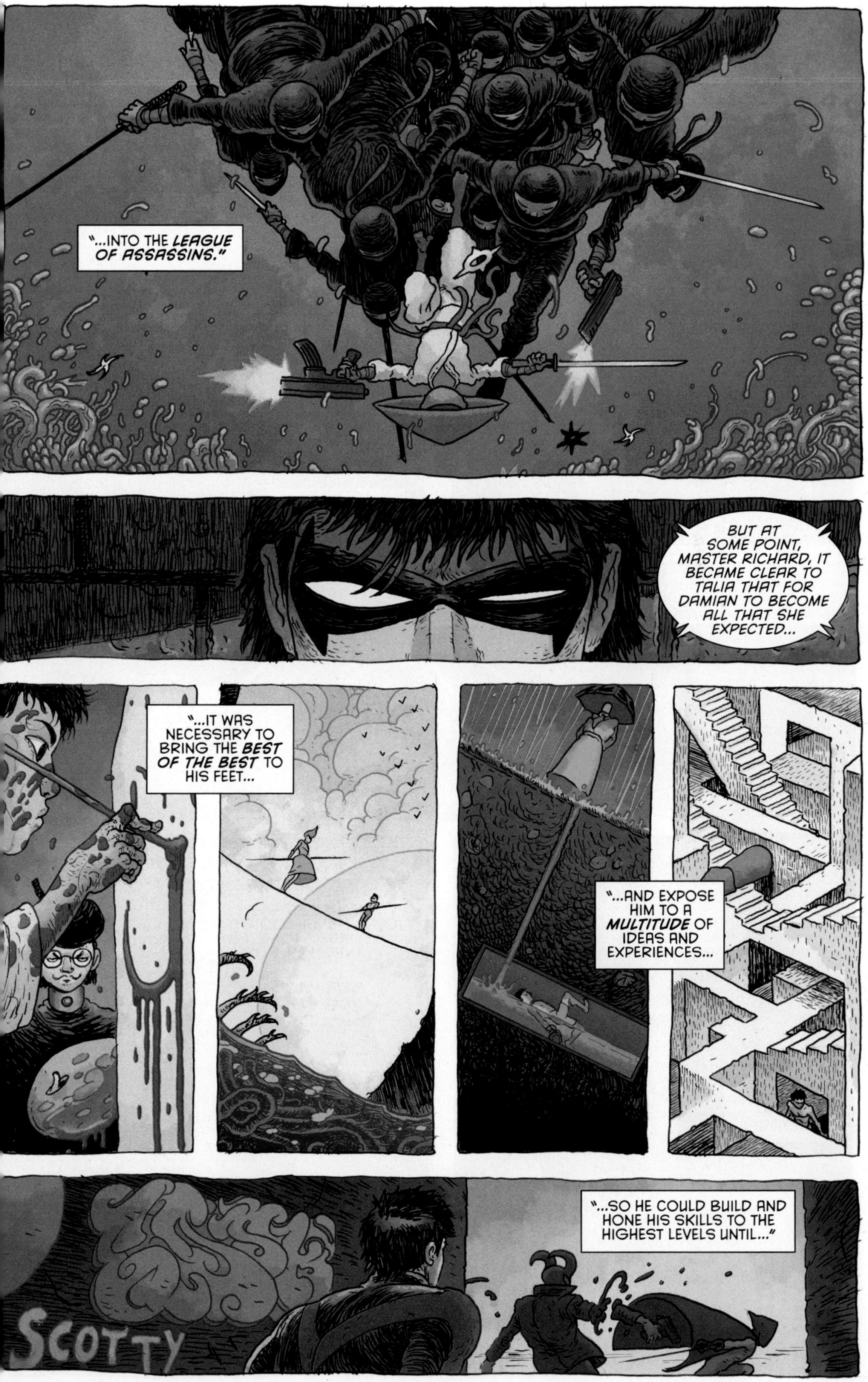
"...INTO THE *LEAGUE OF ASSASSINS.*"
BUT AT SOME POINT, MASTER RICHARD, IT BECAME CLEAR TO TALIA THAT FOR DAMIAN TO BECOME ALL THAT SHE EXPECTED...
"...IT WAS NECESSARY TO BRING THE *BEST OF THE BEST* TO HIS FEET...
"...AND EXPOSE HIM TO A *MULTITUDE* OF IDEAS AND EXPERIENCES...
"...SO HE COULD BUILD AND HONE HIS SKILLS TO THE HIGHEST LEVELS UNTIL..."
SCOTTY

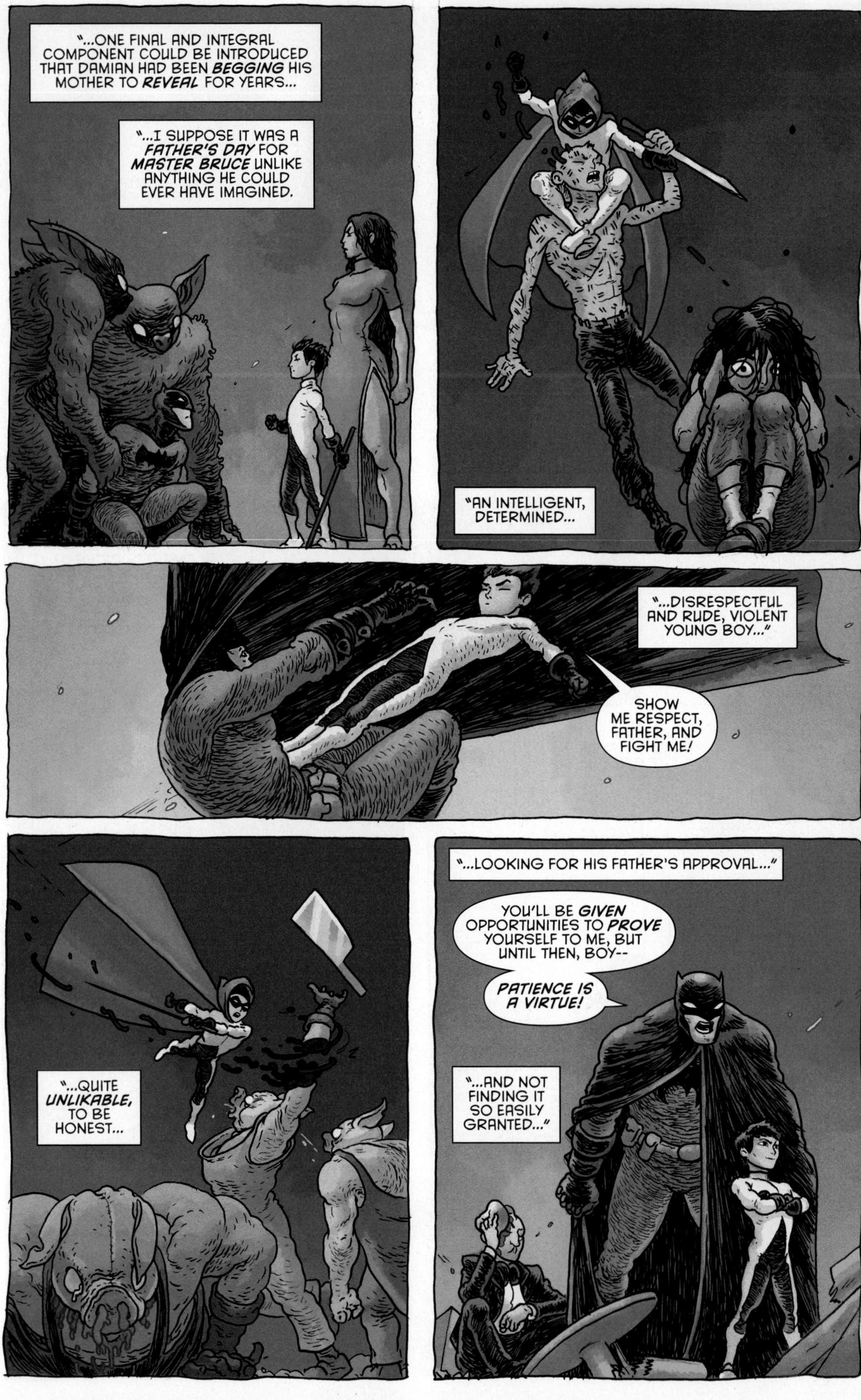
"...ONE FINAL AND INTEGRAL COMPONENT COULD BE INTRODUCED THAT DAMIAN HAD BEEN BEGGING HIS MOTHER TO REVEAL FOR YEARS...
"...I SUPPOSE IT WAS A FATHER'S DAY FOR MASTER BRUCE UNLIKE ANYTHING HE COULD EVER HAVE IMAGINED.
"AN INTELLIGENT, DETERMINED...
"...DISRESPECTFUL AND RUDE, VIOLENT YOUNG BOY..."
SHOW ME RESPECT, FATHER, AND FIGHT ME!
"...QUITE UNLIKABLE, TO BE HONEST...
"...LOOKING FOR HIS FATHER'S APPROVAL..."
YOU'LL BE GIVEN OPPORTUNITIES TO PROVE YOURSELF TO ME, BUT UNTIL THEN, BOY--
PATIENCE IS A VIRTUE!
"...AND NOT FINDING IT SO EASILY GRANTED..."

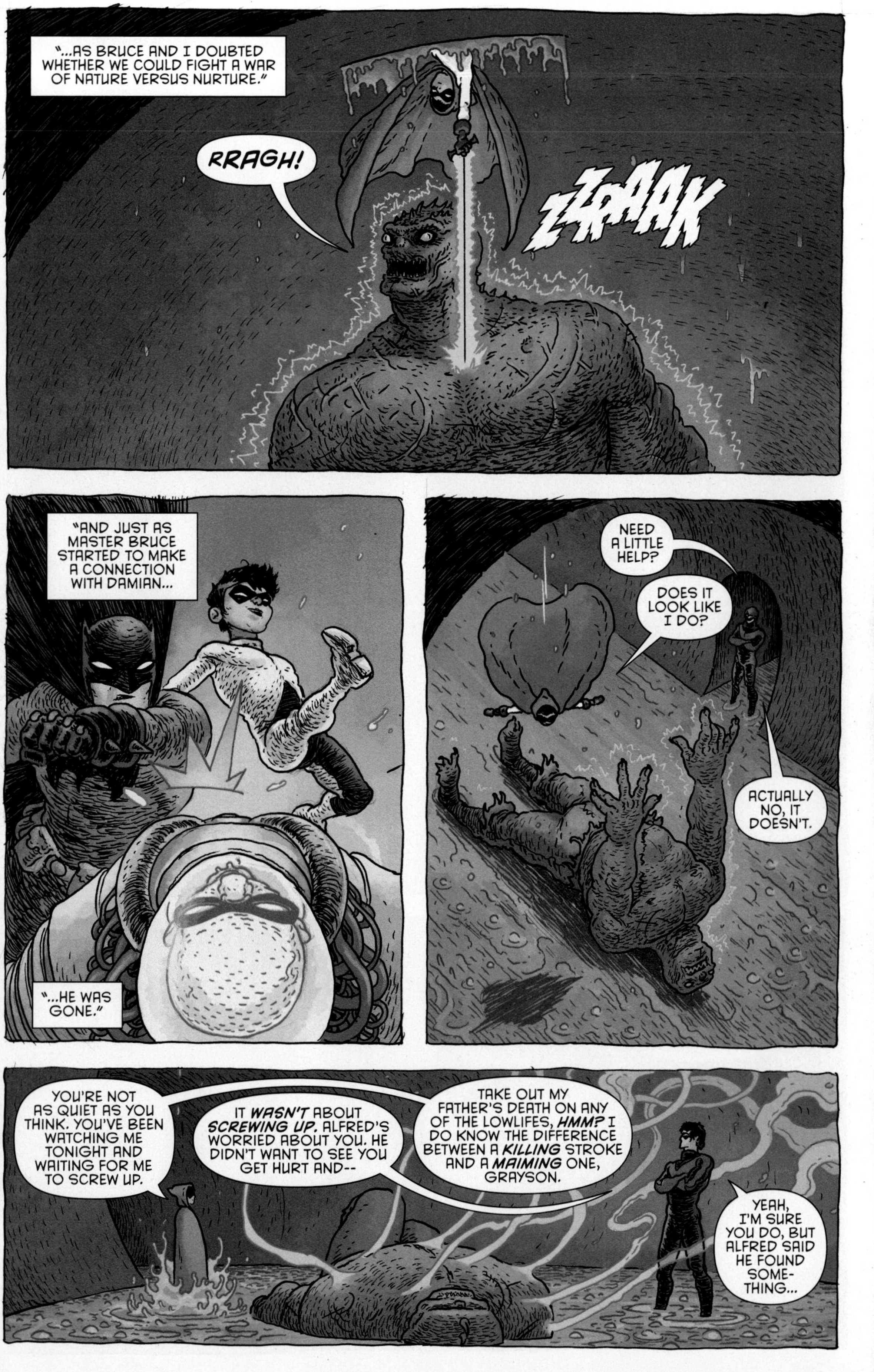
"...AS BRUCE AND I DOUBTED WHETHER WE COULD FIGHT A WAR OF NATURE VERSUS NURTURE."
RRAGH!
ZZRAAK
"AND JUST AS MASTER BRUCE STARTED TO MAKE A CONNECTION WITH DAMIAN...
"...HE WAS GONE."
NEED A LITTLE HELP?
DOES IT LOOK LIKE I DO?
ACTUALLY NO, IT DOESN'T.
YOU'RE NOT AS QUIET AS YOU THINK. YOU'VE BEEN WATCHING ME TONIGHT AND WAITING FOR ME TO SCREW UP.
IT WASN'T ABOUT SCREWING UP. ALFRED'S WORRIED ABOUT YOU. HE DIDN'T WANT TO SEE YOU GET HURT AND--
TAKE OUT MY FATHER'S DEATH ON ANY OF THE LOWLIFES, HMM? I DO KNOW THE DIFFERENCE BETWEEN A KILLING STROKE AND A MAIMING ONE, GRAYSON.
YEAH, I'M SURE YOU DO, BUT ALFRED SAID HE FOUND SOME-THING...

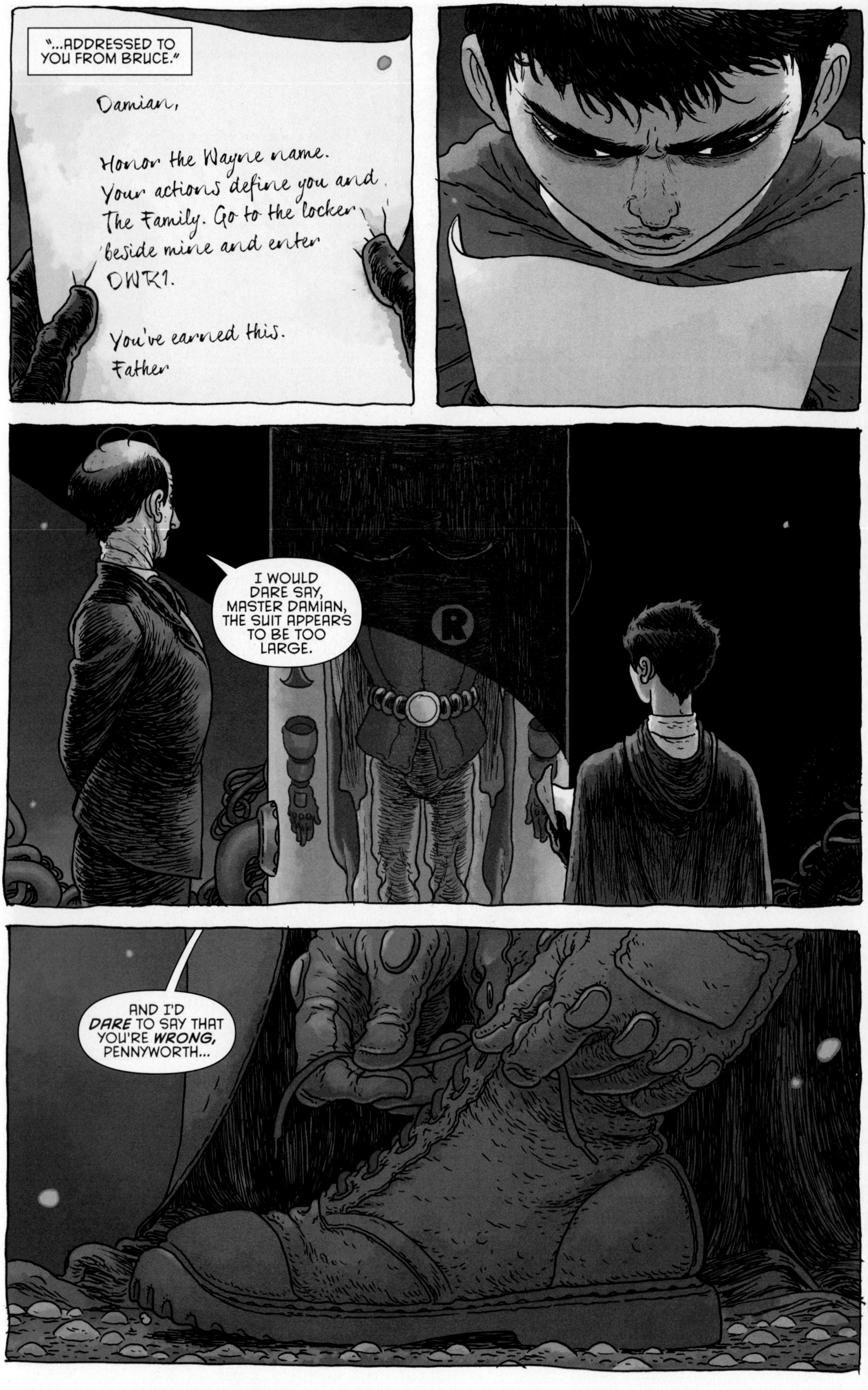
"...ADDRESSED TO YOU FROM BRUCE."
Damian,
Honor the Wayne name. Your actions define you and The Family. Go to the locker beside mine and enter DWR1.
You've earned this.
Father
I WOULD DARE SAY, MASTER DAMIAN, THE SUIT APPEARS TO BE TOO LARGE.
AND I'D *DARE* TO SAY THAT YOU'RE *WRONG*, PENNYWORTH...

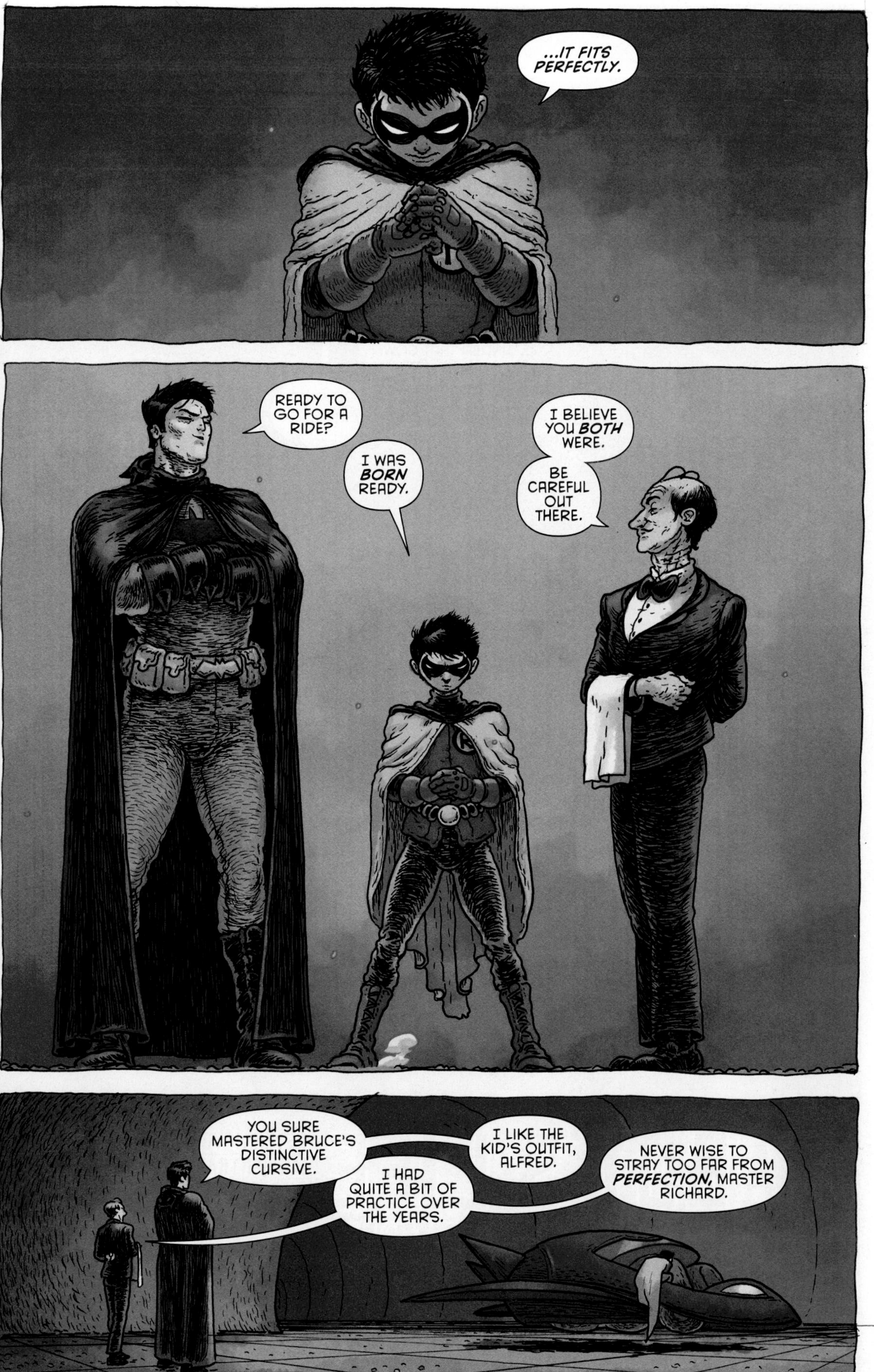
...IT FITS PERFECTLY.
READY TO GO FOR A RIDE?
I WAS BORN READY.
I BELIEVE YOU BOTH WERE.
BE CAREFUL OUT THERE.
YOU SURE MASTERED BRUCE'S DISTINCTIVE CURSIVE.
I HAD QUITE A BIT OF PRACTICE OVER THE YEARS.
I LIKE THE KID'S OUTFIT, ALFRED.
NEVER WISE TO STRAY TOO FAR FROM PERFECTION, MASTER RICHARD.

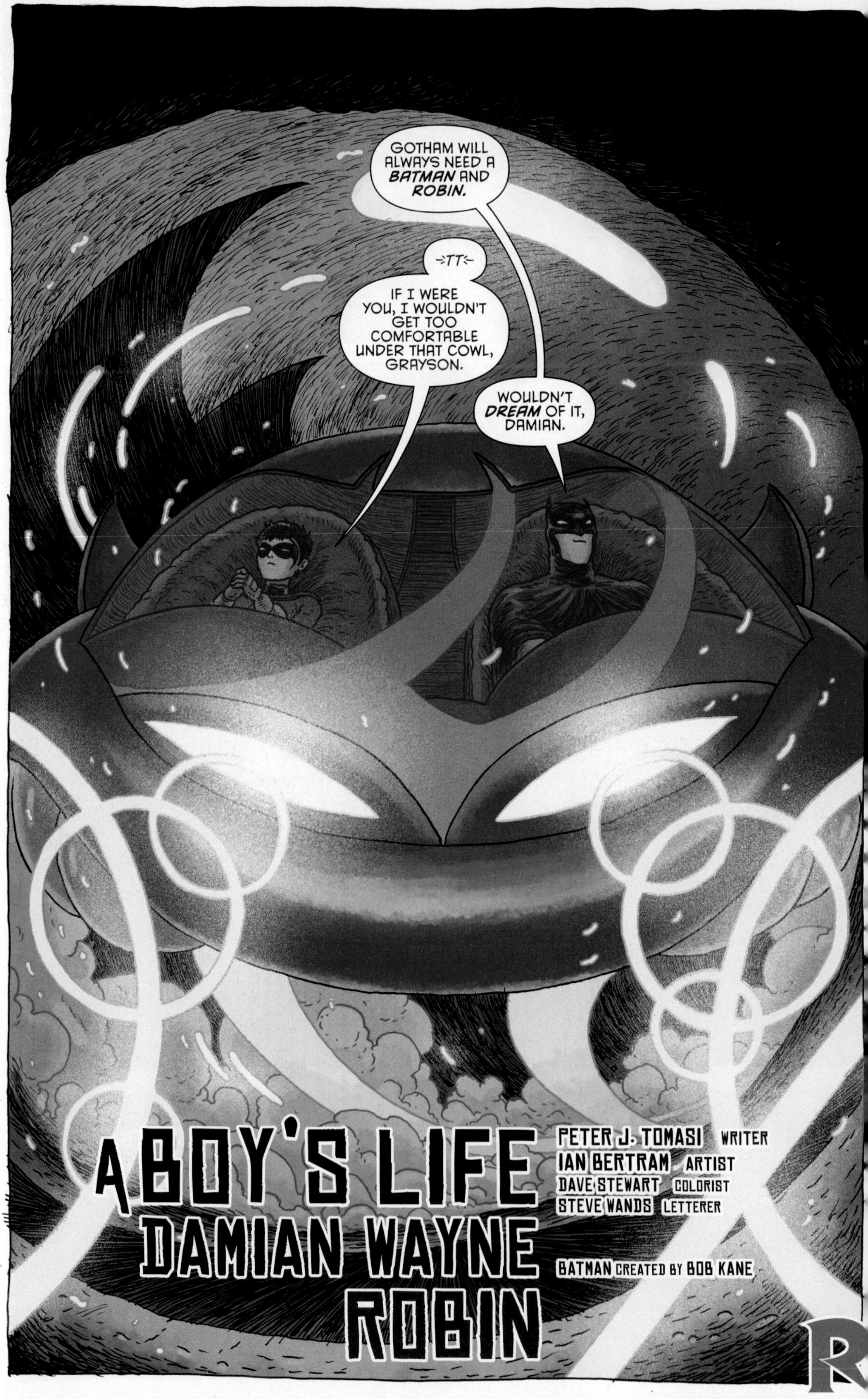
GOTHAM WILL ALWAYS NEED A BATMAN AND ROBIN.
-TT-
IF I WERE YOU, I WOULDN'T GET TOO COMFORTABLE UNDER THAT COWL, GRAYSON.
WOULDN'T DREAM OF IT, DAMIAN.
A BOY'S LIFE
DAMIAN WAYNE
ROBIN
PETER J. TOMASI WRITER
IAN BERTRAM ARTIST
DAVE STEWART COLORIST
STEVE WANDS LETTERER
BATMAN CREATED BY BOB KANE

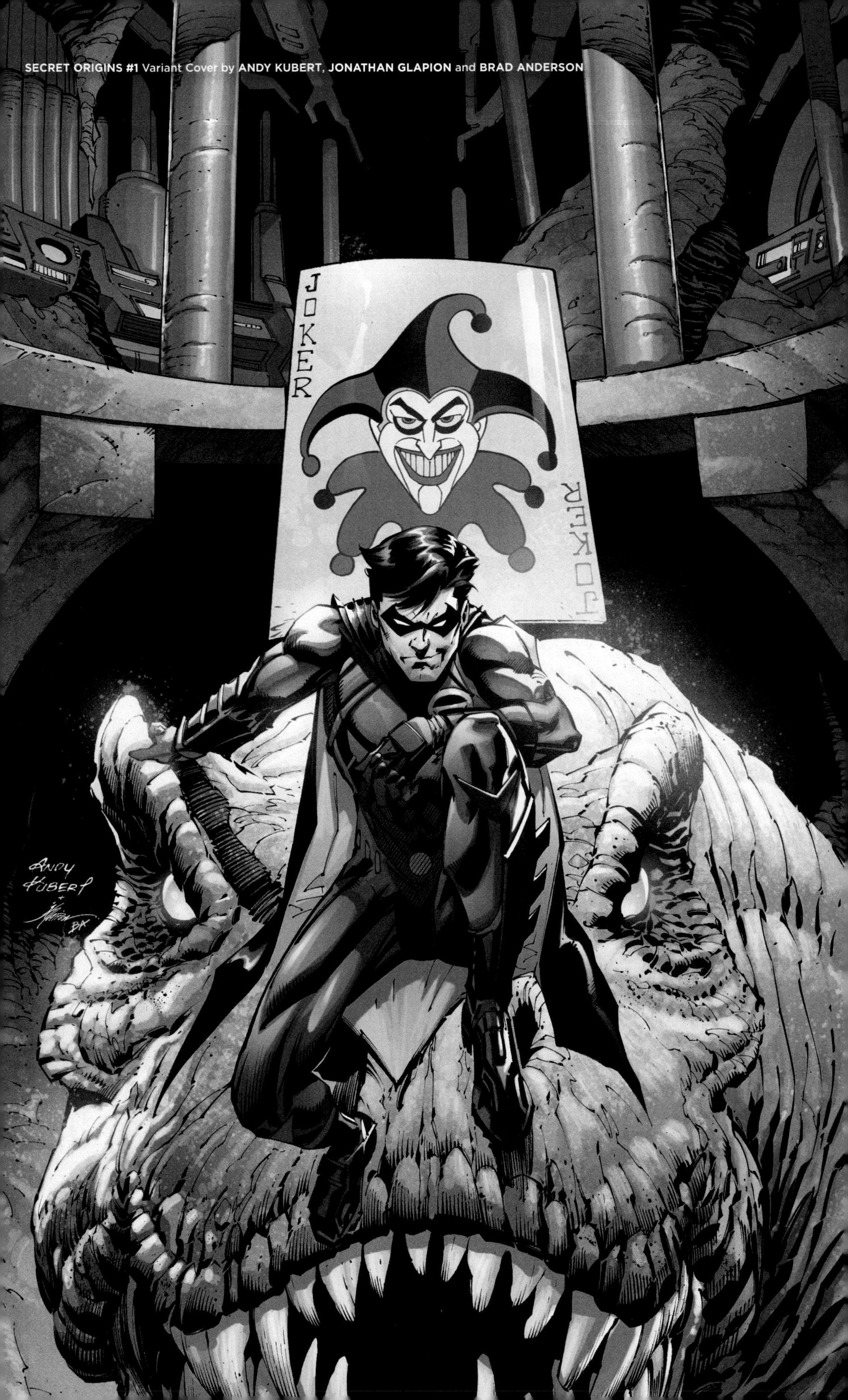
JOKER
JOKER
ANDY KUBERT

SECRET ORIGINS #1 Variant Cover by **ANDY KUBERT**, **JONATHAN GLAPION** and **BRAD ANDERSON**

START AT THE BEGINNING!
JUSTICE LEAGUE
VOLUME 1: ORIGIN
GEOFF JOHNS and JIM LEE

JUSTICE LEAGUE VOL. 2: THE VILLAIN'S JOURNEY

JUSTICE LEAGUE VOL. 3: THRONE OF ATLANTIS

JUSTICE LEAGUE OF AMERICA VOL. 1: WORLD'S MOST DANGEROUS

DC COMICS™

"[Writer Scott Snyder] pulls from the oldest aspects of the Batman myth, combines it with sinister-comic elements from the series' best period, and gives the whole thing terrific forward-spin."—ENTERTAINMENT WEEKLY

START AT THE BEGINNING!

BATMAN VOLUME 1: THE COURT OF OWLS

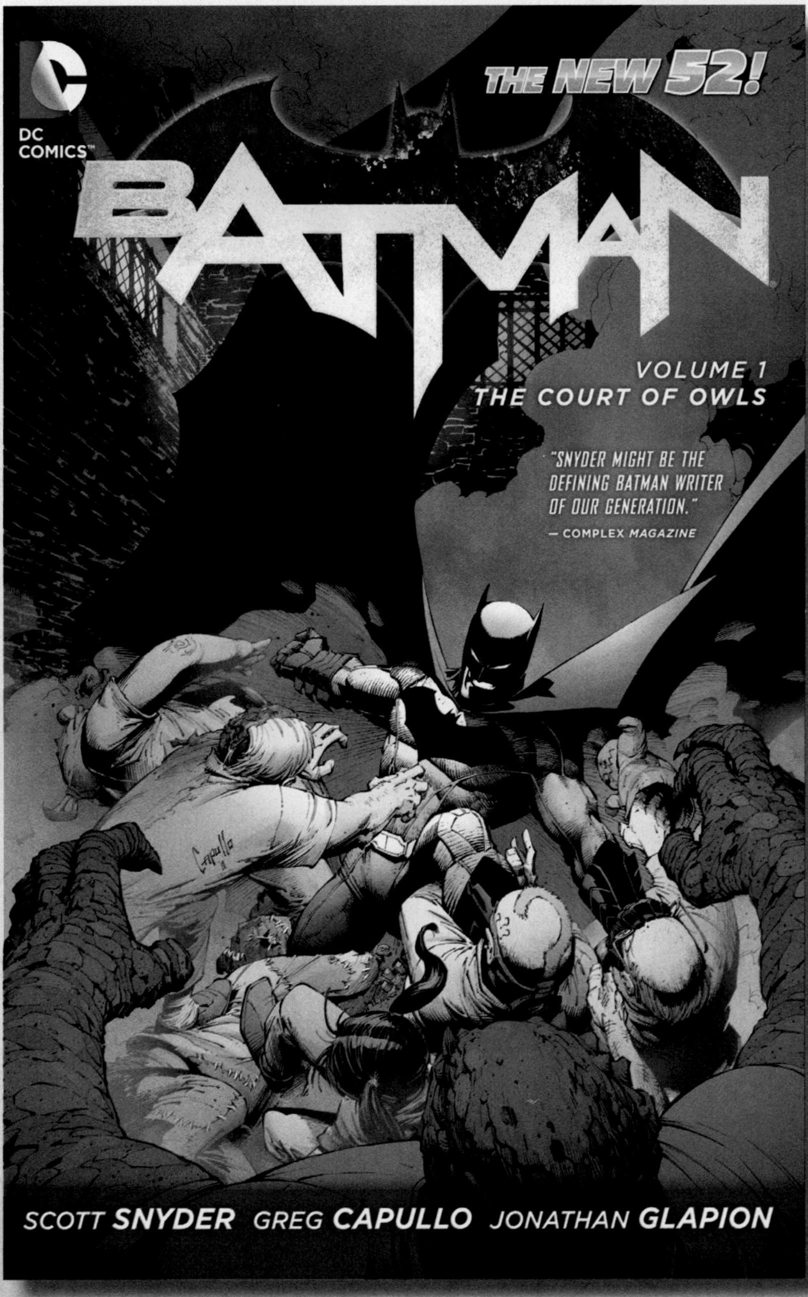
DC COMICS™
THE NEW 52!
BATMAN
VOLUME 1
THE COURT OF OWLS
"SNYDER MIGHT BE THE DEFINING BATMAN WRITER OF OUR GENERATION."
— COMPLEX MAGAZINE
SCOTT SNYDER GREG CAPULLO JONATHAN GLAPION

BATMAN VOL. 2: THE CITY OF OWLS

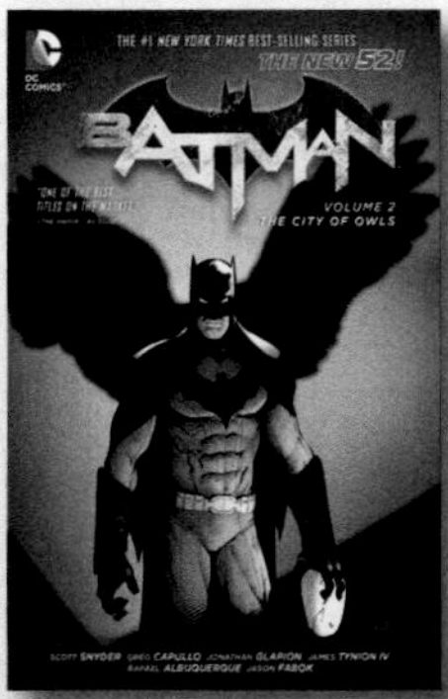
THE NEW 52!
BATMAN
VOLUME 2
THE CITY OF OWLS

with SCOTT SNYDER and GREG CAPULLO

BATMAN VOL. 3: DEATH OF THE FAMILY

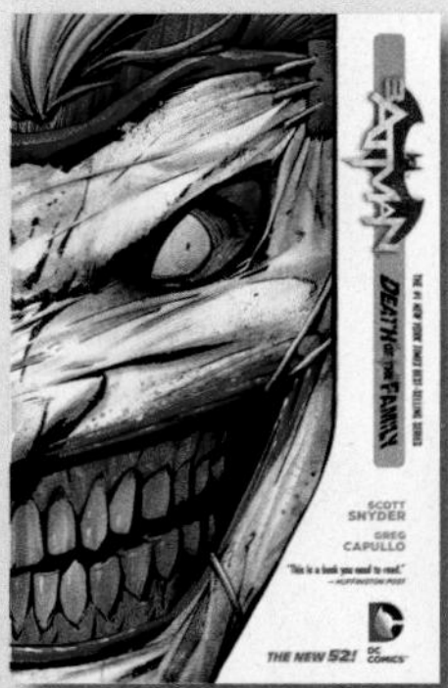
BATMAN
SCOTT SNYDER
GREG CAPULLO
THE NEW 52!

with SCOTT SNYDER and GREG CAPULLO

BATMAN: NIGHT OF THE OWLS

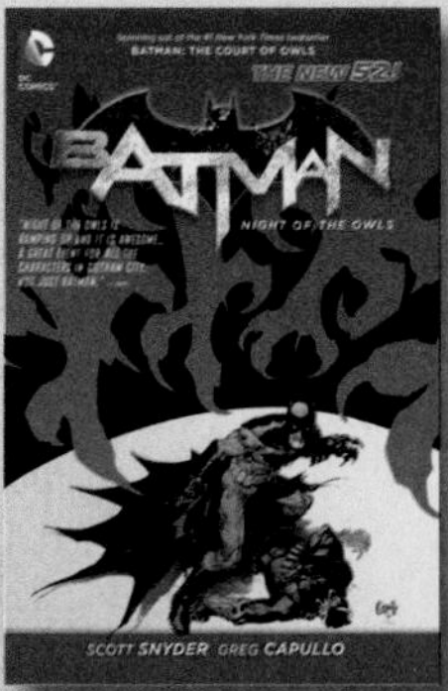
THE NEW 52!
BATMAN
NIGHT OF THE OWLS
SCOTT SNYDER GREG CAPULLO

with SCOTT SNYDER and GREG CAPULLO

START AT THE BEGINNING!

SUPERMAN: ACTION COMICS VOLUME 1:
SUPERMAN AND THE MEN OF STEEL

SUPERMAN: ACTION COMICS VOL. 2: BULLETPROOF

with GRANT MORRISON and RAGS MORALES

SUPERMAN: ACTION COMICS VOL. 3: AT THE END OF DAYS

with GRANT MORRISON and RAGS MORALES

SUPERBOY VOL. 1: INCUBATION

THE NEW 52!
SUPERMAN®
ACTION COMICS

VOLUME 1
SUPERMAN AND THE MEN OF STEEL

"BELIEVE THE HYPE: GRANT MORRISON WENT AND WROTE THE SINGLE BEST ISSUE OF SUPERMAN THESE EYES HAVE EVER READ."
— USA TODAY

GRANT MORRISON   RAGS MORALES   ANDY KUBERT